AF600583

MIGRATION AND THE MEDIA

Debating Chinese Migration to Italy, 1992–2012

Migration and the Media

Debating Chinese Migration to Italy, 1992–2012

GAOHENG ZHANG

UNIVERSITY OF TORONTO PRESS
Toronto Buffalo London

Toronto Buffalo London
utorontopress.com

ISBN 978-1-4426-3043-7

Cultural Spaces

Library and Archives Canada Cataloguing in Publication

Title: Migration and the media: debating Chinese migration to Italy, 1992–2012 / Gaoheng Zhang.
Names: Zhang, Gaoheng, author.
Series: Cultural spaces.
Description: Series statement: Cultural spaces | Includes bibliographical references and index.
Identifiers: Canadiana 20190126043 | ISBN 9781442630437 (hardcover)
Subjects: LCSH: Chinese – Italy – History – 20th century. | LCSH: Chinese – Italy – History – 21st century. | LCSH: Italy – Emigration and immigration – History – 20th century. | LCSH: Italy – Emigration and Immigration – History – 21st century. | LCSH: China – Emigration and immigration – History – 20th century. | LCSH: China – Emigration and immigration – History – 21st century. | LCSH: Mass media and culture.
Classification: LCC DG457.C47 Z53 2019 | DDC 304.8/45051–dc23

This book has been published with the help of a grant from the Federation for the Humanities and Social Sciences, through the Awards to Scholarly Publications Program, using funds provided by the Social Sciences and Humanities Research Council of Canada.

University of Toronto Press acknowledges the financial assistance to its publishing program of the Canada Council for the Arts and the Ontario Arts Council, an agency of the Government of Ontario.

Canada Council for the Arts | Conseil des Arts du Canada

Funded by the Government of Canada | Financé par le gouvernement du Canada

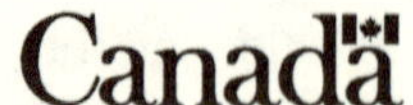

This book is dedicated to my parents,
Yuan Shuijuan and Zhang Erjun.

Contents

Acknowledgments

This is my first book, a milestone for my academic growth as a Chinese-born Italian studies scholar working in North America. It thus gives me immense pleasure to thank the people who have contributed to its making since 2012. I would like to begin with three women. My mother, Yuan Shuijuan, has always worked tirelessly to lend her utmost emotional support to my education and scholarship. After I completed my PhD dissertation (on a topic unrelated to the current book) at New York University, my advisor Ruth Ben-Ghiat very generously chaperoned this book manuscript at various stages and shaped many of its key features. Then, as a postdoctoral fellow at the University of Southern California, Tita Rosenthal gave me meticulous critique and unwavering moral support, as well as guidance crucial to the design of the book. I am grateful for their care and insight.

In the United States and Canada, I further received timely and thoughtful comments on various forms of this manuscript from friends and colleagues to which I am indebted: David Forgacs, Kristina Varade, Valerie McGuire, Aria Cabot, Daniele Forlino, Xin Liu, Alessia Pannese, Piotr Mirowski, Teresa Fiore, Flavia Laviosa, Francesca Vassalli, Áine O'Healy, Marguerite Waller, Graziella Parati, Eugene Cooper, Francesca Italiano, Gianni Chen, Géraldine Fiss, Laura Ruberto, Konrad Eisenbichler, Luca Somigli, Jill Ross, and Donna Gabaccia. Invited stand-alone lectures at University College Cork, Stony Brook University, Smith College, and Columbia University gave me a forum to receive collective feedback on my research. I thank my hosts at these institutions: Silvia Ross, Mark Chu, Chiara Giuliani, Mario Mignone, Anna Botta, and Ernest Ialongo. I also thank the graduate and undergraduate students who participated in my seminars about Italy and China at the University of Southern California, the University of Toronto, and the University of British Columbia. At the University of

Toronto, where I substantially revised my book manuscript, I wish to thank Manda Vrkljan from Kelly Library at St Michael's College for collecting a significant number of books and articles for me. I also thank my colleagues at the University of British Columbia who are curious and supportive of my book project and the Italian-Chinese cultural framework that I continue to develop.

Several granting agencies and institutions from the United States and Canada made the production of this book possible. I would like to acknowledge the University of Southern California's Provost's Postdoctoral Scholarship in the Humanities (now USC Society of Fellows) for a generous fellowship tenure during 2012–14 when I researched and wrote a substantial portion of this book. The publication of this book is graciously supported by two grants: Columbia University's Schoff Publication Fund Award and the Canadian Federation for the Humanities and Social Sciences' Awards to Scholarly Publications Program.

In Italy, between 2012 and 2015, I conducted research in personal and institutional archives and libraries. I appreciate the facilitation of the scholars and librarians who made my visits fruitful. I wish to thank Daniele Cologna for sharing his own collection of news coverage of the 2007 riot in Milan, which gifted me with a first example of substantial evidence of the media attention to Chinese migration to Italy. Our subsequent exchanges have also been crucial to my thinking about this cultural phenomenon. I thank Wu Jie, *Ouzhou Qiaobao*'s then editor-in-chief, and his staff for opening their archive in Milan for my perusal. Likewise, many thanks to Fabiano Magi and Marco Wong for allowing me to consult issues of *It's China* in Campi Bisenzio. Giuseppina Cozzi and Katia De Sensi were helpful at Mediaset's archives at Segrate near Milan. I also thank Cinzia Padovani, Milly Buonanno, and Giorgio Grignaffini for making this contact for me. The staff at Milan's Mediateca Santa Teresa were helpful when I navigated Rai Teche archives. At Rome's National Library, where I researched *Cina in Italia* and consulted books, I thank Gianluca Parisi for his assistance and friendship.

In Italy, I also profited from productive dialogue with people that improved my mature thinking about Chinese migration to Italy as a cultural phenomenon: Marco Wong, Antonella Ceccagno, Sabrina Marchetti, Alessandra Lavagnino, Shi Yang Shi, Francesca Bellino, Mara Matta, Maria Luisa Tornotti, Fan Jiang, Sergio Basso, Vincenzo De Cecco, Andrea Segre, and David Prelini. Although this is not a book about the empirical practices of Chinese migrants in Italy, over the years I have talked to many of them and I appreciate the views they have shared with me. I was also able to speak about the book's subject to university students and to the general public in Italy thanks to the talks Valentina Pedone and Miriam Castorina organized at the University of Florence in 2018, Virginia Cox and Angelica Pesarini at New York University Florence in 2018, and David Prelini and Monica Achille at the Dergano-Bovisa Library in Milan in 2017.

Last but not least, I wish to thank my editors at University of Toronto Press for their continued enthusiasm and support for the project. I am grateful to the late Ron Schoeffel for encouraging me to submit the manuscript, Siobhan McMenemy for accepting the manuscript and commissioning readers, Mark Thompson for guiding me through most of the book-making process, and Frances Mundy for overseeing the production of the book. I also would like to acknowledge the anonymous peer reviewers for their incisive comments and the meticulous copy editing done by Elizabeth Venditto and Carolyn Yates that made the book more reader-friendly and accurate. Don Braswell also edited many previous drafts of the manuscript and shaped my view of academic writing in general. I am extremely grateful for his friendship over the years.

This book encapsulates many of my academic and personal highlights from Hangzhou to Beijing, from New York City to Los Angeles, and from Toronto to Vancouver, with many Italian cities in between. Gazing at Vancouver's mountains and waters from my office building at the University of British Columbia, I am reminded of the permanence and fluctuation of life around all of us. I hope that both the acknowledgments and the book capture this spirit in their distinctive ways.

MIGRATION AND THE MEDIA

Debating Chinese Migration to Italy, 1992–2012

Introduction

Large-scale Chinese migration to Italy has occurred since the 1980s – relatively recently compared with the Chinese diasporas elsewhere in the world. Yet Italy, along with France, has absorbed the highest numbers of those who moved from mainland China to Europe since that decade.[1] In the early 2010s, there were approximately 200,000 legally registered Chinese in Italy. But many more Chinese there were undocumented, and an accurate number is difficult to obtain. The number of Chinese migrants in Italy is small compared with the number in Southeast Asia (around 7.8 million in Indonesia alone) and in North America (around 4.1 million in the United States). In the same period, the Chinese were the fourth largest group of legal foreign residents in Italy, although they lagged far behind the third-largest group, the Moroccans, with a head count of more than 430,000. But this is the first time in history that so many Chinese reside in Italy, which was itself a significant emigrant-sending country until the 1970s. More remarkably, this is the case despite the fact that the Chinese have not enjoyed the European Union migration policies, colonial ties, and geographical proximity that respectively facilitated the cross-border movements of the Romanians, Albanians, and Moroccans, Italy's three largest migrant groups in the early 2010s.[2]

Why did Chinese workers migrate to Italy en masse, and what agendas did they set for their migration? China's Open Door policy, initiated in 1978, loosened previous restrictions on emigration and made transnational movements possible. But why did these Chinese choose Italy as their migration destination? Chain migration was a key factor, as migrants tend to go where friends and relatives have first settled. By the 1980s, unlike other southern European countries, Italy had already seen a well-established network of Chinese nationals, who migrated before the Second World War and were integrated in Italian society.

New migrants could therefore rely on older migrants' family-owned businesses for work. This explains why Italy's Chinese mostly came from the same regions of China: Wenzhou and its surrounding counties. Moreover, in the 1980s and 1990s, Italy's several regularization schemes (sanatorie), which gave residency permits to its large illegal immigrant population, encouraged an influx of migrants, including the Chinese. Most importantly, Chinese workers migrated to Italy to capitalize on entrepreneurial opportunities that were not available in Northern Europe (or in China). The Italian economy was prospering in the 1980s, but the country's laws on legal labour migration were strict. Therefore, employers needed irregular workers to fill positions (in the garment industry, for example), which prompted Italy's underground economy to thrive on Chinese and other migrants (as well as southern Italians).[3]

Indeed, the impact of the Chinese migration on Italian society was intimately linked with their entrepreneurship. As Chinese migrants opened a large number of small businesses based on a self-employment model, they created considerable turmoil for small- and medium-sized Italian enterprises, the pillar of the postwar Italian economy. One sector in particular bore the brunt of the business challenges these migrants and neoliberal globalization posed: Prato's textile and garment industries. From the end of the Second World War through the 1990s, Prato's industrial district prospered in production and reputation, as its versatile fabrics served a worldwide clientele and were used for "Made in Italy" clothing, known for its quality and its brands. The crisis and decline of these Italian textile and garment firms began in the 1990s in tandem with the rise of fast-fashion manufacturing, in which Prato's Chinese migrant entrepreneurship specialized. Chinese-owned workshops received orders from major Italian fashion houses and also made garments out of fabrics imported from China. Later, the Chinese expanded into the design and distribution divisions of the garment sector, further challenging the traditional Italian monopoly on the more profitable segments of the supply chain. Collectively, Prato's Chinese migrant factories and firms morphed into the only migrant business sector in Italy that was able to successfully compete with Italian firms.

Italian firms in Prato and elsewhere also faced stiff competition from China. "Made in China" garments began pouring into the Italian market following China's entry into the World Trade Organization (WTO) in 2001, further exacerbating the perception that the Chinese – including both those abroad and those in mainland China who were often conceived in the media as a single entity – were taking away Italian jobs and intruding into traditional "Made in Italy" trades. Since the mid-2000s, China and Italy have indeed competed for global markets in the labour-intensive, low-tech, and export-oriented textile and garment industries. To be sure, the sale of "Made in China" clothing in Europe has been a form of Chinese economic globalization quite different from the fast-fashion manufacturing of Italy's homegrown Chinese migrant firms. But the two economic phenomena have sometimes been linked. For instance, most Chinese migrants have used "Made in China" and not "Made in Prato" fabrics either by personal choice or at the request of their Italian commissioners.

Despite the fierce business competition that Chinese migrants introduced into Italy's garment industrial districts, a wide spectrum of the Italian public believed that the country should strengthen its ties with all Chinese residents. As Prato became the premier European fast-fashion manufacturing centre, astute Italians capitalized on the expansion of Chinese businesses to sell empty warehouses to migrants at high prices for use as workshops.[4] For many Chinese and some Italians in Prato, the fast-fashion sector remade the city's "Made in Italy" reputation by updating it to suit current clothing trends. Moreover, elite Chinese migrants began to create their own fashion brands by using fabrics made in Prato and by hiring Italian designers and Chinese workers for Italian market rates.

Under these economic and business conditions, it is not surprising that the mainstream Italian media took contradictory attitudes towards Chinese migrants. In general, in reporting on mass foreign immigration in the 1990s, it often adopted a paternalistic tone reducing migrants' migration motives to either poverty or political crises in their home countries. Occasionally, the Italian media interpreted the Chinese migration through these lenses, too. But more often, it sounded the alarm about Chinese competition: how Chinese migrant firms' illegal economic and business practices – such as prolonged working hours and tax evasion – were purportedly forcing Italian businesses out of both Milan's Via Sarpi area and Prato's textile and garment industries. These views were taken to the extreme by the right-wing media, such as *La Padania*, the mouthpiece of regionalist political party Lega Nord (Northern League). In time, because of anti-Chinese news articles' strong condemnation of illegal Chinese economic practices, pro-Chinese journalists emphasized admiration for migrants' ability to withstand harsh working conditions in pursuit of a better future. Some journalists even praised the industriousness said to characterize Wenzhounese migrant workers by comparing it with that of southern and rural Italian migrants during the nation's rapid industrialization in the 1950s and 1960s. Such coverage was supported by a vast and well-established network of pro-Chinese

Italian journalists and academics, some of whom were rather militant in their defence of Italy's Chinese.

Chinese migrants also joined these debates, thereby reinforcing the media polyphony concerning their migration. Particularly since the mid-2000s, migrant elites including entrepreneurs and journalists have been voicing their opinions on the merits and drawbacks of their entrepreneurship and migration in their own newspapers and magazines. These media stakeholders refuted biased Italian news coverage and protested Italian municipal authorities' harsh regulations that seemed to target the Chinese, such as street rules that prohibited the use of pushcarts to transport wholesalers' merchandise in Via Sarpi. These stakeholders argued that they had contributed to Italian globalization by investing economic and cultural capital in Italian cities. The Chinese migrant press also advised migrants on how to best modify their specific business practices and behaviour to counter mainstream society's opinions about them. Major Italian media outlets occasionally referenced and cited these challenges to Italian accusations, as well as recommendations to fellow migrants, showing how, by the mid-2000s, Chinese migrants' well-organized media outlets had considerable clout in Italy's mediascape.

These demographic, social, economic, and media dynamics of this migration were symptoms of a watershed chapter in twentieth- and twenty-first-century Italian-Chinese encounters, and particularly in Italian representations of the Chinese. Among the modern European countries that share a significant relationship with China, Italy boasts the oldest network of written texts, starting with the works of Marco Polo and Matteo Ricci.[5] Later, seventeenth-century Italy's decline in geopolitical importance and eighteenth-century China's policy to censor foreign trade reduced the movements and cultural production by travellers from both places. In the twentieth century, however, Italian journalism and films concerning China again became influential intellectual projects and intercultural texts in the West. These included, among others, Alberto Moravia's and Tiziano Terzani's news articles and Michelangelo Antonioni's *Cina Chung Kuo* (*China*) (1972) regarding the Cultural Revolution (1966–76), as well as Bernardo Bertolucci's *L'ultimo imperatore* (*The Last Emperor*) (1987), which obtained rare permission from the Chinese state to shoot on location in one of the country's most iconic places, the Forbidden City in Beijing.

Unlike in the past, when Italian narratives about the Chinese relied largely on Italians' travel in China, the years between 1992 and 2012 were the first in history that a significant number of people moved from China to Italy, eliciting remarkable media coverage. To be sure,

Italy was rather late in joining the cultural conversation about Chinese migrations in Europe, particularly when compared to Britain, France, and the Netherlands, whose colonial ties with territories where ethnic Chinese resided had experienced large-scale migration throughout the nineteenth and twentieth centuries. But the Italian and migrant news media's coverage of the Chinese migration offers crucial insights into the local-global redrawing of European societies, economies, and national-cultural identities in the age of migration since the 1990s.

In this book, I analyse the Chinese migration as it was conveyed in the news media between 1992 and 2012. During this twenty-year period, both the Italian media and Italy's Chinese migrant media covered this migration extensively, revealing the eye-opening characteristics of the Chinese community. I explain this strong media interest in Italian-Chinese migrant relations by placing it within relevant economic, political, cultural, and linguistic contexts. I examine how journalists, entrepreneurs, and politicians differed in and publicly debated their interpretations of the Chinese migration. I also explore what the debates over recent Chinese migration allowed these stakeholders to achieve within the Italian media and popular culture, in a period in which migrants settled in Italy at an unprecedented rate and in which China increased economic globalization that critically impacted Italy.

From 1992 to 2012, the mainstream Italian and Chinese migrant news media were the dominant source of information for the public on Chinese migration to Italy, which emerged through reporting on a phenomenon and three major social events. The analysis that forms the core of this book consists of four case studies, follows a roughly chronological order, and, except in the first case study (about the "Chinese mafia"), is classified by city (i.e., Milan, Prato, and Rome).

When interpreting the Chinese migration from the early 1990s to 2006, major Italian weeklies and the popular press prominently drew on the Chinese mafia trope, which the media helped to create when it extensively covered Italy's Chinese community for the first time in contemporary history. The "Chinese mafia" functioned not only as a shorthand for this migration, but also as an initial interpretive framework for migrants' entrepreneurship. During the 2000s, as the Italian media increasingly understood this migration as an economic phenomenon in need of better regulation by Italian municipal and police authorities, and as the Chinese migrant media began to protest, discussions about the supposed Chinese mafia gradually lost currency. But this topic, as well as its related discourses, has retained its interpretive appeal in Italian crime reporting about the Chinese.

On 12 April 2007, Chinese migrants and Italian police clashed violently in a dispute concerning parking and the use of pushcarts in the area near Via Sarpi, which had been recently reconceived as Milan's Chinatown, although most Chinese lived elsewhere in the city. The 2007 riot revealed tensions between migrants' economic practices during their settlement and the city government's determination to impose discipline. For the police, some residents of Via Sarpi, and Italian journalists, Chinese wholesaler businesses encroached on Italian spaces and identity. For Chinese migrants and pro-Chinese Italian journalists, the municipal authorities and the police's incongruent implementation of street rules and other regulations were discriminatory acts, a sign of the country's poor management of migrant settlements, and the result of a lack of Chinese participation in Italian politics.

Since the 1990s, Chinese migrant entrepreneurs and workers have transformed Prato into Europe's foremost fast-fashion production site. Meanwhile, the local textile industry, which traditionally supplied "Made in Italy" clothing, became increasingly unsustainable. Likewise, Prato's Italian ready-to-wear clothing firms lost market appeal in the 2000s. These circumstances provoked media debates, leading journalists inspired by nativism to argue that Prato's "Made in Italy" label should be limited to fabrics and garments made by Italian hands. On the contrary, pro-migrant and pro-globalization journalists advocated for a redefinition of "Made in Italy" to include Prato's Chinese-managed fast fashion. These issues were hotly debated in the media before and after the 2009 local elections that resulted in post-Second World War Prato's first right-wing government, which ordered a massive number of police raids on Chinese-owned factories, thereby deepening existing controversies.

The tensions between Italians and Chinese migrants as covered during the 2007 riot and in the Prato case study hardly surfaced in media reporting on a Chinese-organized march following the murder of two Chinese migrants in a working-class Roman neighbourhood in 2012. The random assassination of two migrants, one of whom was a baby girl, incited a media frenzy that drew on various Italian- and Chinese-language narratives of victimhood in order to claim the murder and march as a traumatic event for Italy's Chinese and in the recent history of Italy's migrant populations. Because of the extremely positive image of the Chinese that the media painted on this occasion, it seemed that Italian journalists were poised to integrate Chinese migrants into the Italian mediascape not as members of the Chinese mafia or as unruly and exploitative migrant merchants, but as normalized subjects.

Through analysing media debates in these four case studies, I examine why journalists, politicians, and entrepreneurs engaged in this intense and extensive coverage. Through mobilizing specific representations, what meanings did they make of this migration and what did they stand to gain? To be sure, they aimed to understand the Chinese migration from social, anthropological, criminological, and economic perspectives. Italy's Chinese became newsworthy thanks to both their dramatically increased numbers since the 1990s and the considerable wealth they had accumulated as successful entrepreneurs and dedicated workers since the 2000s. It took police, judges, and several years of scholarly fieldwork in the 1990s to more fully expose the mechanisms of this migration and its entrepreneurship. In those years, a few journalists pieced together disparate information from various credible or dubious sources, which led to criticism about the accuracy and appropriateness of such coverage.

But journalistic examinations of this migration from social scientific perspectives constituted only a small portion of the extensive coverage of Italy's Chinese. Had the utility of covering the Chinese migration been limited to understanding it, extensive coverage would have ceased once such knowledge was achieved. But as my analysis shows, even though accurate journalistic accounts of the migration emerged around the mid-2000s, media interest in it remained intense between 1992 and 2012 and particularly so after the mid-2000s. With this in mind, what were other main purposes of the ongoing enthusiastic debate?

I argue that journalists used the Chinese migration and migrants' entrepreneurship as a particularly effective example through which to approach Italy's stance towards integrating migrant populations and towards its economic globalization. These two umbrellas encompassed topics and perspectives of critical national concern because of how they shaped Italy's national identity, economy, and international reputation in recent decades. To address migrant incorporation, Milan's Chinatown was a dramatic case that could spark conversations on how a single ethnic group managed to insert its commercial centre into a traditional Italian neighbourhood and created the most notable Chinese quarter in Southern Europe. When considering Italy's economic globalization, what other recent migrant entrepreneurship could provide as powerful and controversial an example to ignite debate as the often-cited threat posed by Prato's Chinese-owned fast-fashion sector to local industrial traditions in textile and ready-to-wear production?

To address migrant entrepreneurship's role in Italy's economic globalization, journalists could have chosen to cover, for instance,

Egyptian-owned restaurants in Milan, which received some Italian media attention but no significant international coverage. But compared to the Egyptian-Italian case, Prato's Chinese-Italian tensions were a much more effective way for journalists to illustrate conflicts between localism and globalization, to initiate debate, and to catalogue debate in order to suggest some kind of solution. This is because the manufacturing and symbolic competition between "Made in Italy" and "Made in China" garments remained at the heart of Italy's global competitiveness in a sector in which it used to excel unchallenged. To cite another example, the media has dedicated considerable attention to organized crime involving Italy's various migrant groups and their criminal entrepreneurial and commercial activities, including the Albanians and the Russians. But, as far as I can tell, Italy's Albanian and Russian "mafias" have not received the sustained, intensely racist and orientalist journalistic and cultural treatment that the "Chinese mafia" has since the early 1990s, which pro-Chinese journalists and academics then tried in earnest to dismantle in their own representations of the community.

Therefore, as the first central argument in this book, I propose that the integration of migrants into Italian society and media culture, along with the negotiation of globalization in local business environments, were the two main areas of debate where the Chinese migration gained currency in the news media. This migration was a very effective vehicle for journalists, politicians, and entrepreneurs to persuasively discuss these two rather broad national concerns, in which many news topics and perspectives could be included for debate and then generalized, albeit falsely and often implicitly, to refer to other migrants. Regarding the first area of debate, a broader media discussion about migrants' spatial practices in Italian neighbourhoods could be dramatically articulated through the Chinese migrants' use of pushcarts on the sidewalks and the subsequent riot in Milan's Chinatown. Regarding the second area of debate, Prato's globalized fast-fashion sector, owned by the Chinese who worked very long hours, functioned as a paradigmatic example to debate about migrants' violation of local laws and apparent splintering from local (textile and ready-to-wear) manufacturing traditions.

The second central argument concerns how media texts formulated and communicated such meanings. Which sources were used to explain the Chinese migration? Which methods were adopted to narrate facts and events? Why might a particular construction of an argument appear persuasive to participants – including journalists and readers – in any debate concerning Italy's Chinese? I maintain that as journalists, in addition to politicians and entrepreneurs, debated about migrant incorporation and economic globalization, they created, used, and refashioned an Italian-Chinese migrant cultural repertoire. They turned to this repertoire for available cultural tools and resources that would allow for a sufficient and timely coverage of any of the four case studies at the heart of my analysis. In using this repertoire, which often constrained their interpretations of the Chinese migration, they also remade it; for example, they added new topics, or invalidated and then discarded certain perspectives.

I examine three primary categories of tools and resources in this repertoire. First, journalists focused on newsworthy topics that they considered relevant and important to their stories. A significant topic has been Chinese migrant entrepreneurship and its impact on the Italian economy. Second, journalists used textual mechanisms in specific passages of their articles to approach these topics, including conventionally accepted perspectives, rhetorical devices, and discursive strategies that helped to construct arguments. They deployed the time-honoured criminological perspective on the Chinese diasporas in discussions of the Chinese migration to Italy in the 1990s. In this context, the supposed or real organized crime originating from the Chinese migrant group was used as a metaphor for that entire migrant community. These practices revealed the ethnocultural approach and narratives of victimhood, which are the discursive strategies that I focus on in this book. Third, in the overall arrangement of their news accounts, journalists adopted specific frames when selecting and highlighting topics and textual mechanisms in order to have a common effect on large portions of their audiences. In the Italian-Chinese context, the two most significant frames pertain to Italian-migrant and local-global dynamics.

The last category merits further explanation. For media practitioners and scholars, frames are abstractions that structure message meaning in news coverage. Framing refers to the act of calling attention to certain events and placing them in certain contexts in order to create specific meanings. At the broadest level in this book, by reformulating Robert M. Entman's definitions of frames and framing, I view the Italian-migrant and local-global frames as structuring the ways in which journalists selected and highlighted particular topics, events, and perspectives to debate the Chinese migration settlement in Italy. By using these two frames, journalists reporting on the Chinese migration were able to, for instance, define its problems, diagnose its causes, pass moral judgments about it, suggest remedies for politicians and others to address it, and elucidate its significance for all immigration to Italy.[6]

I use the Italian-migrant and local-global frames to refer to the mechanisms of narrowing debates respectively to those that concern migrant incorporation and to those that concern economic globalization. These frames were by no means applied exclusively to the coverage of Italy's Chinese; since the 1990s, they have arguably been two dominant ways to interpret the general question of immigration in Italy. Yet, the Chinese migration has consistently provided a particularly meaningful example to legitimate these frames for approaching immigration. Compared to the more complex historical and cultural intermingling between Europeans and Africans, or between western and eastern Europeans, the Italians and the Chinese could be easily coded in the media on the basis of their vastly different ethnic and cultural identities. Journalists could then use this coding to argue that the Italian-Chinese migrant case was the most dramatic example of cultural incompatibility between Italians and migrants. Regarding the local-global frame, of all Italy's migrant populations' origin countries, China has posed the greatest threat to the country's standing in the global economy since the 2000s. By viewing Chinese migrant entrepreneurship in Italy as part of Chinese economic globalization, journalists could defend Italian firms; they could suggest that other migrant entrepreneurships in Italy might have a comparable impact on the country's economy if permitted to grow undisciplined, as had occurred when Italian authorities allowed Chinese migrants to import "Made in China" products. Thus, the role of Chinese migrants in the media was to effectively and dramatically set the stage for, and sometimes deepen, debates around larger issues of migrant integration and economic globalization. This book explains these textual, discursive, and framing processes in detail.

In support of my two central arguments, I analyse the media and cultural contexts of recent Chinese migration to Italy by drawing on a large, existing social science scholarship. Several case studies focus on Chinese migrant communities and their economic and social lives in Italian cities and regions. Significant subjects in this body of research include migration (migrants' movement and incorporation), diaspora (connections between a post-migration population, their homeland, and their conationals elsewhere), and transnationalism (ongoing exchanges and movements within the migrant's diasporic networks). However, earlier scholars, including those proficient in Chinese, typically interpret Chinese migration to Italy as a primarily economic and social phenomenon, without placing it within the country's media and cultural milieus, even as they occasionally reference Italian- and Chinese-language newspapers published in Italy.[7] Therefore, rarely do these studies analyse the works of journalists and other cultural practitioners who frame and negotiate migrant transnationalism and economic globalization for the Italian public, politicians, and entrepreneurs. As a result, there is also no systematic analysis of the interventions of the Chinese migrant press into relevant media debates. Even in previous cultural studies that address both Italian and migrant views of Italian-migrant interactions and conflicts, the Chinese case is often glossed over or neglected. This scenario is regrettable; the Chinese migration has generated extensive media coverage in Italy and beyond, and it has also reinforced cultural narratives of recurring issues in Italian-migrant encounters, such as the perceived encroachment of immigrants on Italian national identity and the role of migrant entrepreneurship in the Italian economy.

In providing these missing links, my book is the first to examine both Italian and Chinese migrant coverage, particularly the dialogue that existed between them, in order to show how recent Chinese migration to Italy helped to stimulate media and public conversations on the effects of mass migration and economic globalization on Italy. I wish to demonstrate that, apart from more empirical studies of Chinese migration to Italy, a detailed media and cultural analysis of it is indispensable to understanding how the Italians and the Chinese migrants perceived this migrant community in their social lives and cultural imaginations. Therefore, my analysis is humanistic but borrows concepts from the social sciences, particularly from the study of meaning-making processes in cultural sociology as championed by Ann Swidler, Pierre Bourdieu, Michèle Lamont, and Jeffrey C. Alexander.[8] In my close readings of media texts, I also make collaborative use of theories and insights from scholarship on migration, diaspora, transnationalism, globalization, mobility, race, ethnicity, gender, communication, and cultural studies.[9] Following the call of sociologists Robin Cohen and Gunvor Jónsson for more cultural analysis in migration studies, this book provides the first substantial media and cultural study of Chinese migration to Italy.[10]

Although I do not gesture at the wider implications of the Italian-Chinese migrant case through a comparison with other Italian-migrant and European-Chinese migrant experiences, my emphasis on the media and migration would also be useful for research on other migrations to Italy and on Chinese diasporas elsewhere. Currently, no comparable media and cultural studies address any other migrant group from both Italian and migrant perspectives, including analyses of print journalism and television. As numerous English-language volumes have analysed literary, cinematic, and cultural aspects of non-Chinese migrant communities in Italy, I study the Chinese migration through the news media in Italy.[11] Moreover, I take up the challenge Frank Pieke poses in investigating the role of culture in Chinese migrations in Europe.[12] Through this book, scholars of the global Chinese diaspora will gain a better understanding of how media culture in Italy complicates conceptual and practical problems pertaining to Italian-Chinese migrant encounters.

Although my study does not offer solutions for Italian-Chinese migrant conflict, some of my insights, alongside my methodology and use of theories, may prove instructive for Italian-Chinese intercultural communication, left- and right-leaning political conflicts, and local adaptation to economic globalization. Only with a better understanding of the Italian-Chinese migrant media and cultural landscape can politicians, law enforcement, and the non-migrant public in Italy hope to create more effective programs to interact with migrants. Moreover, only with a firm grasp of these cultural dynamics can the very valid arguments against anti-Chinese slanders be viewed as more than ideological partisanship. For readers who seek a course of action for future Italian-Chinese migrant encounters, my book provides a balanced assessment of media and cultural debates regarding the Chinese migration to Italy between 1992 and 2012.

Overview

In chapter 1, I recount the general sociohistorical background of contemporary Chinese migration to Italy before outlining my methodology and the material I analyse in the rest of the book. I then expand the introduction's explanations of this book's two central arguments. I explore why Chinese migration to Italy became an effective example in media discussions about the country's migrant incorporation and economic globalization. I also theorize what I call the Italian-Chinese migrant repertoire and examine how it enabled as well as constrained media debates concerning this migration.

In chapter 2, I chart the evolving news representations of the Chinese mafia in print and on television from 1992 to 2006. I analyse the sociohistorical and discursive reasons that the Chinese mafia became a favourite prism through which to interpret Chinese migration at this time. In the news media, actual or presumed Chinese criminality in Italy was compared to its counterpart in the United States, as well as to such Italian criminal organizations as the Cosa Nostra and the Camorra.

These parallels helped to create a new metaphor in the 1990s – i.e., the Chinese migrant community was like the Chinese mafia – which Italian journalists used to characterize this migration in their crime reporting and which Chinese migrants subsequently contested.

In chapters 3 and 4, I analyse the implications of the 2007 riot from Italian and Chinese migrant media perspectives. The riot provided the ideologically heterogeneous Italian news media and the Chinese migrant print press with an unprecedented opportunity to reinforce, as well as to modify, positive and negative Chinese stereotypes. This riot fuelled Italian debates on key obstacles to migrants' cultural integration, such as their political marginalization, illegal business practices that supposedly justified institutional disciplinary measures, racism, and migrants' perceived encroachment on Italian national identity. I sequence chapters 3 and 4 to underscore the Chinese migrants' reactions to related Italian coverage and to illustrate how the media reinforced the Italian-migrant frame. While these two chapters examine the widest range of situations that pertain to the Italian-Chinese repertoire as used in this book, they do so for one particular moment: the year 2007.

In chapters 5 and 6, I focus on the political purposes of police raids on Chinese factories and on the dynamic between the restricted and expanded definitions of "Made in Italy." As they discussed Prato's local industries and institutional discipline, journalists claimed to elucidate their significance for other "Made in Italy" industries and for European countries that faced business competition from Chinese migrants and mainlanders. Italian television programs played a key role in the media's attempts to restrategize and republicize Prato as a global competitor. I examine Italian and Chinese migrant perspectives local to Prato in chapter 5 and address international views from the United States, Germany, Japan, and China in chapter 6. Together, these two chapters give a broad view of the local-global framing in media and cultural debate on the Chinese migration. Unlike the previous two chapters, chapters 5 and 6 examine the Italian-Chinese repertoire as it evolved over several years between 2005 and 2012.

In chapter 7, I explain how the Italian and the Chinese migrant media painted an extremely positive image of Chinese migrants following the murder of two Chinese migrants and a subsequent Chinese-organized march in Rome in 2012. Italian photographers and Chinese migrant activists captured moments of mourning and activated victimhood narratives. I suggest that these narratives helped to shape the murder and march into a trauma in the Italian national memory that involves immigrants. This chapter deepens and concludes my discussions of two key issues initially examined in chapter 2: genre requirements of Italian crime reporting, and victimhood narratives based on the supposed parallels between Italian and Chinese organized crime.

Chapter 1

Chinese Migration to Italy, Globalization, and the News Media

A General Background of the Chinese Migration to Italy

Small numbers of Chinese peddlers, probably only a few hundred, travelled to Italy from France during the 1920s and 1930s. These pioneers had chosen Europe over more traditional Chinese emigration destinations such as Southeast Asia and Japan with the hope of being able to move more easily within Europe should business prospects in one place – as had occurred in France – become untenable. By the 1940s, approximately one thousand Chinese resided in Italy. This early migration history made the Chinese community the oldest non-white foreign community in continuous residence in twentieth-century Italy.[1]

Despite this long history, Italy's Chinese population grew markedly only in the late 1980s and early 1990s. According to Italian state records, the number of Chinese residents increased from about 8,500 in 1989 to about 22,900 in 1992, and to more than 200,000 in 2012. But the number of undocumented Chinese migrants, which official statistics do not capture, increased the total Chinese population significantly. Moreover, between 1992 and 2012, Italy hosted the third-largest Chinese community in Europe (excluding Russia), after France (estimated at 500,000 in 2005) and Britain (about 335,000 in 2009).[2]

Since the 1990s, the Chinese have also formed one of Italy's largest migrant groups. While in 1992 they were only the eighth-largest migrant group in Italy, by 2012 they were the fourth largest. Comprising 4.6 per cent of the 4.4 million non-Italian citizens residing in Italy, whose total population was approximately 60 million, the Chinese ranked far below the Romanians, Albanians, and Moroccans, who comprised the three largest migrant groups in Italy in the late 2000s and early 2010s at 21.2 per cent, 10.6 per cent, and 9.9 per cent respectively.[3] Nevertheless, the number of Italy's Chinese is impressive considering that they had no apparent link with the country, unlike the first three groups with connections through European Union membership, colonial history, or geographic proximity.

What, then, accounts for the large-scale Chinese migration to Italy during the 1990s and 2000s? To begin, between the late 1980s and early 2000s, like many migrants who now reside legally in Italy, droves of Chinese migrants sought permits to stay (permessi di soggiorno in Italian) through numerous regularizations. Following schemes issued in 1986, 1990 (Legge Martelli), 1995, and 1998 (Legge Turco-Napolitano), the 2002 law (Legge Bossi-Fini) included the largest amnesty then ever granted in Europe. These regularizations and related laws have remained the basis of Italy's immigration policies to the present. Originally intended to legalize undocumented migrants who already lived in the country, the regulations attracted illegal migrants, including the Chinese, from other parts of Europe to Italy.[4]

Apart from Italy's more favourable institutional milieu for regularizing migrants, the Chinese migrated to Italy during the 1990s and 2000s in order to take advantage of the country's good entrepreneurial opportunities and increase their wealth and social standing. Italy's large underground economy, which employed cheap labour with unofficial contracts, significantly facilitated migrants' economic integration. Within this shadow economy, the Chinese considered the business prospects of their host cities to be a key motivation for migration. In the 1990s, most lived and worked in either major cities with good commercial and transport networks, such as Milan, Turin, Rome, Florence, Bologna, and Naples, or in specialized industrial districts in need of cheap labour and a low-skilled workforce, such as Prato-Florence-Empoli and Terzino-San Giuseppe Vesuviano. In the 2000s, these locations also offered the Chinese new opportunities to grow their businesses, such as in the service sector in major Italian cities and in the fast-fashion sector in Prato's industrial district.

The Chinese in Italy run many kinds of family-owned small- and medium-sized businesses. As a traditional trade for the Chinese overseas, the restaurant industry emerged in Milan and Rome during the 1960s and remains a favourite business activity for migrants today. A related activity in recent years is to manage traditional Italian cafés. Since the mid-1980s, Italy's Chinese have specialized in the manufacture of fast fashion, textiles, and leather goods, particularly in the Prato-Florence-Empoli area. As economic globalization has intensified since the 1990s, migrants have also operated import-export firms in Rome, Milan, and Naples. The growth of the Chinese population in Italy also led to the emergence of service businesses for their communities.[5]

With this variety of business, the Chinese community has always been a leader in migrant entrepreneurship in Italy. Statistics show that in the early 2000s the Chinese owned more firms than any other single migrant group in Milan and in Rome. Nationally, the Chinese operated around 42,703 enterprises in 2012, a number second only to firms owned by the much larger Moroccan migrant community. Moreover, in the same period, Chinese migrant companies dominated in Prato and ranked second in Milan (after the Egyptians) and Rome (after the Romanians).[6]

The legal and economic pull factors that drew the Chinese to Italy during the 1990s and 2000s worked in tandem with push factors in China. In the early 1980s, China's Open Door policy loosened previous restrictions on emigration. Starting in 1986, the Chinese state substantially relaxed its policies on its citizens' right to leave and to return to the country. By 2005, residents of 193 large- and medium-sized Chinese cities were able to obtain passports by presenting their national identity cards and household registration documents to the authorities.[7] Among the first to take advantage of these state policies were migrants from Wenzhou and its surrounding counties – including Wencheng, Qingtian, and Rui'an – in Zhejiang Province in eastern China, which has been one of the most economically prosperous regions in China in recent decades. Wenzhounese migrants to Italy were not typically driven by poverty; rather, most aspired to own businesses but lacked the means to do so back home. Indeed, Wenzhou and its surrounding counties have been time-honoured places of emigration (*qiao xiang* in Chinese), with a well-established transnational network that has made chain migration to Europe extremely desirable, particularly for single young men.[8] Thanks to chain migration, the majority of Italy's Chinese populations hail from Wenzhou and its neighbouring areas. Because most Chinese-identified migrants who reside in Italy, or their parents, were born in mainland China, the Chinese-language newspapers that I analyse in this book originate from a shared cultural tradition. In contrast, the Chinese populations in Britain, the Netherlands, France, and Portugal are of diverse geographical origins (e.g., ethnic Chinese in Vietnam who migrated to France), making the study of their national belonging and ideological leanings more complicated.[9]

The preceding major factors that motivated the Chinese to migrate to Italy between 1992 and 2012 exhibit entrepreneurial zeal. The Chinese are often considered to be the most entrepreneurial among Italy's self-employed migrants, thanks to their explicit, and at times singular, migration agenda to pursue business opportunities in the country. (In this context, "self-employment" refers to the practice of how autonomous employers who are migrants themselves hire from within their own national or ethnic group.) During the 2000s, despite fluctuations in the creation and closure of Chinese migrant firms, it is likely that the Chinese enjoyed the highest percentage of self-employment among Italy's migrant communities. Approximately 27 per cent of self-employed migrants in Rome in the early 2000s were Chinese. In 2012, 14.7 per cent of all self-employed migrants in Italy were Chinese, trailing just behind the much larger Moroccan (16.4 per cent) and Romanian (15.4 per cent) migrant communities.[10]

Since the 1990s, family-owned Chinese firms have absorbed the bulk of migrant labour from China to Italy. The Chinese migrant business network has meant that the numbers of Chinese migrants who obtained residence papers may have increased more steadily than those of other ethnic groups. This observation is related to a particular dilemma that many of Italy's migrant workers faced: initially, migrants benefited from a regularization scheme to obtain a conditional and temporary legal status in Italy for a limited time period. But they could lose this status when their permits expired because an extension required having a new job offer, preferably one more permanent than seasonal or temporary work. Until recently, the migrant entrepreneurship and its strong self-employment pattern provided Chinese migrants with a steady flow of job offers and so helped them to address this problem.[11] In contrast, when negotiating employment, other migrant groups were often only able to count on the support of advocacy groups, including Caritas, which operated on the basis of Catholic humanitarianism; employers' associations, such as those in northeast Italy, which relied on a large number of immigrants in the workforce; and, occasionally, trade unions, when they fought for the universal rights of workers on Italian soil.[12] The net result of the migrants' reliance on these groups proved less reliable than the Chinese migrant business network.

Overall, since the 1990s the Chinese have distinguished themselves from other migrants in Italy through their focus on small business ownership, the high rate of self-employment within the community, and a relatively mature migrant entrepreneurship that resulted from these practices. Wenzhounese migrants to Italy share these traits with contemporary Chinese trade and labour diasporas elsewhere in Europe and within China.[13] The entrepreneurial fervor of Italy's Chinese produced several noticeable corollary effects, including the suppression of personal time in favour of longer working hours. Self-employment also made Chinese with no strong social or employment networks in Italy, particularly those from areas other than Wenzhou, vulnerable to their employers' exploitation. The Italian media avidly covered the positive and negative side effects of this entrepreneurship, cementing the image of Chinese migrants as either "model migrants" or "labor slaves" – in other words, controversially.[14]

After more than two decades of phenomenal growth, Chinese migration to Italy began to slow down in the early 2010s. News reports during these years observed that a significant number of Chinese migrants left the country. According to key observers from Italy's Chinese community, a decade of economic stagnation and recession in Italy during the 2000s had taken its toll on migrant businesses. Some returned to China, while others went on to explore markets in eastern Europe and other southern European countries. Covering the subject prominently for the first time, the *Financial Times* examined the departure of Chinese migrants from Rome throughout 2012 in a story that the mainstream Italian media, including *Corriere della Sera* and Telecom's La7, enthusiastically disseminated.[15]

But the reality of this migration was more complex than the media coverage intimated. Italy's Chinese population did not conform to one category of mobile subject, as it included short-term migrant labourers, members of a trade diaspora, settlers (i.e., those seeking to live permanently in the country), and transnationals who each favoured different modes of mobility that could impact the official population estimates.[16] It is equally difficult to determine the precise number of returnees to China, migrants to other countries, and new arrivals in Italy over the years. Some migrants returned to China even during the 1990s, a decade that is often considered the heyday of Chinese migrant entrepreneurship in Italy, while others, propelled by fast fashion's mobility imperative and by new entrepreneurial opportunities in import-export, moved between Italian cities and European countries numerous times, living in one place only for a limited period, thereby resulting in inaccurate official counts.[17] In any event, in 2012–13 the number of Chinese with Italian residency permits continued to grow as more undocumented migrants found ways to become legalized, particularly those from places in China outside Zhejiang Province.[18]

Nevertheless, I focus on the period between 1992 and 2012 in this book, because it was in these two decades that the media definitively moulded the social perception of and cultural imagination about Chinese migrants in Italy. This period saw a relatively advanced stage in the relationship between the Italian state and its migrant populations, in which conflicts and collaborations became frequent and complicated.[19] In 1992, extensive Italian media coverage of the supposed Chinese mafia peaked for the first time. A demarcation line appeared in 2012, when the most virulent media accounts seemed to have run their course, as both the Italian and the Chinese migrant media were empathetic to the Chinese community after two of its members were murdered. Moreover, media debates concerning the 2007 Milan riot and the 2009 and 2010 Italian-Chinese conflicts in Prato generated a steady supply of films and novels that had refashioned the Italian-Chinese migrant cultural landscape by 2012.[20] Thus, the twenty-year period represents a unique historical moment in the age of information and the knowledge economy, when it became paramount for the news media in Italy to accommodate and offer hospitality to the transnational Chinese migrant community in their coverage.

This book offers a history of these media narratives and the cultural politics they articulated in relation to the three most economically important Italian cities in the landscape of this migration: Milan, Prato, and Rome.[21] The visibility of Chinese migrants in Milan, the oldest Chinese community in Italy, increased significantly during this period. In 2010, the city was home to almost 18,900 Chinese migrants, Italy's largest Chinese community according to official records, outnumbered only by the Filipinos (approximately 33,700) and the Egyptians (about 28,600).[22] The community was spread across Milan and was not confined, as some believed, to the area around Via Sarpi and Via Canonica, which acted as its service and commercial centre.[23] Milan's Chinese migrant entrepreneurship was arguably the most diversified in Italy. While factories and wholesalers have always existed, since the 1990s entrepreneurs have been active in the service sector, like their colleagues in Rome, thereby differentiating themselves significantly from those investing in Prato's textile and garment industries. Working in the service sector presumably intensified interactions among the Chinese, the Italians, and other migrant groups, a condition that led some scholars and the media to claim that the Chinese were the migrants most effectively integrated into mainstream Italian society.[24]

By 2010, Prato had become home to Italy's second-largest Chinese community, with 11,900 registered residents. Scholars believe that Prato's illegal Chinese migrants accounted for 15 to 20 per cent of the city's entire Chinese population, while police reports concerning illegal Chinese businesses estimated 43 per cent. Thus, the Chinese would have constituted about 15 to 25 per cent of Prato's population during the 2000s. In 2010–11, the Italian media estimated Prato's Chinese population to be 50,000, while a Chinese migrant newspaper cited 100,000. Regardless, Prato was very likely the Italian city with the highest Chinese population in the late 2000s and early 2010s. During those years, the Chinese were also the dominant migrant community in Prato, where more than 15 per cent of the local population was foreign-born.

The extremely high concentration of the Chinese in a relatively small city dramatically bolstered their visibility.[25]

As one of the most important textile and garment manufacturing centres in Italy, Prato's Italian firms employ a significant number of migrants. The Chinese entered this highly specialized industrial district in the mid-1980s, and the majority manufactured ready-to-wear and leather garments and bags for Italian suppliers, including local clothing companies and major national fashion houses. Since the 2000s, Chinese migrant entrepreneurs have worked in the entire production process in these sectors, competing with and eventually surpassing a large number of Italian factories, which had already shown signs of crisis. In the late 2000s and early 2010s, seeking other routes to success, some migrant entrepreneurs also began to fill their orders in China and then import merchandise into Italy. But Prato's Chinese have always focused on the garment industry, specifically the fast-fashion sector, where they excelled and became well-known worldwide.[26]

As in Milan, Rome's Chinese businesses have historically been concentrated in the service sector. The Chinese in Rome had an official population of 12,000 in 2010, thereby making them Italy's third-largest Chinese community and Rome's fourth-largest migrant group. Their commercial activities have been focused in Esquilino and other areas east of the capital's historical centre. During the 2000s, import-export firms gradually became the most attractive route to success for Italy's Chinese, with Rome serving as their centre at the beginning of the decade.[27]

What differentiated Rome from Milan and Prato between 1992 and 2012 was its status as the headquarters of important Chinese migrant newspapers and magazines, the setting of some of the first Italian films about Chinese migrants, and the site of high-profile and often state-sponsored Chinese-Italian cultural events and organizations. Founded by Hu Lanbo in Rome in 2001, the magazine *Cina in Italia* (China in Italy) published bilingually for both Chinese migrant and Italian readers. *Ouhua Lianhe Shibao/Il Tempo Europa Cina/Ouhua Italy*, the oldest and most widely circulated Chinese-language newspaper in Italy, has been based in Rome since 1996. Associna was founded in Rome in 2005; it became the most important so-called second-generation Chinese-Italian association, as well as one of the first organizations created by young, second-generation migrants in Italy. The year 2004 saw the screening of one of the first documentary films about the Chinese migration, Gianfranco Giagni's *Un cinese a Roma* (A Chinese in Rome). One of the first Italian fiction films about this migration, the 2008 comedy *Questa notte è ancora nostra* (This night is still ours) was likewise set in the eternal city. In 2006, Italy's Confucius Institute opened in Rome, one of the first of its kind established in Europe. Finally, in 2010 and 2011, a series of intergovernmental cultural events titled "L'anno culturale della Cina in Italia" (The cultural year of China in Italy) took place mostly in Rome.

Given the economic and social importance of Milan, Prato, and Rome for Italy's Chinese migrants, significant media coverage focused on these three cities. In the next section, I discuss my dialogical approach to the large body of material analysed in this book, which shaped my selection of key media accounts and my conclusions. This methodological explanation prepares the grounds for detailing, in this chapter's last two sections, the specific contexts in which this media coverage emerged as well as the cultural and political purposes it served.

Dialogical Analysis and Methodology

The encounters between the Italians and the Chinese migrants between 1992 and 2012 were dialogical processes. A premise of this book is that these processes in the material world were conveyed to the broader public through textual and discursive interactions within the news media. To be sure, individual news articles and television programs about Italy's Chinese population served purposes relative to the specific contexts and cases at hand. However, when taken as a whole, this material was created in order to respond to the more or less bounded social reality of contemporary Chinese migration to Italy. Further, as John Downing and Charles Husband contend, while individual journalists should not be unduly blamed for misinterpreting events because of their institutional and industrial restraints, the profession's betterment ultimately boils down to its practitioners' intercultural media competencies.[28] The best place to demonstrate these competencies, or the lack thereof, to the general public is journalism. Therefore, I view the media coverage produced between 1992 and 2012 as a discursive laboratory in which different journalistic, political, and cultural narratives of the Chinese migration converged and were negotiated. Both sides of the interlocutors in the dialogical process were able to access and contest these media texts and narratives.

Within this framework, my analysis in the following chapters will focus on the textual and discursive aspects of news articles and television programs, including analyses of specific choices in topics, frames, schemata, quotations, lexical and semantic moves, argumentative styles, and rhetoric, as well as the social, economic, and cultural meanings of these choices. On a much smaller scale, I have also incorporated aspects of news production and the profession in general, including hiring, news gathering, and social standing, whenever possible and necessary.[29] This focus guided my research in the archives of the Italian and the Chinese migrant news media for key coverage. I also identified several pivotal accounts in the American, German, Japanese, and mainland Chinese news media that give global perspectives on Italian-Chinese migrant encounters. Altogether, more than three hundred media texts form the core of the primary material used for this book.

These texts represent a wide range of news media formats, including print and online newspapers and magazines, broadcast and internet television news, television talk shows and current affairs programs, online websites and forums, and photojournalism. Italian television news was the dominant source of public information in Italy during the period that I discuss. I researched the archives of the state-owned broadcaster Rai and the private-owned company Mediaset, which have dominated Italy's television industry since the 1990s. I also accessed the archives of a popular local television service, Prato TV, for the two chapters focused on that city. In addition, I consulted several internet television programs available on the websites of *La Repubblica* and *Corriere della Sera,* which were designed to give viewers more flexibility than conventionally broadcast television, and Rai, Mediaset, and Prato TV, which often made their broadcasts available online as video clips.

When examining newspapers and current affairs magazines published in Italy, which were the second most important source for this book, I used accounts that narrated social issues and events from diverse, and at times opposing, political ideologies and cultural perspectives. The mainstream Italian national newspapers I surveyed include the centre-left *La Repubblica* and *La Stampa,* the centrist *Corriere della Sera,* and the centre-right *Il Giornale.* I read articles from such progressive newspapers as *Il Manifesto, Liberazione,* and *L'Unità* alongside those from such main conservative newspapers as *Il Giorno, Libero,* and *La Padania.* To examine media coverage of diverse political persuasions is a necessary exercise for two reasons. First, in the following chapters, I challenge the notion that the Italian left always employed a multicultural rhetoric about Chinese immigrants, or that such rhetoric has been wholly beneficial to them in media debates. Second, I analyse how Italy's mainstream right-leaning media shared and distributed many ideas about Chinese migrants that had originated from extreme right-wing news media.[30]

Different case studies required different primary texts. Leading national weeklies such as *L'Espresso* and *Panorama,* as well as the Christian weekly *Famiglia Cristiana,* enthusiastically reported on the 2007

Milan riot. I used popular local newspapers *La Nazione* and *Il Tirreno* for the Prato case study and *Il Messaggero* for the march in Rome. Given a local-global framework in the Prato coverage, I gleaned additional material from such general-interest news media as *Der Spiegel, Die Zeit, Die Welt,* the *New York Times, Time, Voice of America,* and Japan's national broadcasting company, NHK. Since Prato's Italian-Chinese clashes were primarily caused by economic factors, I also gave prominence to coverage drawn from influential business-focused newspapers, including *Il Sole 24 Ore, Bloomberg Businessweek,* and the *Financial Times,* which took different editorial stances on economic globalization.

With regard to Italy's Chinese migrant news coverage, I privileged more extensive commentaries and editorials, in which elite migrants expressed their opinions more clearly, over day-to-day reporting. I researched the archives of *Ouzhou Qiaobao/Europe China News* in its main office, located in Via Sarpi. Online archives for *Ouhua Lianhe Shibao* and *Xinhua Lianhe Shibao/La Nuova Cina* were available in the early 2010s, although subsequently some of these sources were deleted. I only used a handful of articles published in *Ouzhou Huaren Bao/Europe Chinese News* because its archives were not accessible to me at the time of my research. These four have been the major newspapers published by Italy's Chinese community since the 2000s.[31] Further, I thoroughly researched the archives of the two main Italian-Chinese bilingual magazines, *Cina in Italia* (Rome, 2001–) and *It's China* (Campi Bisenzio, 2003–14), and those of Associna's bilingual website. I also selected several articles from mainland Chinese news media as additional evidence of Chinese migrant perspectives, particularly in reprints and collaborative reporting. Finally, I interviewed a key media professional in the Chinese community in Italy, and I consulted several interviews with Chinese migrants published in existing sociological and anthropological studies.

While this primary material has been widely available to the public, previous scholars have not brought Italian- and Chinese-language texts into dialogue with one another in any significant way. They also have not analysed dialogues between pro-Chinese and anti-Chinese, or pro-migrant and nativist, positions as articulated in this extensive media coverage. My textual and discourse analysis will probe two possible reasons for this omission.

Although a considerable body of scholarship on Italian media depictions of migrants exists, some of which touches on the Chinese case, Chinese migrant media coverage has not always been considered worthy of extensive critical analysis because it largely caters to Italy's Chinese, who Italian society has often viewed as culturally unsophisticated. To borrow a term coined by Rey Chow, I suggest that some critics, including those who are versed in the Chinese language and able to read these newspapers, nurture a "orientalist melancholia" towards Chinese migrants in Italy. That is, some journalists and critics who are knowledgeable of Chinese high culture accuse migrants of failing to rise to the grandeur of their home country's cultural heritage, obsessed as these migrants are with economic pursuits.[32] I wish to avoid this pitfall and examine Chinese-language coverage in order to understand what was economically, socially, and politically at stake for migrant journalists as they countered accusations of illegal business activities and other issues.

Moreover, using the words of Ella Shohat and Robert Stam, previous critics have tended to "take a monolithically hostile attitude towards dominant media." In the present context, this critical approach often does not allow for a nuanced analysis of the polysemy of Italian-language media narratives of Chinese migrants. Too much ink has been spilt on mainstream news media's false claims about Italy's Chinese without detailing the specific contexts and purposes of those claims and without examining alternative media reactions to them. Therefore, still drawing on Shohat and Stam, I analyse the "cultural polyphony" that emerges from existing dialogues among Italian-language media coverage of diverse political and ideological persuasions.[33] Ultimately, discussions of dialogue among diverse Italian news media, as well as those between the Italian and the Chinese migrant media, will take an additional step towards understanding Italian-Chinese migrant encounters in the empirical world.

As I pose the question of how Italians and Chinese migrants with various social backgrounds and political aspirations managed to speak with one another on Italian-Chinese migrant issues between 1992 and 2012, I anchor my dialogical analysis to a solid theoretical base. Following James Clifford's observations about travelling and dwelling, I analyse existing dialogues in the news media between travelling Chinese migrants and settled Italian natives, between Chinese migrants with first-person diasporic experiences and Italian journalists who acquired knowledge of Chinese culture from secondary sources, and between cosmopolitan-minded and nativist-inclined journalists. Likewise, Stephen Greenblatt's analysis of mobility and stasis underscores the value of dialogism. Like Greenblatt, I examine points of debate that pertain to two orders of things: concrete issues in the empirical world and symbolic exchanges through languages, metaphors, and images. (Thus, in relation to the Prato case study, I analyse both debates about Chinese migrants' illegal business practices and those about the competition between "Made in Italy" and "Made in China" based on brand reputations.) In keeping with Homi Bhabha's theorization, I view the in-between spaces, which media coverage of Italian-Chinese migrant social encounters helped to create, as the location of cultural production and negotiation of the Chinese migration.[34]

Admittedly, these critical insights apply more to Chinese migrant elites and Italian journalists and politicians than to less-cosmopolitan migrants and Italians, who experienced power imbalances, discrepancies in knowledge and technologies, and systematic discrimination.[35] Because my book aims to lay the groundwork for future cultural analysis of Italy's Chinese, I focus on episodes concerning Chinese migrants and Italians with significant social, economic, and cultural capital. When describing migrants and Italians with less media and cultural capital, particularly in chapters 4 and 5, I provide a "thick" description of each case: the highly contextualized descriptions of cultural interactions, as Clifford Geertz practices.[36]

My final methodological concern is the following: Is my dialogical analysis of the Italian-Chinese encounters, ostensibly based on the two groups' national and ethnic differences, overly dualistic? As I demonstrate throughout this book, this dualism was what most media coverage assumed or invoked. Thus, my methodology aligns with what the material presents. In order not to fall prey to this dualism, however, I employ three approaches. First, I discuss media debates within the heterogeneous Italian and Chinese migrant communities. Second, I evoke two comparative perspectives – the Chinese diasporas in Europe and non-Chinese migrations to Italy – throughout my book, which help provide a wider intercultural context. Finally, I soften this dualism by analysing American journalism's influence on Italian-Chinese migrant encounters in relevant media coverage. As I show in chapter 2, American sociological studies and popular journalism regarding Chinese Americans influenced Italian coverage of the supposed Chinese mafia in the early 1990s.

Using the dialogical analysis and methodology to study a significant amount of primary texts, I make two broad arguments in this book, which I have highlighted in the introduction and which are synthesized as the titles of the following two sections.

An Effective Example

As my readings of the aforementioned material using a dialogical analysis reveal, between 1992 and 2012 media debates about Chinese migration to Italy were extensive, heated, and, for the most part, in opposition. Many multiculturalist media agencies aimed to provide hospitality to Italy's Chinese in their coverage, and often praised the cultural diversity that the community had brought to the country. In contrast, some assimilationist media analyses virulently attacked Chinese migrant culture, which they deemed unsuitable for mainstream assimilation. Progressive journalists viewed Italy's Chinese migrant entrepreneurship as an exceptional asset for furthering the country's economic globalization. Conservatives viewed it as the fatal blow for local Italian firms and stores, which had been struggling to stay in business since the early 2000s.

In the introduction, when exploring the purposes of intense media debates about the Chinese migration, I have suggested that the community's dramatic demographic increase and successful entrepreneurship initially led the media to examine this migration. But more importantly, many media practitioners used the Chinese example to stimulate debates about how to incorporate migrants and their entrepreneurship into Italian cities. Compared to other migrant groups, then, the Chinese community became a particularly controversial and eloquent way to talk about such critical issues of national concern as migrant integration and economic globalization.

Here, I further explore the following questions: Why did the Italian-Chinese case become such an effective example? That is, what dynamics of migrant incorporation and economic globalization did Italy's Chinese and their entrepreneurship evoke? What about them inspired such oppositional media views and emotional reactions by debaters? Who were the debaters in the media, and why were they so militant and partisan? The combination of three specific circumstances concerning Italy's Chinese set them apart from other migrants in the country in furthering related debates. First, this community enjoyed an exceptional economic power gained through entrepreneurship, which China's economic ascendance in recent decades has only accentuated. The media had very different things to say about this condition. Second, the Chinese community had the support of a vast network of Italian journalists and academics who not only defended migrants against racist and nativist slanders but also extolled Chinese high culture. Finally, Chinese migrant elites published newspapers, magazines, and websites in which they vigorously countered biased mainstream media narratives. Their coverage also engaged in dialogue with the Italian media through quotations and translations. Based on existing scholarship, no other migrant group in Italy possessed the combined economic, cultural, and media capital comparable to the Chinese between 1992 and 2012 that would lead to similar media debates.

In these twenty years, while Italy largely failed to address Chinese economic globalization, the country's Chinese migrant entrepreneurship became the strongest in Europe and started to affect Italy's competitiveness in the global economy. Whether this impact has been beneficial to Italy or not has been at the centre of much media debate. Since the Second World War, the manufacturing sector has been vital in Italy, second in size only to Germany in Europe. In the first decade of the twenty-first century, this sector counted for about 17 per cent of Italy's gross domestic product. Because Italy's manufacturing sector was very export-oriented, it competed with China for exports in such sectors as textiles, garments, furniture, and mechanics. As the decade drew to a close, Italy's share of the global textile and garment market fell from 8.70 per cent to 6.62 per cent. Before Italy adopted the euro in 1999, it had traditionally eased competition with others by devaluing its previous currency, the lira. With this no longer an option, Italy was further impacted by China's persistent artificial undervaluation of its currency, the renminbi. In this scenario, some Italian producers began to pursue a higher product quality in order to distinguish "Made in Italy" from "Made in China" merchandise and to compete more meaningfully in global markets. A higher quality resulted in higher consumer prices, which further diminished the prospects to export effectively despite the higher returns per product.[37]

If Italy faced fierce Chinese competition in sectors in which it used to be a major player, what about exploring the Chinese market as a place to export Italian products? Since China opened to Western market economies in the early 1980s, Italy's economic ties with it have been notably weaker than those of other major European countries. The market share of Italian products among all exporters to China was an unimpressive 0.9 per cent in 2011. But luxury goods by major Italian fashion houses did enjoy a boom in China. Since 2006, Italy has also been the largest exporter of clothing, textile, and accessories to China. But the small- and medium-sized enterprises, which were the driving force of the Italian economy, did not have the clout to operate and protect themselves in that market as Italian and other European multinational corporations did. Finally, the Chinese state's direct investment in Italy was rather small, merely 1.79 per cent among all European Union countries in 2010, far behind Britain (12 per cent) and Germany (10.9 per cent).

Under these circumstances, Italy's vibrant Chinese migrant entrepreneurship has been the country's only conspicuous advantage in its competition with other European countries for Chinese capital through migration or direct investment. To begin with, this entrepreneurship generated considerable tax revenues for various Italian city governments and stimulated local economies by way of property purchases and daily consumption. In Italy, the concept of ethnic business is often used only to describe Chinese migrant entrepreneurship, as that single group dominates the entire industry of fast fashion. Prato's Chinese created the only migrant entrepreneurship in Italy that accumulated considerable wealth and competed successfully with small- and medium-sized Italian firms. This is a stark contrast to ethnic businesses in the United States, which relied heavily on self-employment in the 2000s. There, while Chinese Americans were among the main migrant groups to benefit from ethnic businesses, they were far from being the dominant one.[38] Further, since the 2000s Prato's Chinese factories that manufactured apparel for Italian firms, and not for counterfeits with "Made in Italy" labels, have also competed with mainland Chinese workers specialized in "Made in China" clothing.[39] These observations show how Chinese migrant entrepreneurship contributed much to the Italian economy in Italy's competition with China in the garment sector in the 2000s. Moreover, as pro-globalization journalists emphasized, Chinese migrant entrepreneurship spurred Prato's Italian industrialists to adapt product design in order to satisfy international markets. These journalists also pointed out that Prato's Chinese helped to redefine "Made in Italy" and to restore international confidence in the city's economy. All of this growth would elevate Italy's competitiveness vis-à-vis other European countries in the global quest for Chinese capital, as well as in innovating the textile and garment industries.

However, Italian entrepreneurs and politicians as represented by the media have not always been enthusiastic about Chinese migrants' economic value. A 2008 episode of the Rai Due program *Un mondo a colori* (A colourful world), titled "Foreigners Made in Italy," claimed that among the various "Made in Italy" industries to employ significant numbers of foreigners, Prato's Chinese garment industry was the only one infested with irregular employment and economic exploitation.[40] This episode attributed migrants' illegal business practices to the self-employment and ethnic business network, viewing the practices as traits that differentiated Chinese from other migrant workers and entrepreneurs in Italy. Therefore, as the episode intimated, the Chinese migrant economy in the fast-fashion sector was not an integral or legitimate part of the Italian economy. Such a view about the Chinese migrant and Italian "parallel districts" in Prato was rather widespread in the media in the 2000s. Inherent in this assessment was the notion that the Chinese migrant economy in Italy took part in mainland China's economic "invasion" of Europe, as if none of these migrant businesses had paid taxes to the Italian state, among other things.

Moreover, much Italian media coverage argued that Chinese migrant firms and major Italian fashion houses collaborated on fast fashion to the detriment of Prato's artisan textile and garment producers. The contractors who took orders from fashion companies and commissioned Chinese migrants to execute them did not request either textiles produced in Prato or Italian labour. But migrants produced garments that were still labelled "Made in Italy." In other cases, Chinese migrant workshops simply manufactured counterfeit garments with "Made in Italy" labels. For many journalists, both scenarios undermined the concept and production system of "Made in Italy" garments by bypassing the once-massive Italian textile industry and by damaging the smaller number of Italian clothing firms in Prato. Indeed, Italians tended to perceive local Chinese migrant transnationalism as having an "edge" that, to use the words of Donald Nonini and Aihwa Ong, entailed "an unpredictable wildness and danger" that colonial empires, postcolonial nation-states, and international capitalism had been unable to entirely domesticate.[41] Many Italians viewed the Chinese migrant entrepreneurial spirit as a disregard for the country's hard-won labour laws. They also perceived Chinese people as prioritizing profits above all else.

I examine the veracity of these claims and their rhetorical composition in detail in chapters 5 and 6. It is sufficient to mention here that self-employment, as well as the illegal practices associated with it, is what makes small- and medium-sized, family-managed Chinese migrant enterprises resemble Italian ones in industrial districts. In spite of migrant companies' similar business logic and ethos, as Emilio Reyneri observes, Italians have been reluctant to associate migrants with the social prestige that self-employment and independent entrepreneurship normally carry in Italy.[42]

Above, I analysed how the media debated the economic impact of Chinese migrants in relation to Italy's competition with mainland China and in relation to other European countries. The debates also implicitly compared Chinese migrants with those from other countries. Since the early 1990s, the Italian news media often covered migrant communities by focusing on poverty, social plight, and criminality. The Chinese, however, have received far fewer such depictions in the mainstream Italian media than other ethnic groups in Italy. A brief mention of Italy's other major migrant communities and their media features will demonstrate this point. Chinese migrants have rarely received such visually spectacular news coverage as the landings of Albanian refugees in Bari in the early 1990s, or the interception of refugees crossing the Mediterranean from North Africa starting in the late 2000s. The media fixated upon social disturbances caused by Romany camps in the suburbs and the perceived danger of terrorism from Muslim, or Muslim-looking, migrants in urban centres. Neither case found a parallel in representations of the Chinese migrant community. Further, despite isolated episodes of violence within their own community, the Chinese did not have a history of physical violence with Italians, unlike the African workers involved in the riot in Rosarno in Calabria or the Egyptians and the Latinos in another riot in Via Padova in Milan, both of which garnered prominent media coverage in 2010. Finally, the Italian media did not perceive the large number of Romanian migrants in Italy to be nearly as noteworthy an economic threat as the Chinese.[43] When disseminated via the media, events involving non-Chinese migrants impacted international perceptions of Italy's migrant incorporation. However, they did little to attract the global community's attention to Italy's potential economic prospects in the age of migration and globalization. For many pro-Chinese Italians and Chinese migrants, Italy's Chinese had a more significant role in drawing overall media attention to Italy's economic globalization and the migrants' role in it. In so doing, these journalists capitalized on this implicit inter-ethnic comparison to further underscore Chinese migrants' economic and transnational benefits for Italy.[44]

Pro-Chinese Italians also strongly opposed sensationalist media depictions of the supposed Chinese mafia, the 2007 Milan riot, and illegal Chinese business practices in Prato. They saw the "Chinese mafia" as a grave misinterpretation of Italy's Chinese migrant entrepreneurship. They also saw the 2007 riot as a one-time disturbance borne of specific spatial conditions in Milan's Via Sarpi area and the xenophobic climate fostered by the city's government. Furthermore, migrants' illegal business practices in Prato must be attributed to the demands of the fast-fashion sector and Italy's underground economy.

These cogent arguments on behalf of Italy's Chinese were made possible thanks to the unwavering support of a vast network of Italian academics, journalists, entrepreneurs, politicians, migration professionals, filmmakers, and novelists. Chinese migrants enjoyed an enormously favourable Italian support network based on highly informed activism, which drew on rich and detailed academic studies of both the migrant group itself and the country of origin. A great deal of this scholarship was made available in condensed versions to mainstream Italian media outlets, including more left-leaning newspapers that have always championed academics' viewpoints. Italy's strong tradition of sinology, which draws on Chinese-Italian communication as the oldest written history in East-West exchanges, nurtured this network. Not only has scholarship on Chinese culture been vibrant for centuries, but sociological and ethnographic studies of Italy's Chinese population have also been prolific since the 1990s.

One particular effort of this Italian support network has been finding common ground on which Italian and Chinese people might build bonds or mutual recognition. For advocates, this common ground would facilitate Italian-Chinese migrant relations, while avoiding such inaccurate comparisons as the one between the Cosa Nostra and the Chinese mafia (chapter 2). Italian-Chinese migrant mutual understanding would also put into practice the solidarity with immigrants that advocacy groups and centre-left politicians in Italy often championed. Traditional emigrant-sending southern European countries, including Italy, all brought their emigrant pasts to bear on its initial immigration policy-making.[45]

Indeed, as Graziella Parati notes, discussions about contemporary Italian multiculturalism can be fruitfully put into dialogue with Italy's "long pluricultural history," including Italian-speaking communities outside the country.[46] At the broadest level, pro-Chinese advocates activated a simplified version of this mechanism when they compared Chinese migration to Italy with Italian migration to North America.[47] They argued that just as self-made Italian migrants in North America had realized the American Dream, Chinese migrants in Italy, armed with an unsurpassed entrepreneurial spirit, pursued their Italian Dream. The scales of the two migrations are not comparable. But both migrant groups have claimed that their industriousness is superior to that of other ethnic groups and have argued that to fit into their adopted countries they endured more hurdles than other migrants, including legal discrimination, nativism, racism, and social closure (chapters 3 and 4).

For pro-Chinese advocates, apart from their shared experiences in diasporas, contemporary Italians and Chinese could also bond over respective national pasts in which they perceived themselves to be victims. Only by drawing on national narratives of victimhood in their own culture did Italian journalists and politicians quickly digest Chinese victimhood in the coverage of the 2012 Rome march (chapter 7). Italy's competitors in Europe – mainly France, Germany, and Britain – did not share such narratives with China. In fact, they caused the orientalization of Italy since the eighteenth century and the semi-colonization of China in the nineteenth and twentieth centuries, which deepened narratives of victimhood in the political discourses of both nation-states.[48]

In 1999, the critic Alessandro Dal Lago rightly observed that the Italians must help counter one-sided depictions of migrants as threats and enemies to the country, because the migrants' own voices were rarely heeded in the Italian media.[49] However, since the mid-2000s, Italy's Chinese have actively rejected negative Italian media accounts about them in the Italian and the Chinese migrant news media. Unlike the majority of Chinese migrants, who had limited educational capital and time to engage in media debates, their middle-class and more socially engaged counterparts had, by the early 2010s, appeared in the mainstream media with a certain frequency. These migrant elites also formulated cogent views about their social integration and business strategies in Chinese-language newspapers and in bilingual Chinese-Italian magazines and websites. The 2007 Milan riot provides a case study of the interactions between the Italian and the Chinese migrant media (chapters 3 and 4). The 2012 Rome march is the most significant example of how Chinese migrant journalism and advocacy affected Italian coverage (chapter 7).

During the 2000s, elite Chinese migrant entrepreneurs and intellectuals, including young Chinese Italians, formed a transnational sociocultural community in Italy.[50] They were the backbone of the financial, and editorial, composition of the Chinese migrant news media. Positing themselves as cosmopolitans, they often claimed to be the driving forces behind Italy's economic globalization. In media coverage, these migrant elites fashioned themselves as the opinion-makers for both Italian and Chinese audiences on broader Italian-Chinese migrant issues. They aimed to foster greater Italian-Chinese migrant cooperation that would establish their legitimacy and utility in Italian society, as well as consolidate their powerful position within local Chinese communities. These elites' media practices demonstrated the revival of overseas Chinese nationalism since the 1990s, which Hong Liu describes as derived from "China's economic prosperity, cultural regeneration, and national unification."[51]

Although Chinese migrant elites unambiguously defended their community in media, virulent attacks on Italian stereotypes about the Chinese were rare in the 2000s. Most Italian coverage was not without a factual basis; many elite migrants had profited from illegal business practices in the past, while their less-privileged conationals still did. Rather, Chinese migrant editorials were directed at media coverage that verged on blaming Chinese migrant entrepreneurship for all of globalization's ill effects on failed Italian industries. Such Italian coverage also tended to short circuit a proper discussion of Italy's underground economy and labour laws, which exploited globalization and Chinese workers. Elite migrants also risked inciting discontent between employers and employees within their business network. There had been reports of disgruntled employees who denounced their employers' illegal business practices to the Italian municipal authorities and police, perhaps as a result of exposure to media coverage.

The prolific media production within Italy's Chinese community indicates that since the mid-2000s, migrant elites have nurtured and established their own cultural voice. Media and academic representations of the Chinese migration from exclusively economic and social perspectives are thus inadequate. As Ong notes with reference to Hong Kong migrants in North America in the 1990s, their flexible migration strategies were characterized by the acquisition and deployment of what Pierre Bourdieu calls symbolic value. Within structural and institutional limits, once their settlement in North America had advanced to a comfortable degree, elite Hong Kong migrants consciously converted economic capital (e.g., wealth) into symbolic (e.g., community recognition), social (e.g., political entitlement), and cultural (e.g., academic credentials) capital.[52] While the context differs, I propose that Italy's Chinese during the 2000s exhibited comparable dispositions and practices to those Ong examines. Negative Italian media depictions, in fact, accelerated the conversion of various types of capital, as Chinese migrant elites became increasingly aware of the role of public opinion in their social and economic successes against the backdrop of the exponentially increased police raids on their businesses in that decade. Italy's other migrant groups that have engaged in self-employment since its legalization in Italy in 1998 enacted a similar conversion of capital, as did Chinese migrants in France and in Spain.[53]

What made the Chinese example particularly provocative and eloquent in media critiques of migrant integration and economic globalization? The vibrant Chinese migrant media was a feature of this community's incorporation in Italian society. It was also a way to multiply media debates concerning the migration, as media practitioners actively sought recognition and legitimacy both from mainstream Italian society and media and from within their own community. Another premise, also related to migrant incorporation, was a strong and growing network of pro-Chinese Italians, who exhibited cosmopolitan outlooks and confidence in their support of migrants by defending and nurturing them. Routine detractors accused migrants of exploiting Italy's imperfect migration system and large underground economy in order to conduct illegal business and to practice cultural enclosure. Pro-Chinese Italian and Chinese migrant journalists argued that the Italians should learn about Chinese culture and business practices as a civic competence in a transnational world, which would serve as a prerequisite for providing media and social hospitality to Italy's Chinese. These debates revolved around a common point of departure: both the export-oriented Chinese economy and Italy's Chinese entrepreneurship exerted considerable pressure on Italian small- and medium-sized firms, which were still exploring ways to adapt to globalization from 1992 to 2012.

A Cultural Repertoire

Between 1992 and 2012, localists in Italy were in fact embroiled in the effects of economic globalization. Neither ordinary Chinese migrant workers nor Italian owners of small- and medium-sized enterprises were truly "local" producers. They were not "global" in the ways that elite transnational Chinese migrant entrepreneurs and executives of major Italian corporations were. But as Stuart Hall wrote in the early 1990s, things that were once considered local and national in most places in the world had been thoroughly reshaped to be largely global and transnational.[54] Detractors of Chinese migrants often had sufficient transnational capital to understand this migration. But they deployed specific global cultural resources in order to derive and make meanings that were very different from pro-globalization cultural practitioners. Ultimately, many of Prato's textile and garment factories rejected globalization because, unlike major fashion houses, they could not benefit from a speedy production time for manufacturing export-oriented textiles and garments, and consequently their disadvantaged position in the global network prevented them from taking advantage of it.

Where, and how, did Italian and Chinese migrant journalists, entrepreneurs, and politicians acquire the specific global and intercultural competencies with which they described Chinese migration to Italy? In what ways did these resources mould these cultural practitioners' narratives of this migration? And, most importantly, how did journalists deploy these resources in understanding the Chinese migration and in using it as an effective example to address migrant incorporation and economic globalization in Italy?

In considering these questions, I draw on Ann Swidler's theorization of the multiple cultural repertoires an individual acquires and deploys in order to address various aspects of their social life. Swidler's theory helps unravel how culture affects social life by studying how individuals use culture to achieve goals that have social underpinnings, like love and romance, which is the subject of her empirical inquiry.[55] She explores the "larger questions about culture and meaning: how culture actually works when people bring it to bear on a central arena of their daily experience [e.g., love and romance] and especially how culture is (or is not) linked to action." For the critic, social actors strategically deploy cultural tools at their disposal – the so-called strategies of action – to deal with life, although they do this within specific institutional contexts.[56]

Applying Swidler's theory, I view cultural repertoires as containing tools and resources that cultivated the skills and capacities that journalists, politicians, and entrepreneurs used to narrate Chinese migration to Italy in the media. As I mentioned in the introduction, I focus on three primary categories in these repertoires. The first category concerns the journalists' selection of specific topics of debate about Italy's Chinese – including, most notably, their entrepreneurship – that they presented as newsworthy for the intended audience. The second category pertains to culturally specific textual mechanisms, including the perspectives, rhetorical devices, and discursive strategies that journalists used to organize the selected topics into narratives that conveyed their arguments and were meaningful to the audience. Finally, the third category refers to the Italian-migrant and local-global frames, which selected, highlighted, and created meanings out of these narratives in order to maximize the impact on the audience.

How did these repertoires enable and support media debates about Italy's Chinese? There were many ways. For instance, the repertoires often provided resources to journalists and other stakeholders for constructing competing views of the same phenomenon. With regard to Italy's migrant entrepreneurship, Chinese migrants viewed it positively; it was both a successful accumulation of family wealth and a reflection of their self-esteem and social status. In contrast, Italian competitors of Chinese businesses often viewed it negatively, assuming that it was based on unfair competition through illegal and criminal business practices. In this example, the topic was migrant entrepreneurship, and the discursive strategy to address this topic relied on stereotyping Chinese migrants, whether positive or negative.

To give another example, journalists' use of cultural repertoires often led to schemas in media narratives – for the most part, metaphors and metonyms – that helped to make sense of this migration or used it for narrative and political purposes. As I examine in chapter 2, since the early 1990s, in accusing Chinese migrants of illegal economic activities, Italian journalists often likened Chinese migrant firms to the supposed Chinese mafia, mainly because they drew on influential American nonfiction concerning transnational Chinese criminals, and on the coverage of the Cosa Nostra, a Sicilian criminal organization. The "Chinese mafia" became a metaphor that Italians used to understand Chinese migrants' entrepreneurial success, whose causes had not been clearly articulated in the media or in scholarship in the early 1990s. Right-wing journalists also used this metaphor to denigrate the Chinese in order to appease Italian voters, who were closing their businesses allegedly because of the Chinese competition.

As these two examples indicate, the cultural tools and resources that journalists used to speak about the Chinese migration existed both in the empirical world (e.g., Italy's migrant entrepreneurship) and also in a social actor's cultural experiences (e.g., the use of a metaphor to represent a phenomenon or a community). Moreover, for the media stakeholders I study, "culture" in these repertoires meant for the most part ethnic and national cultures. From 1992 to 2012, the cultural components that journalists deployed came most often from Italian, Chinese, and, to some degree, American contexts.

At this point of my application of Swidler's theory to the case studies, one would legitimately ask whether it is feasible to undertake a project about untangling the complex web of many cultural repertoires from which media practitioners and others might have drawn. My solution to this difficulty is to regard the intersection of these various cultural repertoires as an independent Italian-Chinese migrant cultural repertoire, on the grounds that the area in which these various repertoires intersected addressed a single subject: Italy's Chinese migrants. Thus, the Italian-Chinese migrant cultural repertoire was the toolkit to which media practitioners and other stakeholders turned whenever the need to cover the Chinese migration to Italy arose. It was also a toolkit they helped shape and evolve as they deployed its resources to debate and argue about issues in the empirical world according to changing sociohistorical circumstances. The Italian-Chinese migrant cultural repertoire was dynamic in that media stakeholders reinforced, refuted, highlighted, and devalued the tools and resources it contained, in keeping with exigencies in media debates and in order to narrate key events involving Italy's Chinese.

How, then, did stakeholders create and refashion the Italian-Chinese migrant cultural repertoire? My analysis pinpoints the creation of this repertoire in 1992 when detailed coverage of Chinese migrants first appeared in major Italian news magazines. This repertoire initially contained important topics including the Chinese mafia, rhetorical devices featuring the octopus as metaphoric of the Chinese "invasion" in Italy, and discursive strategies such as a criminological perspective on this migration. From 1992 to 2006, as pro-Chinese Italian and Chinese migrant journalists reacted to the initial repertoire and attempted to destabilize previous interpretations, they added more topics and introduced more discursive strategies. A prominent topic that emerged from this period concerned the Chinese community as a particularly industrious one among all migrants thanks to their successful globalized entrepreneurship. This topic was usually deployed in positive stereotyping of Chinese migrants as good settlers in Italy. The selecting and highlighting of topics and perspectives relating to migrant integration and economic globalization then cemented the Italian-migrant and local-global media frames.

As the first major social event concerning Italy's Chinese widely reported in the media, the 2007 Milan riot illustrated journalists' use of the Italian-Chinese migrant cultural repertoire up until that point. In particular, my analysis emphasizes the Italian-migrant frame in Italian media coverage and how Chinese migrants operated within the same frame but productively reacted to the Italian coverage in arguing for alternative ways of administering migrants. My analysis of the intense coverage of Prato's business dynamics from 2009 to 2012 accentuates its local-global frame. This frame addressed Italy's economic globalization in the age of migration, leading the media to debate about Prato's local form of institutional discipline (i.e., police raids on Chinese factories) and about the identity and reputation of "Made in Italy" clothing for the international audience.

By the time of the media coverage of the 2012 Rome murder and march, the news media had made a very skilful use of the Italian-migrant and the local-global frames. For an example of the first frame, the media conveyed that the murder's randomness indicated how, like the Italians, Chinese migrants were victims of senseless violence. Indeed, for much media coverage, during the march the Chinese acted like dutiful citizens, lawfully expressing their mourning and protesting the state's neglect in public security. For an example of the second frame, both Chinese migrant and Italian journalists extensively employed victimhood narratives to argue that Chinese merchants and workers were not Italians' transnational economic competitors, but rather their neighbours in local business.

So far, I have discussed the Italian-Chinese migrant cultural repertoire's enabling mechanisms, which made tools and resources available to media practitioners who in turn helped to update the repertoire itself. This repertoire also had limiting effects. One strength of Swidler's theorization of cultural repertoires is to analyse culture in action, as it alternately enables and constrains social actions. As I argue throughout this book, the journalists' deployment of the Italian-Chinese migrant cultural repertoire sometimes limited the range and nature of their textual and discursive strategies. While I address culture's restrictions in relation to individual cases in subsequent chapters, here I examine two discursive strategies that had broad appeal to journalists – namely, transnationalism and ethnocultural essentialism.

It is not difficult to understand why Chinese migrants and pro-globalization Italians highlighted their transnational capabilities. In the media, Italy's Chinese often performed a transnational defence against accusations that their economic practices exhibited traits of unregulated capitalism. For them, transborder entrepreneurship would, by definition, challenge practices of mature capitalism in local contexts, and the transnational flow of capital would stimulate local economies. Admittedly, in so doing, Chinese migrants and pro-Chinese Italians appropriated and renewed an age-old northern European and American view of Italy as a backward economy that nurtured nostalgia for local artisan production. But Chinese migrant transnationalism indeed had a rightful place in Italy. Following Anthony Giddens, I believe that historical contingencies from 1992 to 2012 placed this entrepreneurship in a uniquely favourable position to help accelerate global innovations in Italy, particularly because of the increased economic globalization of the migrants' home country. Furthermore, as John Tomlinson eloquently puts it, the "paradigmatic experience of global modernity" is "that of staying in one place but experiencing the 'dis-placement' that global modernity *brings to them.*"[57] The nearness of transnational capitalism has been palpable even for nativist- and protectionist-minded Italians, who could not possibly wish away Chinese migrants and "Made in China" products, as well as their tangible contributions to daily life in Italy.

If transnationalism has been almost a given in Italy and China since the 1990s, then a more vexing question concerns why the Italians resorted to ethnocultural essentialism – indeed, to cultural rootedness – in order to counter accusations of their provincialism and protectionism, and why Chinese migrants used the same mechanism to survive charges of unrestrained globalization and capitalism. For Arjun Appadurai, "culturalism" (here I replace the critic's term with the more readable ethnocultural essentialism) is "the conscious mobilization of cultural differences in the service of a larger national or transnational politics." For the critic, the "deliberate, strategic, and populist mobilization of cultural material" – that is, a migrant group's "identity, culture, and heritage" and, I would add, ethnicity and race – is precisely what "cultural differences tend to take in the era of mass mediation, migration, and globalization."[58] Appadurai's point is further corroborated by Bhabha's analysis of essentialist ethnoculturalism and by Paul Gilroy's discussion of the dynamics between cultural nationalism and creolization in black cultures in the Atlantic, albeit in different contexts. Several critics have already noted forms of cultural essentialism in Italy's multicultural media discourses.[59]

My analysis emphatically shows that the frequent deployment of ethnocultural essentialism was mobilized by Italian and Chinese cultures, sanctioned by the Italian and the Chinese states, and absorbed and performed by the Italians and the Chinese migrants. In terms of cultural attitudes, just as the Italians advanced essentialist formulations of Italian and Chinese cultures in underscoring their fundamental differences, so too did the Chinese. Some Italians claimed that while they appreciated the time spent with their families on vacation, Chinese migrants were encouraged by their government and culture to focus solely on work. Chinese migrants countered that while they had a strong work ethic, Italians were lazy. Some journalists drew on certain essentialist ideas of Chinese culture to denigrate Chinese migrants, while others used the same ideas to praise them. According to a prominent example of this mechanism, on the one hand, the Chinese overworked themselves, breaking labour laws in order to make more garments and earn more money. On the other hand, this industriousness differentiated them from complacent Italians and migrants of other ethnicities.

The Italian state endorsed ethnocultural essentialism by promoting migrants' economic integration without providing them with proper social services, voting rights, or paths to citizenship. As opposed to *ius soli* (birthright citizenship), a combination of *ius sanguinis* (citizenship by descent, institutionalized in 1912), *ius domicili* (citizenship by way of long-term residence, established in 1992), and *ius conubii* (citizenship through marriage with an Italian citizen, cemented in 1992) characterized laws for immigrants of non-Italian ancestry.[60] Ius sanguinis was the dominant factor in granting Italian citizenship in the period under discussion in this book, and its ethnocultural connotations were often used to argue that migrants of other ethnicities and cultures without any Italian blood could neither become Italian citizens nor be included within the imagined community of Italians.

Further, the deployment of ethnocultural essentialism for both positive and negative purposes has served Italy's migrant incorporation at a national level. By positing a specific culture as an insular entity, ethnocultural essentialism plays a crucial role in migrant integration in contemporary European societies. According to the assimilationist model, which France exemplifies, the migrant's previous cultural identity can be assimilated into French national identity. According to the multicultural model, which Britain and the Netherlands embrace, the migrant's previous identity should be preserved and celebrated in their societies. (These countries have not strictly followed the idealized models.)[61] In Italy, the introduction of the 1998 Turco-Napolitano law and the 2002 Bossi-Fini law mostly regulated migration management (e.g., border control and migrants' right to enter the host country), leaving integration largely up to the municipalities. In so doing, the Italian state did not officially adopt either dominant model of migrant integration in Europe between 1992 and 2012 and was thus multipositioned, making specific municipal-level regulations liable to ethnocultural essentialism from the combined forces of both.[62] On the one hand, municipal and non-governmental initiatives often exhibited ethnocultural essentialism as they drew on the multiculturalist model to argue that Chinese migrants would enrich Italian society. On the other hand, Italian politicians, who believed that Chinese migrants would not fit in under the assimilationist model, also employed the rhetoric of ethnocultural essentialism by highlighting the presumably irreconcilable cultural differences between Italians and migrants. In both scenarios, Chinese migrants were made to appear, by default, as deficient in their knowledge of Italian society and culture.

Reacting to this lack, pro-Chinese Italians and Chinese migrants tended to fight negative ethnocultural essentialism by employing a positive version of the concept. In response to anti-Chinese journalists' correlation between Chinese identity and their illegal business practices, pro-Chinese advocates associated Chinese ethnicity with industriousness. Here I view journalists' performance of ethnocultural essentialism as reactive and intercultural.[63] Chinese migrants were largely excluded from the imagined community of the Italian nation-state, and so they fell back on the Chinese identity that offered a solid ground from which to fight Italian accusations. Since the 2000s, moreover, the Chinese government has actively courted overseas Chinese for their potential contributions to the homeland, lauded their achievements in foreign lands in state-sponsored media outlets, and sponsored their visits to rediscover family and cultural roots in China. Drawing on a diasporic nostalgia for Confucian-inspired cultural values and practices, which the Chinese state encouraged through the media, migrant elites often indulged in highly moralistic tones in their 1992 to 2012 coverage, whether when asking the Italian state to create more possibilities for them to participate in politics, or when cautioning the less-privileged members of their community against illegal economic activity.[64]

Ethnocultural essentialism was also used in media accounts regarding Italy's transnational politics and economic globalization. Much of the journalism produced in the United States and Germany that I examine in chapter 6 used essentialist intercultural perspectives to make sense of the competition between "Made in Italy" and "Made in China" in world trade and viewed both the Italians and the Chinese migrants as enmeshed in their own parochialism. According to these views, the former must take responsibility for their slow-paced adaptation to globalization and for their reluctance to incorporate migrants economically and culturally, while the latter overindulged in an unbridled capitalist transnationalism and in a disregard for laws and socially acceptable behaviour in the host society. Although such domineering, essentialist views were open to debate, they were a boon to the moral economy and politics of the Italian-Chinese migrant encounters between 1992 and 2012 because they highlighted the cultural meanings of, in Giddens's words, the "clash between a cosmopolitan outlook and fundamentalism," a fundamentalism that "isn't about what people believe but, like tradition more generally, about why they believe it and how they justify it."[65]

As I have shown, through the Italian-Chinese migrant cultural repertoire, culture has both enabled and constrained the parameters of media narratives of Italy's Chinese in the empirical world between 1992 and 2012. During this twenty-year period, transnationalism and ethnocultural essentialism, insofar as they were discursive strategies in a widely recognized and deployed Italian-Chinese migrant cultural repertoire, were accessible to any cultural practitioners involved in portraying Chinese migration to Italy in the media. We cannot assume that the pro-migrant camp only invoked transnationalism, or that the nativist camp only praised ethnocultural rootedness. The two discourses were symbiotic because media coverage inspired by national and cultural essentialism often could not avoid some consideration of global competencies, even if only as negative examples. The same is true for coverage in favour of economic globalization, which must attend to the phenomenon's benefits in local situations in order to be persuasive.[66] To borrow Ong's observation in a similar context, the tension between the two discourses refers to the dynamic between an insistence on "the modernist imaginary of the nation-state (emphasizing essentialism, territoriality, and fixity)" and a eulogy of the transnational and "entrepreneurial capitalism (celebrating hybridity, deterritorialization, and fluidity)."[67]

In the introduction and in chapter 1, I have explained this book's central arguments and sub-theses in general terms, and I have defined terms, theories, and methodologies that I apply throughout this book. It is now possible to delve into the four case studies.

Chapter 2

The "Chinese Mafia" in Italy, 1992–2006

In the early 1990s, the Chinese migrant community in Italy made a dramatic entrance into mainstream Italian media. The Italian public began to learn about this migration first and foremost through a criminological lens. In 1990, *L'Europeo* reported on a major protest organized by the Italians against Florence's Chinese community, as well as emphatically dismissed certain 1980s coverage of the "Chinese mafia" in Italy as mere speculation.[1] The year 1992 saw substantial media coverage of the first major police investigations into Italy's Chinese community that brought criminals to court. By 1993, *Corriere della Sera* had featured the Chinese population numerous times, often displaying a hodgepodge of social and criminological facts and fantasies based on popular Western archetypes. In this coverage, Milan, the Florence-Prato-San Donnino area, Rome, and Naples were the most frequently reported areas where the Chinese communities grew and their criminality increased.[2]

These initial chronicles concerning the Chinese community were characterized by fixation on the "Chinese mafia," a term Italian journalists used to refer to vastly different types of presumed and real Chinese criminality: the Triad (the powerful Hong Kong-based transnational network of Chinese organized crime), disparate small-scale organized criminal groups that performed illegal activities on commission (e.g., intimidation because of personal or business relations), or individuals who formed alliances with family members or friends in order to facilitate specific illegal activities (e.g., to smuggle their relatives from China to Italy). If the Triad may be labelled the Chinese mafia because it shared traits with the Italian mafia, such as hierarchy, then individuals in the latter two categories were almost certainly not members.[3]

Why did the Chinese migration suddenly become newsworthy in the early 1990s? Why did the media fixate on the criminal and illegal business activities among migrants? How did journalists argue for, and against, the mention of the Chinese mafia when covering Italy's Chinese community? In this chapter, I analyse the 1992 to 2006 evolution of significant media coverage of the Chinese mafia as a single social and cultural phenomenon, exploring its reasons and modalities.

The "Chinese Mafia" as a Metaphor

The media took an interest in Chinese migration to Italy because the Chinese population in the country swelled in the early 1990s thanks to government-authorized regularization schemes. The schemes in 1986 and 1990 inadvertently encouraged many illegal migrants to move to Italy from elsewhere in Europe in an attempt to gain legal residency. Many of them were convinced that Italy was more tolerant than the Netherlands and France, which had stricter migration regulations. In Milan, the number of Chinese migrants who requested regularization during the amnesties of 1995, 1998, and 2002 increased steadily, although it remained smaller than that of the three largest foreign groups to do so.[4] The opportunistic movement of the Chinese encouraged abuses by migration intermediaries and human smugglers, which the media considered to be part of this migrant community's existing network of illegal business activities, including using undocumented workers, counterfeiting, evading taxes, and violating Italian labour laws, among others. In mainstream Italian weeklies and magazines, such as *Panorama*, *Famiglia Cristiana*, *Sette*, *Il Venerdì*, *Ventiquattro*, and *Grazia*, extended coverage of the Chinese community peaked in 1992, 1995, and 2003, coinciding with the regularization schemes. I view this extensive attention as indicative of a greater journalistic urgency to address the Chinese diaspora in Italy.[5]

Furthermore, drawing on George Lakoff and Mark Johnson's insights concerning metaphors, I contend that when attempting to understand the Chinese migration in the early 1990s, journalists created a new metaphor for crime reporting: the "Chinese mafia" represented Italy's Chinese community.[6] This metaphor was based on two rhetorical parallels: the Chinese mafia in Italy was said to resemble those in other Western countries, as well as the Italian mafia. Because the early 1990s police investigations and sociological scholarship were still formulating observations about Chinese migration to Italy, journalists resorted to media and quasi-sociological sources on Chinese criminality in North America, France, and Britain, where the Chinese diasporas had much longer histories than in Italy. Italian journalists also drew on the crime reporting on the Cosa Nostra, the Sicilian organized crime that was then a major news topic. Through this metaphor, journalists organized and disseminated a specific body of knowledge on early 1990s Chinese migration to Italy.

What does this metaphor's criminological emphasis reveal about rhetorical tendencies in Italian journalism that covered the country's early 1990s contact with the Chinese and with mass immigration more broadly? I argue that it indicated and perpetuated journalists' tendency to associate an ethnic group with a specific set of bounded traits, a mechanism that Arjun Appadurai calls "metonymic freezing." Throughout the 1990s and 2000s, Italian readers and journalists believed, as some continue to believe, that the Chinese mafia was such a defining characteristic of Italy's Chinese community that migrants could not, and would not, put an end to it. Thus, for many journalists, the Chinese mafia served both as a "shorthand" for interpreting existing economic and social activities of Chinese migrants and as a "guide" for analysing incoming information about the migration as it continued to evolve.[7]

Up until the mid-1990s, the "Chinese mafia" metaphor was the dominant interpretive lens in mainstream Italian journalism about the Chinese migration. However, its validity was challenged between the mid-1990s and the mid-2000s. Some news articles employed positive ethnocultural essentialism to avoid addressing Chinese criminality and to refocus on migrants' contributions to Italian society and culture. Others interpreted migrants' illegal economic activities not in relation to their supposed root in organized crime, but as economic phenomena in need of more regulation. The Chinese migrant news media countered the metaphor in 2001–3 when elite migrants founded two bilingual monthly magazines, *Cina in Italia* and *It's China*, in which they largely endorsed the practices of Italian police and judicial authorities that disciplined overt economic crimes and human smuggling but made no connection between these criminal activities and the so-called Chinese mafia. The migrant elites' approval was addressed to the two magazines' Italian readers, including politicians and government officials often quoted in their pages. Moreover, by siding with the Italian authorities, migrant journalists wished to regulate the Chinese migrants' conduct. Thanks to the efforts of both Italian and Chinese migrant journalists, by 2003 the supposed Chinese mafia had lost momentum in Italian news coverage of the Chinese migration.

However, with the 2006 publication of *Gomorra* (*Gomorrah*), a hugely popular nonfiction book about the Camorra (Italian organized crime centred in Naples and the Campania region), Roberto Saviano renewed debates about the Chinese mafia. Differing from the then-common approach in the news media, Saviano uses the Chinese mafia as a case study, and a particularly provocative and sensational one at that, to set the stage for his analysis of his main subject, the Camorra. Therefore, he interprets the Chinese migration mainly by exploiting orientalist discourses that correlate its gains and losses with Italy-centred social issues, in particular the Camorra.

In the rest of this chapter, I unpack these nuances of the metaphor of the "Chinese mafia" between 1992 and 2006 and illustrate how the Chinese migration spurred Italian journalists to rethink their country's migrant integration and economic globalization.

Paralleling Organized Crime in Italian Reporting, 1992–1995

From 1992 to 1995, Italian media coverage of the Chinese migrant community featured the supposed Chinese mafia by making two assumptions about it. The first was that Chinese criminality in Italy was parallel to, if not actually affiliated with, the Triad in the United States, France, and Britain. Evidence of highly organized Chinese criminal associations in the United States was widely circulated in the British and Dutch media in those years and was cited by Italian journalists when referring to the Italian case.[8] The second was that, since these Chinese criminals operated in a system not unlike the Cosa Nostra, journalists should apply conclusions and methods from years of reporting on the latter to address the former. Some of the first extended coverage of Italy's Chinese community, a 1993 *Spazio 5* program on Mediaset's Canale 5, extensively drew on these two parallels.[9]

The two parallels illustrated the Italian mass media's criminological approach to immigration, which emerged from the larger media and political cultures in major European countries in the early 1990s. With high-profile unrest between migrants and natives in Germany and France, most European media accentuated the correlation between immigration and public security.[10] In that period, the Italian media also adopted the criminological lens on immigration for political reasons, as it was grappling with two major crises that threatened the stability of its national identity. The European Union demanded that Italy better manage its migrant integration and its national budget, in order to maintain a national profile in line with the rest of Western Europe. Meanwhile, the country was in the midst of what the press called Tangentopoli (Bribeville), with court trials for widespread political corruption in all of its then-major political parties, which eventually eroded its post–Second World War political system and weakened its citizens' credibility in world politics and global business. Under these circumstances, according to Russell King and Nicola Mai, when addressing the early 1990s' most dramatic social event concerning immigrants – namely the emergency landings in Puglia of refugees from post-Communist Albania – much Italian media coverage criminalized the Albanians because they played the role of the "'constitutive other' within the country's renegotiation of a viable national identity." In other words, the media criminalized the Albanians in order to "articulate a civilized and democratic Italian identity in relation to Italy's aspirational belonging to Europe and the West."[11] Chinese migrants also served as the Other in this reformulation. The Chinese-Italian case tellingly illuminated how media professionals, under great pressure to cover immigrants in the early 1990s, drew on existing migrant narratives from non-Italian contexts, as well as on crime reporting.

The news coverage of the Chinese diasporas in other European countries and in the United States that Italian journalists referred to tended to have heavily criminal connotations. When applied to the Italian context, Chinese organized crime was said, without any credible proof, to be ready to infiltrate Italy. A 1992 *Corriere della Sera* article, "Allarme 'sole rosso,' racket cinese," traces the Triad's expansion from China to North America, Australia, and Europe, but fails to explain the story's relevance to Italy. Similarly, a 1992 article in *Sette* (*Corriere della Sera*'s magazine) titled "Yellow Milan" does not distinguish between documented Chinese criminal activities in Chinatowns outside Italy and the lack of analogous events in Milan. In "Yellow Milan," observations about the example most geographically close to Italy, France, remain generic: Chinese owners in Paris "are suspected of favouring the infiltration of the Triad and even that of secret agents from the Communist regime." The writer uses the simple future tense to enhance the veracity of their claims about Italy's Chinese, and cautions that "if speculation becomes reality, then the risk is that [the Chinese mafia in Milan] will reveal itself to be proportional to that in New York City's Chinatown where the racket in 'slaves' is rampant." Italy's Chinese supposedly operated "in close collaboration with their Californian counterparts and with the Triad, the criminal organization based in Hong Kong that employs men worldwide, wherever there is a Chinese community."[12]

In the 1990s, Italian journalists across the political spectrum also adopted an old metaphor about the Chinese mafia from their American colleagues, namely, the octopus. As the aforementioned 1992 *Corriere della Sera* article relays, nineteenth-century Chinese secret societies penetrated Western societies with their "tentacles." A 1995 *Famiglia Cristiana* article, titled "The Octopus with Almond-Shaped Eyes," invokes the same imagery: Chinese restaurants and service stores were "all paid with cash and were often owned by the same Chinese families. This made us suspect that the 'yellow Octopus' ['Piovra gialla'] was extending its tentacles throughout Europe." In 1995, both *TG 2 Dossier* on Rai Due and *Verissimo* on Canale 5 employed this metaphor in coverage of Chinese migrants in Milan and in San Donnino.[13] This metaphor was part of a 1990s mainstream Italian media trend of applying moralizing adjectives, including "slave-like" and "desperate," to immigrants in coverage of social deviance and public security.[14]

The octopus metaphor effectively conveyed the allegedly invasive and sneaky nature of the Chinese and other Asians, a stereotype with a prodigious written and iconographic history in the West.[15] The re-emergence of this metaphor in Italian popular culture between 1992 and 1995 had a more immediate cause: American journalism about Chinese organized crime. A prime example was the 1988 book *Warlords of Crime: Chinese Secret Societies – The New Mafia* by the American journalist Gerald Posner, which was quickly translated into Italian in 1990 as *Il sole bianco: La mafia cinese sulle piste della droga* (The white sun: The Chinese mafia on the path to drugs). Following the trail blazed by Posner, in 1994 Patrizia Dionisio and Francesco Sisci published their nonfiction account of Chinese organized crime, *Piovra gialla: La mafia cinese alla conquista del mondo* (Yellow octopus: The Chinese mafia conquering the world).[16]

The immensely successful American-influenced Italian television miniseries on the Cosa Nostra, *La Piovra* (*The Octopus: The Power of the Mafia*) (1984–2001), also helped to popularize the octopus metaphor in the social imagining of the Chinese in Italy. According to Milly Buonanno, initially the serial's title was meant to invoke the octopus metaphor from popular Western novels and movies so that the audience would understand it. Then events involving the Cosa Nostra in Italy during the 1980s and 1990s created a greater demand for fictional representations of them on television. This condition nurtured a short circuit between reality and fiction through *La Piovra*, which helped to introduce the octopus-Cosa Nostra metaphor into journalism and nonfiction.[17] As the octopus metaphor became an effective shorthand in 1990s Italian culture, journalists increasingly viewed the Chinese and Italian mafias as parts of the same news topic: organized crime. Indeed, Italian media coverage of the Chinese mafia coincided with intense reporting on the Cosa Nostra, a timing that further validated their paralleling for the Italian public. In 1992, the high-profile assassinations of anti-mafia magistrates Giovanni Falcone in May and Paolo Borsellino in July occurred when the initial news articles about the Chinese mafia in Italy emerged.

What did the media see as the parallels between these two types of organized crime? *TG 2 Dossier*, dated 1995, features an interview with

Pino Arlacchi, then vice president of the parliamentary anti-mafia commission, who gave a lengthy list of them: the two organizations' supposed symbolisms, organizational structures, working procedures, long histories, stated intentions to defend the poor, rituals, devotions, and oaths of silence. But Arlacchi did not elaborate on this analogy in his interview, leaving the viewer with only a vague impression of various similarities between the two criminal organizations that allegedly threatened ordinary people's lives and Italy's democracy. In reality, these supposed parallels could not sustain their validity under rigorous scrutiny, as many subsequent academic studies and police reports would reveal.

In the 1990s, Italian police were unable to find concrete evidence of any large-scale Chinese criminal organization or the Triad in Italy, and so journalists were only able to hint at the existence of the "Chinese mafia." They did so by manipulating verbal and visual techniques, as well as by drawing on American imagery of the Triad and of the Cosa Nostra. In "Yellow Milan," the journalist cautions that the collaboration between Italy's and California's Chinese criminals was "only the tip of an iceberg, whose true proportions are yet to be ascertained." He writes that Italian authorities sanctioned the owners of several Chinese restaurants and leather workshops in Milan and Monza because of irregular migration and illegal job placement. He further observes that "[this is] judicial euphemism to indicate that they [i.e., the Chinese owners] are the main organizers of this trafficking of labourers, to which the Chinese mafia is not unrelated ['al quale non è estranea la mafia cinese']. It is a secret for no one [literally 'it is no mystery for no one'; 'non è un mistero per nessuno'] that the hands of the Chinese mafia have long extended to Europe." These two statements use the double negative, with the latter a negative concord frequently used in the Italian language. But this grammatical construction does not elaborate on the content of these statements. Instead, it winks at readers, encouraging them to call on their experiences living with or reading about the Cosa Nostra to complete the Italian-Chinese parallel via the mafias. Through this mechanism, the journalist did not need to offer examples of highly organized Chinese crimes, which was fortuitous as they did not exist in Italy.

Another example of using language to cover up conceptual incongruities concerns verb tenses. In the following sentence, excerpted from the aforementioned 1992 *Corriere della Sera* article, the journalist uses the historical present tense to recount the history of the Triad (the first three conjugated verbs) and the simple present tense to relay what the journalist takes to be sociological findings of the criminal organization (the fourth conjugated verb): "Disciplined and trained in martial arts, the pious men *establish* mysterious secret societies that *protract* their tentacles in all of China. With the passage of time, they *transform* from organizations of political resistance to powerful clans dedicated to a thousand kinds of trafficking. The oath of silence [omertà], family loyalty, and ethnic ties *are* the pilasters of a capillary structure, ready to serve regimes and the powerful in exchange for economic favors. [Italics mine.]" As the two tenses appear grammatically similar, this approach creates a high degree of textual and temporal continuity. As another example, a police report about Operation Asia Trading in Bari's Chinese migrant community in 2000–1 also describes the Triad by using a similar textual transition from the past to the present.[18] Both texts assign essentialist traits, often laden with ethnic connotations, to the Chinese mafia and to the Chinese. Reading these two texts together gives an inkling of how mainstream journalism and police investigations used similar verbal manipulations, as well as uncritically drew upon historical accounts in non-Italian contexts, in order to explain current events in the country.

The Italian press also used visual language to reinforce the supposed existence of the Triad. Two large photographs that ran with "Yellow Milan" feature two Chinese men posing like mafia bosses or, in the Chinese context, like elders ['laoda'].[19] Middle-aged Harry Chan sits in his warehouse filled with Chinese art objects. Several young men, each holding a vase, stand behind him. According to the caption, Chan was then the wealthiest Chinese man living in Milan and was a relative of the last Chinese emperor's master, in an explicit reference to Bernardo Bertolucci's 1987 film and to the opulent aesthetics and decadent morality that it conjured for Western viewers. The other photograph depicts middle-aged Hu Che Chan as an imposing figure in a low-angle shot. A "president of the Chinese community," this Chan (or Hu, as it is not certain whether the article follows the Chinese convention of putting a person's family name first) "performs the role of support and control of members of the community." As the reader wonders whether these two men belong to the same family by virtue of their last name, the two photographs nod at a passage from the article: "A large and hard-working [Chinese] community is open to dialogue, but it is jealous of its own traditions and culture. But a couple of 'families' from this community are organized in ways quite similar to our homemade mafia ['di casa nostra']."

Cinematically inspired visual signposting also invoked Chinese criminal groups. The title of a 1992 *Panorama* article, "Cosa Nostla," refers to the Cosa Nostra while mocking how many Chinese migrants failed to roll the Italian "r" and instead replaced it with an "l."[20] In this article, we learn that two criminal groups with operations in Rome, Milan, and Florence marked several places in these cities with their symbols. The article draws on the narrative and visual conventions of crime cinema when explaining these marks: "In Rome there is the Sole rosso. In Milan, the Drago and the Tao. Hurriedly painted with a stencil and a bit of paint, they are small signs that appear at night on the shutters or on the mantels of entrance doors. They mean only one thing: Pay." The person who left the marks was charged with collecting protection money from the owners of two Chinese restaurants, who offered their supposed insiders' perspectives on Chinese criminality to the article's reporters.

However, these marks were also a staple in the popular Fu Manchu novels and movies set in Britain and the United States during the 1920s and 1930s. In Charles Brabin's influential film *The Mask of Fu Manchu* (1932), extreme close-ups of one such mark occur at various moments, indicating its narrative significance. Only through a proper reading of this mark was the British secret agent able to find clues, identify the Chinese criminals, rescue the British captives, and, ultimately, defeat Fu Manchu.[21] In fact, the two photographs examined above also distantly recall Fu Manchu in Brabin's film, which frequently depicts the creature sitting on a throne in his bizarrely orientalist palace or pacing about in a palace room filled with oriental objects and Western laboratory equipment that he used for sinister experiments meant to destroy the white race. The photographs broadly drew on the Western tradition of portraying the evil "Chinaman" in order to talk about Chinese migrants to Italians. It is not surprising, then, that the British writer Sax Rohmer's creation of Fu Manchu as that figure incarnate was one of the most prominent twentieth-century embodiments of the octopus metaphor.[22]

Why did journalists employ the two parallels in the above specific ways? Why did they seem to delight in speculation about the Chinese mafia when covering Chinese migrants? In the early 1990s, Italian journalists lacked experience writing about large, heterogeneous communities of foreign migrants, a phenomenon that was occurring in Italy for the first time in the contemporary era. Contact between Italian journalists and foreign migrants, which would have otherwise provided more accurate or objective information, was scarce.[23] Furthermore, professional training and experience, Italian journalists were better-versed in covering crimes and court cases, including those involving Chinese migrants, than in addressing other facets of immigration. Answered simply, the Chinese mafia was a new subject to which journalists could apply their existing crime reporting expertise.

Symptomatic of the profession's gap in knowledge and competencies was the 1995 media practice of covering judicial evidence of criminal activities involving Italy's Chinese without thorough investigation. Crime reporters continued to rely on the Italian-Chinese organized crime parallel from the early 1990s in their coverage. In a 1995 *Corriere della Sera* article, the journalist Lavinia Di Gianvito set out to validate the 1992 police and media speculation about Italy's Chinese criminal groups: "The Roman tribunal confirmed the existence of the yellow-colored 'octopus' ['piovra'] in a sentence which condemned its association with mafia-related crimes ['associazione a delinquere di stampo mafioso']: For the first time, the famous Article 416 bis, which was created to break up the Cosa Nostra, was applied to someone who was not Sicilian, Calabrian, or Campanian." Di Gianvito writes that, while these groups were unrelated to the Triad since the captured criminals belonged to "three gangs ['cosche'] of secondary level," "these minor organizations could make the big leap to seize control of the international drug trafficking."[24] However, in accounts such as Di Gianvito's, the reader learns very little about how criminal activities associated with Italy's Chinese, ranging from human smuggling to illegal labour, were primarily driven by economic factors related to the movement of transnational Chinese capital. Instead, the reader is once again asked to comprehend this migration by recalling the octopus metaphor, the gratuitous specialized vocabulary concerning the Cosa Nostra here used to describe the Triad, and the visual evocation of the Chinese mafia's imminent but unspecified threat to Italy.

The Italian-Chinese mafia parallel was particularly relevant to journalists in the 1990s because they were increasingly influenced by crime fiction. In "Yellow Milan," the yellow colour used to print the headline points both to the article's content (i.e., the supposed skin colour of the Chinese race) and to its stylistic inspiration in the literary conventions of Italian crime fiction (called the *giallo* in Italian; literally, the yellow colour). In this and other articles, crafting entertaining and memorable news accounts supersedes scrupulously collecting and interpreting pertinent evidence. More seriously, by confirming an unfounded thesis about the Chinese mafia in Italy without offering any substantial new information, "The Octopus with Almond-Shaped Eyes" and similar articles increasingly steered serious journalism away from first-hand sources. It refocused on the mechanism of news-making and even on journalistic sensationalism, which I intend here as the prevalence of the tabloid format and spirit over objective information analysis. Indeed, the 1992 reporting about Falcone and Borsellino marked a watershed moment in contemporary Italian journalism when sensationalism became rampant and clearly affected coverage of immigrants.[25] All of these practices made crime reporting vulnerable to the influence of crime fiction.

In depicting the Chinese mafia in Italy, crime reporting drew on the literary genre's narrative conventions, for the basis was often a real crime case. The genre's logic also provided a key because often there was a recourse to conspiracy theory in the journalistic texts. Last, crime fiction's rhetorical viability was articulated in crime reporting insofar as the attention tended to focus on the crimes' impact on ordinary people. A case in point is an article Di Gianvito wrote in 1997 that followed up on her aforementioned 1995 piece.[26] There, she uses first-hand sources to analyse all three semantic levels of the Chinese mafia: individual criminals, criminal groups, and the Triad. She employs terms specific to the Cosa Nostra to refer to two recently captured Chinese criminals who decided to collaborate with Italian police: "pentiti" and "collaboratori di giustizia," which indicate former members of the Cosa Nostra, often highly ranked in the criminal structure, who informed on the organization to the magistrates in exchange for the court's protection. As Di Gianvito reports, according to these criminals there were two criminal groups in Rome, each composed of "six, seven persons," with one group a "clan which, in pure mafia style, never abandons its very faithful members." The association of these groups with the Triad comes next. For the ferocity of the Cosa Nostra-like Chinese mafia bosses, "maintaining 'order' within the organization is the only system to guarantee respect for the rules imposed by its heads." Only after exploiting the full semantic range of the Chinese mafia does Di Gianvito elucidate its implications for Rome: "In our city where more than five thousand citizens of the oriental country reside, there have been many episodes from the past few years that confirm the existence of a precise strategy." She closes with a summary of these episodes, which were "mysterious but all connected with the Triad."

In invoking the Triad's influence in Italy in their accounts without presenting relevant evidence, Di Gianvito and other journalists did not presume innocence. This failure to assume defendants are innocent until a judgement is made violated a principle of the 1993 "Carta dei doveri del giornalista" (Norms of the journalist's duties) issued by Italy's Consiglio Nazionale dell'Ordine dei Giornalisti (National Council for Journalists) and Federazione Nazionale della Stampa (National Federation of the Press). The "Carta" concerns journalists' deontological behaviour, that is, their duties as opposed to their ethical obligations, in reporting. The "Carta" was born in response to the excessive and often inaccurate coverage of Tangentopoli that journalists were churning out in 1993.[27] The principle of "presumption of innocence" was not effectively applied in news reporting on the supposed Chinese mafia in the 1990s. While Di Gianvito in her aforementioned 1995 article dutifully noted that the two criminal groups in Rome were considered organized associations from a judicial standpoint, she did not mention the likelihood that they might really be individual criminals who worked together for convenience, a view later supported by research on Chinese human smuggling into the United States in the early 2000s.[28] Rather, this article was symptomatic of the journalistic tendency to identify Chinese criminals with the Triad or related large-scale criminal groups. By extension, the Chinese migrant community as a whole was criminalized in this media coverage.

Fast-forwarding to the year 2003, most coverage of Chinese migration to Italy in the mainstream news magazines explicitly invalidated the parallels between the Chinese mafia in Italy, the Chinese mafia in the United States, and the Cosa Nostra in Italy and abroad. The tendency towards excessive crime reporting and the use of metaphorical language for Chinese migrants also abated. The media's knowledge of Chinese migration to Italy had visibly advanced, primarily thanks to an increase in detailed police reports and sociological studies, which relevant news articles cited with considerable precision. In a December 2003 *Panorama* article, Francesco De Ciccio of the Italian police's foreign crime section explained that "if [by the 'Chinese mafia'] we mean an organization residing on our territory, with a pyramid structure comparable to that of our mafia, or to that of the Triad, then the answer is no. But we can easily define various organizations as having a mafia nature ['di stampo mafioso'] because of their operational mode. We have already obtained some results." The reporter of a November 2003 *Panorama* article cites the sociologist Daniele Cologna and assures readers that "the *carabineri* teams in Italy do not believe that the Triad (the Chinese mafia) is present in Italian provinces. The mafia phenomenon affects metropolitan areas more, and it is not yet very widespread in Italy. In the provinces, the problem is instead with criminal gangs." A similar observation, which appeared to originate from Cologna as well, informs the December 2003 article: "The Triad exists ... But they are completely different from criminal gangs and Chinese mafia associations operating in Italy ... No contacts between Chinese organized crime in Italy and the Triad, which has Paris and Lyon as its European operation centres, have ever emerged from police investigations."[29]

At this time, the Italian media also identified the real culprits of criminality emerging from within the Chinese migrant community: criminal groups composed of unemployed young men who had recently migrated from China. Using relevant police reports and sociological studies, and in particular those about gang members already available in the late 1990s, the aforementioned *Panorama* articles were precise about what Chinese criminality in Italy meant for them: young men who often worked on commission independent of larger criminal organizations. In the early 1990s, the problem involving young male migrants also occurred in the so-called Zhejiang Village in Beijing, a major migration destination for the Wenzhounese in China.[30] As reported in the December 2003 *Panorama* article, these men threatened members of Milan's Chinese community; in Rome, they also exploited prostitution, a business recently opened to Italian and other non-Chinese customers.

Therefore, by 2003 the availability of up-to-date police reports and detailed sociological studies concerning the Chinese migration had helped journalists to become more sophisticated in interpreting the phenomenon. What other factors conditioned this media shift, which forcefully delegitimated the 1992 to 1995 media discourse about the supposed Chinese mafia? In the next three sections of this chapter, I explore several explanations for this media change between 1995 and 2003, including ethnocultural, economic and institutional, and Chinese migrant perspectives.

Positive Ethnocultural Essentialism, 1995–2003

The two parallels examined in the previous section had strong connotations of negative ethnocultural essentialism. The Chinese mafia in Italy was said to resemble that in North America because their members were conationals who allegedly acted according to tenets of the same Chinese ethnic and cultural heritage. In Italian crime reporting, the Chinese mafia in Italy had deep roots in Chinese history and culture, just like the Cosa Nostra did in Italian culture. To refute widespread negative ethnocultural essentialism around the Chinese, the first extensive use of positive ethnocultural essentialism emerged in Italian news magazines in 1995.

Media coverage that drew on positive ethnocultural essentialism often viewed this mechanism as a genuine gesture of sympathy and hospitality for migrants, as journalists often explicitly intended to amend the previously excessive focus on criminality. In a 1995 *Grazia* article, the journalist elucidates this objective first through an example from Milan's Chinese community: while Italian authorities criticized an unauthorized Chinese-owned hospital, she argues that patients needed it because they were more accustomed to Chinese doctors who understood their culture.[31] Thus, the journalist highlights the migrants' cultural distinction, which outsiders are said to easily misconstrue as criminal activities. Moreover, she blames certain colleagues for failing to interpret these behaviours within the context of Chinese culture and ethnicity, as well as for defaming migrants tout court by associating them with the Chinese mafia: "And so, we are back to speak of Chinatown, the mafia, parallel worlds, and mysteries. It is always like this when something happens in the Chinese community." Instead, she intends to enlighten the reader on Chinese social and cultural details through, among other strategies, featuring several large photographs depicting vibrant Chinese festivals and other social aspects of migrants' lives in Italy.[32]

Having demystified migrants' seemingly criminal social behaviour by attributing it to ordinary Chinese culture, how did journalists explain this community's often-reported existing criminality, such as the human trafficking that the Chinese mafia supposedly conducted in order to supply businesses with illegal migrants? Quoting a statement from Milan's Office for Foreigners, the journalist behind the *Grazia* article defines irregular migration from China to Italy as human smuggling and not as human trafficking. This conclusion is confirmed by recent sociological findings. In most cases, in the 1990s Chinese migrants initiated the process of smuggling themselves and paid intermediary smugglers in order to travel illegally or to help them procure Italian tourist visas with the intention to overstay. During the 1990s and 2000s, there was a ready market in Italy's Chinese community for illegal labourers. Elite Chinese migrant entrepreneurs continued to open factories but were often unwilling to hire formally when they could instead exploit the low cost of newly arrived migrants. In other cases, they were unable to hire formally, owing to the restrictions posed by Italian labour laws on hiring procedures and labour contracts for migrant-owned enterprises.[33]

Once the news media established that human smuggling was the progenitor of much of the criminality within Italy's Chinese community, a further question arose: What attracted the Chinese migrants to Italy? In the 1990s and 2000s, Italian news magazines showcased one factor in particular: *guanxi*, a trait said to be characteristic of Chinese migrants and of Chinese people more generally. In an interview for a 2003 *Panorama* article, the criminologist Renzo Rastrelli attributed the sudden influx of illegal Chinese migrants in Italy during the 1980s and 1990s to the relative ease of their insertion into Italy's Chinese ethnic business thanks to guanxi.[34] Guanxi was said to typify interpersonal relations in China and to denote a social and community network based on family, personal ties, economic interests, and reputation. According to Rastrelli, Italy's Chinese migrant entrepreneurs, who were mainly from Wenzhou and its surrounding counties, relied on guanxi to borrow large sums of money from friends and business partners as start-up capital, often with little or no interest. However, according to the two economists cited in the *Panorama* article, by 2003 that system had begun to erode, owing to high competition among Chinese enterprises in Italy. Funds for new businesses and jobs were less available, and some job-seekers without adequate money, legal documents, or social ties formed gangs. This and other Italian news coverage identified guanxi as the main financing for Chinese migrant businesses in Italy, making it a powerful concept to counter speculation around the Chinese mafia offering migrants in need loans with high interest rates and employing them in businesses.

The scholar Aihwa Ong criticizes such a use of guanxi by transnational Chinese and their spokesmen as positive ethnocultural essentialism. Instead, she views it as a "mix of instrumentalism (fostering flexibility and the mobility of capital and personnel across political borders) and humanism ('helping out' relatives and hometown folk on the mainland)" that was not unique to Chinese culture. Indeed, according to Ong, guanxi and other perceived "Asian values" may well be "sociopolitical effects of an array of strategies, programs, and techniques that regulate society in a way that reflects the liberal logic of economic competitiveness." For Ong, rather than an illiberal tactic intrinsic to communist China and in opposition to Western democracy and economic liberalism, guanxi is an efficient network among diasporic Chinese for achieving optimal economic performances at a minimal economic and sociopolitical cost.[35] The case of Italy's Chinese was no different.

The media also considered other factors in China that set this migration in motion. In the 1990s, certain journalists exhibited Cold War thinking in examining the subject, such as in the aforementioned 1992 *Sette* article, which prominently discusses human rights in China as a reason for the Chinese to leave their homeland, a theme that would have resonated with readers familiar with the 1989 Tiananmen Square protests. Chinese individuals were "taken away from their houses in the poorest and most depressing regions of the PRC [People's Republic of China], with the promise of a new life in a free country where democracy does not have only one colour or one party." The rhetorical viability of the article's Cold War thinking was enhanced by the recent cultural memory of an alleged display of China's diplomatic style based on intimidation. In 1992, China publicly blamed Italy when the latter withdrew its promised investment in Shanghai's Pudong district, a diplomatic failure that was a result of Tangentopoli.[36] Moreover, the *Sette* quotation illustrates an intellectual practice concerning supposed cultural clashes resulting from the end of the Cold War political system. Best illustrated by Samuel P. Huntington's 1993 essay "The Clash of Civilizations," this practice promoted monolithic views of cultures, sweeping generalizations, and an alarmist tone, which all meshed together to rhetorical effect.[37] Indeed, journalists like the one behind the *Sette* article and others from the early 1990s were essentially speculating about whether the recent breakdown of the Cold War system had unleashed an influx of ex-Communists from the former eastern bloc into Western Europe, with the Chinese following in their footsteps.

The multiculturalist camp loudly opposed this alarmist rhetoric, often through positive ethnocultural essentialism. For example, a 1995 article in *Il Venerdì* (the magazine of *La Repubblica*) titled "Chinese Neighbors Next-Door" draws cultural borderlines to argue in favour of the desirability of Chinese migrants in Italy.[38] The journalist praises the balance that Chinese migrants struck between maintaining traditional Chinese customs and practicing a strong Western capitalist work ethic. While family, religion, and traditional Chinese medicine helped them remain grounded in their native culture, the journalist opines, the Chinese came to Italy in search of "a real capitalism." To be sure, such juxtapositions based on traits said to be intrinsic to Italian and Chinese cultures were meant to support Italy's multicultural project. As the journalist argues, the heritage and culture of Chinese migrants and their offspring would ultimately enrich and diversify Italian society precisely because Chinese culture was fundamentally different from Italian culture. Before that would occur, the journalist implies, Italian society should understand that most of migrants' illegal business activities and habits, such as spitting on the ground, could be explained by placing them within the context of Chinese culture and customs.

A further point about ethnocultural differences in this context refers to mobility. In support of a multicultural vision of Italy, and in reaction to depictions of the Chinese as highly mobile economic profit-seekers, "Chinese Neighbors Next-Door" paints a positive portrait of Chinese migrants as potential permanent residents rather than as temporary sojourners. From the journalist's perspective on fashioning a multicultural Italy through immigration, if Chinese migrants intended to settle permanently in Italy and did not regard it as merely a place to accumulate wealth before returning home, then they should be considered members of the Italian nation-state like Italian citizens who were assumed to be sedentary. This was a reasoning validated by history, because permanently settled residents were often distinguished from unsettled nomads based on essentialist ethnic differentiation. According to Hyun Jin Kim, this distinction was important for defining the Self through the Other in ancient civilizations. In *Histories,* Herodotus sets the Greeks apart from the Scythians by contrasting settlers who were civically conscious and nomads who were inclined towards expansion and invasion. Similarly, in *Shiji* (Record of the grand historian), drawing on contrasting settlement patterns, the Chinese historian par excellence Sima Qian shows the superiority of the sedentary Chinese in cultural and other achievements over the nomadic Xiongnu.[39]

These ancient and contemporary examples contain much wishful thinking about the assumed sedentariness of settlers and residents in a given area. But the facts point to the contrary. Significant numbers of recent Chinese migrants to Italy are diasporic in that they move back and forth between Italy and China and reside in both for extended periods of time. Other Chinese are transnational entrepreneurs and workers in that they move from Italy to live in Chinese migrant communities in other European countries, ever sensitive to entrepreneurial opportunities and political climates. Only a small portion of Chinese migrants reside or intend to reside in Italy for their entire lives as migrants; even then, they tend to move from city to city within Italy.[40]

I do not question the truthfulness of the examples of Chinese residents cited in the news accounts that celebrated a multicultural Italy. Rather, I suggest that the news focus on the permanent residents within the heterogeneous Chinese migrant community inadvertently endorsed highly ethnoculturally essentialist depictions of Chinese migrants in public discourses. This multicultural thought process risked ascribing Chinese migrants with more or less fixed traits that were associated with their ethnicity and native culture, even though such positive traits were said to benefit Italian society. These faulty characteristics of the 1990s multicultural discourse in Italy would continue to play a key role in later Italian media coverage of the Chinese, as I show in chapter 3.

Migrant Entrepreneurship and Institutional Discipline, 1995–2003

Quite early on in the Chinese migration, the local governments, the police, and the courts were all engaged in regulating illegal activities and in prosecuting migrants' economic misconduct, prompting concerns. In 1995, in a major televised debate on the *Maurizio Costanzo Show* on Canale 5, the Italian priest Don Momigli underscored how the local government's disciplinary actions in containing the flow of Chinese migrants and their businesses should be replaced by policies aimed at promoting their better integration into local society. Momigli made the recommendation based on his experience in providing social and religious assistance to the Chinese community in Campi Bisenzio, near Florence.[41]

This example illustrates another dominant media perspective that, like positive ethnocultural essentialism, distanced itself from the previous focus on the Chinese mafia. This perspective interpreted the Chinese migration by focusing on migrants' illegal business activities and on Italian municipal and police regulations. By covering disciplinary actions applied to Chinese migrant entrepreneurship, the Italian media refocused on how to best govern it and jettisoned its previous emphasis on the role the supposed Chinese mafia played in managing this entrepreneurship.[42]

I discuss the specifics of this perspective on economic crimes and institutional discipline in relation to the 2007 Milan riot and to the Prato case study in subsequent chapters. Here, I am concerned with how this news emphasis was born of historical and economic dynamics in the late 1990s and early 2000s. In the mid-1990s, the image of Chinese migrants as underdogs in Italian capitalism was widely accepted as they still mainly worked for Italian business owners as contractors and had only just begun to establish their own firms in Prato and elsewhere. In the same period, as mainland China began to explore the global market, migrants imported "Made in China" products into Italy, which arguably benefited the average Italian's personal wealth. Starting in the late 1990s and stimulated by the legalization of migrant self-employment in Italy in 1998, Chinese migrant businesses began to compete with both mainland Chinese and Italian firms.[43] Italy's economic confidence in the late 1980s and early 1990s was all but gone by the early 2000s. In those years, with a two-digit annual GDP growth, China's momentum was evident to all. China's entry into the World Trade Organization in 2001, which gave impetus to the country's economic globalization, greatly impacted Italy. While small- and medium-sized Italian enterprises were generally not well-prepared for globalized economy at that time, several industries in which the country had traditionally been a leading exporter, including textiles and furniture, met with stiff competition from mainland China and from Chinese migrants in Italy.

Under these circumstances, not only did the early 1990s news coverage of the Chinese mafia look hackneyed, but a continued recourse to it as an explanation for Chinese ascendance vis-à-vis Italy's declining position in the global economy seemed naive and irresponsible. An adequate understanding of migrants' routes to success and business practices, and Italians' institutional reactions, became pressing issues for Italian journalists and readers. Italian journalists might also have been wary about offending and provoking Chinese authorities, including the Chinese embassy and consulates in Italy, by referring to controversial issues like the Triad in Italy which had been repeatedly proven untrue, or by insisting on a stark dichotomy between Western democracy and Chinese communism whose rhetorical viability was weakened at a time when the Cold War system had ended more than a decade before.

Therefore, by 2003 the Italian media had unambiguously come to view the Chinese migration as a primarily economic phenomenon. According to the aforementioned 2003 *Panorama* articles, this phenomenon was impressive: in that year, Italy's Chinese owned 12,000 companies and paid about 1.3 million euros in taxes: "This is an invisible army that marches silently. With the rustling sounds of euros, they conquer the real estate, commercial activities, and industries. Pieces of cities like Prato, Rome, and Milan too." Moreover, the Chinese conquest depended on such economic crimes as irregular migration, counterfeiting, working more than legally allowed, underpaid and illegal labour, violating labour legislation, and even extortion. Therefore, as these articles emphasize, municipal governments and police must dedicate more efforts than in the past to regulating this entrepreneurship. In this respect, Prato was a model, having mobilized forceful operations to curb illegal Chinese business activities from 1998 to 2003.[44] In the early 2000s, journalists were rightly concerned with how Italian authorities at various levels addressed Chinese economic crimes and labour law violations – not insofar as these firms were involved in the Chinese mafia, but in relation to their business practices and their impact on local Italian businesses. Indeed, in providing a historical perspective on the contentious relationship between start-up capitalism and law enforcement, in 2001 *Ventiquattro* (*Il Sole 24*'s magazine) argued that the exploitation of Chinese labour in Italy in the late 1990s and early 2000s was comparable to the experiences of Italian labourers in the Veneto in the 1950s and 1960s during Italy's postwar Reconstruction, when its labour laws increasingly matured.[45]

The refocus on economic crimes and institutional discipline was an important novelty in the mainstream Italian magazines in the early 2000s and would be prominent in the coverage of the 2007 riot (see chapters 3 and 4). However, the establishment of a particular media perspective did not invalidate previous angles entirely, as subsequent media analyses about the Chinese in Italy proved, where concrete evidence was not always given to substantiate claims about migrants' crimes or illegal activities and the term "mafia" was used indiscriminately.[46] Nevertheless, as the discussion in this section shows, an influential group of Italian media texts examined Chinese migration to Italy in relation to economic globalization in Italy, reflecting the changing economic and historical landscapes in and between the two countries.

Reactive Chinese Migrant Reporting, 2001–2003

In the early 2000s, two major bilingual Chinese-Italian monthly magazines, *Cina in Italia* and *It's China*, launched.[47] Reacting to previous Italian news coverage about the Chinese population in Italy, the magazines avoided any mention of the Chinese mafia, addressed human smuggling to some degree, and discussed Italian institutional disciplinary actions against Chinese migrant merchants at length. This content focus was directed at Italian readers, especially the government officials, police chiefs, and other institutional figures who the magazines also frequently interviewed. Articles that endorsed institutional discipline showed the desire of elite and legal Chinese migrants to live and conduct business in Italy according to the country's laws.

We can appreciate the function of the Italian-language magazine editions through Mary Louise Pratt's concept of "autoethnography." This concept describes how colonized people's texts were coded in the colonizers' written conventions, and therefore were addressed "both to metropolitan readers and to literate sectors of the speaker's own social group ... Often such texts constitute a group's point of entry into metropolitan lettered culture."[48] A quasi-colonial relationship emerged as the Italian municipal authorities and police often took top-down disciplinary actions against the Chinese migrant community, as the Chinese migrant media justified various misunderstood aspects of their entrepreneurship to Italian readers in Italian, and as migrant elites conveyed their opinions in Italian-language articles. As the Chinese migrant media understood early on, the only effective way to question the legitimacy of this institutional discipline was to set up their own discursive regime. This regime offered counterarguments in Italian to Italian detractors and made recommendations to fellow migrants in an attempt to correct their behaviour.

During the 2000s, irregular migration to Italy was a major concern for the country's legal Chinese migrants. Chinese migrant journalists rarely associated irregular migration with Chinese organized crime, much less with the Triad. Rather, their coverage ascribed criminality to individuals or small groups engaged in human smuggling. In a 2001 *Cina in Italia* article, a journalist warns potential human smugglers about the harsh legal consequences in Italian courts and discourages potential migrants in China from using such services. He describes the dire fate of certain *shetou* (literally snakeheads, the Chinese slang for human smugglers) who were lured into the trade because penalties for it were not yet severe in China. However, he adds, the Italian law previously reserved for the Cosa Nostra had recently been applied to Chinese migrants, as the crime reporter Di Gianvito had relayed in 1995. In addition, Italian judges tended to charge Chinese migrants with mafia-associated crimes even though they mostly worked together for convenience and not as part of a larger criminal structure. Therefore, the journalist urges young Chinese contemplating becoming snakeheads not to make the decision lightly out of ignorance of the Italian law's severity.[49] *Cina in Italia*'s criticism of the emigration brokerage system in China was timely after the 1990s, a decade in which illegal migration flowed unchecked from China to Europe.[50] The moral high ground that the magazine took against human smuggling indicated the perceived urgency of eradicating it. It was also an important issue for a magazine published in collaboration with the Confederazione Generale Italiana del Lavoro (Italian general confederation of labour).

In the first half of the 2000s, *Cina in Italia* and *It's China* often explained why and how to address the implementation of Italian laws, which in principle aimed to fight human smuggling and migrants' illegal business practices, but in practice also hurt legal business transactions by slowing them down with frequent police investigations. The 2003 inaugural issue of *It's China* (then called *Wan Li*) features an interview with Giacomo Dentici, the head police commissioner in Prato, who admonishes migrants to respect Italian laws because "now that the situation is notably ameliorating and many Chinese became legalized, it is in their interest to approach the police in case of need." Dentici was addressing middle-class legal Chinese migrants whose initial entrepreneurship in the country must have involved illegal economic practices. From the standpoint of reactive communication, the main purpose of such coverage was to show how Chinese migrants collaborated with Italian police to combat irregular migration and economic crimes.

Apart from these cautionary words from Italian police, elite migrants often made similar recommendations to their fellow entrepreneurs and workers in the two magazines. Indeed, when addressing Chinese migrants, news stories about human smuggling and economic crimes were cautionary, didactic tales, in keeping with the Confucian tradition of Chinese-language newspapers. The July 2004 cover story of *It's China* presents the results of the Prato police department's Operation Surprise 2, and notes that both Italians and Chinese were jailed for facilitating unlawful migration and irregular labour. Careful not to offend Chinese readers, the journalist euphemizes what the Italian media would normally label as the Chinese mafia as "international mafias." But Chinese criminals' names are listed on the cover, a form of public shaming in the Chinese tradition meant to denounce or warn those on the margin of legality. The cover story also cautions Chinese entrepreneurs against mistreating their workers, who could report such misconduct to the Italian authorities and cause disciplinary actions against their businesses. Indeed, according to this report, Italian financial police succeeded in their operation with "the help of certain migrants who decided to collaborate."[51]

Concerned with establishing a proper work ethic within their community, educated and established Chinese migrants often adopted a rather harsh and patronizing, and sometimes intimidating, tone towards fellow migrants in news commentaries. At times, elite migrants regarded those whose businesses systematically committed economic crimes as the community's internal enemies. In the 2001 inaugural issue of *Cina in Italia*, the journalist Shi Yi congratulates the entrepreneurs on their great success in the import-export businesses that had flourished since the mid-1990s. However, as these firms mushroomed, all with a very similar configuration, a vicious price competition quickly emerged and engendered more illegal economic practices. Migrants who succeeded in the 1990s, through legal or illegal channels, became models for newcomers who would run any risk in profit-making. This was a phenomenon that Shi Yi criticizes:

> Undeniably, racist prejudice against Chinese migrants exists. There is no way to escape it. In debates, the left-leaning and right-leaning political parties always sharpen their points by referring to migrants who rarely fight back because of their limited rights in Italy. However, Chinese migrants themselves repeatedly display their mistakes, which would satisfy the Italian institutional curiosity for the Chinese mystery [i.e., their entrepreneurial success in Italy]. Migrants continually provide ironclad evidence to the Italian authorities, encouraging them to desire for ever more control. Consider the fractured state of a great number of import-export companies that follows any police investigation. Chinese migrants offer the most authoritative statistics and records for the latest Italian understanding of their community.[52]

In keeping with the antagonistic and moralistic modes of expression used by editorials in *Ouhua Lianhe Shibao*, one of the oldest Chinese migrant newspapers in Italy and their previous employer, Shi Yi goes on to voice concerns about the future of Italy's Chinese migrant entrepreneurship.[53] For the journalist, this entrepreneurship was being destroyed by certain migrants' illegal business practices, which resulted in more police raids and damaged the entire community's public standing in Italy.

Since the early 2000s, when the Chinese migrant media gradually and firmly established itself in Italy's mediascape, the editorial teams and financial backers of *Cina in Italia* and *It's China*, in addition to those of the four major newspapers I will discuss in subsequent chapters, have been the ultimate opinion-makers within their community. These elites benefited from the fact that the magazines spoke to both Italians and fellow migrants. Successful Chinese migrant entrepreneurs, journalists, and educators positioned themselves as intermediaries between the Italian government and police and ordinary Chinese migrants, interpreting Italian laws for migrants and negotiating with authorities when conflicts arose. For these elites, it was important to maintain a good media reputation for themselves and for their community. That reputation could help ensure laws were applied fairly and other discriminations were prevented, and thus ease their business practices, professional activities, and daily lives. Elite migrants' concerns were not different from those of the emerging elite business class in China around the same period. Wary of international restrictions on their transnational mobility, this class pressured the Chinese state to fight irregular emigration.[54]

Under these circumstances, ordinary Chinese migrant workers and their perception of the Chinese mafia and economic crimes were often obscured in the Chinese migrant print press. Published in *Cina in Italia*'s inaugural issue, several articles about the experiences of a clandestine migrant were very similar to the aforementioned Italian news articles.[55] These Chinese accounts contain no particular insights into this individual migration trajectory, except for the pronounced use of Chinese populist pathos as the migrant recounts the sacrifices his dying father made to fund his trip to Italy, his remorse about using this money that could have saved his father's life, the inhuman journey he endured, and his isolation and economic obstacles after arrival. These ostensibly first-person accounts supported the magazine's opinion that migrants should not leave China for Italy on impulse and must not pay human smugglers to help.

Because of a lack of relevant research, it is difficult to determine whether such accounts represented a majority of ordinary migrants' views of their migratory experiences. As interviews conducted in the late 1990s by the critic Antonella Ceccagno reveal, migrants did not always view snakeheads as evil intermediaries and they did express indignation at the apparent ease with which the Italian media wielded the "Chinese mafia" label.[56]

Undoubtedly, the tendency to censor alternative viewpoints of members of a heterogeneous migrant community showed how elite Chinese migrants were eager to establish authority within their community. But along the way, *It's China* and *Cina in Italia* offered self-representations that formed a unified rhetorical front in addressing increasing accusations of Chinese migrants' illegal business practices in the 2000s Italian media. This journalistic practice proved to be a necessary evil when the Chinese migrant press mounted a full-scale counterattack on negative Italian media depictions of the 2007 riot, as I examine in chapter 4.

Orientalizing the Chinese in Roberto Saviano's *Gomorra*, 2006

One of the most well-known journalistic accounts of the Chinese mafia in Italy appeared in the first two chapters of Saviano's 2006 nonfiction *Gomorra*. News commentators and critics regard this book as the narrative that brought the Camorra's economic and criminal activities to international attention. Saviano denounced the Camorra so effectively that he had to be put under protection because of several death threats made by Camorristi. What has not been scrutinized in news analyses and critical literature is the role of the Chinese in Saviano's book.[57]

As I have examined previously, by the mid-2000s pro-migrant news articles had clarified migrants' contributions to Italian society. Media coverage had become quite precise about the nature of Chinese economic crimes and entrepreneurship. The Chinese migrant media had defended migrants' settlement. Thus, by that time, the validity of addressing the Chinese migration by focusing on the Chinese mafia had been seriously challenged. Why, then, did Saviano do just that in 2006?

Did Saviano use the Chinese mafia as a sensationalist topic because of his apparent lack of familiarity with the Chinese migrant community? The Chinese migrant media that reacted quickly to Saviano's depictions seemed to embrace this interpretation. In one article, Hu Lanbo, the editor-in-chief of *Cina in Italia*, takes issue with the expression Saviano uses in *Gomorra*'s opening paragraph ("The Chinese never die") and then explains the specific Chinese cultural practices and migration patterns that helped to keep migrants' funerals out of sight in Italy. Hu is mainly concerned with whether Saviano's view of Naples's Chinese would impact the average Italian reader's opinion of this community, given the book's realism. In another article, Associna rebukes Saviano both for knowing little about Naples's Chinese and for not hesitating to discuss them sensationally.[58]

Indeed, Chinese migrants were quick to identity the problematic stereotypes of the Chinese and the simplistic dichotomy between the Italians and the Chinese migrants in *Gomorra*. However, by unduly focusing on the sociological and anthropological accuracy of how the Chinese lived in Naples in the mid-2000s as a way to fight journalistic sensationalism, Hu and Associna seemed to ignore the possibility that Saviano in *Gomorra* never aims to examine Naples's Chinese on their own terms in the first place.

In probing Saviano's agenda in depicting the Chinese, I maintain that the Chinese mafia serves as the first and most effective case study in *Gomorra* to address the subjects that concern him for the rest of the book: the Camorra and globalization, both Italy-centred social issues. Saviano's intent is not to investigate the illegal economic activities of Naples's Chinese on their own terms, unlike most of the journalists who felt it was their duty to unravel them for the Italian reader and from there to cover the Chinese migration (as well as to exercise their expertise in crime reporting). Instead, he aims to stimulate the reader to make an approximate, but emotionally powerful, association between two types of transnational organized crime – the Camorra and the Chinese mafia – in order to better contextualize the former at the opening of his book. Ultimately, Saviano is not especially concerned with an accurate account of the Chinese mafia: the topic still informs his second chapter but it disappears suddenly and totally from the rest of the book.

To borrow Edward Said's words, Saviano's depiction of Chinese migrants in *Gomorra* manifests orientalism through "ideological suppositions, images, and fantasies" of China. But more importantly, again following Said, this depiction is orientalist in reconsidering "the changing historical and cultural relationship between Europe and Asia" during the 2000s in order to suggest that, if we were to follow Saviano's visceral and mostly fact-based arguments, the Chinese global economy was expanding to the detriment of the Italian economy. In rhetoric, Saviano's use of China in *Gomorra* is similar to that of such contemporary critical theorists as Giorgio Agamben, Michael Hardt, and Antonio Negri in their projects, where, as Daniel F. Vukovich notes, they "betray no serious engagement with the question of China through intellectual rigor."[59]

Saviano orientalizes migrants as members of the Chinese mafia when, despite the profuse statistics and first-hand investigations at the core of his book, his realist narrative does not tangibly increase the reader's knowledge of this migration; it refers only to relevant information circulating within the Italian media, and not to that within the country's Chinese migrant media. He opens *Gomorra* with the image of frozen bodies, discussed below, and notes that this eye-witness account is a transcription of what a crane operator told him. Subsequently, in the overview of the transactions at the port of Naples, Saviano uses statistics (e.g., "the largest cargo terminal" and "almost all the traffic," 5) whose sources are omitted, leaving the reader with no clues about the criteria used to substantiate such superlative claims.[60] (Elsewhere, Saviano sometimes mentions his sources.) Later on, Saviano uses the second-person imperative to invite the reader to call on their somatic experiences in daily life and on their familiarity with crime reporting in order to understand the Chinese migration and the Chinese mafia. In the rest of the first chapter, Saviano narrates a first-person eyewitness account of his activities in a Chinese migrant warehouse, underscoring the authenticity and values of his own observations. Following these details, Saviano finally concludes that the Chinese mafia operated in Naples and collaborated with the Camorra.

Saviano's first-person accounts, use of statistics, address to the reader, and conclusions based on inconclusive evidence were widely practiced techniques throughout the 1990s and 2000s in the Italian media milieu. Several of his points in the first chapter had precedents in the mainstream Italian media, which had already created a cognitive map of the Chinese migration for most of Saviano's readers. For example, the two aforementioned 2003 *Panorama* articles referenced the recycling of deceased Chinese migrants' passports, the low number of Chinese funerals in Italy, and the Chinese-Italian competition in the garment industry in San Giuseppe Vesuviano, near Naples.[61]

An extended example of Saviano's reliance on existing media coverage concerns his speculation about how the Camorra and the Triad-controlled Chinese migrants collaborated in Naples's garment industry. In his second chapter, the Chinese employed the Neapolitan tailor Pasquale to teach them to manufacture higher quality garments. These migrants were then ready to emulate the quality produced by Neapolitan sewers. For Saviano, the Chinese could easily come into conflict with the Camorra who financed many local garment workshops. As no overt Camorristi intervention into Naples's Chinese businesses were reported, Saviano draws on a journalistic tradition of speculating about cooperation among the world's transnational criminal organizations to posit that the two criminal organizations secretly agreed to cooperate. Naples's garment industry often hired Italian workers on the black market, and the industry was, according to a 2003 *Panorama* article, "a business traditionally controlled by the Camorra, who had nothing to say on this. Strange, no? This is how the anti-mafia investigators reason.

They fear for an agreement between Chinese organized crime and the Camorra."[62] The basic logic for this media interpretation, to borrow the critic Massimo Introvigne's observation, is to consider whether or not Chinese organized crime existed in Italy, even when countering negative stereotypes of the Chinese.[63] From 2000 to 2003, speculation around potential Chinese collaboration with the Camorra also prevailed in mainstream Italian media outlets other than *Panorama*.[64] Ultimately, Saviano asked his readers to draw on these narratives in order to digest his analysis. His rhetoric was tautological in its recycling of old media content and methods. At its publication in 2006, *Gomorra* added no particular insight into the 2000s Chinese migration to Italy.

In the book, Saviano's realist strategy works in tandem with his affective strategy, which exploits pathos. The latter contributes even less factual information to the public understanding of Chinese migration to Italy and relies even more closely on past textual techniques of distinguishing the Chinese from the Europeans. Saviano's affective strategy is particularly effective in his notorious opening paragraph, in which he shares an eyewitness account from a crane operator at the port of Naples:

> The container swayed as the crane hoisted it onto the ship. The spreader, which hooks the container to the crane, was unable to control its movement, so it seemed to float in the air. The hatches, which had been improperly closed, suddenly sprang open, and dozens of bodies started raining down. They looked like mannequins. But when they hit the ground, their heads split open, as if their skulls were real. And they were. Men, women, even a few children, came tumbling out of the container. All dead. Frozen, stacked one on top of another, packed like sardines. These were the Chinese who never die. The eternal ones, who trade identity papers among themselves. (3)

The trafficking in Chinese dead bodies through the port of Naples was a media cliché that widely circulated in Italy from the late 1990s. The image was specifically associated with Naples, which, prior to Italian state restrictions in 2003, had been the largest European port of entry for "Made in China" merchandise. The French news media had begun to use this visually evocative detail, though in a different geographical context, in the early 1980s.[65]

In Saviano's retelling of this classic image, the third-person account creates a social distance between normal Italian readers and bizarre Chinese migrants, an example of the orientalist discourse of the Other. In the history of Western depictions of China, affective and moral distances are created between the Europeans and the Chinese in a familiar formula to differentiate good Westerners from evil Chinese. In a shot-and-reverse shot scene from *The Mask of Fu Manchu,* the titular devil concocts a poison as the white British captive looks on with horror. In *Gomorra,* a similarly constructed distance juxtaposes the norm and the deviance. While Saviano acknowledges that "kimonos, Marco Polo's beard, Bruce Lee kicking in midair" were commonplace stand-ins for China, the country was in fact "more closely linked to the port of Naples than to any other place" (4). Further, the "proverbial slowness that makes the Neapolitan's every move molasses-like" (5) was nowhere to be found in the port, as "Made in China" merchandise had to be unloaded quickly and silently before customs arrived. In *The Mask of Fu Manchu,* Fu Manchu reveals that the poison would be used to control the captive's body and mind in a quest to destroy the white race. In *Gomorra,* Saviano suggests that China has been cultivating the easily corruptible portion of the Italian economy for its own economic purposes, and that the Italians' moral outlooks and social behaviour have changed for the worse. As Saviano argues, because the Camorra damaged the healthy and morally upright portion of the Italian economy in similar ways, a collaboration between Camorristi and Chinese migrants was inevitable.

Another prominent example of Saviano's affective strategy concerns his use of a sexually charged metaphor – i.e., the port of Naples as an anus – to accentuate Chinese migrants' negative economic impact on Italy. He compares the port to an "open wound" and to "the hole in the earth out of which what's made in China comes" (4). This "hole gets bigger and deeper" (4) as "the sheet metal and screws slowly penetrate the tiny Neapolitan opening" (6). Figuratively speaking, as Chinese bodily fluids (i.e., the flow of fleets carrying "Made in China" merchandise for Chinese migrants' import-export business in Italy) were injected into the Italian body (i.e., the port of Naples), the Chinese invaded Europe. As if to address questions raised about the economic value of transporting Chinese goods through the port, Saviano's anus metaphor also comments on the non-procreative nature of the sexual act and thereby on the commercial transactions at the port of Naples.

For the critic Alessandro Dal Lago, Saviano uses a "gastroenteric vocabulary" to denigrate the Chinese by associating them with abjection, to which I add that the anus metaphor is a prime example. For Dal Lago, this vocabulary is part of a larger discursive project, which Saviano undertakes in this book and elsewhere, that draws on cultural populism, dilettantism, and stereotypes to uphold a heroic image of the writer and journalist as the public denouncer of morally controversial social issues.[66] The anus metaphor provides Italian readers with an outlet to express their frustrations at the cost of Chinese migrants' reputation: the menacing army of Chinese fleets was only equipped with cheaply made merchandise, which the Italians would consume and then discard. By condemning a complex social phenomenon through metaphors that evoke disgust and abjection, Saviano provides a potent form of psychological compensation for readers who may well face real-life problems resulting from globalization in Italy, in which the Chinese migration has played a key role.

While Saviano's realist and affective strategies do not enlarge his readers' knowledge of the Chinese mafia and Chinese migration to Italy, in *Gomorra*'s narrative these strategies reflect on Italy's perilous positions in economic globalization and migrant integration, both of which are crucially linked to the Camorra. Chinese-Italian commercial conflicts, as Saviano examines in his first chapter, serve as an opening example to tease out his arguments about the Camorra's global economic empire. When he expresses disgust at the image of Chinese dead bodies and at the port of Naples as an anus, he sets the stage to denounce the Camorra in the ensuing chapters, which he does with even greater intensity. The psychological distance he creates between the Italians and the Chinese in the first chapter of *Gomorra* prepares the groundwork for a similarly emotionally charged distance between ordinary Italians and Camorristi in the rest of the book.

Here I examine in detail one particular orientalist modality of using the Chinese Other to better reveal aspects of the Italian Self: the parallel between the Chinese mafia and the Camorra in Naples. Xian was the only Chinese migrant insider in *Gomorra* who was in charge of Chinese-owned warehouses near the port. Through the interactions Saviano had with Xian, he claims that the Camorra shared similar traits with the Triad. At one point, Saviano tried to engage Xian in a conversation about the Triad and the latter satirically offered up the euro, dollar, and yuan. In interpreting Xian's silence on the matter, Saviano states a main thesis of *Gomorra*: like the Triad, the Camorra advocated for its low-ranked members who often suffered from considerable economic and social hardships, and who often supported or were complicit in the criminal organization. Indeed, a characteristic of Saviano's condemnation of Chinese migrants in his book is to target the elites in the Triad's hierarchy who do not figure in the book, rather than lower-level intermediaries like Xian or migrant workers, who do. On the contrary, in the Chinese migrant press, transnational elites tended to associate the local underclass – including the Italians, the Chinese, and other migrants – with economic crimes.[67]

Saviano uses this insight from the Chinese migrant context and applies it to the dynamics between the Camorra and the Neapolitans. Already in the first chapter, he believes that Xian as a go-between was precisely how the Camorra, like the Triad, controlled the "intermediate stages, financial transfers, and investments – everything that makes a criminal economic outfit powerful" (12). In a later chapter titled "The Secondigliano War," he describes how residents of Secondigliano depended on the Camorra for a living, detested state negligence of their social plight, and protested a large-scale police raid in the area, and the reader would recall the similar relationship between Xian and the Triad. *Gomorra* intimates that Neapolitans' loyalty to the Camorra parallels Xian's to the Triad in that both were misdirected, yet essential, for the survival of socially disadvantaged people.

The orientalist punch of these narrative details fulfills the ultimate goal of the Triad-Camorra parallel in *Gomorra*, which is to argue that the Camorra, not Chinese organized crime, was at the time of his writing a significant social malaise in Italy. To be sure, from a conventional perspective, Italian journalism has a mandate to critique social phenomena that occur on Italian soil for Italian readers. Moreover, as Said notes, since the orientalist's vocabulary and language often do not even try to be accurate, there is really no reason to examine the accuracy of Saviano's empirical knowledge of the Chinese migrant community. Rather, for Said, the critic's task should be to show for whom and for what reasons such an account is written, a recommendation that I follow in the present analysis.[68]

But my view is also that immigration to Italy and its multicultural social reality during the 2000s made such a conventional perspective on national journalism obsolete and even dangerous. Italian journalism would be compelled to develop intercultural and transcultural competencies able to adequately address the diversity of the non-Italian Other, as well as to re-evaluate the assumptions of the Italian Self vis-à-vis the Other. Consider that, unlike in the colonial-era texts Said analyses, *Gomorra* was vehemently contested by some Italians and Chinese migrants, because the book's readership faced a Europe composed of very heterogeneous communities of migrants and natives, intellectuals and laymen, and artists and journalists. A socially engaged author like Saviano would certainly appreciate this point.

As media representations of Chinese migrants between 1992 and 2006 indicate, the Chinese mafia functioned as a metaphor that journalists used to organize debate about the migration. To borrow Appadurai's words, the Chinese mafia was a compelling idea "around which to organize *debate*, whether such debate is about method, about fact, about assumptions, or about empirical variations."[69] The ability of this metaphor to construct new narratives concerning Italy's Chinese was also evident in several television serials that catered to a wide range of viewers and aired on Mediaset and Rai. These included "Un cinese di nome Gioia" (A Chinese named Gioia) in *Carabinieri* (Raffaele Mertes, 2002) on Rete 4, *La moglie cinese* (The Chinese wife) (Antonio Luigi Grimaldi, 2006) on Rai Uno, "I tuoi rimorsi" (Your remorses) in *La nuova squadra* (The new team) (Claudio Corbucci, 2008) on Rai Tre, and "L'invasione cinese" (The Chinese invasion) in *Tutti per Bruno* (All for Bruno) (Francesco Pavolini, 2010) on Canale 5. Saviano's *Gomorra* drew on, and inspired, these television shows, all of which arguably orientalized Chinese migrants in order to explore Italy-centred issues or the complexity of Italian characters.

The phenomenon of the Chinese mafia marshaled together several notable topics and perspectives in the Italian-Chinese migrant cultural repertoire, chief among which were the history of the Chinese diaspora in the United States, Italy's own organized crime, a multicultural vision of addressing immigration, negative and positive ethnocultural essentialism, and Italian institutional regulation of Chinese migrants' economic crimes. The last topic would be particularly dramatized by Italian media coverage of the 2007 Milan riot, to which I turn in chapter 3. Increasingly drawing on positive ethnocultural essentialism of the Chinese people, Chinese migrants' reactive reporting, which first became assertive between 2001 and 2003, would grow into maturity during the coverage of the riot, to which I turn in chapter 4.

Chapter 3

Milan: The 2007 "Chinatown" Riot in Italian Debates

In 2007, Milan hosted the largest Chinese migrant community in Italy by official counts, with approximately 14,700 registered residents.[1] Located in Via Sarpi, one of the city's most popular shopping districts, Milan's Chinese neighbourhood has been home to diasporic businesses since the 1920s and 1930s. Beginning in the 1990s, hundreds of Chinese migrant wholesalers operated in this area. As most migrants only went there for work, the Italians still comprised the majority of the neighbourhood residents. Thus, the journalists' appellation of the neighbourhood as "Chinatown" would seem erroneous, since the term usually describes an area with a majority Chinese residential population in a non-Chinese place. Moreover, "Chinatown" often refers to the history of discriminatory laws forcing the Chinese to live in confined areas, as well as to the phenomenon of the Chinese residing in specific areas due to family and social relationships, neither of which applies to Milan's Chinese neighbourhood.

On 12 April 2007, Bu Ruowei, a Chinese migrant, quarrelled with Italian traffic officers in the neighbourhood over parking fines and the confiscation of the registration certificate for a double-parked car. When the Chinese community heard that Italian officers had hit Bu when she and her husband refused to surrender the certificate, the dispute escalated into a dramatic face-off between hundreds of migrants and the Italian police. The riot showed how Chinese merchants resented Italian traffic officers, who had overzealously and uncompromisingly fined them for breaches of contested street regulations in the prior months. The strategy was meant to address the difficulty for traffic circulation and pedestrian mobility in the neighbourhood that migrant wholesalers' activities had created: vehicles double parked in narrow streets, merchandise transported from cars to stores and vice versa throughout the day, and pushcarts used to move goods on narrow sidewalks. In the mid-2000s, these activities were intense as, thanks to migrant wholesalers, the commercial area in Milan's Chinese neighbourhood prospered and attracted clients from many corners of Italy and Europe. Therefore, Chinese merchants had reasons to be concerned about the economic impact on their stores when, in early 2007, Milan's centre-right municipal government led by mayor Letizia Moratti announced its plan to turn Via Sarpi into a pedestrian zone and to move Chinese wholesalers to Arese, a city north of Milan. Moreover, the merchants felt entitled to their commercial activities because they had invested in this neighbourhood: they had bought the properties from Italian store owners at high prices and had paid to obtain permissions from previous city governments to operate wholesale stores in the neighbourhood. Few doubted that institutional measures adopted to restrain Chinese commercial activity in Via Sarpi were also meant to appease Italian residents, who protested against migrant merchants and who the Moratti government needed to court for future elections.

Promptly recognizing the riot's historical significance, the media in Italy enthusiastically covered it as a great novelty in the history of immigration to Italy and Europe: it was the first time that a single ethnic minority group clashed with the police in a major violent protest in contemporary Italy, the only notable violent clash involving Italy's Chinese and one of the very few involving overseas Chinese generally, and the first major Chinese riot in continental Europe. Because media outlets worked under time pressure to explain the riot's newsworthiness for the public, their coverage formed a privileged site in which to examine the topics and approaches concerning Chinese migration to Italy already in circulation. Indeed, the riot presented the Italian and the Chinese migrant media with a unique opportunity to consolidate, and modify, existing Chinese stereotypes in order to further understand this migration, as well as to elucidate its significance for immigration to Italy in general.

In chapters 3 and 4, I argue that the media debate over the riot drew on and deepened social, institutional, and cultural conversations on migrations to Italy that the news media disseminated throughout the 2000s. Relevant coverage addressed key issues within the existing media knowledge of immigration to Italy, including migrant criminality, migrant integration in the context of refashioning Italian national identity, racism against migrants, tension between migrant economic crimes and disciplinary actions from Italian police and municipal authorities, and the need for migrants to participate in Italian politics and to nurture a multicultural society. In reporting on these issues, the media adopted an ethnocultural approach from both Italian and Chinese perspectives and covered both negative and positive connotations. Through narrating the riot, Italian and Chinese migrant journalists also made the Chinese migration an effective case study in rehearsing and sharpening existing polemics over migrations to Italy as a whole.

Topics and Approaches

The Italian media used topics from the Italian-Chinese migrant cultural repertoire (indicated in italics below) in order to depict Milan's Chinese community and the riot. The *violence of Chinese migrants* supposedly derived from the *Chinese mafia* that controlled Chinese gang members who operated in Milan's *Chinatown*. Thus, the riot articulated *Chinese spatial invasion* in the capital of Lombardy, which became a *threat to Italian national identity* as it was expressed in spatial and gendered terms. In this interpretation, there was a considerable degree of underlying *Italian racism against the Chinese*, although it was explicitly articulated only rarely in news coverage in part because by 2007 the Italian media had more reasons to focus on entrepreneurship when covering the Chinese migration (see chapter 2). This entrepreneurship was said to be characterized by pervasive *illegal economic and business practices*, which required *disciplinary actions from Milan's police and municipal authorities* through patrols and regulations on the transport of merchandise in Via Sarpi. Not surprisingly, Chinese migrants and Italian activists perceived the ways in which the police implemented the regulations as excessively harsh, fast, and unfair. As a result, a severe communication gap emerged between the perceived *self-enclosed Chinese migrant community* and Milan's centre-right government, which was intent on tightening its grip on migrant economic practices and on appeasing the Italian residents' growing protests against Chinese merchants. In searching for a solution to this lack of communication, activists and politicians promoted Chinese migrants' greater political participation in Italy's migrant incorporation and urged the institutionalization of a citizenship law for migrants. The *multicultural project* aimed to increase the political stakes of Milan's economically powerful Chinese migrants, who in 2007 were an insignificant electorate for Milan's political parties as most Chinese residents did not have Italian citizenship.

As Stuart Hall puts it, the news media "define for the majority of the population *what* significant events are taking place, but, also, they offer powerful interpretation of *how* to understand these events."[2] In covering these topics, the media across a wide range of political and ideological affiliations adopted the ethnocultural approach, a specific discursive strategy drawn from the Italian Chinese migrant cultural repertoire. By the ethnocultural approach, I mean the processes of ethnocentrism and ethnogenesis. Ethnocentrism refers to an ethnic group's tendency to view the world and to evaluate other groups exclusively from its own perspective. Some Italian media displayed Italocentric perspectives on Milan's Chinese community when accusing it of wreaking unprecedented havoc on local Italian merchants and store owners, who therefore needed more municipal protection. Meanwhile, some pro-Chinese Italian media – as well as Chinese migrant media – analyses exhibited equally powerful Sinocentric views and argued that theirs was a model migrant community that had contributed to the local economy in ways other migrant groups had not.

Ethnocentrism is different from a related and more widely used mechanism in relevant media coverage: ethnogenesis, which differentiated the Chinese from other migrants and the Italians by constructing a distinctive Chinese ethnic group.[3] For example, many media accounts claimed that Chinese migrants worked long hours in factories, totally cut off from Italian society and laws. Depending on media outlets' specific ideological positions, this issue was either critiqued as a reason for migrants' failure to integrate or praised as proof of their industriousness. But both interpretations tended to view the combination of extreme social isolation and work ethic as a distinguishing characteristic of the Chinese in Italy. It thus became an ethnic stereotype about Chinese migrants, alternately negative or positive depending on the context. As I use it in this book, ethnogenesis is part of the larger project of ethnocultural essentialism, which I defined in chapter 1 as social actors' conscious mobilization of dichotomized differences between Italian and Chinese cultures.

The "Chinese Mafia"

In keeping with the general trend to criminalize immigrants in the Italian media, the supposed Chinese mafia remained a somewhat prominent topic in 2007.[4] Several *Corriere della Sera* articles about the riot were reminiscent of the content and rhetoric of coverage of the Chinese mafia in Italy examined in chapter 2. One sensationalist headline announces: "Chinese Criminality: Sex, Illegal Migrants, and Counterfeit Merchandise: Thus the 'Triad' Manages Human Trafficking and Money." Although the title points to the Triad's activities in Italy, the journalist concludes by admitting that no connection between the Triad and various Chinese criminal groups in Italy could be established. Elsewhere, Chinese migrants' alleged insolence during the riot is attributed to Italian politicians' impotence in migration management and to the "most powerful mafia, that of the Triad, which directly manages the Asian migration." In another case, the journalist re-enacts the unverified connection between criminal organizations and economic crimes, which was a key topic in the 1992 media accounts: "Dirty affairs, strange rounds, constant illegality that the police forces often bring to light. All this money comes from who knows where. The Chinese mafia controls everything and moves everything. The Triad has its own rules and laws. The omertà [oath of silence] of many people."[5] *Un mondo a colori* on Rai Due, a program exclusively focused on migration issues, more explicitly attributed the source of the money that Chinese migrants used to purchase Italian property in Via Sarpi to the Chinese mafia.[6]

By the mid-2000s, migrant entrepreneurship and the institutional disciplining of it had become part of how the media covered the Chinese migration (see chapter 2). But as the examples above show, in the immediate aftermath of a crisis such as the riot, the virulent stereotype concerning the parallel between the Italian and the Chinese mafias resurfaced in the Italian press. The parallel gained some momentum in 2007 because it seemed to confirm Roberto Saviano's depiction of Italian-Chinese criminal collaborations in *Gomorra*, published a year prior (see chapter 2). The *Stampa* article, "The Other Gomorrah," cautions Milan's city government against a potential expansion of Chinese migrants' illegal economic activities. Positing *Gomorra* as a factual source, *La Padania*, the mouthpiece of the right-wing and of regionalist political party Lega Nord, comments on the extremely low mortality rate of Italy's Chinese. A *L'Espresso* article employs *Gomorra*'s themes and style, jarringly mixing sociological statistics and first-hand observations with assumptions and generalizations. The journalist argues that the need to curtail economic crimes was urgent, for after Milan, Prato, and Rome, Sicily was in danger of becoming "the new land to be colonized [by the Chinese]."[7] In line with Saviano's rhetoric, the journalist's omniscient and totalizing view of migrants' economic activities, as well as his "discourse of reverse discrimination" by the Chinese against Italy, reveal the extent of Eurocentrism at work.[8]

These accounts are also examples of how crime reporting borrowed techniques from crime fiction. Like the early 1990s media coverage of the Chinese mafia, the reporting on the 2007 riot frequently employed evocative metaphors. According to *Corriere della Sera*, following the riot Italian police renewed their surveillance of potential criminal alliances formed by Chinese, Albanian, and Nigerian migrants, as well as of clashes among Chinese youth gangs. On 28 April, a Chinese migrant was murdered by a conational in Via Sarpi. Covering the murder, *La Repubblica* likens Chinese criminality to an "immense and tangled" spider's web in which each individual gang was ready to "imprison and suck its preys, that is, the spiders." Left to their own devices in uncoordinated operations, these gangs became dangerous "loose dogs."[9] The article does not use older metaphors such as the octopus, nor older visual signposting such as the cinematically inspired Chinese mafia marks. Nevertheless, in 2007 the spider's web proved to be an equally memorable and literary metaphor for journalists who used the Chinese mafia to signify the entire Chinese community in Italy.

Space, Masculinity, and Italian National Identity

On 13 April, *Il Giornale*, Italy's major conservative newspaper headquartered in Milan, deployed the spider's web to refer to the Chinese diaspora in Italy more generally, for the complexity of this web mirrored the "multiple and oppositional readings" of Milan's "Chinatown" as an "ethnic enclave."[10] Compared with the 1990s coverage in which journalists employed the metonym between the Chinese mafia and Italy's Chinese community, in the 2007 coverage journalists spatialized this metonym through a tangibly growing "Chinatown" in Milan. Chinatowns, the most visible evidence of Chinese diasporic settlement, became the physical and metaphorical embodiment of the Chinese mafia. Rather than tell the nature of the Chinese mafia, media operators opted to show its supposed workings in Italy's Chinatowns, often by resorting to what they knew about Chinese criminality in other countries.

On 14 April, the journalist Maurizio Stefanini claimed in *Libero* that one out of five Chinese people overseas were affiliated with the Triad. He drew on his views of historical representations of Chinatowns and on Chinese criminality worldwide. He also leaves the impression that the article was based on statistics produced by the International Criminal Police Organization. Dwelling on the brutality of the Triad and on the animosity of locals in certain Asian countries, including Malaysia, towards Chinese migrants, Stefanini paints a gruesome portrait of these Chinatowns, before issuing a warning against a similar fate for Italy's Chinatowns following the riot. On the same day, *La Padania* also published an opinion piece comparing Chinatowns worldwide with such "ethnic ghettos" as the Jewish quarters, evoking the undesirability of both locations in popular imagination.[11]

These extremely negative and ahistorical readings of Chinatowns did not go uncontested. On 15 April, Federico Rampini offered a rebuttal in *La Repubblica*.[12] Like Stefanini, Rampini starts by recounting the melancholic and violent past of Chinatowns in San Francisco, Paris, and

Saigon. But his account is meant to highlight the chic images of these same places in contemporary postcards and guidebooks. Such a juxtaposition allows Rampini to ask how Italy could build on these positive experiences of urban transformation. Contrary to Stefanini's vision of the future of Milan's Chinatown as dominated by youth gangs, Rampini suggests that the city should nurture the nationalistic pride of a new crop of highly educated and successful Chinese migrants already living in Italy, the counterparts of those working in entrepreneurship and in the tech industry in San Francisco's Chinatown. Here he refers to Italy's elite Chinese migrants, who were already becoming businessmen and professionals. His argument resorts to the idea of Chinese migrants as a model minority, the most recent in a series of positive stereotypes applied to the Asian Americans.[13]

Rampini often argues in ways typical of the ethnocultural approach: While the Jews and the Chinese have been the ethnic minorities most vilified in their adopted countries, they have also been the "most educated, entrepreneurial, and courted [ethnic groups] for their talents." At times, he takes on a Sinocentric tone, particularly when he warns Italians about the price of *Libero*, *La Padania*, and the Italian police damaging the image of Chinese: "Like in the heydays of the Celestial Empire, which treated its neighboring countries as vassal states and guaranteed protection for its countrymen, today the Chinese diaspora is able to count on an economic, political, and military superpower. New hostilities against Chinese overseas would not pass without consequences."

The two opposing interpretations suggest how Italian journalists may differ greatly in their knowledge of the Chinese migrant community and in their approaches to migrant integration; yet may still share the basic view that "Chinatowns" mirrored this community. Most differences between Stefanini's and Rampini's articles are centred on the details of the Chinese diaspora in Italy and on the best ways to govern it for Italy's benefit. The metaphorical linkage that associated the Chinese community with the supposed Chinese mafia and Chinatowns was not questioned. The task of dismantling this false link fell on several scholars and China experts in Italy. From their perspective, the Chinese neighbourhoods (i quartieri cinesi) in Italy should not be labelled Chinatowns because the term indicates areas with definite geographical confines due to institutional discrimination where residents enjoyed close social and family ties, circumstances not applicable to Italy's Chinese communities.[14]

By 2003 most journalists had realized that the Chinese mafia's impact on Milan's Chinatown could neither be conclusively gauged nor convincingly argued by referring to physical threats to Italian residents, who were rarely the casualties of the isolated Chinese gang clashes (see chapter 2). Moreover, following the 2007 riot *Corriere della Sera* published a study of Milan's so-called ethnic enclaves, showing that public criminal activities had been very rare in Via Sarpi. In other words, overt local Chinese criminal activities could not have been the main spatial practice that had deepened social antagonism between Italian residents and Chinese merchants. Rather, as Christian Novak, an urban studies professor, explained in *Panorama*, a key contributing factor was the "use of public space" by migrants and Italians in the neighbourhood.[15]

Indeed, relevant media reporting on the riot was replete with references to migrants' everyday spatial practices, which many Italian residents deemed inappropriate, unpleasant, or uncivilized. In Via Sarpi, the most controversial of these practices was the coming and going of a large number of vans and pushcarts, which transported merchandise from narrow streets to wholesaler stores and vice versa, and which was disruptive to other traffic. The police's draconian implementation of street rules to reduce this traffic and the municipal government's plan to make Via Sarpi into a pedestrian zone were among the key factors that had turned an individual altercation into a riot. Other minor complaints included unhealthy and offensive habits and conduct that were said to be typical of Chinese migrants; examples included spitting in public, dumping garbage on the streets during the night and on Sundays, and even making loud noises by cutting chicken.[16] For the complainants, these were unacceptable "Made in China" behaviours, like the similarly labelled goods that migrants helped to bring to Via Sarpi and to Italy that weakened the local businesses' competitiveness.

As some media coverage reasoned, by living in such urban squalor, local residents nurtured nostalgia for a nicer environment in the area from decades ago. To show the transformation of the neighbourhood over time, *Il Giornale* juxtaposed two photographs of a particular section of Via Sarpi on the front page on 14 April. According to the caption, in 1966 the area was a chic neighbourhood with Italian stores, but in 2007 it became a chaotic "Chinatown" with incomprehensible Chinese ideograms on most storefronts. This article was emblematic of media coverage that attempted to erase Chinese migrants' decades-long contributions to the neighbourhood from local memory.[17]

Other conservative media outlets recalled distant memories of Chinese contributions to the neighbourhood in highlighting the current discord between residents and merchants. *Il Giorno*, a conservative newspaper with a sizable circulation in Italy, attributed the improvement of public security of Via Sarpi to Chinese migrants. For the newspaper, by settling into this neighbourhood starting in the 1980s,

Chinese migrants helped to combat the muggings and crimes that used to beleaguer it. Likewise, Rete 4, Mediaset's adult-oriented, third-largest channel, interviewed an elderly Italian man who discussed Italian proprietors of his age selling their properties to the Chinese before retiring. He also reminisced about seeing Chinese men selling ties in the neighbourhood before the Second World War and about witnessing the social harmony between Italian residents and Chinese migrants during that time. Thus, these conservative media used the more peaceful times to throw into sharper relief the neighbourhood's current downgraded quality of life, said to have resulted from the recent Chinese migration.[18]

From a psychological perspective, complaints of urban degradation and nostalgia for the past exposed how certain Italian residents felt an acute sense of disorientation and loss around the blossoming of Chinese migrant businesses in Via Sarpi. This loss justified a desire and a responsibility to enforce a rigid boundary between Chinese wholesaler stores and traditional Italian retailer stores, particularly when the commercial Chinatown and the Italian residential area formed a spatial continuum. The following passage from *Corriere della Sera* is emblematic of this sentiment, depicting the Chinese migration as a spatial and economic "invasion":

> It is the revolt of a city within the city, of another Milan called Chinatown. Having grown in the midst of a migration without rules and a commercial abusiveness which was tolerated through bribery, recently Chinatown privatized streets and sidewalks occupying them and filling them with vans and carts. It also evicted historic stores and bookstores to make space for wholesalers dealing in jeans, handbags, and pajamas … The quantity, the commercial strength, and the power of Chinese money created so robust an enclave in the Via Paolo Sarpi area that at the first sight of the police forces, at the first attempt of restoring legality to the neighborhood, the Chinese community rebelled … Today, the presence of the Chinese in the neighbourhood has become dominant, whereas the Milanese are the minority.[19]

Right-wing media outlets exaggerated this popular perception of Chinatown as a city within city. Calling Via Sarpi a "fortress," *La Padania* emphasized the migrants' supposed aversion towards their host country: "Today, entire neighbourhoods of our cities are in the hands of a community which does not show any intention to integrate." Matteo Salvini, then Lega Nord's representative in Milan's city government, accused Chinese migrants of setting their own rules in their "conquest" of this area. The vice president of *Panorama* appeared on Rai and argued that they "made themselves bosses of the neighborhood." *Il Giornale* even charged that they protested as violently as if their "territory had been invaded by alien oppressors [i.e., Italians]." Like *Il Giornale*, which viewed Chinese migrants' expansionist ambitions as "yellow colonization," *Libero* warned against the financial and geographical penetration of Europe's Chinese through its "soft stomach" of Italy.[20] These comments were reminiscent of popular early twentieth-century "Yellow Peril" imagery, according to which the Chinese mounted a robotic invasion of Western countries.[21]

In making these vindictive remarks, the right-leaning media momentarily abandoned their more typical masculinist attitudes towards immigrants, which had previously feminized them regardless of gender. This move aimed to accentuate what this media claimed to be the Chinese migrants' perverse masculine vigor, citing economic aggression towards local Italian stores and violence during the riot as evidence. Typically, *La Padania*'s language tends to be domineering over women and migrants. As Michel Huysseune notes, Lega Nord's rhetoric oscillates between the misogynist language used to refer to Italian women in speeches and news articles, and the actual acceptance of women's participation in the party in order to claim their political emancipation as a sign of northern Italy's modernity.[22] Similarly, Lega Nord's populist interpretive framework often pits the Italians against the migrants using a symbolic North-South (masculine-feminine) divide, a strategy that Federico Faloppa rightly views as a way to "excite the savage appetite of the electors" through "lexical and iconographic stupidities."[23]

However, in covering the 2007 riot, most right-leaning Italian mainstream and alternative media underscored how uncontrollable the Chinese male violence in defence of Bu was a threat to Italian citizens and particularly Italian men. On 12 and 13 April, television news broadcasts on Canale 5 and Italia 1, Mediaset's first- and second-largest channels respectively, repeated an iconic violent episode from the riot. In it, an Italian woman approached Chinese protestors and, pulling down the banner they were carrying, apparently sought to reproach them. A moment later, she was hit by an empty plastic bottle. Startled, she backed off. These broadcasts often only showed the woman being hit by the bottle, sometimes in slow motion, to emphasize the violence she suffered. *Il Giornale* described a similar incident in graphic terms. An Italian man, who shouted that it was right for the police to beat the Chinese, "was attacked and knocked down." He was "saved from lynching by the police forces." Likewise, a *Giorno* article titled "The Yellow Fever" accentuated the frenetic zeal of angry Chinese young men, who were photographed excitedly waving their arms and Chinese national flags. *La Padania* compared the "overbearing" and "arrogant" Chinese men from Via Sarpi to the rebellious Frenchmen of North African and Asian ancestries from the outskirts of Paris during the mid-2000s riots.[24] Indeed, most of this coverage drew on an unsubstantiated "tribal knowledge" of Chinese ethnic and cultural traits in order to differentiate the Chinese from the Italian nationals, as well as to align Chinese migrants with other migrant groups who were more conventionally believed to have an unruly and violent nature.[25]

Further contributing to public perception of male Chinese violence, Rai Due, then under the direction of Antonio Marano of Lega Nord, showed only footage of Chinese migrants' attack on Italian police. In particular, Federico Carrozzo became the symbol of a dutiful and innocent ordinary Italian policeman who fell prey to Chinese violence. He appeared on Rai Tre to discuss his physical injuries and psychological shock following the confrontation earlier that day. *Corriere della Sera* gave even more prominence to Carrozzo's first-person account: "A vase of geraniums launched from a balcony only scraped me. But I was not able to avoid the assault of thirty Chinese persons: I was surrounded, kicked, and punched. I had to crouch on the ground to protect myself and to make sure that they did not steal my pistol."[26] Carrozzo's instinct to preserve his masculine dignity is paralleled by the protection of his pistol, a symbol of male sexual and destructive powers.

However, this depiction of extensive Chinese violence towards Italians was only part of the story. Other coverage of the riot in Italy's major national newspapers showed that migrants' violence was incited by the Italian police's repressive measures and that the Italian police also used extensive violence. Alongside terms such as "revolt," "urban guerrilla," "battle," and "garrison," *La Repubblica* provided detailed visual evidence of the physical confrontation. *Corriere della Sera* published a first series of photographs online in which crowds of unarmed migrants confronting armed cops are captured in panoramic shots and close-ups, indicating the high tension between the mob and the oppressors. A second series documents a sequence of chaotic moments as several Italian police agents brought down a Chinese man. In *La Stampa,* the sinologist and journalist Francesco Sisci cited these photographs as grounds to denounce the brutality of Italian police.[27] As this and other coverage described violent acts and injuries on both sides, it generally refrained from blaming Chinese migrants. Instead, it juxtaposed migrant and police accounts of the riot by printing them side by side on the same page.[28]

If both the Italians and the Chinese committed equally extensive violence, then why did the Italian media highlight that from the Chinese?

Because damaged Italian masculinity was spectacular proof of migrants' threat to Italian bodies and to the masculine sense of personal safety. By extension, the Chinese violence also encroached on the Italian character of Via Sarpi and on Italian national identity. This media analysis served as a further call for Milan's municipal authorities and police to discipline unruly migrants. What these journalists had in mind could be something similar to Rome's forceful interventions to curb Chinese investment in Piazza Vittorio and to protect Italian stores between the early 1990s and 2005.[29]

While Milan's government continued slowly taking steps to redesign Via Sarpi, some Italian natives staged symbolic repossessions of their neighbourhood just after the riot. These public acts often had a theatrical flair. The Associazione ViviSarpi, formed by disgruntled Italian residents in 1999, displayed Italian national flags and orange sheets with "No to Illegality" written on them. *Il Giornale* interpreted this act as indicative of the locals' will to "take possession of the neighbourhood again." Forza Nuova, an extreme right-wing political party, signed anti-Chinese graffiti and posters and left them in "Chinatown." Indeed, according to *La Padania*, a bonifica (reclamation), a term that invokes fascist social engineering and eugenics, was overdue in the neighbourhood. Similarly, on his blog, the Italian comedian/actor/politician Beppe Grillo suggested that "we will integrate them [i.e., Chinese and other migrants] and prohibit ghettos. In addition to Italians, a neighbourhood should not be made possible to host more than a certain percentage of North Africans, Chinese, and Filipinos."[30]

As Grillo's comments suggest, through references to perceived spatial invasion, urban degradation, and threatened masculinity, the 2007 riot was nimbly knitted into a media narrative that pointed to migrants' undesirability. As a journalist writing for *Corriere della Sera* put it dryly: "Milan cannot accept the existence of enclaves with reduced sovereignty (be they the miserable Nomad camps, or the rich Chinatown), in which law is domesticated rather than implemented." In *La Padania*, a journalist compared the Chinese "invasion" in Milan with the presence of migrants in Italian schools, mosques, and Romany camps. A few Rai broadcasts, after reporting on the 2007 riot, covered the landing of illegal migrants in Sicily, the robberies committed by male immigrants who threatened public security, and the arrest of male African migrant criminals.[31] To be sure, such pairing of Milan's Chinese with Italy's other migrant groups revealed the implicit political legitimation of cross-referencing migration, marginality, and crime.[32] As I have examined, this pairing also illustrated the Italian media's general preoccupations with immigrants' challenge of spatialized and gendered Italian national identity. Milan's riot became the most illuminating example of this challenge in that period.

Racism

A photograph captured during the riot and published in *Il Giornale* shows two Chinese women holding sheets of plain white paper that read "enough with racism and repression" and "the police will not beat women."[33] The laconic and improvised style of the slogans and protest materials supported these women's claims of racism and victimization by the police and traffic officers. However, *Il Giornale*'s readers could also view these public acts, which were intended for the Italian media, as evidence of these women's disproportionate sense of racism and self-victimization that blamed Italian authorities and police for the riot.

Another rare coverage of overt Italian racism following the riot concerned Forza Nuova's anti-Chinese graffiti and posters in "Chinatown," which aimed to symbolically retake the neighbourhood. Both the method (i.e., public visual signposting) and the content (e.g., one Nazi-inspired slogan read "Cinesi Raüs," or Chinese out) demonstrated racism as commonly defined. But the media often glossed over the significance of this manifest racism. The front-page coverage of the 15 April Milanese edition of *Corriere della Sera* featured this incident with the title "Racist Slurs in Chinatown." But the article itself downplays Forza Nuova's racism by juxtaposing photographs of the slurs with those of anarchist graffiti about "Killing Policemen" taken in the same neighbourhood on the same day. The editorial intent of the article was to criticize the absurdity of both extreme right-wing and extreme left-wing ideologies.[34]

As the two examples illustrate, while Chinese migrants considered certain Italian actions to be racist, in general the Italian media avoided discussing racism when it was not denying its existence outright. How and why did this phenomenon occur?

To start, Chinese migrants and their Italian advocates often viewed insults directed at China and Chinese ethnicity, as well as the Italian police's abuse of power, as acts of implicit and institutional racisms.[35] Following an insight by Philomena Essed, I contend that in differentiating between racist and non-racist acts in everyday situations and specific events, migrants and journalists deployed knowledge of "everyday racism." To use Essed's observation, they mobilized a "general knowledge of racism" – a space for memories that they acquired in school and in life and then activated when assessing new experiences of potential racism. This general knowledge can be more precisely defined as "generalized episodes or scenarios of racism."[36] Many generic, populist news comments on racism during the riot implicitly referred to two archetypical scenarios in Chinese culture: narratives of how ordinary Chinese suffered oppression during the Japanese occupation of China and those of Jews in Nazi Germany. According to *La Repubblica*, a Chinese merchant complained: "You have to explain to me why the police give me a fine every day. I'll tell you why; because the police want to see the Chinese coming to a bad end."[37] Although this observation was vague, it established a dichotomy between Chinese merchants and Italian police, as well as between victims and oppressors.

Further, Chinese migrants' experiences with the recent intensification of police investigations and enforcement of street rules in Via Sarpi provided additional generalized episodes of racism. In *La Repubblica*, a Chinese merchant named Jian relayed a typical scenario of Italian police searching for counterfeit merchandise in the area's Chinese stores: "They enter the store, look around, check on the merchandise, and see a kitchen knife that does not have a 'kitchen knife' label on it. Only this one, all other knives had the label. Result: a 300-euro fine. We kept quiet, but certain things hurt you. This is not common sense; this is something else."[38] In a *Corriere della Sera* article, citing a document issued by the Chinese government in response to the riot, the sinologist and journalist Paolo Salom referred to the Chinese "impression that the Italian public security authorities persecuted Chinese migrants in particular ... Milan's Chinese residents noted that this treatment was reserved only for them, while other migrant communities violated the rules on a daily basis with no punishment."[39] In both examples, specific recent experiences with the police were articulated in general terms in order to underscore either the frequency with which similar events had occurred in the past, or the likelihood that they would occur in the future.

In stark contrast to the Chinese denunciation of Italian racism, most mainstream Italian coverage did not engage with racism in any meaningful way, neither as a vocabulary in news reports, nor as a conceptual tool to interpret the police's behaviour during the riot and the pre-riot policies about pushcarts. In other words, the Italian media was generally reluctant to attribute street laws and their enforcement in Milan's Chinatown to racism within the city's government and police. This was not surprising. Surveying major Italian weeklies from 1980 to 2007, academics found that racism conspicuously framed media discussions only during 1990 to 1992 and 2000 to 2002. In particular, the 1989 assassination of Jerry Masslo, a black migrant from South Africa, was one of the first cases of overt Italian racism against migrants that the mainstream Italian media examined.[40] Despite national coverage similar to that of the Masslo incident from 1990 to 1992, why was racism not a key issue in media accounts of the 2007 riot, particularly in left-leaning, pro-Chinese media outlets? While *Il Giornale* ridiculed the interpretations of the riot in Rai TG3, *Il Manifesto*, and *L'Unità* for drawing from Marxism and communism, racism was entirely off the radar for these left-wing media outlets.[41]

To my mind, the left-leaning Italian media failed to critique the Milan riot from a racial perspective due to ethnogenesis in media discourses about migrants. To be sure, by focusing on commercial activities and behaviour said to characterize the Chinese, journalists shed light on the causes of the riot by examining Chinese culture and the inner mechanisms of the Chinese migration. For instance, readers were told that Chinese wholesalers had much to lose from the street rules because they had purchased properties in Via Sarpi using capital gained through guanxi. Often such statements did not surface in the right-wing media. Nevertheless, ethnogenesis adopted by left-leaning journalists ended up replacing a proper consideration of Italian racism with a multicultural discourse. The journalists advocated for the fair treatment of Chinese migrants by Milan's government and police not by arguing against the systematic racism that many migrants viewed as inherent in the implementation of the street rules, but by highlighting the Chinese as a model minority in Italy.

A case in point is Rampini's 13 April commentary for *La Repubblica*, in which he correlates migrants' use of Chinese national flags during the riot with a generational change in Chinese diasporic communities worldwide, in a period when the Chinese Central Government had become the touchstone for the nationalist and ethnic pride of overseas Chinese youths. Referring to both Chinese ancient values and economic modernity, the journalist depicts the average Chinese migrant as performing both "ancient Confucian values of social cohesion" and "the pride of someone who comes from a superpower." For Rampini, "in the Beijings of Italy," by which he means Italy's Chinese neighbourhoods, migrants were "busy reproducing the virtues and vices of today's China: industriousness and clannishness, the flexibility and ruthless exploitation of their hard work, dynamism and *omertà*." Given the unfortunate circumstances of the riot, Rampini advises Italian readers to take more advantage of the "virtues" rather than mindlessly combating the "vices," all the while essentializing these qualities as intrinsically Chinese. Various Rai news broadcasts at the time made similar points.[42]

Ethnogenesis was deemed a legitimate tool to approach Chinese immigration to Italy because most pro-Chinese and Beijing-centred news analyses in the country were penned by journalists with knowledge of China and the Chinese diasporas gained through work experiences or research. Undoubtedly, these Italian journalists used their intercultural media competencies to analyse the Chinese migration from the perspectives of its sociological and anthropological details and of the migrants' home culture. Recall that the lack of such competencies was the primary reason that Chinese migrants rejected Saviano's superficial treatment of the Chinese in *Gomorra*. Migrant journalists themselves also enthusiastically embraced ethnogenesis as an intercultural media practice (see chapter 3). In other words, as many journalists aimed to better inform Italian audiences on Chinese migration to Italy from more Chinese perspectives, they often relied on ethnogenesis: migrants did these things because they were Chinese. This perspective was widespread in Italy's pro-Chinese mediascape, making ethnogenesis a quasi-racist practice, in that it became an unquestioned assumption and a normalized interpretive way to address the Chinese migration.[43]

Indeed, to me, ethnogenesis was part of inferential and everyday racisms in the media's depiction of Italy's Chinese. For Hall, inferential racism occurs in "representations of events and situations relating to race, whether 'factual' or 'fictional,' which have racist premises and propositions inscribed in them as a set of *unquestioned assumptions*." According to Essed, everyday racism "involves racist practices that infiltrate everyday life and become part of what is seen as 'normal' by the dominant group."[44] For many Italian and Chinese migrant readers and journalists, to attribute essentialist and supposedly intrinsic traits to the Chinese in explaining their migratory experiences was an everyday practice during any discussion of the Chinese migrant population. As ethnogenesis itself was deeply implicated in these racist practices, it could not effectively critique racism.

Given that ethnogenesis is such a problematic practice, from which angle and in what way can we best analyse Italian racism against Chinese migrants during and after the riot? A combined analysis of race and gender provides one route. I suggest that biased coverage of Chinese women displayed the most explicit expression of racism, which was particularly well-articulated in relation to Bu, the protagonist in the dispute with Italian traffic officers that led to the riot. For the benefit of an Italian audience, the media's depiction of Bu's gendered histrionics brought to mind the behaviour of Turandot the virago and Cio-Cio

San the victim. Her behaviour was racialized based on such operatic archetypes of "oriental" women.[45]

In right-wing news accounts, there was a concerted effort to incriminate Bu for inciting violence. These accounts share striking similarities in content and style and omit her name as a way to show their contempt for Chinese women. In *Il Giornale,* Bu is characterized as hostile and cunning in an eyewitness-like account of the initial dispute: "She got out of the car with the baby in her arms and then pushed one of the two agents. It was she who made the policewoman and her own baby fall. Then she started to yell to draw the attention of other Chinese. In just a second, dozens of them arrived, circling and hitting the agents' car." *Il Giorno* and *La Padania* replicated the same approximate scenario.[46] These details proved effective for the reader because of shared psychological and somatic experiences. The depiction of Bu's allegedly heartless treatment of her child was in keeping with the newspapers' thinly veiled neo-fascist orientation in denouncing "deviant" women, who were supposedly led astray either by socialism and modernity during fascism, or by present-day Chinese communism and economic globalization.[47] All of these reports conclude by informing us that because of her violent actions, Bu was charged with resisting arrest, causing injury to public officials, and maltreatment of a minor.

The image of Bu as an aggressor and provocateur was contested by other news articles in which she and other Chinese women repeatedly represented themselves as victims at the hands of Italian police. *Corriere della Sera* interviewed Bu online, under the headline "Clashes in Milan, 'I Was Offended so I Reacted,'" and quoted her in the article "The Grit of Ruowei and Other Women." In her statements, which were translated into Italian in both cases, she described her quarrel with the traffic officers and her attempts to negotiate with them to prevent the registration certificate of her car from being confiscated. According to Bu, a male traffic officer insulted Chinese migrants and behaved aggressively towards her. All of this evidenced her discontent with the way she was treated in Italy. In oral testimonies reported in the left-wing newspaper *L'Unità,* female Chinese protestors shared Bu's sentiments. Photographs showing Chinese women using megaphones to attract a crowd or raising their arms in anger underscored the intensity of their efforts to express victimization in public.[48] As these examples show, Bu's racialization as either of the two archetypes – aggressor, or victim – was a widespread racist premise and practice in everyday Italian media discourses on the Chinese in 2007.

Apart from the employment of ethnogenesis, the Italian media's silence on the question of race relations occurred in part because other issues that emerged from the riot were deemed more newsworthy and urgent. According to a rumour, the Chinese had premeditated the riot. Many newspapers referred to this rumour, and some, like *Il Giornale*, featured it and claimed that the Chinese mafia had fomented the riot. Italia 1's television news showed images of a Chinese woman shouting into a megaphone and advising the crowds to "stay calm, or else we will lose." Riccardo De Corato, Milan's vice mayor, mentioned the rumour but presented no evidence, prompting a rebuke from Limin Zhang, Chinese consul in Milan. In *Uno mattina* on Rai Uno, in response to De Corato's claim, Luigi Sun, a long-time resident of Milan's Chinese community, attributed the riot's spontaneity and intensity to the community's frustration with the city's top-down handling of street rules in Via Sarpi. Responding to complaints that street laws targeted the Chinese and were implemented at an unreasonable speed, Letizia Moratti, then Milan's mayor, underscored her intention to strike a balance between hospitality and integration, and between security and legality. As a member of Silvio Berlusconi's centre-right party Forza Italia, Moratti's remark adhered to the conservative tendency to classify migrants' social integration as a public security issue.[49] Indeed, this rumour framed the riot as a public security issue, a key modality for interpreting migration and making it into a "problem" in the Italian media.[50] This mechanism thus subordinated a racial issue to a legal and criminological matter.

The riot furthermore highlighted two other issues of greater public concern than racism in the news media, which I will discuss in the next two sections.

Migrant Entrepreneurship and Institutional Discipline via Economic Crimes

If the riot was a threat to public security, then what made these migrants become bold enough to defy law enforcement? What was at the heart of Milan's thriving Chinatown? In much of the media coverage of the riot, the answers lay in Chinese migrants' tremendous economic capital through entrepreneurship, as well as in the real and perceived illegal business practices that created their wealth. Both right- and left-leaning journalists extensively covered this topic, although they often weighed its pros and cons differently. Indeed, the Italian media largely considered economic crimes to be the distinguishing characteristic between Chinese and other migrant groups. This case of ethnogenesis occurred primarily because, since the 2000s, the Chinese community has had Italy's most vibrant migrant entrepreneurship that significantly engaged with economic globalization, which crucially involved China, the migrants' home country and Italy's major trade partner. This entrepreneurship was a persuasive example for journalists when debating Italy's efforts to address globalization and govern migrants.

Conservative newspapers often used migrants' economic and illegal practices to scapegoat their entrepreneurship for failures attributable to Italy's ineffective economic policies and business ecosystem. In *La Padania,* a journalist made a causal link between migrants' need to earn money as quickly as possible and their decision to enter the underground economy, skipping a proper discussion of Italy's large informal economy where Chinese migrant businesses operated. This comment was apparently based on police reports and on the website *Chinatown Italia,* which both referred to the difference between Milan's more homogeneous and unified Chinese community in the 1960s and 1970s and its current heterogeneous and fractious counterpart, a difference considered the root of the steep class and economic divisions within the community that had led to labour exploitation.[51]

Similarly, drawing on sociological sources and focusing on Chinese migrant entrepreneurship's internal dynamics, a *Libero* article passed its verdict on the community in its sections titled "A Quiet Community," "The Migratory Career," and "A Closed Market," reinforcing popular notions about the supposed economic autonomy (i.e., Chinese ethnic businesses) and territorial independence (i.e., Chinatown) that migrants enjoyed in Italy. As the journalist argues, "Thanks to *guanxi,* communism, together with its collectivist logic, embodies an utmost anarchic liberalism, which interprets and uses possibilities within its enclosed world." Couched in a jarringly academic vocabulary, the simplistic and pedantic thesis camouflages the article's recourse to Cold War thinking, which its main title makes it explicit: "The Revolt of the Chinese: The Children of the Most Ruthless Communism Look for a Liberalism Without Rules."[52]

In blaming illegal Chinese business practices without referring to structural issues in the Italian business environment, these reports used sociological studies superficially. In more progressive venues such as *L'Unità* and *Liberazione,* the sociologists Daniele Cologna and Antonella Ceccagno countered the usurping of legitimate research for the purpose of scapegoating Italy's Chinese migrant entrepreneurship. By 2007, both Cologna and Ceccagno, as well as other Italian scholars, had conducted extensive fieldwork in the Chinese communities in Milan and Prato. In their news commentaries, the academics aimed to transform the politically charged debate about economic crimes into more sophisticated sociohistorical analyses conducive to Italy's migration policy-making.

Rejecting the prevailing media depiction of the riot as a clash of cultures, Cologna contended that its main cause was the escalating tension between Italian residents' use of social spaces and Chinese merchants' business needs in Via Sarpi. While the neighbourhood symbolized Chinese identity in Milan and was the city's Chinese business centre, for Cologna it was not an "ethnic ghetto" or "Chinatown" because the specific historical meanings of these terms came from non-Italian contexts and largely did not apply. Debunking the practice of ethnogenesis, Ceccagno suggested that traits commonly associated with Chinese migrant economic practices were not intrinsic to this community, but rather were developed to accommodate social and economic circumstances in Italy and China. The critic explained the dramatic growth of Italy's Chinese migrant businesses from the perspective of emigrant-sending China and concluded that clashes with Italian locals resulted from a model of transnational Chinese business encouraged by the Chinese government. She called for state-level migrant integration in Italy that would differ radically from the current paradigm of linking migration to public security and, therefore, to disciplinary actions against migrants.[53]

Indeed, considerable media debates after the 2007 riot concerned Italian control, discipline, and punishment concerning Chinese economic crimes. This emphasis illustrated what Giovanna Zincone identifies as the "repressive-legalitarian" attitude towards immigrants, which both liberals and conservatives in Italy adopted. This attitude made the link between illegality/criminality and control/punishment the raison d'être of the country's migration policy-making.[54] By the time of the riot, the Italian media had already documented, and even mythologized, what it saw as the illegal and unfair competition from mainland Chinese and Chinese migrant businesses in Italy. Municipal and police measures to counter such illegal activities were considered either too harsh or too lenient, depending on the commentator's political orientation. The reporting on Chinese migrants' other illegal social behaviour and practices – including prostitution, underground hospitals, child labour, and food safety in Chinese restaurants – further legitimized harsher disciplinary measures. Not surprisingly, the aforementioned information about illegal activities was provided by Mediaset television news. In 2005, Italia 1 first reported on these issues, which all three Mediaset channels recycled in their coverage of the 2007 riot, sometimes image for image.[55]

What legitimated the "repressive-legalitarian" attitude with regard to immigration to Italy is a complex question. Here I discuss it by considering the media's articulation and validation of diverse political opinions and ideological positions on Italy's Chinese migrant entrepreneurship around the time of the riot. To begin with, relevant debate was set against larger issues of political economy and international trade between Italy and China. As the Chinese global economy had boomed since the beginning of the twenty-first century, the Italian media adopted an alarmist rhetoric that blamed mainland Chinese for the Italian economy's stagnation. In 2007, the centre-left Italian state government, headed by Romano Prodi, was frequently portrayed as a Chinese ally. It was an alliance that influential centre-right city governments, including Milan's, perceived as detrimental to Italy's own growth in the global economy. Giannelli's 14 April satirical cartoon published in *Corriere della Sera* illustrated this popular view. In it, Prodi shouts: "The recovery is near ['vicina']." People around him only hear the last four letters of the word "vicina," namely "Cina" (China), and protest it.[56] As the cartoon intimates, the left-leaning Italian state government facilitated China's increased presence in the Italian economy, and most Italian people were against this economic infiltration.

Il Giornale published two more satirical cartoons about the riot, showing that the populist sentiment about Italy's international trade and political economy, based on xenophobia and fear of communism – indeed a type of Sinophobia – ran deep in the mid-to-late 2000s. In the first, the Chinese flag flies over Milan's cathedral, visually overwhelming it because of their almost equal size. The phrase "China Is Near," a reference to Marco Bellocchio's film and Enrico Emanuelli's book of the same title, appears underneath the cathedral, further rattling its foundations. The second cartoon more explicitly equates communism with Chinese identity. A green Chinese dragon with the head of a presumably Italian communist member spits out red fire that forms the shape of a hammer and a sickle. The fire menaces the cathedral, as the sky is lit by five yellow stars arranged in the same manner as those on the Chinese flag. A slogan reads: "Let us found the PCI again: Italian Chinese Party ['Partito Cinese Italiano']!" By satirizing Italian politicians who allegedly sympathized with communism and the Chinese, here the punch line insinuates that they offered Italian sovereignty in exchange for economic favours from the Chinese state.[57]

Meanwhile, journalists wondered whether the Chinese in Italy who practiced illegal economic activities had official backing from their home country. After all, with an ethnogenic perspective, mainland Chinese and Italy's Chinese migrants could be viewed as a single ethnic group of workers practicing the same illegal business activities. After the riot, Dong Jinyi, then the Chinese ambassador to Italy, was quoted as saying that China's economic power, and specifically its direct investments in Italy, was an important bargaining tool in seeking a balanced solution to the riot from Italian officials who had sanctioned police violence on migrants. Dong hoped that Italian authorities would pay more attention to migrants' legitimate business needs in Milan and elsewhere.[58] Right-wing media interpreted Dong's comments, originally published in *Corriere della Sera* on 15 April, as blackmail by the Chinese government and as proof that it supported its nationals' economic crimes in other countries. *La Padania* attempted to expose the hypocrisy of China's admonition to Italy by evoking the 1989 Tiananmen Square protests and the more recent social unrest in China's countryside, where the state, which had claimed to care about its citizens' political rights, used brutal means to discipline them. According to *La Padania*, since China was not a democratic country, it had no business telling Italy how to treat migrants.[59] Thus, initial questions about the Chinese government's economic relationships with Italy's Chinese were eclipsed by analyses of the riot based on an irrational fear of China and communism.

Chinese migrant economic activities in Italy were largely independent from the Chinese government's direct investments in the country. But Chinese migrant firms remained on good terms with the Chinese government because an amicable relationship would ensure better import-export opportunities, including competitive prices for textiles. However, the bulk of the mainstream Italian coverage of the riot was not concerned with investigating these real-life economic situations. Rather, it helped to endorse stricter street regulations on Chinese merchants from Milan's centre-right city government. Indeed, when disparaged and caricatured as in the aforementioned satirical cartoons, the centre-left Italian state government also faced greater pressure to discipline breaches of the law with greater force. This practice must have seemed the most expedient way to placate Italians and to avoid legal quarrels with migrants.

While both left- and right-leaning Italian politicians and journalists endorsed the principle of curbing economic crimes and related activities such as the use of pushcarts in Via Sarpi with laws, they differed greatly over how to do so. Opinion-makers resorted to newspapers and television programs to legitimize specific rules and their implementation. In a web television program produced by *La Repubblica*, Riccardo De Corato of the neofascism-inspired party Alleanza Nazionale (National alliance), then Milan's vice mayor, reiterated the importance of applying the same street laws to both migrants and Italians. In contrast, Dario Cresto-Dina, *La Repubblica*'s vice director, asked viewers to consider whether the street rules should be established in consultation with Chinese merchants from Via Sarpi or through a top-down approach. Though Cresto-Dina offered comments in support of migrants, the program did not include any Chinese migrants, and thereby reserved explicatory power exclusively for Italian commentators and revealing Eurocentrism.[60]

The Italian media frequently explores the tension between left- and right-leaning views of the same issues as a way to approach Chinese migration in Italy. Using the Milan riot as a springboard for discussing immigration to Italy, Rai Tre showed a debate between Matteo Salvini of Lega Nord and Flavio Zononato, Padova's left-wing mayor. Rai Tre also broadcast an episode, "Chinatown's Two Faces," which juxtaposed the opposing views of the riot of Ignazio La Russa of Alleanza Nazionale and Leonardo Domencini, Florence's left-leaning mayor.[61] Predictably, these discussions proceeded in accordance with the political agendas of the parties to which the speakers belonged.

These programs exemplified what Gianpietro Mazzoleni and Anna Sfardini term "pop politics" on contemporary Italian television. As the most significant conveyer of politics in Italy in recent decades, television created visually appealing, energetic debates in order to sate the audience's appetite for pop politics.[62] Conceivably, Italian television viewers were able to access both sides of the arguments on an issue related to migration. By presenting the Italians as victims of Chinese businesses, these audiences could better understand why Chinese migrants were their arch-enemies. Alternately, by depicting Chinese migrants as scapegoats of the Italian state and its political inefficiency, audiences could be moved to side with migrants in a country that did not usually heed their voices.

Pop politics and its simplistically dichotomized models allowed audiences to identify with Italians and Chinese migrants as they desired. More often than not, the ease of accessing the Other's world through social fantasies set back, rather than moved forward, media and political discussions about devising better ways to implement rules that would impact migrants' business practices and social conduct. Not surprisingly, the television programs I have just examined all concluded by acknowledging the diverse opinions concerning Italy's Chinese, but not with a workable proposal for future political deliberations about this migration. Indeed, in connection with the riot, the mainstream Italian media was not keen to solve concrete problems about implementing street rules or other policies that could have impacted migrants economically. Instead, it set as its primary agenda the public legitimization or delegitimization of various political parties and governmental authorities' proposals regarding the execution of specific institutional disciplinary actions to curb Chinese merchants' illegal activities in Via Sarpi. A telling example about these dynamics concerned the symbolic contestation in Milan's Chinatown between public surveillance cameras installed by Italian authorities and the use of personal cameras that yielded a different narrative about the police and their conduct.

When the media raised concerns about the street laws' potential discrimination against migrants' commercial activities, conservative politicians routinely evoked the principle of equal law enforcement for both Italians and Chinese in Via Sarpi and elsewhere in Milan. Key audiovisual evidence disputed this claim by showing the traffic officers' patrols in the neighbourhood in the week before the riot. Two Italian journalism students, Vittorio Romano and Andrea Sceresini, hid a camera inside a cardboard box on a pushcart and walked it through Via Sarpi. Recall that one street rule that traffic officers were supposed to enforce was prohibiting the use of pushcarts on the area's narrow streets. The first four patrols ignored them entirely, while the fifth patrol was forced to stop them because they met head-on on Via Sarpi. In Romano and Sceresini's video clip, the officer talked about his obligation to fine the two Italians as he believed that the Chinese were filming him from within their stores. That imagined footage would have undermined the municipal administration, if it had shown that the officer was not applying the street rule to everyone.

Posted on *Corriere della Sera*'s website and shown on Mediaset's Italia 1 on 13 April, Romano and Sceresini's footage revealed the hypocrisy of Italian politicians' post-riot rhetoric about equal treatment for offenders, giving credence to migrants' complaints of discrimination in *Il Manifesto*. More seriously, according to migrants' oral testimonies reported by *La Stampa*, certain Italian police openly asked for cash from migrants in exchange for not issuing a fine for the use of pushcarts or for double parking.[63]

Romano and Sceresini's method also protested the CCTV surveillance systems that Milan's city government had installed in Via Sarpi on 5 April. These cameras were purportedly used to combat illegal activities by anyone in the neighbourhood, in keeping with the normalizing conception of contemporary surveillance technology and crime. In reality, they were used to map the spatial-temporal coordinates of the traffic caused by migrants' vans and pushcarts. The resulting information might help police Chinese wholesalers' commercial behaviour and support other normative practices, such as other street rules and the municipal government's plan to relocate merchants to Arese.[64]

Ironically, according to the Milanese police, these cameras malfunctioned during the riot's first few hours and yielded no footage that revealed whether Bu or the Italian traffic officers started the physical confrontation. The press speculated about three possibilities. If the police cameras simply malfunctioned, then they exhibited the limits of surveillance regimes that employ digital technologies. But the other two possibilities give us cause to reflect on institutional disciplining and its technology: if the cameras were intentionally damaged before the riot, presumably Chinese migrants were preparing for a pre-planned riot; or, if the police hid the footage and made a false announcement, then they wished to protect the real culprits, presumably the Italian officers.[65]

Drawing on Michel Foucault's theorization of the panoptic in prisons and in other social institutions via a concept by Jeremy Bentham, I view these cameras as embodying the institutional power and authority to control and correct migrants' commercial activities, often claimed to be illegal or criminal. From this perspective, if migrants rebelled against the surveillance and avoided institutional disciplining by disabling the cameras, then they would have failed to survey themselves, a condition central to the panoptic surveillance that Milan's municipal government hoped to achieve with these cameras.[66] If, instead, the Milanese police retained the footage, then they would be covering up their failure in crime management (i.e., violence during the riot) by withholding specific knowledge of the crime (i.e., the information about who started the bodily assault), leading to serious questions about social justice.

The question of who used violence first would illuminate our interpretation of the riot. But this information would neither invalidate the logic of linking entrepreneurship via economic crimes to institutional discipline nor improve the methodology of applying street rules in any foreseeable future. Similarly, the counter-surveillance moves by Romano and Sceresini, as well as by Chinese migrants who were said to film patrols from their stores, would only increase the police's sense of insecurity, which could then justify more brutal means of discipline, like the clubs used to beat the rioters on 12 April. Rather, the takeaway message is that the 2007 riot became an opportunity for the Italian media to rehearse and reinforce its pattern of framing migrants' illegal business activities via the official disciplinary and legal measures devised to curb them. In 2007, media coverage of Chinese migration to Milan organized and diversified debates about transnational migrants' economic integration in Italy.

Migrant Self-Enclosure and the Multicultural Project

The episode concerning surveillance and hidden cameras revealed the extent of the mistrust among Chinese migrants, Italian police, ordinary Italians, and Milan's municipal government. To address the existing distrust, most Italian media, progressive or conservative, tried to promote more meaningful dialogue among these groups. What were some of the obstacles that had prevented such dialogue from taking place previously? And what solutions did the media propose to make that dialogue happen?

To begin, Italian journalists often claimed that, despite their economic integration, Chinese migrants lacked the proper cultural capital to become incorporated into Italian society and culture.[67] According to this coverage, the majority of first-generation Chinese in Italy were too busy working, and so devoted little time to learning the Italian language and culture in order to interact meaningfully with Italians. Working mostly for Chinese employers and with Chinese coworkers deepened their Italian social and cultural isolation. In the aforementioned *Repubblica* web television program, Cresto-Dina called this phenomenon Chinese migrants' "self-referential logic," which he claimed differentiated them from other migrants with more exposure to Italian society, including the Romanians who worked as chauffeurs, the Egyptians as cooks, and the Filipinos as caretakers. Further support for the perceived and real self-enclosure of Chinese migrants included their apparently self-contained ethnic entrepreneurship as well as Milan's Chinatown, which the media often depicted as an ethnic business enclave closed to outsiders.

To address this widespread perception of a Chinese community imprisoned within its own social and cultural confines on Italian soil, journalists and politicians frequently suggested engaging with, as the media called them, bilingual, second-generation Chinese migrants or Chinese Italians. Giuliano Amato, then Italy's minister of the interior, held this view and encouraged younger Chinese to become the "icebreakers." Rai Tre interviewed young Chinese-Italian protestors who said they were ready to communicate with the city government, for they too felt like part of the Milanese citizenry. In interviews with *La Repubblica*, several young Chinese Italians severely criticized various Italian authorities for their racism and superficial execution of street laws. These migrants, who were born or grew up in Italy, held out hope for a common ground on which migrants and Italians could work together towards greater social cooperation. In particular, they spoke of a parallel between Italy's diasporic past and the Italian Chinese diaspora today as the basis for improved mutual understanding. As *Liberazione* reasoned, second-generation Chinese Italians lived in the difficult border zone between two cultures. Moreover, since these young people felt betrayed by racist slurs against the Chinese presumably left by the Italians, they went on to more explicitly declare their allegiance to Italian cultural heritage.[68]

In 2007, the media portrayed such young people, some of whom came from elite migrant families, as enthusiastic supporters of a multicultural Italy, quite a departure from the media coverage of young Chinese gangs only a few years prior. In covering the riot, the Italian media did not always acknowledge that a heterogeneous community of young Chinese migrants or Chinese Italians resided in the country. This oversight was likely intentional, because the persuasive premise of any integrationist proposal would need to postpone addressing more problematic issues, such as real criminal activities associated with Italy's Chinese.[69]

This media coverage of Chinese Italians conveyed the idea that self-enclosure only occurred among certain members of the Chinese migrant community, who were usually monocultural, older, and first-generation migrants.[70] When speaking in the news media, elite and bicultural Chinese Italians and second-generation Chinese migrants often made it a point to distance themselves from this group of individuals. The pro-Chinese Italian media used this distinction to emphasize how some Chinese residents were culturally proficient and socially well-inserted in Italy as a way to promote multiculturalism. Young Chinese Italians also participated in these efforts, with a sharper focus on image management and a struggle for greater media visibility.

In realpolitik, young Chinese Italians would bridge the gap between the Italians and the Chinese migrants only if the Italian municipal authorities and police were open to consultation and collaboration with them. Indeed, the other major obstacle to greater dialogue between migrants and authorities concerned city-level politics and administration in Italy.[71] According to the Italian media, in the opinions of Italy's Chinese communities, in 2007 the centre-left governments in Rome and Prato were more tolerant than Milan's centre-right government. *Liberazione* remarked that the riot could not have occurred in Rome or Prato because of the local governments' politics. A Chinese migrant in Rome was quoted as commenting that the laissez-faire attitude of Rome's mayor, Walter Veltroni of the left-leaning party Democratici di Sinistra (Democrats of the left), was a far cry from Moratti's intense street regulation in Milan. In fact, they noted that more police patrols were needed in the Esquilino area where Chinese migrants were subjected to petty crimes. For another Chinese migrant, thanks to Prato's mayor, Marco Romagnoli, who was affiliated with Democratici di Sinistra, more dialogue between migrants and city officials took place in Prato than in Milan. These accounts paint an image of Milan quite different from a place that was "historically open, hospitable, and generous with regard to migrants and to those who are 'different,'" as *Panorama* puts it in relation to the riot. For the weekly, the riot was only the latest episode of several clashes between long-time Milanese who wanted more security and laws, and newcomers to Milan who needed equal rights, citizenship, and respect.[72]

As these media accounts made clear, without a national policy on migrants and multiculturalism, as was the case in Italy in 2007, it was difficult to ensure social justice for the country's minority groups, because local governments and their ideologies were in charge of the creation and implementation of specific rules that directly impacted migrants' lives. Most of the municipal-level policies I discuss in this book were not expressly created to regulate migrant incorporation in Italian cities. On the surface, the street rules were meant to facilitate mobility in Milan's Chinatown as well as in other neighbourhoods. Police raids on Prato's illegal Chinese migrant factories aimed at cracking down on crimes in the city's textile and garment industries as a whole. Although these policies were not designed to discipline the Chinese migrant community, in reality they regulated its economic and business activities and behaviour, which many commentators argued was the governments' real agenda in ensuring electoral victories and saving local Italian businesses.

Moreover, the umbrella term "multiculturalism" has been an ill-defined policy in the Italian context at both the national and municipal levels. When Italian journalists employed this term and its derivative adjectives, such as multicultural and multiculturalist, they did not typically mean the systematic, state-sponsored policies and political philosophies of multiculturalism in countries like Canada. Unlike French republicanism and British or Dutch multiculturalism, Italian journalists, policy makers, politicians, and ordinary citizens did not have a state-sanctioned integration model to which they could choose to assent or contest. In Italy, as Stefano Allievi notes, "the debate on (against) multiculturalism has been imported, and locally produced, before any multiculturalist politics were even proposed, imposed or existed."[73] Thus, during the media reporting on the riot, few journalists or politicians referred to concrete multicultural policies concerning Chinese migrants, such as bilingual education and the promotion of Chinese-run migrant associations. Instead, they most-often discussed Chinatowns in North America. The lack of a common reference model in Italian media discourses on migration crucially accounted for the diverse disciplinary actions by regional and city governments, as well as for the varying degrees of severity with which discipline was applied to individual migrant groups.[74] To my mind, this lack also gave rise to the polyphony in media coverage about Chinese immigration to Italy that I have discussed in this chapter.

Identifying what cultural actors meant by using multiculturalism and its correlated vocabulary in specific journalistic contexts can be a taxing job, as this work would entail unravelling the many perspectives on multiculturalism as a political philosophy. Instead, I discuss several guiding principles for a practice of multiculturalism for the news media. According to Steven Vertovec and Susanne Wessendorf, state governments' multicultural principles should aim to "reduce discrimination; promote equality of opportunity and overcome barriers to full participation in society; allow unconstrained access to public services; recognize cultural identities (as opposed to assimilation) and open up public spaces for their representation; and foster acceptance of ethnic pluralism and cultural understanding across all groups."[75] Most of these tenets were articulated and debated in Italian media accounts about Chinese migrants, such as those in the television show titled *Le iene* (The hyenas) on Italia 1.

Similar to what I examined above in relation to Italian-Chinese international trade and political economy, the Italian media's answer to messy national politics about immigration was satire. Addressing pluricultural Italy with humour and surrealism, *Le iene* offered a panoramic and evocative account of the country's three largest Chinatowns in 2007. Conceived in the format of "politainment," by which critics mean intentionally blurry boundaries between politics and entertainment, the program focused on a lively presentation of current affairs in keeping with Italia 1's young target audiences.[76]

In one episode, while clumsily practicing taiji (tai chi) with a group of Chinese, the host Alessandro Sartino half-seriously announced his intention to integrate as an Italian native into the Chinese community in Piazza Vittorio, the community's symbolic centre in Rome. During a police raid on a factory in Prato, the Chinese continued to stitch garments, as if to spite the ineptitude of Italian administrators who were unwilling or unable to eradicate the root causes of illegal practices in the city's fast-fashion sector. In a hilarious sequence that critiques Italian provincialism in cosmopolitan Milan, Sartino looked on as an old Italian woman asked an Italian young man why his wife was Chinese, rather than Italian.[77]

These episodes in *Le iene* allotted considerable screen time to second-generation Chinese migrants, who debated with Italian residents and offered their perspectives on the riot. Moreover, *Le iene* incorporated the Chinese into its narrative space through comic sketches, irreverent remarks, and satires, departing from the often overly didactic and politicized news accounts by Chinese migrants during the same period (see chapter 4). Therefore, *Le iene* poked fun at both left- and right-leaning media representations of Italy's Chinese in a meta-media vein, commenting on the political decisions the news outlets sought to endorse or refute.

That *Le iene* belonged to the Berlusconi-owned Mediaset group would come as a surprise to readers who unproblematically correlate right-wing media with anti-immigrant attitudes in Italy. Lega Nord's lack of moderation in expressing anti-immigrant racism, which my previous analysis has exposed, was frowned upon by many right-wing politicians and journalists. Already in 2003, one of the cosigners of the rather restrictive 2002 Bossi-Fini immigration law, Gianfranco Fini of Alleanza Nazionale, proposed a bill in support of the migrants' right to vote in local elections. In the critic Zincone's estimation, like Fini, Berlusconi would have exhibited more pro-immigrant attitudes had he not needed substantial support from Lega Nord to form centre-right coalitions. A move towards a centrist position would have secured both Fini and Berlusconi much more support in European political circles.[78]

Having examined some of the multicultural practices in action in the Italian media after the riot, it is possible to critique the ethnocultural rhetoric inherent in Italy's multicultural project and its discontents. Much of pro-Chinese commentators' riot coverage assumed the immutability of Chinese cultural traits in migrations across geographies. Writing for *La Repubblica*, the sinologist Renata Pisu discussed what she viewed as the deep-rooted Chinese scepticism towards authorities, although she correctly noted migrants' multiple and fluid allegiances to their host country, their families, and their home country. Father Giuseppe Chang, referred to in the media as a chaplain in Italy's Chinese communities, explained on Rai Uno that compared to Italians, Chinese were "passive" by culture and more willing to avoid direct confrontation with authorities and to pay fines so that they could move on with their business.[79] Ultimately, the multicultural discourse appreciated Chinese migrants in order to encourage them to preserve their cultural distinctiveness in Italy.

Meanwhile, nativist-inclined riot coverage endeavoured to preserve the present and future purity of the Italian nation-state from foreign contamination. A great number of journalists and residents argued that since migrants lived in Italy where laws applied to everyone, they should either obey those laws or go home. In extreme right-wing thinking, if the Chinese felt subjected to racism merely because they must respect the law, then they should go back to China where they could enjoy unlawful conditions more freely.

Libero charged that the Italians were "stupid cultivators of tolerance and multiculturalism" who allowed criminal organizations to proliferate and gave Muslim migrants the nerve to ask for public funds to construct mosques in Italy. Accusing Chinese migrants of failing to assimilate, integrate, and settle, a journalist in *Libero* went so far as to call Milan an "anthropological encyclopedia" of foreign communities that "assaulted what was left of milanesità," a term used to denote a strong work ethic and a strong sense of hospitality in domestic but not foreign migrants.[80] Such argumentation proclaimed migrants' undesirability by emphasizing the host society's refusal to adapt to, or accommodate, them. Italocentric arguments often proceeded as if their sole goal was to keep Italian-migrant mistrust alive by demanding unreasonable, or morally dubious, integration. As such, nativist discourses dogmatized the superiority of Italian natives over Chinese migrants.[81]

Nativist views of migration had a pronounced connotation of xenophobia and racism. *Vita* satirized these views by referring to classes reserved exclusively for the Chinese in certain Italian schools, for fear that "they could slow down the education of the Italian intelligentsia." Specialized in social analyses, this magazine cited research results from the Cooperation for the Development of Emerging Countries (Cospe) when explaining widespread fear of a rising Chinese economy. *Altrenotizie*, an independent Italian news website, pointed out that behind the riot, politicians were using the issue of immigration to attract electoral support by appealing to the "very human envy of the Italians who are poorer than the Chinese in question."[82]

In making these claims, both multicultural and nativist journalists largely attributed fixed traits to the Chinese and the Italians in order to accentuate their ethnic and national differences, thereby to reach a prolonged political stalemate. This situation not only obscured the intricate economic, strategic, and political negotiation at play in the media coverage of the riot, but also ultimately delayed the task of finding new avenues to more efficiently integrate migrants.

Variations of the many points made by the pro-Chinese Italian media were featured in Italy's Chinese migrant media. Through print and online journalism, Chinese migrant activism opened up another area for debates about the riot. Because of the limited existing archival materials, I find it difficult to determine with precision the extent to which Chinese migrants were engaged in self-representation prior to 2007 (except for what I have examined in chapter 2). But during and after 2007, there was an explosion of Chinese migrants' interventions into media debates concerning their community. This media coverage helped to cement Italian-Chinese encounters as a culturally significant process in media debates around migrant incorporation and economic globalization in Italy. In the next chapter, I reconsider the riot from Chinese migrant perspectives as conveyed in their news outlets.

Chapter 4

Milan: The 2007 "Chinatown" Riot in Migrant Debates

As Russell King and Nancy Wood suggest, in order to better examine migration in the media, we may explore representations in host-country media, in country-of-origin media, in migrant communities' media, and in global media.[1] Following this suggestion, in this chapter I analyse the riot as it was covered in Italy's Chinese migrant media and, to a lesser degree, in mainland Chinese media. Given the poor Italian-language literacy of most Chinese migrants, these two types of media can reasonably be posited as their main source of information. According to an empirical study conducted in Turin in the 2000s, while migrants watched Italian and Chinese television programs almost equally, they read mostly Chinese-language newspapers. Roughly half of the respondents read newspapers every day, and the rest at least once a week.[2] For Wanning Sun, the availability of Chinese-language news media forms a key condition for overseas Chinese identities to function. (Other conditions are commerce as well as community-building activities that include migrant associations and Chinese-language schools.)[3]

In 2007, Chinese migrants possessed considerable media clout: they published four major newspapers, two Chinese-Italian bilingual monthly magazines, and a great number of websites in which they confidently promoted their interests.[4] The Chinese migrant media wielded substantial influence in shaping the community's views of the riot and other issues. Some of these views were also known to Italian readers through excerpts in Italian newspapers. However, the existing scholarship on Italy's Chinese has largely ignored their contributions to the country's mediascape.[5] Here, I offer the first detailed scholarly account of the intense Chinese migrant media coverage of the riot.

The Chinese Migrant News Media in Italy

The four leading Chinese migrant newspapers operating in Italy in 2007 were created with seed funding from the community's successful entrepreneurs, with *Ouhua Lianhe Shibao/Il Tempo Europa Cina* (1996–) and *Xinhua Lianhe Shibao/La Nuova Cina* (2010–) based in Rome, and *Ouzhou Qiaobao/Europe China News* (2001–) and *Ouzhou Huaren Bao* (Europe Chinese news) (2004–) based in Milan.[6] These newspapers derived the bulk of their revenues from local and national advertising targeted at migrants. Such unabashed promotion of business interests distinguishes the Chinese migrant press in Italy and elsewhere from Western and other migrants' media.[7] The 2005 circulation statistics put *Ouzhou Qiaobao* in first place with seven to eight thousand copies, followed by *Ouhua Lianhe Shibao* with five to six thousand copies.[8]

In 2007, *Cina in Italia* and *It's China* were the two bilingual monthly magazines about Chinese culture and current affairs concerning China and Chinese migrants. *Cina in Italia* collaborated with the Confederazione Generale Italiana del Lavoro while maintaining close ties with mainland Chinese media outlets and with the Chinese government. Compared with *Cina in Italia*, *It's China* was a general-interest magazine with a more pronounced focus on migrant issues in Italy. While the four newspapers were readily available in Chinese-run stores in major cities in Italy and in other European countries, the two magazines offered reader subscriptions and operated websites. Furthermore, a very active bilingual website maintained by Associna served as an information and opinion hub. Established in 2005, Associna is Italy's largest organization for so-called second-generation Chinese migrants and Chinese Italians, and one of the largest and earliest associations created by second-generation migrants or Italians of foreign ancestries.[9] Associna also hosted a forum, an example of virtual diasporas: migrants interacted online, extending their diaspora in the empirical world.[10]

Italy's Chinese migrant media provided information on the riot to mainland Chinese media outlets, which were state-controlled but to varying degrees. Thanks to media globalization and communication technologies, the mainland Chinese media, which are part of China's soft power abroad, exerted a considerable influence on Chinese migrant journalism in Italy through ideology and, occasionally, funding. By and large, in 2007 Italy's Chinese migrant press followed the Chinese state's communist ideology – a result, among other things, of the conscious but piecemeal globalization of the Chinese state media. Building on Pál Nyíri's observations of similar cases in other European contexts, we note that Italy's Chinese newspapers frequently employed discourses of patriotism, success, and modernity that the Chinese state nurtured. The state also provided guidance on forming migrant associations based on areas of origin, made its economic assets available to migrants, and cultivated new migrant elites. By realizing these initiatives and through these elites, the Chinese state made essentialist notions of "Chineseness" a commodity for both Chinese and non-Chinese living outside of mainland China. Therefore, still following Nyíri, rather than dilute contemporary China's nation-building and nationalism, in many cases the worldwide Chinese diaspora contributed to them.[11]

Indeed, during the 2000s, the mainland Chinese news media devoted much attention to overseas Chinese, most notably the Communist Party's official organ, *Renmin Ribao* (People's daily), and China's main news agency, Xinhuashe (Xinhua news agency), which published several newspapers. *Xinhua Lianhe Shibao* and *Cina in Italia*, in particular, exhibited high ideological alignment with Xinhuashe, owing in no small part to their collaborations with several mainland Chinese media outlets. *Xinhua Lianhe Shibao* was partially financed by a Chinese governmental initiative to set up newspapers and news websites outside China, and in 2010 *Cina in Italia* became the Italian edition of the mainland Chinese magazine, *Zhongguo Xinwen Zhoukan* (China newsweek), published by China's other main state-owned news agency, Zhongguo Xinwenshe (China news service).[12] There were other mainland Chinese news outlets that covered the riot but were not apparently affiliated with state media agencies, including the influential *Nanfang Zhoumou* (Southern weekly) and the website *Sohu*. Based in Guangzhou, the capital of a traditional emigrant province, *Nanfang Zhoumou* was considered the most liberal newspaper in mainland China. Often consciously positioned to counter *Renmin Ribao*, it frequently criticized Chinese official authorities by reporting on their misdeeds and on national social malaises.[13]

As Frank N. Pieke et al. note, in European contexts, Chinese state and migrant media texts "are written against a background of the same assumptions, in the same style, and sometimes even by the same people as their own. New migrant media form a continuous narrative space with the official media in China, amplifying their impact among the Chinese populations abroad." To be sure, according to Pieke et al., neither the Chinese state nor the migrant associations and their media outlets wished to be entirely influenced by one another because they remained divided on many practical migration issues, such as human smuggling from China to Europe.[14] However, the Chinese state and provincial media shared information, rhetorical devices, and discursive strategies with Italy's Chinese migrant media to such a degree that the similarities appear obvious even to the untrained eye. Even though Italy's Chinese may not have read mainland Chinese coverage in print, they may have accessed it online, and the gist of it was often reformulated in their newspapers and magazines.

Elite Chinese migrants in Italy spent enormous energy nurturing their news media. As the new millennium began, media culture – not political participation in Italian governments, which was largely unavailable to these migrants – was their most potent weapon against bias in the Italian media and society. The Chinese migrant media was also a necessary communications tool for migrant elites to consolidate their authority within their own communities. These economically and culturally privileged Chinese took advantage of a positive media rhetoric of globalization to further improve their social standing in Italy.[15] When addressing the Italian media and public, elite migrants distinguished themselves from their less-privileged conationals through status markers, such as their global entrepreneurial, media, and cultural competencies, which were said to put them on par with middle-class Italians. Moreover, as relevant coverage often revealed, these elites showed sympathy and empathy for less-privileged Chinese on the basis of their common experiences and interests: they shared national, ethnic, or geographical identity; a similar migratory history; a moral imperative to defend the weak; and the experience of being stereotyped in the Italian media and society. From this perspective, migrant elites and pro-Chinese Italians believed they were right to claim to speak for all the Chinese in Italy.

Predictably, the perspectives of socially disadvantaged Chinese in Italy rarely crept into public view. To be sure, their quotations populated the Italian- and Chinese-language media texts that I examine. But their views were filtered by Italian and Chinese migrant journalists' reporting, and sculpted by migrant elites' commentaries in Chinese-language newspapers. Moreover, migrants who were not from Wenzhou and its surrounding counties – the traditional origin areas of the Chinese in Italy – may have been subjected to further hardship at the hands of their Chinese employers, who were mostly likely from these places. These circumstances would lead these least-privileged Chinese, who made up only a small percentage of the overall community, to form very different opinions about the dynamics between Italians and wealthier Chinese.

Despite these gaps, it is important not to over-emphasize the tension between elite Chinese entrepreneurs and their employees, particularly those from the Wenzhou area. During the 1990s and 2000s, Wenzhou fostered a culture of migration. While this milieu created social pressure on Chinese migrants whose agenda was not so clear-eyed, and while during the 2000s most migrants were stuck in low-skilled jobs that had no clear path to economic prosperity, these individuals still conceivably aspired to elite entrepreneurship. The success stories of some present-day wealthy Chinese migrant entrepreneurs, who had first worked in the lowest ranks of the restaurant industry in the 1980s, in garment manufacturing in the 1990s, and in the import-export sector in the 2000s, circulated widely in the news media and through word of mouth.[16]

The vast majority of Chinese migrants regarded migration to Italy not as a survival strategy, but as a quick means to economic prosperity and social mobility. Most Chinese in Italy were not from among the poorest populations from the poorest areas in China; on the contrary, they were only at a relative social and economic disadvantage compared to conationals who remained in the rather prosperous Zhejiang Province. These migrants mustered enough material resources to pay for their trips to Italy, and once there could borrow start-up capital at little or no interest from their fellow migrants through guanxi (see chapter 2).

Within Italy's network of Wenzhounese migrants, most workers did not regard the relentless pace of work for and the submission of some personal rights to employers as labour issues, as the Italian media tended to depict. Most workers understood that in exchange for these rights, employers ensured their collective well-being in times of trouble. For example, workers gave up their passports to their employers for "safekeeping" during their time in a particular workshop. During police crackdowns, not revealing their identities as printed in their passports, which were stored off-site, would help illegal migrants evade law enforcement. Employers were supposed to form a paternal relationship with employees, and everyone had a moral obligation to build a prosperous Chinese migrant economy for everyone's benefit.[17] This may be a problematic view of employer-employee relations, and in practice they were not always functional or ideal. But as the Chinese migrant media often argued, it was a powerful ideology for creating consensus and better managing the Chinese migrant labour force.

Decoding and Encoding

Given the diversity of ideological positions present in both the Chinese migrant and the Italian media, how can we best study migrants' construction of the riot in relation to Italian narratives? Here, I focus on the discursive and rhetorical dimensions of this media process. In terms of creation and interpretation, or encoding and decoding, of texts from mass communication, following Stuart Hall's formulation, I contend that there were two scenarios in which the Chinese migrant and mainland Chinese media operated simultaneously after the riot.[18]

First, this media decoded the professional code in which the Italian media had portrayed the riot by offering different interpretations of the same topics, including perceived Chinese encroachment on Italian national identity, racism against Chinese, Chinese economic crimes and Italian institutional discipline, and Chinese migrants' lack of political representation in Italy's multicultural project. The Chinese media's repeated references to Italian misrepresentations of the riot prepared the grounds from which migrant journalists launched their rebuttals. Presenting themselves as equal players in the competing narratives of the riot, the Chinese migrant media reacted to negative Italian depictions of their community, correcting them mostly for the benefit of Chinese readers, but also for Italian audiences through bilingual texts. Most migrant news commentaries avoided topics such as the Chinese mafia and criminal and illegal economic activities in order to contest harsh Italian institutional discipline more efficiently. They also downplayed their own community's negative and dissenting views of migrants' social and business conduct. The result was a rhetorically unified front for tackling the Italian media's mounting accusations of the community's economic and social illegitimacy. The nature of this communication process conforms to the findings of a comparative study conducted in the early 2000s, which describes minority media policy as "resistant/restrictive" in Italy, as opposed to pluralist in France and accommodating but restrictive in Britain.[19]

Second, the Chinese-language media represented the riot in their own professional code by raising new issues, as well as by adopting a Chinese-centred, and sometimes Sinocentric, ethnocultural approach. Undoubtedly, this code was a reaction to the dominant Italian professional code, insofar as it aimed to enlarge the range of topics with which to approach the riot. For example, the Chinese-language media emphasized the violence and racism that the Chinese in Italy and worldwide endured in order to contextualize the intense Chinese reactions to both issues during the Milan riot. Moreover, in addressing concerns raised by Italian residents and authorities regarding socially accepted conduct in Italy, migrant newspapers developed a guide for Chinese from cultural, behavioural, and business-related perspectives.

But more importantly, the Chinese migrant professional code grew out of elite migrants' efforts to legitimate their opinions about their community's present and future, as well as to convey those opinions to the community's less-advantaged members and to the Chinese state government. The media helped to build consensus in a community deeply divided by class, education, and individual business interests, with an aim to nurture a cadre of well-educated and well-regarded migrants, be they journalists or entrepreneurs, to present to mainstream Italian society. These elites would have the community's support as they actively participated in Italy's local and national politics. In this way, the riot further encouraged Chinese community activism in Italy.

In constructing this community, migrant journalists resorted to age-old Chinese populist rhetoric that gained momentum as Hu Jintao made it a central concern of the Chinese government after he became the country's leader in 2002, a position he held until 2012. Spurred on by this rhetoric, Italy's Chinese migrant press tended to examine current affairs in moralizing terms, which ultimately promoted the interests of Chinese migrant elites and their businesses.[20] Indeed, this media legitimated the opinions of well-integrated elites by adopting an essentialist interpretation of migrants' business and social practices based on supposed ethnically and culturally "genetic" differences between the Italians and the Chinese (i.e., ethnogenesis), with which average Chinese readers could easily identify. First-generation Chinese migrants likely formed a firm idea about Chinese national and cultural identity during their school years in China. Furthermore, starting in the 1990s, the Chinese state often publicly praised its migrants' achievements in European countries, in keeping with a long-time strategy to inculcate a sense of national belonging among overseas Chinese. As Aihwa Ong notes, globalization in Asia "has induced both national and transnational forms of nationalism that not only reject Western hegemony but seek, in panreligious civilizational discourses, to promote the ascendancy of the East."[21] These official endeavours must have strengthened Chinese identity for many first-generation migrants residing in Italy and fostered it among their offspring.

Through the processes of decoding and encoding, Italy's Chinese migrant media showed considerable editorial confidence, which reflected their owners' financial stability and elevated social rank within the community. The elites invested heavily in promoting a positive and up-to-date image of their community, which was oriented towards its other members and towards mainstream Italian society. This press's vitality was also due to China's current economic and political prowess, which more-established migrants capitalized on to enhance the community's image and particularly to support their entrepreneurship and potential political empowerment. Some of Italy's elite Chinese migrants also collaborated with the mainland Chinese media, using their networks to reach Chinese readers there and in other Chinese diasporic networks. In 2007, no other migrant communities in Italy and their origin countries could hope to replicate the favourable economic, political, and media conditions that Chinese migrants enjoyed when combating negative Italian media depictions of them, as well as when nurturing favourable ones both in their own and mainstream Italian news media.

Strategic Silence

A close look at Chinese coverage of the riot reveals a strange case: neither the Chinese mafia nor young criminal gangs were discussed in detail. This occurred despite the legitimate assumption that, given the antagonistic positions the Chinese media assumed towards the Italian media, Chinese journalists must have been aware of vigorous Italian debates on these topics. As I examined in chapter 2, when the Chinese mafia held an unparalleled appeal for Italian journalists, *Cina in Italia* and *It's China* addressed it indirectly but did not view it as a legitimate issue to explore. These magazines may have been silent on this issue in order to curb sensationalism. This absence also typified "saving face" in public, especially when journalists confronted such unpleasant topics as young men who were led astray into criminality.

In Chinese migrant newspapers, the lack of extended accounts of Chinese criminality was paralleled by the suppression of less-than-flattering views of "Chinatowns." Only overwhelmingly positive depictions were presented. Writing in *Cina in Italia*, Xu Jianguo believed that, as Italy's oldest Chinese neighbourhood, Via Sarpi symbolized the community's success. While some Italians viewed this Chinatown as undeniable evidence of Chinese spatial and economic invasion in Italian residential areas and identity, Xu regarded the Milan government's unilateral decision to ask local Chinese businesses to relocate to Arese as an act of encroachment on their lawfully acquired premises, for which they had paid Italian proprietors handsomely. For these payments, migrants used their years of savings and sometimes also borrowed extensively from friends and relatives. For Xu, relocation would mean business losses for merchants because after years of savings and intense labour, they might end up obtaining storefronts in warehouses in Arese that could take years to become commercially viable for wholesale businesses.[22]

In conclusion, Xu praises Chinese migrants' industriousness and perseverance in building a prosperous Chinatown in Milan, which significantly elevated their social and economic standing: "In the beginning, who did not come to Italy with nothing to his name? Gradually, in merely ten years, we relied on our hands to work hard. With tenacity and an entrepreneurial spirit, we created today's prosperity! Apart from Chinese ethnicity, what other races in the world can be so industrious? Undoubtedly, the Chinatown in front of our eyes stands as a testimony to our amazing achievements abroad." Xu's epideictic register, especially the exaltation of Chinese "ethnicity" or "race," is characteristic of journalistic writing about overseas Chinese in the Chinese rhetorical tradition. In this description, Milan's Chinatown also took on a ceremonial significance in the history of the Chinese diaspora in Italy. Xu never mentions any urban degradation in Chinatowns allegedly caused by migrants' commercial activities. He also screens out potential oppositional views by Chinese migrants on the proposed relocation to Arese, so that a united front from within the community can emerge, at least textually and rhetorically, in order to challenge the Italian prejudice witnessed in the previous chapter.

Xu does not take issue with the derogatory connotations of the term "Chinatown," which Italian journalists and politicians employed to designate Via Sarpi as a space reserved for a minority group with a long history of being considered undesirable by the hegemonic classes in host countries. Rather, Xu wishes to preserve Via Sarpi, which is centrally located in Milan, as a place to commemorate his own and his conationals' entrepreneurial achievements, to continue to serve as a gathering point for Chinese migrants and tourists, to showcase Chinese culture and heritage, and to keep functioning as Chinese migrants' commercial and service centre in the city. For Xu, Milan's "Chinatown" became a place of protest against Italian biases. Xu's concept of this space aligned with the conventional functions of migrant associations and organizations in more established Chinatowns in North America, except that in 2007 most of Milan's Chinese did not reside in Via Sarpi.[23] That year, for elite migrants, the legitimization of the Chinese commercial presence in this neighbourhood was a much more pressing issue than its name and historical connotations. These migrants seemed to be oblivious to the fact that a great deal of the negative narratives about the neighbourhood's Chinese drew on previous, similar narratives of Chinatowns in North America, as I have shown in chapter 3.

In addition to the absence of negative views of Chinatowns and the Chinese mafia in the Chinese migrant media, there was a silence about economic crimes. In Italy, like in other countries, the Chinese migrant press promoted their financial backers' business interests and defended the communities' economic interests in host countries. The press genuinely believed and sought to prove that migrant firms had stimulated and revitalized local Italian economies. Therefore, they valorized the price advantage of "Made in China" products and services for the Italian middle and lower classes. *Ouhua Lianhe Shibao* reported on these views, which had emerged from interviews with Chinese migrants, pro-Chinese Italian residents, and an Italian policeman in Milan. Similar arguments also appeared in *Guangzhou Ribao* (Guangzhou daily), the official newspaper of Guangdong Province, which dedicated a special insert to the riot based on information drawn from *Ouhua Lianhe Shibao*. Using a familiar ethnocultural approach, articles in this insert attribute migrants' success to their industriousness and entrepreneurial spirit, said to be distinguishing features of the Chinese that would remedy the global recession.[24]

An efficient way for the Chinese-language news media to counter the Italian accusation of Chinese economic crimes would have been to explain migrants' business configuration and working mechanisms in the Italian economy, as Cologna and Ceccagno had done for the left-leaning Italian newspapers examined in chapter 3. However, the Chinese media rarely mentioned these things following the riot; since it targeted predominantly Chinese migrants, doing so would have been redundant. Chinese journalists were also concerned that more ink spilt on this subject would further tarnish migrants' reputation. During our interview, the chief editor of a major Chinese migrant newspaper in Italy suggested that I not write about migrants' illegal practices. The editor believed that while Italy's Chinese readers knew how to handle discussions about illegal activities with a measured attitude, North American readers might question the legality of Chinese migrant businesses in their cities if they were to learn about the Italian-Chinese case from my book.[25] As I explain in chapter 5, for example, migrant journalism was forthcoming about the inner mechanisms of Prato's Chinese migrant garment industry only when the money they earned in Italy and sent to China through money transfer agencies was confiscated by authorities on a massive scale, largely because this money was the fruit of their labour and the source of sustenance for their families in China and in Italy.

To recapitulate, on the one hand, the Chinese migrant media's silence on such topics as the Chinese mafia, negative views of Italy's Chinatowns, and Chinese economic crimes was strategic and a reaction to Italian depictions. The resulting positive stereotyping of Chinese migrants and their firms attempted to minimize the negative social effects of Italian media bias or misinformation. Through this strategic silence, the Chinese hoped to distance themselves from the image of the arch-enemy who had destabilized Italian national identity and damaged ordinary Italians' economic well-being. Instead, migrant editorials underscored how Chinese firms had socially and economically benefited Italian neighbourhoods and their working-class residents. While not explicitly pointing the finger, they showed that the Chinese migrant community would not stand by waiting to be scapegoated for the inefficient economic planning and migrant incorporation that were duties of Milan's municipal and Italy's state governments.

On the other hand, it was a rhetorical necessity for the Chinese migrant press to smooth out heterogeneous – or obscure negative – views on these three topics within its own community. Such views must have existed, for the community's members were positioned hierarchically in its entrepreneurship and wealth distribution was extremely uneven. What is significant in these dynamics is not so much how this class tension was glossed over in accounts by migrant elites, but how this discursive strategy and the unified picture it painted helped the community address the intense Italian criticism after the riot. The Chinese migrant press posed itself as the official educator for uniting Chinese individuals of diverse backgrounds on the basis of their overall positive economic and cultural contributions to Italy, a typical consensus-building strategy in modern Chinese political discourse.[26] Through this process, this media aimed to legitimate its place in Italian society as the community's public persona.

Counterarguments

The strategic silence examined above should not obscure the fact that Chinese migrant newspapers offered spirited counterarguments, particularly with regard to violence. While Italian police violence was generally frowned upon in the mainstream Italian media, and occasionally exalted in the right-leaning and alternative media, it was unanimously condemned in the Chinese-language media. Based on a generic knowledge of European racism, migrants condemned Italian violence according to Chinese rhetorical and discursive conventions. Chinese accounts depicted Bu and other women as victims who counter-attacked in a way that strongly recalled historical narratives about Chinese people's resistance to the Japanese invasion during the Second World War. According to *Ouzhou Qiaobao*, Bu "painfully fell to the ground, as if injured." A young man was struck on the left temple, which created "a very deep indentation, very cruel indeed." Italian police were "armed to the teeth, and the atmosphere seemed to hark back to WWII and to the era of Hitler and Mussolini." "How can a country extolling human rights repress unarmed ordinary citizens with such bloodthirstiness?" At that juncture, "a Chinese woman bravely stood in front of a police car, becoming the backbone of the protestors."[27] The specific semiotic correlations between the signifiers (i.e., fascism and Nazism) and the signified (i.e., Italian violence) were powerful in the Chinese cultural context because, to borrow from Neil Renwick and Qing Cao, "metaphoric references are, for individuals and masses alike, triggers to formulaic memories and to a particular, constructed discourse and official 'grand narrative' [in China]." This was a narrative of Chinese victimhood and heroism, which emerged from condemning the injustice from European colonialism and Japanese imperialism.[28]

Through such narratives, the Chinese media constructed a malicious and awkward masculine Western Other, thereby reversing the depictions of the wounded masculinity of Italian police in the Italian media as I have analysed in chapter 3. Journalists created this Western Other by reappropriating the prevalent Western construction of a feminized China. A satirical cartoon published after the riot on *Sohu*, a Chinese website, is a telling example, which *Corriere della Sera* and La7 avidly reprinted.[29] In the cartoon, a Mussolini-looking fascist soldier is about to strike a Chinese woman and her baby with a club, one reminiscent of those Italian police wielded during the riot. To convey the police's masculine domination of the feminized ordinary people, the artist places the Italian man sitting on a horse and the Chinese woman kneeling on the ground. This visual dominance recalls the same techniques used in the previously discussed Italian satirical vignette, in which the Chinese flag overwhelms Milan's cathedral. The soldier's club bears the Nazi swastika, a symbol of racism. This grotesque caricature calls to mind comparable Italian depictions of Chinese migrants as octopuses and spiders, with both metaphors serving to urge readers to distance themselves from these creatures. From the perspective of Xiaomei Chen's concept of official Occidentalism, the cartoon essentializes the Italian fascist to invoke nationalist sentiments in Chinese readers.[30]

The vignette's emphasis on the violence and injustice endured by Italy's Chinese throughout the 2000s was not as anachronistic or exaggerated as it might appear. The Chinese media offered the personal safety of overseas Chinese as a new perspective from which to analyse Italian violence and to stimulate community activism. This news topic was well-documented and timely for the Chinese government during the 2000s. Since 2006, *Nanfang Zhoumou* has published annual reports on the safety of overseas Chinese and issued advice for mainland Chinese travellers abroad in collaboration with the Chinese Ministry of Foreign Affairs. In its 2007 report, the Milan riot was listed among a very select number of incidents, out of approximately thirty thousand, that were considered "harmful" to overseas Chinese and Chinese travellers, including violent attacks, deaths, and robberies.[31] Moreover, the riot was the headline of a special page on *Sohu*, which drew on the *Nanfang Zhoumou* report. This page showcased the riot with photographs of violent clashes between Chinese migrants and Italian police. *Ouhua Lianhe Shibao* also viewed the riot as part of a wave of recent violent acts against overseas Chinese in Spain, Brazil, Russia, and Indonesia, and pointed to the local anxieties triggered by migrants' entrepreneurial success.[32]

While condemning Italian violence, Chinese migrant newspapers justified Chinese violence by highlighting how the riot was supported by the civilians and others against the police and elites who abused power. Many were perplexed by why the riot turned violent, as overseas Chinese were known for keeping a low public profile and for readily cooperating with local authorities during conflicts. This was the main question directed at Fang Manqing, or Sarah Fang, then *Ouhua Lianhe Shibao*'s vice president, during an interview with the BBC Chinese Channel. In her reply, Fang explained that Milan's Chinese merchants needed an outlet for their anger: "There are over 500 Chinese-owned firms in Milan's Chinatown. Everybody had been fined once and everybody was angry." In a matter-of-fact tone, she went on to discuss how the Chinese found the recent escalation of parking fines and the confiscation of vehicle registration certificates to be "discriminatory" and "unreasonable."[33] The premise of Chinese violence was therefore constructed as a response to excessive fines and aggressive conduct on the part of Italian traffic offices and Milan's municipal government.

Chinese newspapers moreover tried to show that the riot's goal was to ensure economic survival and equal treatments for Chinese migrants as Milan's citizens. In other words, violence was its means, not its end, a statement made to dispel the public's doubt about how Milan's Chinese seemed prepared to use violence to convince the Italian authorities to meet their demands. For example, in covering a Chinese-organized protest of Italian police's conduct in front of Milan's cathedral on 15 April, *Ouhua Lianhe Shibao* conspicuously stressed the event's peaceful nature and reaffirmed migrants' desire to live in harmony with the rest of the city.[34]

Furthermore, in justifying its own community's violence, the Chinese migrant press emphasized the need to respond to the enemy using the same means, a key ethnocultural explanation that was entirely absent in the Italian media. *Ouzhou Qiaobao* quoted a well-known statement by Mao Zedong, which expresses a traditional Chinese notion later appropriated by the Chinese communist government: "We will not attack unless we are attacked; if we are attacked, we will certainly counterattack." The same newspaper also claimed that the Chinese "would rarely protest and argue unless cornered."[35] These emotionally charged Chinese idioms, expressions, and images aimed to awaken in Chinese readers an acute memory of threatened nationalism, a lofty sense of good over evil, and a populist approach towards an eye for an eye and a tooth for a tooth.

Indeed, in these accounts, a generic knowledge of feudal and Republican China became the nexus in which victimhood narratives, ethnocultural arguments, and nationalist incitements converged. A member of Associna proposed staging a "small Chinese-Italian May 4 Movement" in Italy, referring to the student agitation in Beijing during the May Fourth Movement in 1919, which opposed the Republic of China's further concession of the country's sovereignty to foreign powers during the negotiations for the Treaty of Versailles. *Ouzhou Huaren Bao* also valorized violence, implying that using it to obtain equal rights, even without provocation, was legitimate: "Silence is not cowardice, patience is not numbness, the unyielding Chinese will not let others decimate them."[36] Ultimately, as this press and its discursive space functioned as a rhetorical site for migrants to express their frustration and anger, it discouraged any spillover of this sentiment into the empirical world, as that would cause further turmoil.

In reassuring Chinese migrants about their personal safety within the Chinese migrant community, the Chinese press was apt to point out that violence during the riot was unplanned and short-lived, and that the Italian media was to blame for turning it into a spectacle. Associna members relayed how the riot was mostly peaceful except for a concentrated moment of violence. In their opinion, the extent of violent clashes between Chinese migrants and Italian police was incorrectly amplified in Italian television news, especially on Canale 5, which repeatedly sensationalized the few direct confrontations. In another case, while the question of whether Bu or the Italian traffic officers used violence first was not settled, Mediaset's other influential channel, Italia 1, quoted an Italian store owner who claimed to have witnessed Bu initiating the fight.[37]

Indeed, the Italian news media was pinpointed as the principal disseminator of inaccurate information about the riot and Italy's Chinese. On 18 April, *Ouhua Lianhe Shibao* was indignant at two photographs taken from Italian newspapers that showed contrasting views of the riot. In one photograph, Chinese and Italians held a piece of white cloth with "Italians and foreigners united against racism and repression" written on it in red. In the other photograph, Lega Nord's supporters waved Crusade-inspired white flags with red crosses on them and vowed to defend Italy from foreigners. Commenting on these two photographs, *Ouhua Lianhe Shibao*'s authoritative editorial voice charges, in an unusually confrontational and sarcastic tone: "Is this the so-called 'democracy' of which Westerners are so proud? How is it possible that two starkly opposing conclusions coexisted about an event which occurred in broad daylight and in the presence of photographs, video clips, and over a thousand witnesses?"[38]

The two photographs in *Ouhua Lianhe Shibao* appear side by side on the editorial page, a style that mimics and satirizes the typical layout of views on the Chinese community as used in the Italian press and on Italian television, an example of pop politics in the Italian media (see chapter 2). Perhaps sensing this media's indifference to improving conditions for Italy's Chinese, the editorial ends on a Sinocentric note, providing catharsis for its Chinese readers and asking them to band together: "In this world, where there is a place, there are Chinese people. As the sun will never set, the Chinese will never fall! We should hold our heads high and be proud to be Chinese!"[39]

Moreover, *Ouzhou Qiaobao* fought disparaging and morally ambiguous Italian depictions of the riot by putting forward its own account. The newspaper made strategic use of discursive and physical spaces to better acquaint Chinese migrants with its perspectives on the riot. It published a special issue on 13 April that offered a narrative of the riot in Chinese; featured numerous articles informing readers about how its take differed greatly from Italian ones; and protested Forza Nuova's anti-Chinese racist slurs. *Ouzhou Qiaobao* displayed copies of the special issue on the walls in Via Sarpi, using a Chinese custom familiar to migrants. This visibility performed a community victimhood narrative, which the newspaper used to seek consensus on its reading of the riot from its heterogeneous audience.

The publicization of the *Ouzhou Qiaobao* issue also helped its perspectives enter into various anti-Chinese Italian media. Television news on Italia 1 showed images of the display. Starting on 14 April, *Il Giornale* and *La Padania* published photographs of migrants reading the issue in Via Sarpi. *Libero* excerpted and translated three pieces from the special issue that addressed how the Chinese felt ambivalent about the proposed relocation to Arese, Bu's account of the initial quarrels, and the riot itself.[40] With no editorial commentary to orient a particular reading of these translations, what the three right-wing Italian newspapers intended to achieve by referring to Chinese perspectives is not immediately ascertainable. Likely, however, this operation reiterated the conservative view about migrants being misguided by their own media outlets, which were said to draw more on propaganda than on social reality.

Criticism of the Italian media as a political instrument was extensive in Associna's online forum, which provided unfiltered platform for ordinary Chinese migrants (and Italians) to express opinions about the riot. Compared to printed news editorials, the observations in the forum were much less concerned with consensus-building within the Chinese migrant community. Pop psychology and conspiracy theories regarding the Italians' motives abounded. In particular, we witness discussions about whether the Italians used the fight against migrants' economic crimes as a pretext to rein in Chinese business growth. We also see speculation about how Chinese migrants' extremely successful entrepreneurship had engendered jealousy in the Italians, thereby provoking retaliation.

As a forum member named federep argued, by making the riot a media spectacle yet failing to propose any concrete solution, mainstream Italian journalism reinforced the public's fixation on illegal Chinese business practices. To illustrate his argument, federep referred to similar recent events, including a violent clash between North African migrants and Italian police in Turin's Porta Palazzo neighbourhood, which did not attract widespread media attention. Indeed, in federep's opinion, insults directed at non-Chinese migrants in the Italian media rarely reached the same degree of offensiveness: "Tell me, how many Italians will take to the streets to defend the rights of overseas Chinese? ... The Italians only respect certain migrant communities, usually those who do not seem to be more successful than themselves." As federep implied, ever since it had become apparent that Chinese migrants would pay fines for using pushcarts in Via Sarpi because they wished to avoid direct clashes with Italian police, Italian law enforcement had unethically collected fines.[41] It is difficult to gauge the validity of this dark interpretation. Rumours abounded about the municipal governments' profit-making by fining the Chinese for street rules in Milan, and by confiscating their factories and facilities in Prato.

Recommendations

Apart from producing counterarguments to the Italian news media and for the benefit of its own community, the Chinese migrant media spent considerable time making recommendations to fellow migrants. They urged migrants to better integrate into Italian society in order to avoid the police's disciplinary actions in Via Sarpi and ordinary Italians' implicit racism. Specifically, news outlets sought to explain the cultural, behavioural, and business-related advantages of greater social integration to the average migrant. The main audience for these recommendations were Chinese residents in Italy, although when the texts were printed in bilingual editions, they also accommodated Italian readers in a display of the community's willingness to dialogue with the host society.

Media accounts painted a portrait of a conscientious and self-critical Chinese migrant community, showing a decorous way of suggesting reforms to politicians. In a key article published after the riot, *Cina in Italia*'s editor-in-chief, Hu Lanbo, uses a popular Chinese saying to warn migrants against the media's appetite for newsworthiness: "A dog that bites a person is not news, but a person who bites a dog is." While Italians should cultivate a better awareness of Chinese Italian cultural differences, Hu suggests, migrants should reflect on their own defects and conduct and on the positive things the Italian government had done for them. According to Hu, the low level of education of most of Italy's lower-middle-class Chinese remained the main obstacle to their integration. Therefore, an increase in migrants' cultural capital was of paramount importance. Hu also urges Italy to recruit highly skilled workers from China, especially Chinese students in Italy, by providing a more amiable work environment.[42]

Hu's article is a prominent example of the ethnocultural codes employed by migrant journalists who, like their pro-Chinese Italian colleagues, drew on Chinese and Italian cultures and customs to interpret state management of migrant incorporation. The example illustrates how an intercultural perspective risked ethnogenesis, even as it avoided ethnocentrism. Published in both Chinese and Italian, Hu's article adheres to *Cina in Italia*'s mission to cater to both Chinese- and Italian-speaking readers, an editorial practice that effectively removes any ethnocentric premise, as the text is accessible to readers of both languages with no apparent preference for either. However, Hu tends to assume that all Chinese migrants in Italy would identify with specific markers of Chinese high culture that arguably have geographical limitations. The text features an image of a mask with the left half face painted in the tradition of Beijing Opera and the right half face as a Venetian carnival mask, suggesting that Chinese-Italian conflicts masked deeper commonalities. Drawing on the Chinese government's official rhetoric of social harmony, Hu concludes: "China and Italy did not have conflicts in absolute terms in history. Instead, they share many things in common. Since both races are humanitarian, there is no reason why they cannot live together peacefully. Through concerted efforts on both sides, the Italians and the Chinese will undoubtedly overcome the current clashes and misunderstandings, and will live together in harmony."[43] Couched in ethnocultural terms, this passage assumes that the majority of Italy's Chinese identify with cultural and political references associated with Beijing (e.g., Beijing Opera) and the Chinese Central Government (e.g., a political discourse that exalts social harmony, tout court), even though they migrated from Zhejiang Province in search of a better entrepreneurial environment not attainable at home. Indeed, Hu tends to lump Chinese migrants into an ethnically and culturally coherent Chinese whole, erasing their geographic and any potential ideological differences.[44]

To rework an insight by Hall, the "rediscovered, essential identity" had the power to define a single perception of the Chinese diaspora in Italy. Through the mechanism of ethnic and cultural self-essentialization, this and other similarly conceived articles consolidated discourses about Beijing-centred hegemony within China and the Chinese diasporas and reenacted the basic tenets of Western orientalism about uncontaminated and unchangeable cultural essences. Meanwhile, Hu unproblematically posits Italy as a country with morality at its core. This assessment draws on official Occidentalism, by which Chen describes how "the Chinese government uses the essentialization of the West as a means for supporting a nationalism that suppresses its own people." Seen from this perspective, Hu aims to cultivate a positive opinion of the Italians among its Chinese readers by constructing fossilized versions of well-meaning Italians and Chinese.[45]

In the passage quoted above, Chinese "race" refers to Chinese ethnicity created by the Chinese state as an imagined community – namely, the "big Chinese family" whose members include not only mainlanders but also Chinese-identified persons outside mainland China. The references to this concept in the Chinese migrant and mainland media was a result of the Chinese government's programs to reconnect with overseas Chinese since the 1990s, when it viewed these individuals both as the racial embodiment of Chinese traditional culture and nationalism, and as amoral capitalists who might undermine Chinese national interests.[46] As Kevin Latham notes, for reasons related to entrepreneurship and to the preservation of Chinese identities, migrant newspapers often discussed the Chinese migrant community in Italy by associating it with mainland China and with the Chinese diasporas in Europe.[47] Indeed, Hu points to diverse interpretations of "homeland" in the triangle formed by the home country, host country, and migrant community. Was the migrants' homeland their native city, Zhejiang Province, mainland China, the Italian city in which they lived, or Italy?[48] By asking readers to consider "homeland" allegiances, Hu endorsed the concept, articulated in the ideology of the "big Chinese family," that no matter what migrants considered their homeland, their ethnocultural identity entitled them to feel Chinese and to be part of the global Chinese community. To what extent Italy's Chinese accepted or internalized this form of contemporary Chinese nationalism is difficult to gauge, owing to a lack of research. We do know that the rivalry between mainland China and Taiwan for overseas Chinese's political allegiance played out in Italy and elsewhere in Europe. This circumstance made indoctrinating patriotism among Chinese migrants a pivotal issue in the Chinese government's political approach to juggling domestic with foreign affairs.[49]

From a rhetorical perspective, the point here is not whether Italy's Chinese conformed to this ideology, but how Hu presented a unified and positive image of this community to its host society as well as to itself. Indeed, while Hu's many essentialist assumptions were conceptually problematic, they effectively helped to both protest negative Italian depictions and propose positive Chinese versions. The form of Chinese cultural nationalism Hu puts forth in the article was a continuation of what Arif Dirlik calls the Confucian revival during the 1990s economic ascendance of Asian societies: "an articulation of native culture (and an indigenous subjectivity) against Euro-American cultural hegemony."[50] In other words, ethnogenesis, as manifest in Hu's and other articles, provided Chinese migrants with a solid ground – the powerful Chinese cultural heritage – from which they could then mount Chinese-centred counterarguments to Italian criticisms of their community. Chinese culture also provided resources for migrant elites to articulate Chinese-centred interpretations of the riot and of the community's standing in Italian society.

Apart from recommendations based on Chinese culture and heritage, the press provided migrants with practical advice concerning social and business activities. These recommendations were meant to counter what Italian sources often called Chinese merchants' nagging ethnic and cultural behaviour. Indeed, they were mostly directed at new migrants from China who had to be quickly incorporated into the hierarchical Chinese migrant economic system in Italy, as well as at old-time migrants thought to persist in habits learned in China. To connect with a wide spectrum of readers who may have had limited education, these recommendations were usually blatantly pedagogical and moralistic. For example, in its news analysis, *Guangzhou Ribao* advocated the following: first, Chinese migrants should do more to integrate into the local culture by overcoming the language barrier and obeying Italian laws. Second, they should avoid being opportunistic with laws like those in the past who had tarnished the entire community's reputation.

Third, they should refrain from behaviour that Italians considered uncivilized. *Ouzhou Huaren Bao*, *Nanfang Zhoumou*, and the overseas edition of *Renmin Ribao* had similar observations.[51] Chinese migrants themselves often made these comments in keeping with the long-standing Chinese cultural requirement for self-reflection on conflicts.[52]

Further, when this behaviour blocked the advancement of migrants' business activities or social mobility in Italian society, most Chinese were forced to conform to social norms. Being disciplined for irregular conduct could be costly to their finance and migration agendas. *Guangzhou Ribao* quoted a migrant as observing that the merchants "all have borrowed money in their hometown to venture out. They would be harmed and trapped by the implementation of regulations [in Via Sarpi] in such a [strict] way."[53] An even more damaging consequence of blocked migration life impacted migrants' sense of self-worth. For instance, Chinese male migrants, in Italy and elsewhere, became businessmen in order to elevate their class status and masculine esteem. Positing *wen* (originally cultural attainment, but also cultural and educational capital) and *wu* (originally martial valour, but also athletic ability) as popular yardsticks of Chinese masculine identities, Kam Louie shows that in contemporary China wen has primacy over wu, and that a man's wen can be enhanced by the possession of greater economic capital.[54] In the Chinese migrant media, being a successful entrepreneur meant, for the most part, being a successful man, with all the symbolic values attached to this image. To lose this painstakingly built image over social and business behaviour that could be corrected with relative ease would be reckless.

For the Chinese migrant press, then, when migrants modified unbecoming behaviour, they improved and expanded the community's business prospects. Chinese merchants commonly perceived the Milanese city government's proposal to relocate wholesaler stores to Arese as detrimental to their businesses. *Ouhua Lianhe Shibao* intimated, however, that more opportunities might become available for merchants there, because Milan intended to capitalize on the construction of the Corridor Rotterdam-Genoa railway in order to replace Rome as Southern Europe's transportation hub. Such an analysis placed Italy's Chinese migrant entrepreneurship at the centre of Milan's future economic prospects, as the newspaper considered migrants' business strategies in relation to Italy's role in the European Union's integrated economy. In providing comprehensible and relevant business analyses, the newspaper clarified how migrant entrepreneurs and workers needed to further integrate with the mainstream Italian economy and society in order to take full advantage of emerging opportunities. In the Chinese migrant media, this intra-European perspective on migrant entrepreneurship was a distinctive topic; in the Italian media, it was barely raised.[55]

Political Representation and Participation

Ouhua Lianhe Shibao questioned the efficacy of violent protests in protecting migrants' rights, and *Ouzhou Qiaobao* critiqued the stringent implementation of street rules in Milan's Chinatown as a pretext for certain politicians to gain votes among local Italian residents, a scheme in which Chinese and other migrants mattered very little because most of them, as non-Italian citizens, could not vote.[56] For these newspapers, without adequate political intervention there was no mechanism to keep Italian police and municipal authorities from taking drastic actions against Milan's Chinese. For many news commentators, Italian local and state governments neglected to assist migrants and ignored their legitimate requests because the political benefits of devising and implementing policies that would improve migrants' daily life, such as their day-to-day concerns about petty crimes and racist slurs, were few. The stringent implementation of street rules in Via Sarpi was neither considered nor deliberated as an immigrant-related policy, even though the rule almost exclusively impacted Chinese migrants. Ultimately, these newspapers called for a direct representation for Chinese migrants in Milan's city council, as well as for a path to Italian citizenship so that migrants could confidently vote in elections, a form of political participation.

Political representation was necessary because Italian politicians' mediation between Milan's government and the Chinese migrant community was neither adequate nor interest-free. Stefano Di Martino was a case in point. Then the vice president of Milan's city council and a member of Alleanza Nazionale, Di Martino was the only prominent right-leaning politician who participated in the riot and spoke positively about the Chinese in the Italian media. In 2008, the Chinese government recognized Di Martino's contributions by naming him an ambassador of friendship with the Chinese People in the World. However, in 2010 Di Martino's credentials were questioned when news came out that – with the cooperation of Emanuela Troisi, then the director of a Chinese-Italian cultural association named Alkeos – he had misused Milan's city funds intended for Chinese-Italian intercultural projects. In 2012, Di Martino and Troisi's misconduct was proven in court.[57]

To prevent such cases in the future, the Chinese migrant media argued that members of their community should serve on Italian municipal government committees on civic matters. At least one such example existed at the time of the riot. In 2006–7, Liu Cheng served as the adjunct foreign city councillor (consigliere straniero aggiunto), a position that was meant to represent immigrants' interests, on Ancona's city council. More recently, in 2014, the first city councillor (consigliere comunale) of Chinese origins, Angelo Hu, was elected in Campi Bisenzio.[58]

While forms of Chinese migrants' direct representation in Italian politics were emerging, the political participation of the vote still eluded most because they lacked Italian citizenship. Italian nationality laws put stringent and elaborate regulations on becoming citizens, even for young Chinese Italians who were born or grew up in the country, not to mention the vast majority of first-generation Chinese migrants. As demonstrated by posts on the website of the popular second-generation migrants' association Rete G2, Chinese Italians were keenly aware of the consequences of their lack of political capital in everyday life in Italy.[59] A more extended example of this concern came from Associna's online forum after the riot. At the time of my research, a forum post dated 12 April and titled "Milan: Revolt in Paolo Sarpi" had received approximately 25,000 views and 490 replies.[60] The development of discussions there from 12 to 16 April spoke volumes about the users' activation of the Italian-Chinese migrant cultural repertoire: the presentation of specific topics, the ethnocultural approach, and, most importantly, the institutional milieu in which Chinese migrants in Italy came to recognize political participation and representation as the most effective routes to fight discrimination.

The initial posts primarily offered a more comprehensive and impartial account of the riot than the one available in the mainstream Italian media. Later, several users started to denigrate the Chinese, drawing on Italian stereotypes of migrants such as the Chinese mafia. In countering these comments, other users offered Chinese stereotypes of the Italians such as their infamous laziness. What ensued from these formulaic altercations was an acrimonious debate on supposedly irreconcilable cultural differences between the Italians and the Chinese. *feilong*, a forum member who identified himself as an Italian native, lashed out with provocative anti-Chinese and anti-Zhejiangnese slurs, for which he immediately received indignant rebuttals. As a Chinese Italian, *lichunhaug*, conscious of their generation's responsibility to "become spokespersons for our community and to emphasize our rights and justifications," stressed that "above all, the system does not work. To be Chinese is not an easy trade ['mestiere']." Using the word "ethnocentrism" to critique the presumed inability for Chinese migrants and Italians to communicate because of their cultural differences, lichunhaug underscored the need for migrants to have voting rights if they were to negotiate effectively with Milan's government.[61]

In this example, we witness, on the one hand, how the issue of citizenship rights came back to the vertical relationship between the state and migrants.[62] That is, if Chinese migrants and Chinese Italians had had more political power to vote as Italian citizens, then Milan's city council would have had to deliberate more about the consequences of harsh street rules in Via Sarpi. This reasoning would oppose the ethnocultural impulse in the current media discourses on multiculturalism and citizenship rights in Italy, because the heart of the debate would revolve around whether migrants were entitled to become citizens, and if so via what path. In other words, the debate would not focus exclusively on whether or not Chinese migrants were capable of incorporation into Italian society based on the cultural and social values of their home country.

We also witness, on the other hand, how the multicultural project through nationality can also return to a horizontal relationship among members of different groups: how Italians and Chinese migrants relate to one another. As I have underscored in this chapter, the application of stringent street rules to Milan's Chinatown was not a policy created for the Chinese only, even though it functioned that way. At the core of the discontent that led to the riot was the ways in which Italian residents and Chinese merchants in Via Sarpi were not entirely able to accommodate one another in their social, commercial, and spatial practices. As I have shown, a great deal of anti-Chinese coverage stemmed not only from a dissatisfaction with the city government's inefficient institutional disciplining of migrants' economic behaviour, but also from a critique of their encroachment on Italians' social welfare, including the enjoyment of familiar neighbourhood spaces and stores. Had a state-level multicultural project aimed to build a democratic citizenship between the Italians and the Chinese, and between locals and migrants in general, would we still have witnessed anti-Chinese media comments that appeared to breach basic tenets of human rights, civil liberties, and accountability?

I view this as the fundamental question beneath many Italian and Chinese migrant media suggestions on how to move the Italian-Chinese relationship forward after the riot. However, Chinese migrant media coverage rarely tackled this question directly, and instead focused on social agents with the potential to help induce a change in Italian citizenship laws from the bottom up. Like in the Italian media previously examined, the most frequently proposed group was young, predominantly second-generation Chinese Italians. They were the ideal candidates to enter Italian politics as representatives of the community and as career politicians. Their mediation would greatly diversify the cadre of Italian-Chinese intermediaries, which at the time of the riot was largely composed of better educated first-generation elite Chinese migrants, Italian experts on China, and unqualified politicians like Di Martino. To borrow a term that Mary Louise Pratt uses in the colonial context, Chinese Italians worked in "contact zones" in which they and the Italians had already met and negotiated their encounters and would continue to do so.[63]

Ouzhou Qiaobao even promoted Italian youth as the bridge generation that would foster a better multicultural project in Italy. Such youth were pro-Chinese Italian allies who sympathized with Chinese migrants because of their shared social marginalization. To develop this line of thinking, the newspaper covered the anti-racist campaigns of the Italians associated with the Centro Sociale Cantiere, an organization formed by Italian students and individuals with precarious work. According to *Ouzhou Qiaobao*, these young Italians staged music performances in a demonstration following the riot to show their love for the Chinese and their hatred of the Italian police's brutality. A special issue of the same newspaper published two photographs in which two Italian young men were depicted protesting alongside Chinese migrants. One man wrapped the Chinese flag around his body, while the other held a piece of paper that read "The Chinese are not the Sick Men of East Asia."[64]

The irony of proposing second-generation Chinese Italians and young Italians as intermediaries was that neither had a say in realpolitik. An environment that would accord Italian political participation and citizenship to migrants could only be created with the consent of Italy's ruling class. As I examined in the previous chapter, certain elite Italian politicians, such as Giuliano Amato, did support the Chinese migrant community, if not in action at least in spirit. But Amato's 2006 proposal to reform Italy's nationality law failed, which highlighted a political stalemate that Giovanna Zincone characterizes as one "between citizenship conceived mainly as an instrument of integration (typical of the left) and citizenship conceived as a reward for accomplished integration (typical of the right)."[65]

Indeed, in 2007, the institutional obstacles to migrants' political incorporation outnumbered the incentives. Consider the activities by older Italian male citizens often associated with ViviSarpi, who were part of an important electorate, and those by Gian Paolo Gobbo of

Lega Nord, then major of Treviso, around the time of the riot. ViviSarpi posted several video clips, titled "Between Degradation and Illegality," on its website, accusing the entire spectrum of Chinese business operations of damaging Via Sarpi's local community. Footage in these clips, which exclusively focused on illegal Chinese activities, fleshed out the sensational and defamatory slogans used against migrants. Edited interviews of Italians' negative experiences with the Chinese further underscored the necessity of the association's campaign to pressure Milan's city government to implement stricter regulations on Chinese businesses. In May 2007, Gobbo approved a regulation in Treviso that prohibited Chinese restaurants from hanging red lanterns, on the grounds that they exhibited excessively "oriental characteristics." In response, *Ouhua Lianhe Shibao* jokingly remarked that by this line of reasoning, the Italian team should not be allowed to show their national flag upon entering the stadium at the opening ceremony of the 2008 Olympics in Beijing, because that gesture, too, would be a blatant exhibition of their Italian national identity.[66]

In June 2010, the final court verdict on the riot proved to be a major disappointment for Chinese migrants. Thirty-seven Chinese individuals were charged, and Bu was jailed for five months and twenty days for her aggression towards the traffic officers. The *Repubblica* article that announced the news focused on the incident involving Di Martino. Upon the verdict's announcement, *Xinhua Lianhe Shibao* alerted readers to the importance of respecting Italian laws when interacting with the authorities, citing the charges against Di Martino as a proof of the Italian court's impartiality.[67]

Rampini's description of San Francisco's Chinatown as an ethnic tourist Mecca anticipated Milan's urban project in Via Sarpi in the late 2000s and early 2010s. Following the riot, *Il Manifesto* also recognized the area's desirability as a tourist destination: "Milan's Chinatown is Italy's most multi-ethnic showcase, a place that would be included in every tour guide, had it been in a normal city." Even *La Padania* endorsed this view after the riot.[68] Meanwhile, most of the Chinese wholesalers agreed to relocate to Arese, as a portion of Via Sarpi was remodelled as a pedestrian area that opened to the public in 2011. The redevelopment of Milan's Chinatown as an ethnic shopping and tourist area garnered consent across a wide political spectrum. This was the result of neoliberal urban planning in contemporary Western societies, which focuses on the knowledge, finance, entertainment, and culture industries that can be brought to repurpose and revitalize specific locales.[69]

Whether these efforts would raise the prestige of Milan's Chinatown to those in other European and American cities in the years to come remained dubious, as *Corriere della Sera* and La7 covered the project's less-than-stellar success in 2011.[70] In 2012, the final year that I examine in this book, I observed that several Chinese wholesaler stores still operated in Via Sarpi, but with much lighter merchandise transport, particularly on the neighbourhood's main commercial street. In December of that year, red lanterns adorned the street lamps in preparation for the Chinese New Year.

Having examined the Italian-migrant frame in chapters 3 and 4 that focuses on various issues regarding migrant integration, in the next two chapters I turn to the local-global frame that addresses Chinese migrants in relation to Italy's economic globalization by using the fast-fashion manufacturing in Prato as a case study. This switch in focus is for analytical purposes, and does not imply that the newsworthy topics, discursive strategies, and other approaches and perspectives examined in this and the previous chapters are invalid for the Prato case study. Quite the contrary; in chapters 5 and 6 I show that the basic Italian-Chinese migrant frame persisted: after all, migrants' insertion in the Italian economy is part of their incorporation. But the great novelty of the conflicts in Prato was that international news outlets intervened in debates about a migration that initially appeared to concern only Italy and China. Not surprisingly, Prato's Italian and Chinese migrant media also addressed international audiences and attempted to sway their opinions and rebrand the city in their eyes.

Chapter 5

Prato: Local Debates on "Made in Italy" by the Chinese, 2005–2012

Following a medieval tradition, since the end of the Second World War Prato's industrial district has focused on textile production.[1] Between 1940s and 1980s, a majority of local workers, many of whom had migrated from the countryside and Southern Italy to Prato after the Second World War, turned regenerated carded wool into fabrics. In the mid-1980s, a crisis occurred in the carded wool sector, causing some of Prato's entrepreneurs to upgrade the quality of their wool fabrics and yarns, and others to make medium- to high-quality fabrics out of other fibres. Many local contractors, particularly those who specialized in spinning and weaving, closed down: they were unable to work with new types of fabrics, and it was more advantageous for manufacturers to import semi-finished materials than to produce them in Prato. However, the entrepreneurs who successfully offered new products worked with acclaimed Italian ready-to-wear fashion designers to build the "Made in Italy" trademark and acquire a worldwide clientele.[2]

Therefore, in the early 1990s Prato's textile industry re-established its economic status and diversified its product profile, enjoying a positive expansion, which then supported a few clothing firms and a knitwear sector. Chinese migrants played a crucial role in this revival in both textile and garment industries. As fast fashion gradually grew in Europe in the same decade to more quickly respond to customer tastes, its much shorter production and delivery time required that many design choices, such as colour and trimmings, be made at the end of the production cycle, creating an opportunity for Chinese migrants to own dyeing and finishing firms. Moreover, clothing workshops commissioned Prato's Chinese primarily as contractors in various standardized phases of garment manufacturing – such as cutting, sewing, finishing, and ironing – because unlike leading garment firms that could outsource globally to drive down production costs, small Italian enterprises were only able to use local resources, such as cheaper Chinese migrant labour provided. As Italian companies from other parts of the country, including major fashion houses, also entered fast fashion and maintained lower-priced lines, Prato's Chinese contracting firms began to work for their orders. In the late 1990s, Prato's fast-fashion sector became the largest concentration of Chinese migrant enterprises and factories in Europe.

In the late 1990s and early 2000s, elite Chinese entrepreneurs in Prato transformed from specialized contractors in various phases of garment manufacturing into owners of final-good firms specialized in product design, marketing, distribution (e.g., wholesale and import-export), and management of contracted work within the Chinese migrant entrepreneurial network. As Antonella Ceccagno observes, Prato was "the only place in Italy where Chinese migrants have managed to become manufacturers themselves in large numbers," as contractors for both Italian and Chinese migrant manufacturers.[3] Thus, during the 2000s, the specialties of Prato's Chinese factories ranged from fabric dyeing, tailoring, and fashion design to garment manufacturing and wholesaler product distribution, although the scope of fabric production and design remained limited. In 2006–7, Chinese migrants operated 300 to 500 final-product firms in the city. By 2009, they operated between 4,000 and 5,000 garment firms in Prato, and one out of four companies in the city was Chinese-owned. In the late 2000s and early 2010s, they owned about 80 per cent of the market share of Prato's garment sector. By then, they had already become the dominant migrant community in Prato, and officially constituted about 50 per cent of its total migrant population throughout the 2000s.[4]

Meanwhile, how did the Italian-owned firms in Prato perform? From the early 2000s onwards, many clothing firms and many more textile firms have gone out of business, causing many workers to experience early retirement and mortgage foreclosures. According to Ceccagno, the reasons for the diminishing number of Italian-owned businesses in Prato are complex and partially unclear. To be sure, the downsizing of Prato's native textile industry occurred because Chinese migrant and Italian companies often did not use Italian textiles as fabrics, preferring to rework semi-finished products imported from China, Turkey, or eastern Europe. Moreover, as Chinese contractors gradually replaced Italian ones in Prato's apparel sector, and as Italians moved to upper-end production or hired Chinese migrants, the overall number of Italian firms declined. However, it is not certain whether the closures occurred primarily because of competition from Chinese migrants, or because of other factors such as Prato's younger generations' disinterest in continuing their family businesses, which caused an acute generational gap.[5]

Prato's recent economic and industrial restructuring presented a problem of symbols and values. The city, together with its textile industry, was a celebrated postwar symbol of the Italian economy, driven by successful small- and medium-sized enterprises in competitive industrial districts. However, since the 1990s, as Ceccagno observes, "the Prato centre has developed as a loosely connected fast fashion global value chain along with major European brands such as Zara and H&M."[6] By the early 2010s, Prato had become primarily known as the foremost European exporter of low-end "Made in Italy" fast fashion produced by Chinese migrants. The locals witnessed such changes in its national and international reputations with trepidation. According to the critic Gabi Dei Ottati, "After approximately two decades since the start of the downsizing of the Prato textile system, the latter remains the heart of the district, not only because of the number of workers employed and the added value produced, but also for reasons of identity and of production knowledge embedded locally."[7] When local entrepreneurs, politicians, and journalists nurtured such an image of Prato, they viewed the Chinese input in fast fashion as non-Italian and exceptional, despite the Italians' involvement in the sector and the migrants' overall contributions to the city's economy.

The larger global garment manufacturing trends and Chinese migrants' business practices in Prato seemed to only give the Italians more reasons to resist the industrial, economic, and reputational transformations. The city's Chinese reaped considerable economic profits and gained a European-wide influence relatively quickly by working in a single sector: fast fashion. Fast fashion yields high profits due to its responsiveness to consumer desires and short production time: market tastes change quickly and garments must be designed and manufactured within a strict timeframe to satisfy them, sometimes within weeks. Fast fashion also requires highly organized transnational distribution networks, and largely depends on relatively free access to local markets in countries where low-end but trendy garments are in demand and can be quickly consumed. Finally, the low-cost labour and low- to medium-quality fabrics ensure low pricing. In order to enhance productivity and employment, Prato's Chinese adopted a mobile regime in which they slept in or near the workshops and moved frequently among them.[8]

While many journalists both in Italy and abroad had a basic understanding of how fast fashion had led the Chinese to adopt sweatshops, illegal labour, and other questionable business practices, they nonetheless interpreted the success of Italy's Chinese in such a stressful industry as the result of economic crimes. As media coverage often depicts, migrants typically lived in enclosed spaces that served as both workshops and living quarters, and that frequently lacked basic hygiene and safety measures. Many Chinese worked in these sweatshops for very long hours and on most days of the year. When orders had tight time constraints workers quit sleeping to fulfill them, causing noises day and night and ignoring regulations for garbage disposal. Chinese migrant entrepreneurs sometimes mislabelled garments imported from China as "Made in Italy," counterfeited Italian fashion brands, hired conationals without work authorization, enforced unreasonable rules that infringed on sweatshop workers' human rights, paid these workers salaries below the standard rates for similar jobs done by Italians, evaded taxes, laundered money, hired criminals to settle debts, and so on.

During much of the 1990s and 2000s, Italian institutions often tolerated illegal economic practices within Prato's Chinese migrant entrepreneurship, because they ultimately benefited Italian fast fashion manufacturers and other garment and accessories sectors. However, beginning in the mid-2000s and under increasing pressure from local textile producers and business owners, government officials and police could no longer take a laissez-faire attitude towards Chinese migrants' real or supposed illegal business activities. Between 2009 and 2011, after Prato's first post-Second World War right-wing government took office, Italian institutional surveillance and punishment of Chinese illegal workshops became extremely severe. The police raided factories, arrested illegal migrants, confiscated sewing machines, and closed sweatshops. Although the outcomes of these activities were mixed, the stated goal was to curb illegal businesses practices so as to protect the native Italian textile industry and the "Made in Italy" label. Against this backdrop, in chapters 5 and 6, I examine how and why the local and international news media shaped and disseminated specific views of the Prato case study.

Key Media Debates and the Master Narrative

From 2005 to 2012, Prato's economic and social drama spurred two main media debates. These were additional examples of two essential topics and their related discursive strategies in the Italian-Chinese migrant cultural repertoire that I examined in chapters 3 and 4 – namely, Italian institutional disciplinary actions against illegal Chinese migrant business activities, and the competition between the multicultural and nativist approaches to Italian national identity that migration increasingly challenged.

The first media debate concerned the use of police raids to constrain the activities of Prato's Chinese migrant entrepreneurship. Influential Italian industrialists and politicians claimed that economic crimes were behind migrants' entrepreneurial success, the collapse of Italian factories, and social unrest. For these Italians, increasing police crackdowns in the late 2000s were necessary to curb this unfair competition. In response, Chinese migrant entrepreneurs attributed their success to their timely responses to global market developments and to their familiarity with the Italian economy's inner workings. By 2009, Italian journalists generally admitted that neither all Chinese garment factories nor the entire fast-fashion sector engaged in economic crimes. They had also covered the widespread collaboration between Chinese migrants and major Italian fashion houses that embittered Prato's provincial industrialists whose fabrics the latter no longer desired.

Were the raids meant to combat Italy's underground economy in order to ensure equal opportunities for Chinese migrants, major Italian fashion houses, and artisan fabric producers in Prato? Were they meant to assuage the sense of failure among Italian industrialists of small- and medium-sized enterprises? Were they meant to help Prato's government continue to exploit Chinese migrants' low-cost labour and global export networks for tax revenue and for the city's economic gain?

The second media debate concerned whether Prato's "Made in Italy" label was sufficiently distinguished from the "Made in China" industry that garments made by the city's Chinese were often perceived to represent. For some, Prato's Chinese were dedicated to self-employment, and shunned any Italian participation in their production lines. From this perspective, the migrants' only agenda was to exploit the city's "Made in Italy" reputation by manufacturing low-end garments, which tarnished the label's prestige. For others, local Chinese significantly helped to remake "Made in Italy" fashion, first by working in Prato's clothing and knitwear factories in the 1990s and then by manufacturing garments for major Italian fashion houses in the 2000s, because both modes decreased the outsourcing that had become the norm in the fashion industry. Indeed, in *Panorama*, Ceccegno observed that some illegal activities within Italy's Chinese companies, such as working overtime to satisfy rapidly shifting consumer tastes, "became fundamental to the competitiveness of 'Made in Italy'" because of their adaptability to the "flexibility and externalization of costs, which are characteristic of a new, globalized production."[9] Moreover, the media praised Chinese entrepreneurs for creating their own high-quality fashion brands in collaboration with Italian designers, a phenomenon that helped to diversify the "Made in Italy" system.

No one disputed that Prato's family-owned textile businesses were the traditional suppliers of high-end "Made in Italy" fashion predominantly made outside the city. But should low- and middle-quality garments carry the "Made in Italy" label if they were made in Prato by Chinese migrants, with fabrics imported from China, and on behalf of major Italian fashion houses and international brands? Should Chinese-owned fashion brands in Prato and elsewhere in the country carry the "Made in Italy" label, especially when they employed Italian designers and Italy's Chinese workers, and used both Italian and Chinese textiles?

To address these questions and debates, in this chapter I focus on Italian and Chinese migrant media perspectives in Prato and across Italy (local debates), while in chapter 6 I examine American, German, and Japanese media perspectives (international debates). I emphasize police investigations in this chapter because they were locally oriented disciplinary measures, while in the following chapter I examine the competition between the "Made in China" and "Made in Italy" labels that was vital for Prato's globalized businesses. However, this division of analytical foci does not imply that raids were only discussed in the Italian media, or that "Made in Italy" was only discussed in the international media. Rather, I underscore that raids disrupted the lives of Prato's Chinese and stimulated heated local media discussions, laying the groundwork for the success of a right-wing candidate in the 2009 local political elections, which then deepened the ongoing controversies. Meanwhile, the debate regarding the "Made in Italy" label had a global resonance, for it concerned Italy's and China's roles in the global apparel sector where both countries excelled and competed.

In chapters 5 and 6, I contend that in untangling the complexity of Prato's Italian-Chinese migrant encounters, journalists produced a master narrative that was articulated locally and globally. At the local level, the narrative accentuated the specific economic and political circumstances of Prato's fast-fashion and ready-to-wear textile industries. Police raids were considered a necessary way to preserve the knowledge, expertise, and labour of those working for "Made in Italy" textile and garment industries. At the global level, the narrative argued that Prato was a prime example for other "Made in Italy" industries and for European countries because they faced tremendous competition from Chinese migrants and mainlanders as well. In particular, in journalists' accounts, the Prato case study illuminated problems that could arise for other labels and industries through its coverage of the use of police raids to crack down on migrants' illegal business activities in the name of preserving the internationally known "Made in Italy" fashion label and its associated manufacturing traditions and specializations. The symbiosis of the local-global emphases in journalistic narratives can be best appreciated through John Tomlinson's observation that "culturally informed 'local' actions can have globalizing consequences," and global processes inform and condition local actions.[10] Ultimately, this local-global master narrative validated and publicized concerted business and political strategies in Prato since the 2000s that had aimed to restrategize the city's competitiveness in the fashion and garment industry.

In this and the next chapters, I also propose that while the Italian versus Chinese migrant media, hegemonic versus counter-hegemonic, and decoding versus encoding model examined for the 2007 Milan riot held true for Prato in 2009 and 2010, these debates were not pronounced outside this time period. To be sure, the performative aspect of speeches that injure the Other remains clear in the Prato case study. As Judith Butler writes, the "offensive call runs the risk of inaugurating a subject in speech who comes to use language to counter the offensive call." That is, Chinese migrants continued to contend with discriminatory speeches in the Italian media that were "vulnerable to failure," a "vulnerability that must be exploited to counter the threat" to the legitimacy of their settlement in Prato.[11] Despite this media tension, mainstream Italian media was not particularly biased towards Prato's Chinese before 2009. In 2011 and 2012, the media also focused on migrants' successful economic and social insertion into the city. Thus, the Chinese migrant versus Italian media debate was most evident in times of perceived economic conflict, such as the police confiscation of Chinese-owned money transfer agencies' assets in 2010, and during political crises, such as the 2009 election of Prato's first right-leaning government since the Second World War. In this chapter, I focus on these local Italian-Chinese migrant media debates.

Towards the 2009 Local Elections

Prato's 2009 local elections made Roberto Cenni, who was supported by Il Popolo della Libertà (The people of freedom) and Lega Nord, the first conservative mayor in the city's postwar history. Having defeated his centre-left opponent, Massimo Carlesi, by a small margin (51.32 per cent for Cenni versus 48.68 per cent for Carlesi), Cenni assumed office on 22 June 2009 for the following five years.[12]

In February and March 2009, two emotionally charged televised events articulated the conservative political agenda supported by

Prato's increasingly discontent voters. Both events aimed to protect the city's "Made in Italy" reputation and to endorse frequent police raids. Television was the primary medium for discussing widely shared anti-Italian state and anti-Chinese sentiments, as the events' protagonists claimed that the state's negligence and Chinese migrants' supposed takeover of the local economy had caused Prato's crisis. In such media interpretations, the city's declining textile industry often stood in for all small- and medium-sized entrepreneurship in Italy, a synecdoche necessary to request state interventions including direct financial assistance, lower taxes, reduction of energy costs for manufacturing, and so on.

Prato witnessed its most cathartic moment of popular nationalism in recent local memory on 28 February 2009. Eight thousand textile workers and business owners, along with representatives of labour unions and public institutions, demonstrated and demanded state financial assistance comparable to that already given to Italian automobile and home appliance companies. The rhetorical devices used during this event were primarily visual and televisual. As memorably caught on camera and shown on Rai and Prato TV, protestors circled the Piazza Mercatale, the city's main square, with a one-kilometre-long banner of the tricolour Italian flag. The white part of the banner contained the slogan "Prato non deve chiudere" (Prato must not close). The same slogan appeared on another banner in the centre of the square. As many sequences in the television coverage and news photographs can attest, these banners were intended for an aerial view, such as from the helicopter that filmed the central slogan before panning to reveal the full extent of the larger banner, which stretched out into the city's streets.[13]

The demonstration's pathos lay largely in evoking Italian identity as the core value of "Made in Prato" fabrics. On this topic, however, the demonstration sent a contradictory message. On the one hand, by asking for greater state interventions into their family-owned businesses, the protestors seemed to contradict the dominant social fiction about Prato because, following Costis Hadjimichalis, "the success of small-scale flexible capitalism, with its highly individualistic and competitive character … creates employment, increases family income and boosts exports without assistance from central state."[14] On the other hand, the locals expected greater state financial assistance to help them preserve and strengthen the artisan production model, thereby keeping the heroic social fiction alive. This contradiction pointed to symbolic ambivalence of the "Made in Italy" label: it was both a mark of individualistic artistry in a place like Prato, and also a globally oriented product associated with the Italian nation-state and Italian identity.

Like the 28 February demonstration, Prato's workers and industrialists staged their protest on the popular Rai show, *Annozero* (Year zero), providing another example of the conscious and collective dramatization of a social trauma through contemporary Italy's dominant media: television. The show offered in-depth commentaries on social and political issues on Rai Due, the traditional Rai channel of political opposition to Italy's governing parties, with ratings just behind those of Rai Uno and Mediaset's Canale 5. On 19 March 2009, *Annozero* aired an episode titled "The Red and the Black," with two parts respectively focused on Chinese migration in Prato and on Italy's informal economy.[15] The episode's title gives away what Maurizio Ambrosini notes as the fallacious association of Italy's migrant workers with the black market, rather than with the production logic of the industrial districts in central and northern Italy, including Prato. Indeed, as Michael Blim argues, the Italian underground economy was fed by and served postwar industrialization in these areas, which was "at once spontaneous, small scale, and flexible in production method, export-led and niche-finding in its marketing, familial in organization, and petty entrepreneurial in character."[16]

The presentation of Prato in "The Red and the Black" only makes the erroneous association of migrants with the underground economy more apparent. In the first part of the episode, we see workers and entrepreneurs gathering in the city's Santo Stefano factory where the Italian flag used in the 28 February demonstration is spread out on the floor. Meanwhile, left-wing and right-wing politicians and journalists sit with the program's host on opposite sides of the television studio, showing the tendency towards pop politics in *Annozero* and in Italian talk shows as a whole (see the similar formula examined in chapters 3 and 4).[17] The dramatic set-up gives a pleasurable viewing and listening experience to contrasting opinions.

The segment's narrative features the locals' denunciation of the Italian state and of Chinese migrants. Several interviews with Italian textile workers and entrepreneurs relate the trauma of their failing businesses and their apprehension about the future. The head of the Santo Stefano company complains about the state's mismanagement of small- and medium-sized enterprises in Prato, Italy's 1995 entry into the World Trade Organization, and the usurpation of the "Made in Italy" label by China and other countries. As if to show evidence, the camera pans from the industrialist to a Chinese factory located next door to the Italian factory. What are the workers in the Chinese factory doing at this hour of the evening? Rather than move inside that particular factory, the camera cuts to pre-recorded footage of a police raid in a Chinese sweatshop, where the main investigator explains how such factories operate. In another clip, a journalist makes a brief trip to Prato's Chinatown but fails to engage migrants in her cursory investigation into the matter, as no Chinese seems willing to offer their perspective. The explanatory power passes to Italian journalists and politicians in *Annozero*'s studio, who debate following the video clips. Later, the debates are jarringly interrupted by the second part of the episode, which focuses on Italy's underground economy.[18]

The episode's narrative relies on the two video clips to inform the audience about the causes and current state of Prato's textile and garment industries. Similar to coverage of the same subject aired on Rai Tre in 2010 and 2011, the clips are the building blocks of the viewer's visual memory of migrants' illegal business practices.[19] Their visual economy draws on the Italians' mobility in Chinese spaces. The first clip was shot in a mostly participatory style from the perspective of the Italian financial police on-site in the sweatshop. Driven by a desire to uncover illegal practices, the camera dwells on the unusual arrangement of space: the workshop, dormitory, leisure quarters, and kitchen all jammed into one airtight, enclosed warehouse. The camera also captures the Chinese, who look on as though the raid is a common occurrence. Although three undocumented migrants are taken away, the head officer explains that further evidence would be needed before permanently closing the sweatshop. Thus, this video clip makes two widely accepted, yet imprecise and controversial, points for the average viewer. First, Chinese economic crimes in counterfeit and other illegal activities were indisputable and pervasive, as demonstrated by their abusive use of the workshop spaces and enhanced by the police discourse that turned one episode into a generic scenario. Second, the "Chinese invasion," a metaphor often used in the mass media to refer to either Chinese migrants or Chinese mainlanders in Italy, resulted both from these migrants' illegal activities and from the complex bureaucratic procedures required to effectively implement Italian regulations and eradicate irregular business practices.

The second clip is equally biased: it shows a journalist's visit to several Chinese retailers and to a street in Prato's Via Pistoiese area, where she attempts but fails to visit a factory. The camera captures long shots of many houses in the area, in which the first floors are workshops and the second floors are living quarters. Previously belonging to Italian artisans, these houses had been purchased and occupied by Chinese migrants.[20] Such knowledge of the changing work-living arrangements in the neighbourhood must have already conditioned many viewers' negative judgments of the Chinese invasion. Most migrants give curt answers to the journalist's blunt questions about how many people they employ and about the Chinese origin of the fabrics they transport. They repeatedly turn down the journalist's requests to visit their property. To the average viewer, the clip thus makes these Chinese silent on their illegal business practices. There could well have been a legitimate explanation of the phenomenon had it been fully explored. However, reasons such as migrants' concerns with protecting their business tactics from outsiders and from one another within the community, for instance, are not adequately considered before drawing conclusions.

Furthermore, in associating unlawful business practices with Chinese ethnicity, these clips confuse Prato's Chinese with mainland Chinese in order to address economic globalization and migrant entrepreneurship. When these two groups were construed as a homogeneous entity, media discourses on the competition between mainland Chinese and Italian firms could be recycled with little modification to address conflicts between Chinese migrant and Italian firms. In this view, "Made in Italy" fashion faced challenges from two major sources that were, in fact, one. On the one hand, Prato's Chinese manufactured low- and middle-quality "Made in Italy" garments, a sector said to be part of the "Made in China" production chain. On the other hand, mainland China manufactured counterfeit "Made in Italy" garments as either final or semi-final products, which migrants then imported to Italy for various European markets. Indeed, Ceccagno posits that "in a global context where diasporas are more and more depicted as part and parcel of their country of origin's transnational strategies, [Chinese] migrants will increasingly bear the burden of perceptions and dominant discourses at global, national, and local level about their home country."[21] The erasure of crucial differences between these two groups based on their shared ethnicity drew on ethnocultural essentialism.

"The Red and the Black" demonstrates this erasure when the host solicits comments on the Chinese migrant entrepreneurship from three journalists, namely Silvia Pieraccini of *Il Sole 24 Ore*, Nicola Porro of *Il Giornale*, and Fabrizio Gatti of *L'Espresso*. Pieraccini, the author of a 2008 book titled *L'assedio cinese* (The Chinese siege), neatly blames Chinese economic crimes for causing the failure of many Italian firms and for tarnishing the "Made in Italy" label. She identifies two kinds of "Made in Italy" fashion: the genuine kind produced by Italians who now faced unfair competition from Chinese migrants and mainland Chinese; and the fake kind produced by Chinese who were only interested in taking advantage of the prestigious label to export "Made in China" fashion, repackaged in Italy, to other European markets. Pieraccini's central contention about "Made in Italy" is that it must be made by native Italians.

In the episode, while the other two journalists contradict Pieraccini when she resorts to rather bold and exaggerated language to make her arguments about Italy's underground economy and about migrants' supposed tax evasion, her ethnogenesis-based thesis on migrant entrepreneurship remains unchallenged.

Pieraccini's stance here on Prato's Chinese migrant entrepreneurship is a nativist and ethically ambiguous journalistic interpretation of the "Made in Italy" label. The journalist worked at *Il Sole 24 Ore*, the newspaper of the Confindustria with one of the most complete "Codes of Self-Discipline" regulating reporters' ethical behaviour in Italy.[22] But Pieraccini's repeated enunciation of the same arguments in *Il Sole 24 Ore*, and occasionally on Italian and international television, emboldened anti-Chinese individuals, particularly the corporate decision-makers who were the main readers of the leading national business newspaper.[23] Pieraccini was especially problematic because she belonged to the Ordine dei giornalisti (Order of the journalists), one of the organizations that issued the 2008 "Carta di Roma," an important deontological document about how to address immigration to Italy and how to discuss immigrants.[24] While Pieraccini's was an extreme case, as "The Red and the Black" shows, many journalists and editors, whether consciously or not, were responsible for allowing a narrow definition of "Made in Italy" to go uncontested in 2009.

Television coverage of the February demonstration and the March "The Red and the Black" *Annozero* episode not only gave an early indication of the rightist turn in Prato's local elections in June, but also indirectly provided a platform for politicians to legitimate the intensifying police raids on Chinese factories in the months leading up to the elections. Journalists often referred to these raids using the word "blitz," of German etymology, which evokes efficiency, rapidity, strategy, and violence.[25] Raids conducted by Italian financial police on Chinese-owned factories had already begun by the mid-2000s, which the city's previous left-leaning government first ordered. Starting in 2007–8, as a result of the "Pact for a Secure Prato," the city government used agents from public security agencies for the raids.[26] But in 2009, because of the imminent election, the police investigations reached a climax and became the most concrete form of local institutional discipline of Chinese migrants.

Called the largest-ever "maxi blitz" to combat illegal Chinese migrant businesses in Italy, Operation Secure Economy took place in Prato on 29 April 2009 and continued throughout the following day. More than two hundred financial police were aided by canine units and by a helicopter from the Financial Police's Aerial Section in Pisa. Together, they inspected fifty companies, seized six companies' assets, found seventy irregular workers, and expelled fifty clandestine migrants. In addition, they uncovered 30,000 toys without the European Union's CE (Conformité Européenne) safety marking; 200,000 pieces of bags and accessories; seven kilometres of counterfeit Louis Vuitton fabrics; and 50,000 articles of clothing, of unclear origin, labelled "Made in Italy." As shown on Prato TV, the financial police provided the statistics.[27]

According to *La Nazione*, the raid's stated objectives were twofold: to uncover mainland Chinese counterfeits stitched with "Made in Italy" labels, and to break up Italy's Chinese migrant underground economy, which enslaved Chinese labourers. While "The Red and the Black" on *Annozero* focused on the factory's irregular use of space, *La Nazione* accentuated Chinese workers' inhuman working conditions. Like *La Nazione*, Rai and Prato TV offered similar readings of the situation, with commentary on labour exploitation over shots of sweatshops in disarray. Surely, the exploitation that irregular Chinese workers experienced at the hands of their Chinese employers deserved denunciation. However, such media narratives conveniently obscured the history of Chinese migrants' gradual insertion into Prato's economy in the previous twenty years or so, a history amply covered in the media prior to 2009, as I explore in the next chapter.[28]

The 2010 and 2011 Carrot-and-Stick Political and Business Negotiations

Once in office in June 2009, Cenni implemented policies to address both Chinese Italian cooperation and conflicts: the use of Italian fabrics in Chinese fast-fashion manufacturing, and the distinction between legal Italian and illegal Chinese business practices.[29] To my mind, drawing on business pragmatism and institutional repression, Cenni's strategy was a prime example of a carrot-and-stick policy. Insofar as he framed his stick policy as a way to curb illegal Chinese migrant and Italian factories, it appealed to legal business owners. Cenni astutely realized that Prato could not afford to shun Chinese migrants, who had become major players in its economy and had international standing. Raids would mitigate the ire of the city's Italian industrialists without alienating legal Chinese migrant elites, who controlled the bulk of investment capital and supported much of the Chinese migrant media. While the stick policy based on police investigations was locally oriented, the carrot policy about the collaboration of Italian textile producers and Chinese garment workers in the fast-fashion sector addressed the international reputation of "Made in Italy." Cenni's carrot policy was topical for Italian, other European, and American news outlets that were eager to observe how Prato's industrial district would offer desirable fabrics and garments within the current global economic and manufacturing systems, while preserving its unique geographical and cultural identity. The carrot-and-stick policy was calculated to win the endorsement of a wide spectrum of stakeholders in Prato's textile and garment industries, including Italian and Chinese migrant workers and entrepreneurs, as well as potential international employers and customers. In order for this strategy to work, Cenni needed to cogently argue in the news media that Prato had both a local specificity and a pan-European impact.

For his carrot policy, Cenni advocated the creation of an Italian-Chinese collaboration based in Prato in order to incentivize large fast-fashion retailers, such as Zara and H&M, to move their production to the city and to create products that combined Italian style and Chinese work. How are we to understand Cenni's direct appeal to middle-brow, non-Italian, transnational fast-fashion companies? Prato's Italian artisan producers sold much less fabric to Italian clothing companies than they did in the past because, for many Italian- and Chinese-migrant-owned firms, "Made in Italy" fashion meant garments partially manufactured in China but finished in Italy, a process that made using Prato's fabrics economically undesirable as China provided both the primary materials and the labour. In fact, as both the Italian and the Chinese migrant media reported, Cenni outsourced some of his own company's production to China; his Sasch was one of the city's few surviving medium-sized clothing companies in the late 2000s. In addressing outsourcing and declining market demands, Cenni envisioned an ostensibly win-win scenario for his city: Prato's Italian industrialists would create and sell fabrics to Chinese migrants, who would then manufacture for an authentic "Made in Italy" brand that would enjoy a secure distribution through these global fashion companies; meanwhile, Chinese migrants would be able to completely legalize their businesses and become workers for a legitimate fashion production network. Cenni's proposal differed starkly from Pieraccini's definition of the "Made in Italy" label, as she continued to insist that "Made in Italy" fashion be restricted to high-quality, Italian-made ready-to-wear garments. While her opinion was quoted by the *Financial Times* in 2010, it was no longer the official view sanctioned by Cenni's government.[30]

Journalists enthused over the implications of Cenni's carrot policy for Prato's manufacturing industry. According to local and national newspapers, Cenni's intention to formally incorporate Chinese migrant entrepreneurship into the "Made in Italy" fashion production line won the approval of many Italian industrialists and politicians across the political spectrum. Referring to the low-cost Chinese labour with which Italy was no longer able to compete, *La Nazione* quoted an Italian resident who seconded Cenni's proposal: "Se non puoi batter il tuo nemico, fattelo amico" (Keep your friends close, but your enemies closer). Approving Cenni's strategy, Lamberto Gestri, then the president of the Province of Prato and a member of the left-leaning Partito Democratico (Democratic party), suggested "strengthening relations between the city and the 'healthy' part of the Chinese entrepreneurship that has been legal for some time." Two left-wing members of Parliament agreed with Gestri on providing a path for migrants to legitimize their businesses. At least one Chinese entrepreneur who appeared on Prato TV spoke approvingly of Cenni's strategy. Already in 2008, some Chinese entrepreneurs agreed with the policy Cenni would eventually put forward.[31]

Several reasons accounted for the media success of Cenni's carrot policy among many Italians and some Chinese migrants. To republicize Prato as the European fast-fashion centre, but with a "Made in Italy" reputation, it was necessary for Cenni to incorporate the Chinese into the local economy. As a businessman-mayor, he recognized the need to collaborate with migrants to ensure Prato's current and future economic prosperity. To quote *Corriere della Sera*, "as a businessman, Cenni understands that Prato cannot afford to lose the Chinese. The city would become a museum of de-industrialization, and no special law sanctioned by the crisis state would be able to save it."[32] Cenni's idea about globalization with a nationalist or parochial accent was in keeping with what Stuart Hall calls "the global post-modern," which contrasts with the older form of globalization that "[had] to go back to nationalism and national cultural identity in a highly defensive way, and to try to build barriers around it before it [was] eroded." Indeed, to draw on Roland Robertson's insight into globalization, the new form of protectionism that Cenni implemented in 2009 showed a high "consciousness of the global economy as a whole," for the local must be attached to the global in re-proposing "Made in Prato" textiles and garments for the current consumer markets.[33]

Further, the carrot policy was attractive because several news outlets, including *La Nazione* and the regional weekly *Toscana Oggi*, unambiguously explained that Chinese migrants had helped to revitalize Prato's industry by working for the Italians during the 1980s and 1990s, and that the Italians and migrants benefited one another in garment manufacturing.[34] It would have been difficult and foolhardy for Cenni to blatantly dispute Chinese migrants' role in the city's garment industry. Many Italians' endorsement of the carrot policy underlined the overall transformation of Prato's Chinese from temporary migrant workers into a permanent workforce, as migrants' initially contractually limited employment gradually became a structural feature of the city's economy.

In *Xinhua Lianhe Shibao,* Dai Xiaozhang, then the secretary general of a consortium of Chinese merchants in Italy, used an extended gendered metaphor to encourage his fellow entrepreneurs to further learn about the market economy and the Italian economy in order to open up new avenues of entrepreneurship.[35] Dai's addressees were likely newly arrived Chinese migrants who had heard stories about quick profits through illegal work in Italy's underground economy. In the article, Dai believes that up until then Chinese migrant entrepreneurship had played a youthful home wrecker who insinuated herself into the happily established Italian economy with little space for her ascendance. Here Dai refers to the first Chinese migrants who arrived in Prato in the 1980s and provided Italian employers with cheap labour throughout the 1990s. Therefore, Dai reasons, like a home wrecker, Italians perceived Chinese as immoral and illegal intruders in Prato's economy. Dai's observation is supported by anti-Chinese graffiti that appeared in Prato's Chinatown around the time of the 2009 local elections: "Hello, I am a Chinese whore. I live at No. 45" on Via IX Agosto; and "Here lives a Chinese whore with three notices to leave" on Via Pistoiese."[36] These slurs fed on the social imagination of a feminized and low-cost Chinese migrant community up for sale.

Nevertheless, continues Dai, "like the 'home wrecker' in the face of life's cruelty, if we could use the influence of successful people with power and wealth, then the pressure on our existence would be reduced and the goals that are hard to reach via regular channels could be achieved." Dai implies that the Italian economy needed illegal Chinese migrant labour, just as it needed its informal sector. Chinese entrepreneurs were successful because they understood and acted upon these market impulses. Drawing on the complementariness of Taoist yin and yang and on the Confucian ideal of social harmony in an ethnocultural vein, Dai praises Chinese migrants' ability to navigate the grey area of the Italian economy, guided as they were by survivor instinct. For Dai, while Chinese migrants were assigned the yin (female) quality and Italian entrepreneurs the yang (male) quality, the two groups increased their vitality by absorbing one another's natural quality, much like the metaphor of heterosexual intercourse suggests.[37]

Having abandoned pedantic conventional family morality and justified the mutual attraction between the "successful people of power and wealth" and the "home wrecker," Dai ends this metaphor abruptly. He then cautions that this production mode became outdated because the market and fashion trends had changed, and so had the local politics, in an overt reference to Cenni and his endorsement of increasingly harsh police investigations into factories. Dai suggests that fellow migrants branch out into fast-fashion sectors other than manufacturing in order to expand their entrepreneurship. *Xinhua Lianhe Shibao* advocated the creation of more retail stores over wholesale stores and, based on the similarities between business environments and battlefields, compared such a switch with the transition from a "guerrilla army" to a "regular army."[38]

Xinhua Lianhe Shibao's second proposal in response to Cenni's carrot policy was to advise Chinese migrant factories to update from manufacture of low-end and counterfeit garments to that of medium- and high-quality fashion. This switch would avoid the damage caused by frequent police raids that targeted mislabelled "Made in Italy" products. Moreover, this new focus would allow Chinese entrepreneurs to compete in a higher-profit market. For illustration, the newspaper examined Zenobi, previously an established Italian shoe company, which had been purchased by a Chinese migrant, Wang Yongjia. Wang believed that after the initial capital accumulation – that is, Dai's home-wrecker phase – entrepreneurs seeking to expand had two options: they could either purchase established Italian brands, as Wang had done, or create their own, a phenomenon that pre-2009 Italian media coverage discussed but that 2009 coverage mostly neglected.[39] The trend for the Chinese to tap into higher-end fashion market would be more frequently covered in the media following Cenni's carrot-and-stick proposal. For example, a 2011 article in *L'Espresso* discussed Prato's Chinese-owned, medium- and high-quality "Made in Italy" labels, including Xu Qiu Lin's Giupel and Francesco Zhang's Koralline.[40]

While Cenni's carrot policy stimulated media discussions around the potential future of "Made in Italy" fashion and the migrants' role in it, his stick policy led to immediate, acrimonious polemics. In late 2009, he endorsed frequent police investigations into Prato's Chinese factories, especially those in the industrial district of Macrolotto. The mastermind of many of these raids was Aldo Milone, the newly appointed head of Prato's municipal department of security and police, who had previously served in the position for years. In an interview with *It's China*, Milone repeatedly denied that he nurtured animosity towards Prato's Chinese, although he correlated migrants' wealth with their illegal business practices and reiterated migrants' negative influence on Italians, using both as reasons to justify more raids.[41]

The raids provoked acute social tensions in Prato. On 5 January 2010, *Corriere Fiorentino*'s editorial office received a flyer ostensibly signed by the Brigate Rosse-Partito Comunista Combattente, a faction of the Red Brigades since 1981, which was a prominent left-wing terrorist organization that conducted assassinations, kidnapping, and other activities during the 1970s and 1980s. The flyer states: "Time is running out. You are only dirty fascists and racists ... Keep on blaming the new Chinese proletariat and migrants, Mayor Cenni and Councilor Milone. Your days are numbered. Very soon you'll pay for your xenophobic politics." According to *Il Tirreno*, as a response to this flyer, which was later proved to be a forgery, police investigations climaxed on 19 January 2010. The spectacle was evident to all. Aided by a helicopter, 120 Italian agents from various institutions entered Via Rossini, the heart of Chinatown just outside the city's medieval walls, "in a grand style." *La Nazione* considered this raid the "largest anti-clandestine operation ever carried out in Tuscany." *Il Sole 24 Ore* called it "the most imposing one that the city has ever witnessed in the war against illegality during these years." In Cenni's opinion, it provoked Italian-migrant tensions in Prato comparable to those in Rosarno, where North African migrants rioted against Italian residents and police for days in early January 2010.[42]

The media criticized the style in which the 19 January 2010 raid was conducted and the aura of a police state it conjured. Both the Italian and the Chinese migrant news detailed the Italian police's extreme measures. *Il Tirreno* used the Italian word rastrellamento, which indicates a Nazi-style systematic and organized search, to describe the raid: "Scenes of a room-to-room search ['rastrellamento'], the one that started early this morning in the heart of Chinatown, the first in a grand style in the urban centre. From 8:30 a.m., an army of uniformed agents besieged the 250 metres of Via Rossini, sealing off the street's two ends. This was a kind of bloodless tuna-fishing net, from which few illegal Chinese migrants (those seen fleeing in pyjamas) managed to escape without being stopped and identified." According to *La Nazione*, "While the Italians applauded from balconies, the military penetrated dozens of oriental artisan companies ... With a helicopter surveying the area from above, the police sealed off entrances to the street. For a few hours, no one was able to enter or leave."[43]

The Chinese migrant media generally viewed this police operation as an arrogant show by an economically weakened and yet politically dominating local government that exercised executive power over the economically powerful and yet politically insignificant Chinese community. Describing the raid as a "sweeping search," *Xinhua Lianhe*

Shibao employed a Chinese approximation of "rastrellamento." Unlike the focus on illegal migrants in *Il Tirreno* and *La Nazione*, the Chinese-language newspaper highlighted the unfair treatment of legal Chinese migrants. One man was made to stand in the courtyard, "shivering from the winter cold," for hours during the investigation. "In the end, seeing that we had permits to stay, the agent shook his shoulders and sent us away without offering a word of apology." Many migrants also had no place to sleep that night because the warehouses, which contained both workshops and living quarters, were cordoned off. Indeed, according to *Cina in Italia*, despite the raid's justifiable aim to eradicate economic crimes, it deeply "hurt Chinese migrants' feelings."[44]

This investigation disrupted normal life for Chinese migrants in the weeks leading up to the 2010 Chinese New Year, prompting a widely publicized outcry from Gu Honglin, then the Chinese consul in Florence, which originally appeared in *Il Sole 24 Ore*. Although *Il Tirreno* cited Gu as having "no intention to ask for a suspension of control," but rather for an equal treatment of Chinese and Italian nationals, the newspaper generally depicted Gu as a Chinese leader requesting lesser Italian discipline. Gu denounced the excessive and repressive police methods, comparing the crackdown to Nazis going door to door and to the 1978 search conducted for the abducted Italian politician Aldo Moro by the aforementioned Red Brigades. Gu was further discredited in *Il Tirreno* as a representative from China, "one of the most ferocious dictatorships in the world that, with a stick, governs a billion and half of a population that has no freedom or rights."[45] Such a comment was reminiscent of remarks and satirical cartoons that I examined in relation to the 2007 riot and the 1990s Cold War thinking, which had interpreted the migration as an escape from socialist China to democratic Italy. In the aftermath of the 19 January 2010 raid, journalists resuscitated topics and discursive strategies gleaned from the Italian-Chinese migrant cultural repertoire because of a similar need to defame Gu and other Chinese officials.

Militant Rebuttals to the 2010 Raids

In keeping with his stick policy, in May 2010 Cenni vowed to conduct five hundred police investigations in Prato in the following fiscal year.[46] His new target was Chinese-owned money transfer agencies, which allegedly facilitated money laundering as the Chinese mafia supposedly transferred a huge amount of money from Prato to mainland China. The 28 June 2010 raid was the first of three significant raids charged with this mission; the other two occurred on 21 June 2011 and

11 July 2012. According to *Corriere Fiorentino*, the Chinese mafia ran the Italian-Chinese agency Money2Money, which recycled approximately five million euros' worth of dirty money in five years. The majority of this money came from counterfeiting, commercial frauds, falsified industrial products, tax evasion, and labour exploitation – all familiar Chinese economic crimes. Among those arrested were members of the Chinese Cai family and the Italian Bolzonaro family, who co-owned Money2Money in Italy.[47]

The Chinese mafia resurfaced as a leading topic in the coverage of the 28 June 2010 raid, owing to Italy's then national anti-mafia prosecutor, Pietro Grasso.[48] In *Corriere Fiorentino*, Grasso explained the resemblance he saw between the Italian and the Chinese mafias based on analogous structures and similar ways of corrupting legal economies. In interviews on Prato TV and in *La Nazione*, he offered vague statements about Prato being besieged by the Chinese mafia. This was reminiscent of a mechanism I examined in chapter 2 in relation to Saviano's *Gomorra*. While on Prato TV Grasso admitted that not all Chinese migrants were mobsters, his comments were rather perfunctory because of the newscast's criminal angle: we see a large quantity of cash stocked at a Money2Money agency while the voice-over explains its illegal origins. In such a media climate, Lega Nord felt entitled to call Ding Wei, then the Chinese ambassador to Italy, the godfather of Prato's Chinese mobsters.[49] As I examined in chapters 2 and 4, when the Chinese mafia previously became topical in the Italian media, the Chinese migrant media did not engage with it in any meaningful way. This pattern recurred in 2010, as *Ouzhou Qiaobao* criticized certain Italian media's dissemination of false information about Chinese organized crime only in passing.[50]

In chapter 4, I noted that Chinese migrant coverage of the 2007 riot maintained a strategic silence on the community's illegal economic activities. A similar situation occurred in coverage of police raids on Prato's Chinese factories before 2010. However, following the 28 June 2010 raid, *Xinhua Lianhe Shibao* and *China Newsweek*, an influential mainland Chinese weekly whose feature on the raid was reprinted in *Cina in Italia*, made the most cogent counterarguments to Italian accusations of economic crimes yet by detailing the inner workings of Prato's Chinese migrant entrepreneurships from the migrants' perspectives. The Chinese migrant press's stance on the Italian raids had shifted from tolerance to rebuttal. This change indicated that police investigations into Chinese migrants' money transfer agencies had much higher affective and economic stakes than those into factories. Migrants were concerned with the destiny of the millions of euros confiscated by Italian police. This was money earned, to quote a migrant, with "xue han" (blood and sweat), a Chinese expression frequently used to indicate how underprivileged individuals toil under harsh circumstances to make a modest living.[51]

Previously, Italian journalists referenced Chinese media practitioners' comments on the 2007 riot. And the international media later circulated migrants' two proposals in response to Cenni's carrot policy starting in 2010 (see chapter 6). However, the detailed explanations of Prato's Chinese-owned entrepreneurship in 2010 appeared only in Chinese-language newspapers. Why were mostly Chinese community members, rather than Italians, the intended audience? By the late 2000s, established Chinese migrants had felt it necessary to explain the history of their entrepreneurship to new Chinese migrants, who had differing origins and cultures in China. These established migrant elites needed a common understanding of this entrepreneurship to stabilize its dynamics and hierarchy. Such stability would also give community representatives more leverage in negotiations with Italian politicians and entrepreneurs on issues such as how police raids should be effectively conducted in order not to affect legal Chinese factories.

How did the money, which Prato's Chinese wired through Money2Money and similar agencies from Italy to China, become illicit? According to *Xinhua Lianhe Shibao*, most money was used to purchase materials or goods from Chinese suppliers, and wiring through Italian banks was too time-consuming for merchants who prioritized a timely response to market needs. Since the Italian authorities often perceived migrants as asylum-seekers or poor, when merchants needed to pay for merchandise imported from China, their money was not always acknowledged as their legitimate income in Italy. As Italy had not standardized its consumer market, occasionally money wired from Prato to China did not have accompanying sale invoices to prove that it was merchants' legal earnings. This occurred because Italian customers who wished to avoid the 20 per cent merchandise tax requested no invoices be issued. Since the Italian government purposefully monitored and unreasonably restricted "Made in China" merchandise, and so delayed its delivery to warehouses and stores, the Chinese were forced to resort to underground customs and imports via other European Union countries. All of these practices, *Xinhua Lianhe Shibao* argued, resulted in murkier records in migrants' bank accounts.[52]

Drawing on this self-defence, *Xinhua Lianhe Shibao* and *China Newsweek* embarked on confrontational and razor-sharp analyses of the political and economic aims of police crackdowns in Prato. A trove of reasons emerged: the Italian media was hypocritical in castigating

Chinese migrants for their illegal business practices, because Italy's large shadow economy made it difficult for anyone to fully avoid any economic crime; Prato increased tax revenue by seizing assets belonging to Chinese migrant workshops; because of the wealth Chinese merchants accumulated and their tendency to flaunt it, Prato profited by confiscating their properties including money transfer agencies, an action supported by jealous Italians; Italy exaggerated the impact of migrant economic crimes on social welfare; the lack of solidarity among Chinese migrants and their poor Italian language skills prevented them from effectively protesting like other migrants did; Italy wished to pinpoint migrants' shortcomings in order to have more bargaining power in trade talks with mainland China; and Italian newspapers, seeking to sell more copies, made the 28 June 2010 raid on Money2Money agencies a media spectacle.[53]

Like the coverage of the 2007 riot, the Chinese migrant press recommended tactics and changes in behaviour in order to better address Cenni's stick policy. For *Xinhua Lianhe Shibao*, the tradition of *pai chang* (public extravagance and ostentation) and *mian zi* (face, or public persona) led migrant elites to excessively show off their wealth, such as by driving luxury cars, dining in expensive restaurants, and speaking loudly while drinking expensive wines, all of which were frowned upon by Italians and zealously reported in the Italian media. The solution, the press offered, was to keep a low profile in public, "a true wisdom in life, and a tactic that shows the tenacity and virtue of being a man."[54]

Further, the press asked migrant workers to respect their employers and to work with them to prevent crackdowns. *Xinhua Lianhe Shibao* took a rather patronizing stance on what can be conceived as a class struggle between workers and employers, privileging the interests of the latter over those of the former. For the newspaper, the Chinese tendency to show satisfaction at the misfortunes their fellow countrymen suffered should be discouraged. Journalists also cautioned workers against sneering at employers harmed by the raids, because workers and employers depended on one another for the health of migrant entrepreneurship.[55]

Xinhua Lianhe Shibao also called on other Chinese migrant news outlets in Italy to speak favourably of their community and of China whenever possible, contributing to China's soft power abroad. Implicit in this advice was a hope for more active political participation and representation in Prato, especially from second-generation Chinese migrants or the Chinese Italians, a familiar recommendation I have already examined in relation to the riot.[56] Indeed, as a politically insignificant minority group in Italy, the Chinese felt that the Italians ignored their emotional and historical connection. Migrant journalists recalled the Chinese contributions to revitalizing Prato's textile industry as early as the 1960s and to institutionalizing Prato as the capital of a new province in 1992 because of its growing economy and population.[57] This sense of betrayal partially explained why Chinese migrant individuals, associations, and news outlets tended to seek recognition from the Chinese government, as they often felt that they could not obtain acknowledgment of their contributions from the Italian authorities, particularly with Cenni in office.

Above all, the Chinese migrant media argued in favour of tighter discipline for various economic crimes, although they found Cenni-endorsed and Milone-style raids distasteful and immoral. *Cina in Italia* urged migrants to respect Italian laws and praised Prato's government and police for curbing unlawful economic activities. *Xinhua Lianhe Shibao* emphasized the need to accelerate the legalization of the city's Chinese sweatshops to the benefit of their long-term economic growth. *Xinhua Lianhe Shibao* also encouraged migrants to "re-adjust 'hidden rules' internal to the community, eradicate economic crimes, and redeem the negative social impact they engendered." As that commentator bitterly noted: "To be honest, it is because dark aspects of the Chinese migrant community existed that we are unable to confidently defend our rights."[58] As these remarks clarified, the Italian media and governance perspective that correlated migrant entrepreneurship via economic crimes to institutional discipline aligned with the economic and political needs of elite Chinese migrants who supported the community's news media.

The Chinese coverage of the Prato case study concurred on two major points. First, since Chinese migrants were legitimate producers of the redefined "Made in Italy" apparel in Prato, they must not be blamed unilaterally for illegal business choices germane to Italy's larger institutional and economic environments as well as to market and production logic of fast fashion. Second, as the city's many Chinese migrants legalized their businesses as much as possible and expanded a complete production line in fast fashion, thereby contributing to the city's economy, the increasingly harsh raids to target migrant factories and money transfer agencies were not justifiable.

The Italian, American, German, and Japanese media reported on both of these viewpoints through referencing and quoting Chinese migrant newspapers, interviews with successful migrant entrepreneurs, and

Chinese Italian journalists who worked for Italian newspapers. In the next chapter, I explore the international media's construction of the Prato case study as a prime example concerning the competition between the "Made in Italy" and "Made in China" reputations, as well as that between wider European-Chinese commerce.

Chapter 6

Prato: Global Debates on "Made in Italy" by the Chinese, 2005–2012

As Prato became a leading European fast-fashion manufacturing centre in the 2000s, the international media covered the city's Italian-Chinese relations in depth.[1] In particular, American and German newspapers devoted considerable attention to the Prato case study, likely because the United States and Germany were Italy and China's largest non-European and European trading partners between 2005 and 2012. Equally influential was the coverage on Japanese and mainland Chinese television. Japan was the first east Asian country to successfully challenge the postwar Euro-American economic hegemony. Japan's concerns for tradition and innovation during much of its modern history also made it more attuned to Prato's dilemma about localism and globalization. Mainland Chinese television viewed Prato with interest because the case exposed the vexing relationships between Chinese migrants' worldwide economic pursuits and their impact on China's international reputation and globalization. My discussion of the media debates that emerged from these four countries will put local Italian-Chinese migrant dynamics into global perspective, emphasizing the global dimension in the local-global media frame regarding Chinese migration to Italy.

In German and American news coverage, which sometimes relied on or influenced their Italian counterpart, two controversial issues around "Made in Italy" fashion were notable. The first was the relationship among Chinese migrants, Prato's artisan producers, and Italy's major fashion houses that contracted orders, via various intermediary suppliers or contractors, to Chinese migrants. The second was the creation of middle-brow brands by the city's Chinese migrants and the subsequent impact on the redefinition of the "Made in Italy" label. In addressing these two topics, the German and American news media argued that the Prato case study was a synecdoche of Italian-Chinese competition in the garment and fashion sector, as well as in other industries where the two countries competed directly. Moreover, they viewed Prato as an effective example for initiating debate on European-Chinese competition in the global market. In these interpretations, the drama in Prato was a cautionary tale about globalization, Chinese style, which ill-prepared European countries survived by improvising short-term solutions. But many of these media analyses remained sympathetic to Chinese migrant capitalism and urged Italian firms to accelerate innovation in the textile and garment industries in order to follow or lead international market trends. The energetic debates indicated that these news outlets regarded the Prato case as a way to strengthen their nativist, or pro-migrant, views of contemporary globalized manufacturing and international trade.

Through quotations and reprints, and through comments by individual journalists, the American and German media influenced Italy's news production. The Japanese television documentary and the mainland Chinese television serial that I examine in this chapter did not directly intervene in the Italian mediascape – but they did contain the most extended and emotional articulations of pro-migrant views of the Prato case. The global-local interpretive framing first nurtured in the Western media influenced these east Asian productions. In their depictions, Italy's Chinese became model migrant-entrepreneurs, skilled as they were at negotiating local economic and political responses to the global restructuring of manufacturing, which their labour and capital, as well as Chinese economic globalization, helped to accelerate.

Complementing chapter 5, my discussions here further show that specific media discourses in the master narrative about the global-local dialectic evolved considerably along with the changing political, social, and cultural circumstances between 2005 and 2012. As the 2007 riot was a one-time, spontaneous event, the topics and rhetorical parameters of discourses around it drew on knowledge of Italy's Chinese, China, and immigrants in Italy in general that the media had formed between the early 1990s and the mid-2000s. By examining media discourses around police raids and "Made in Italy" over eight years, I reveal how they were malleable and open for debate. Further, with regard to the riot, the positions that Italian and Chinese migrant news outlets adopted can often be analytically categorized as anti-Chinese or pro-Chinese. As the Prato case study clearly shows, these ideologically and politically driven positions were not always sustained because more stakeholders, including major Italian fashion companies, were in play, and because considerations about business pragmatism and the international reputation of "Made in Italy" often could not afford to offend any buyer including the Chinese, migrants or otherwise.

"Made in Italy" versus "Made in China," 2005

Around 2005, the media increasingly covered the various manufacturing sectors in which Italy and China competed directly. For instance, in his 2005 *Time* feature story titled "Twilight in Italy," Peter Gumbel interpreted "Made in Italy" versus "Made in China" in chair manufacturing as a conflict between artisan production and mass production. For Gumbel, "If the Italians can find a way to carve out an upmarket niche for themselves as the most successful chair manufacturers are attempting to do, there's every reason to believe that Europeans and Chinese can coexist and flourish, with each building on its respective strengths."[2] His point is aptly expressed by the issue's cover, on which Michelangelo's *David* and a Xi'an terracotta warrior arm wrestle.[3] The two figures are not offered merely as icons of their respective countries. Consider how, *David* is a single original piece, despite its numerous later copies, whereas the terracotta warrior is a close replica of many similar pieces within its category in the army. From this perspective, the cover alludes to the conventionally accepted dichotomy between "Made in Italy" design handicrafts and artisan production on the one hand, and the largely imitative, mass-produced "Made in China" merchandise on the other.

Starting in 2005, the textile and garment industries figured prominently in the coverage of "Made in Italy" versus "Made in China," and eventually became an iconic case of this competition in the news media.[4] This attention occurred mainly due to an industry-specific circumstance in a year when China surpassed Italy as the world's sixth-largest economy. On 1 January 2005, the World Trade Organization's Agreement on Textiles and Clothing expired. To quote the WTO regulations, this meant that "trade in textile and clothing products is no longer subject to quotas under a special regime outside normal WTO/GATT rules but is now governed by the general rules and disciplines embodied in the multilateral trading system." China joined the WTO in 2001 and began to export much more fabric to the European Union after 2005. According to a report from the Directorate-General for Trade of the European Commission, that year "China increased its exports to the EU by 42% in value and by 36% in volume … at the expense of traditional EU suppliers, mainly in Asia but also in North Africa and the ACP (African, Caribbean, and Pacific Group of States)."[5] The influx of Chinese fabrics and clothing in the European Union countries noted in this report, however, did not fully capture the stress it put on the Italian textile and garment industries. Not only was this sector one of the largest suppliers to the European Union market and the traditional supplier to "Made in Italy" fashion companies, but in the 2000s Italy was also the only significant apparel exporter among developed countries, as well as the second-largest global exporter of clothing after China.[6]

A media focus on mainland China's challenge to Italy in the textile and garment industries also led the media, since the late 1990s, to identify fast fashion as the focus of Chinese migrants' investment in Italy, and Prato its centre. A 2006 *Newsweek* article, titled "The Chinese Are Coming," cited Prato as the first of several examples of recent Chinese migrant investments in Europe, and asserted that "more than 2,000 Chinese-owned enterprises have helped revive Prato's flagging textile industry."[7] Furthermore, the Italian media increasingly covered how Chinese migrant enterprises matured and Italian businesses declined in Prato in the age of fast fashion. A 1999 *Panorama* article noted Italians' concern with migrants' unfair competition: "Always at the cutting edge of innovation and competitiveness, Prato's textile district, the model of Made in Italy studied in American universities, is in distress." The media also covered the institutional discipline of the migrants' perceived economic crimes, often associated with fast fashion. In 2003, both *Panorama* and *It's China* considered Prato a model city with comparatively efficient migrant firm regulations.[8]

After 2005, the media increasingly turned to Prato as an example of Italian-Chinese competition in the textile and garment industries, of Italian-Chinese competition in manufacturing more generally, and of European-Chinese competition in manufacturing. In the next two sections, I analyse these media narratives in detail, with a focus on specific issues and problems that the "Made in Italy" label and reputation faced in this period.

Provincial Industrialists versus Major Fashion Houses via Chinese Migrants, 2006–2008

In the 2000s, ready-to-wear companies such as Prada, Versace, and Giorgio Armani shifted a portion of their production from global outsourcing to contract work that employed local workers in Italy. Prato's Chinese stood out in this workforce for their speed and economy. According to a 2007 *Newsweek* article, titled "Made by Foreign Hands," this shift allowed these fashion houses to take legal advantage of the symbolic capital of "Made in Italy": "Many high-end designers believe that the MADE IN ITALY label, evoking a long history of artisanship, justifies premium prices – even if the items are produced by foreigners [in Italy and beyond]." Furthermore, as a 2010 article in the *Guardian* revealed, a good portion of the garments commissioned by Italian fashion houses and sewn by Prato's Chinese were not made of Italian fabrics.[9]

The pragmatic redefinition of "Made in Italy" by the country's major ready-to-wear companies was extremely lucrative for them. But it worsened the crisis among Italian workers and entrepreneurs in Prato's textile and garment companies, who respectively now sold less fabric to major fashion companies and could not compete on price. Italian journalists generally decried the dominance of multinational corporations over small- and medium-sized enterprises, revealing at once a moralizing distaste for globalized businesses and a deliberately restricted vision of "Made in Italy." A prominent example concerns two episodes in 2007 and 2008 written by the journalist Sabrina Giannini for *Report*, a well-respected investigative journalism program on Rai Tre.[10] Giannini examines the manufacture of garments and leather goods by Chinese migrants in the Prato-Florence area. She accuses major Italian fashion houses of tolerating and exploiting migrants' illegal business practices to the detriment of Italian producers in specialized industrial districts. She draws on the resentment of the provincial industrialists interviewed to complain that fashion houses schemed with Italian suppliers in order to commission Chinese migrant contractors and to concoct inauthentic "Made in Italy" labels. Giannini further laments the erosion of the proper "Made in Italy" work ethic and production under pressure from globalization and consumerism, and calls for the preservation of the provenance, legal status, and Italian identity of "Made in Italy" brands.

In so doing, Giannini allows Prato's small- and medium-sized producers to assume a higher moral ground than Prato's illegal Chinese migrant factories and Naples's underground Italian-owned workshops, which both received commissions from Italian suppliers with the implicit endorsement of certain big Italian fashion houses. Giannini's interpretation others the Southerner and the foreigner to salvage a particular idea of Italian authenticity under threat – an idea that had served the interests of provincial industrialists in Prato as elsewhere in central and northern Italy. Moreover, her nativist vision of the "Made in Italy" label, following Andrew Ross's observation, "romanticizes small, craft-based firms competing against all the odds on the forgiving field of hardscrabble capitalism."[11] This social fiction was expressively captured on camera during the 28 February 2009 demonstration in Prato (see chapter 5).

Why did the Chinese migrant entrepreneurship become a scapegoat in the discord between Italy's major fashion houses and Prato's artisan producers? What role did it play in the revival of Prato's garment industry in the 1980s and 1990s, in relation to the Chinese community's migration, and against the dominant trend of fast fashion since the 2000s? German journalism from 2006 to 2008 clarified these questions. For a 2008 *Die Zeit* article, the city's Chinese saved the local Italian textile industry from disintegration and from mainland Chinese competition. Significantly, the article establishes two sequential developments in Prato's industrial district, countering popular opinion that Chinese economic expansion caused the failure of Prato's Italian businesses. According to the article, Prato's Italian textile industry crisis preceded the increased mainland Chinese competition that occurred after 2005. It was to address this existing crisis that many small- and medium-sized Italian enterprises sold their unused production space to migrant entrepreneurs. In other words, Chinese migrants did not drive out these Italian producers by offering high prices to purchase their properties; Italians, particularly retirees, profited from this real estate speculation, as recent sociological scholarship confirms.[12]

While *Die Zeit* examined the Prato case from the perspective of the Italians coping with globalization, Fiona Ehlers, in a 2006 article for *Der Spiegel*, approaches the issue through Chinese globalization and examines the past, present, and future of Prato's Chinese in three stories.[13] Luigi was a first-generation Wenzhounese migrant who became legalized thanks to Italy's regularization schemes in the 1990s. He then prospered in the import-export sector, capitalizing on Italy's growing demand for "Made in China" goods. Thus, Luigi typifies the first stage of globalization, Chinese style, when "China took away Europe's jobs" through exports. In the second stage of globalization, Chinese migrants were "now conquering the cities of the old continent." Meng, a young girl and "slave labourer," was sent by her family against her will to work in a Prato sweatshop. Ehlers focuses on the physical and psychological stresses to which Meng and the majority of Prato's Chinese were subjected. Xu Qiu Lin, "a model Chinese entrepreneur," embodied the third stage of globalization, in which Chinese entrepreneurs in Italy were beginning "going back to produce their goods inexpensively in China."

Compared to their Italian counterparts, *Der Spiegel* and *Die Zeit* took a rather critical view of Prato's provincial industrialists, as well as a more sympathetic stance on its Chinese migrant entrepreneurship. What validated this interpretation? The two news magazines are widely read, influential weeklies in Germany, the country whose Nazi past postwar

Italians often invoked to claim their own innocence and victimhood in committing war atrocities. The stereotypical evil and corrupting Nazi Germans functioned as a foil against which good-natured Italians became a trope to exculpate Italians' responsibilities for war crimes.[14] This historical condition might have sensitized the German media to a similar narrative about Italian victimhood, which was now claimed vis-à-vis China and its globalization and migrant transnationalism. In *Der Spiegel*, Ehlers notes that "now that their city is once again in demand, Prato's residents are suddenly claiming that Pronto Moda [fast fashion] was their idea all along. The Chinese, they say, are ruining the Italians' reputation with their cheaply made versions of Italian-style garments." Wryly, Ehlers mocks the Italians' self-victimization in this comment, and goes on to highlight how Prato's Chinese worked for the Italians in the early 1990s, thereby helping the city take on a significant role in then-emerging fast fashion.

Further, Ehler's observation teases out the jealousy many of Prato's artisan producers felt towards Chinese migrants and mainlanders, who had seized upon a golden opportunity to prosper economically at the right moment in history. This envy was related to widespread depictions of a youthful China leading globalization and an aging Italy lagging behind in post-2005 international and Italian media coverage. Gone was the arm wrestling of the 2005 *Time* cover. Taking a pro-globalization stance on the Chinese migrant economic investment in Europe, *Die Zeit* joined *Der Spiegel* in regarding the new breed of transnational Chinese entrepreneurs, exemplified by those in Prato, as harbingers of China's future as an economic super power. Like *Der Spiegel*, *Modern Times*, a 2007 documentary broadcast on Mediaset's Rete 4, posited Xu Qiu Lin as the representative of the new Italian-Chinese generation. A 2008 *L'Espresso* article called this generation "a real Chinese-Italian entrepreneurial bourgeoisie," for whom the two symbols of social status were, ironically, "Made in Germany" and "Made in Italy" – namely, luxury German cars and major Italian fashion brands.[15]

Nativist versus Pro-Migrant Views of "Made in Italy," 2010–2011

After Cenni became Prato's mayor in 2009, his pursuit of the carrot-and-stick strategy heightened the newsworthiness of his city's Italian-Chinese relations. Cenni was always keenly aware of the media's power to shape public and institutional opinions. For him, more media debate would lead to more visibility for Prato, which would in turn gain more political and business leverage. For instance, in July 2010, Cenni opined that more national and international media coverage of the city would help solicit stronger state intervention to curb Chinese migrants' illegal business practices.[16] Coincidentally or not, following his statement, a spate of feature stories about Prato appeared in influential American and European general-interest and business-focused newspapers. Cenni astutely promoted the city on the international news media circuit, a key move to restrategize the place of Prato's "Made in Italy" reputation in the global fast-fashion markets and to posit Prato as a prime example of European-Chinese business competition.

Indeed, most international media accounts focused on the global resonance of Prato's reputation, portraying it as a cautionary tale of globalization's impact on Europe, the globalization that brought "Made in China" products and Chinese migrants to Europe. In September 2010, the *New York Times* set this renewed interest in Prato in motion: "It is a 'Made in Italy' problem: Enabled by Italy's weak institutions and high tolerance for rule-bending, the Chinese have blurred the line between 'Made in China' and 'Made in Italy,' undermining Italy's cachet and ability to market its goods exclusively as high end." Other media outlets followed suit in reporting on Prato by discussing "Made in Italy" and also the competition between Europe, which was catching up with product innovation, and China, on its way to becoming a leader in market capitalism. The *Financial Times* regarded the city as an "example of how economic globalization and weak government have combined to fuel the development of black economies on the southern and eastern fringes of Europe." For *Voice of America*, Prato was a "microcosm of the challenges facing Europe," which was juggling tradition and innovation. For *Bloomberg Businessweek*, the Chinese-Italian conflicts in Prato were a "metaphor for the cultural collisions" that frequently occurred between locals and newcomers who were driven by global capitalism.[17]

Later, Italian and Chinese migrant readers learned these international perspectives from their own news outlets' enthusiastic digestion. Prato's appraisal in the *New York Times* and *Bloomberg Businessweek* was referenced and cited. The popular Italian weekly *Internazionale* translated and republished the latter's article, which Associna then reposted on its website.[18] The journalist Silvia Pieraccini, whose opinions about Prato I examined in the previous chapter, also bridged Italian and non-Italian media perspectives by appearing on Italian television, writing for *Il Sole 24 Ore*, and giving interviews to *Bloomberg Businessweek* and the *BBC News*. In this way, local and international journalists often cross-referenced these viewpoints about Prato's supposed exemplary position in European-Chinese business competition. I argue that the fundamental motivation behind this phenomenon was journalists' performative and strategic use of their intercultural media competencies. During this process, journalists enriched the Italian-Chinese migrant cultural repertoire, making media discourses about Italy's Chinese more nuanced.

Virtually all the news coverage discussed the "Made in Italy" label and debated the pros and cons of the role played by Prato's Chinese, making the contention between nativist and pro-migrant readings conspicuous. Both perspectives further cemented the city as the go-to example in media analyses of globalization and migrant economy in Europe in the late 2000s and early 2010s. A 2011 article titled "Italian Jobs, Chinese Illegals" in *Bloomberg Businessweek* endorses Italian protectionism by adopting an ethnocultural perspective towards economic clashes: "The Chinese substitution of cheap and fast for the Italian tradition of slow, fine, and expensive, has cut into the heart of Italy's fashion industry and, by extension, into Italy's economic culture as a whole." By citing Pieraccini, the article draws on the correlation between migrant entrepreneurship and institutional discipline through economic crimes and discusses how globalization and Italy's economic recession amplified the effect of migrants' illegal activities in Prato, leading to frequent police raids. The article takes the "Made in Italy" label to mean only products produced by Italian artisans, arguing that this is not a "nativist explanation" but a legitimate interpretation because family-owned Italian businesses were "struggling, and the way of life and the Italian craftsmanship they support are under threat."[19]

Drawing on Italian victimhood narratives, this international analysis aligned with earlier views of Italian journalists who had called for protection against Chinese encroachment on the Italian economy and national identity. Stressing the romanticized prestige of "Made in Italy," a 2005 *Panorama* article observes: "Not only sweaters and pants, but also furniture, jewelry, refrigerators, and taps: The champions of Italian exports to Europe run the risk of being overwhelmed by an 'impossible' competition. Is it time to block it?" In this and another 2005 *Panorama* article, a "Made in Italy" expert, Marco Fortis of Fondazione Edison, blamed the crisis almost entirely upon Chinese competition, with the European Union's ineffectual trade policies and the Italian textile and garment industries' lack of innovation a distant afterthought.[20]

In contrast, following German journalists who had highlighted accomplished Chinese entrepreneurs in Prato, many post-2009, pro-migrant media accounts argued that "Made in Italy" could not be limited to local Italian producers and that the Italians' self-victimization should be taken with a grain of salt. In support of its views, this coverage quoted Xu Qiu Lin who, in 2010, was the only Chinese member of Prato's Chamber of Commerce and of the Confindustria, Italy's main association that represents manufacturing and service companies, which he had joined in 2004. Particularly powerful Chinese migrants in Italy have always published Chinese-language books about their heroic, migratory lives.[21] But for a Chinese migrant in Italy to be widely recognized as a model migrant-entrepreneur by non-Chinese sources was a novelty in the late 2000s.

As part of a series on migrant integration in Europe published in the *Guardian*, an article titled "Made in Little Wenzhou, Italy: The Latest Label from Tuscany" focuses on Chinese-Italian collaboration. While most migrants used fabrics from mainland China for their "Made in Italy" fashion, Xu's company was an exception and therefore, as the article praises, a harbinger of future developments in Prato. A *BBC News* report jettisons the cliché of poor-quality merchandise made by the Chinese, stating instead that, among the city's five thousand or so Chinese factories, many produce garments that matched "Italian quality" and beat "Italian prices." The clip opens and ends with Xu conversing with Italian designers in his own factory, conjuring an image of the cosmopolitan entrepreneur. While Pieraccini and an Italian entrepreneur explain unfair competition by Prato's Chinese, and some screen time is devoted to a police investigation of an illegal Chinese warehouse, the report takes a reconciliatory attitude towards Italian-Chinese competition and celebrates Chinese migrants' achievements in Italy. Xu is again singled out as the "symbol of a future reconciliation between the two worlds" in a *Le Monde* article, titled "Made in Italy, Chinese Style." It portrays Prato as a zealous keeper of various markers of Italian cultural identity, including medieval architecture, advanced social policy, and the "Made in Italy" label that "makes the entire world dream." With very sparing reference to police raids or to economic crimes, this French analysis, like its counterparts in the British and German media, leans towards exposing the contradictory attitudes that Prato's Italian industrialists held towards migrants.[22]

On the one hand, following Pierre Bourdieu, as Xu appeared in these news outlets as an elite migrant with secure economic capital, he was disposed towards a riskier, but potentially more profitable, investment in creating a positive cultural image of himself for the Western media's consumption and circulation.[23] On the other hand, the increased coverage of accomplished migrants in Italy and beyond contributed to his newsworthiness as the personification of Italy's legal and successful Chinese migrant entrepreneurship. To borrow from Sara Ahmed, Xu's case became emblematic of "how migration can allow identity to become a fetish under the sign of globality," and an extremely positive global identity at that.[24] As Xu owned his self-created fashion brand Giupel, founded in 2000, the post-2009 media coverage of his story countered the provincialism of Cenni's carrot policy that attempted to keep the Chinese confined to manufacturing for Italian and other European brands.[25] But without the international media's enthusiasm for Prato, fuelled by the businessman-mayor's policy, Xu's international media profile would have been unimaginable.

The Model Local-Global Migrant Entrepreneurs, 2012

In the late 2000s and early 2010s, Xu was the most prominent of the Chinese whom the media portrayed as Italy's model migrant entrepreneurs. In media coverage, because these model migrants successfully navigated Prato's political, institutional, and economic dynamics, they also deserved a globally circulated image as Italy's more innovative transnational entrepreneurs. The positive stereotyping of the Chinese as Italy's industrious ethnic group par excellence culminated in two television programs produced by east Asian media outlets and aired in 2012.[26] While sharing the German and American media's pro-migrant views, the two programs' emphasis on the Chinese as Italy's model minority reprised a strategy already manifest in pro-Chinese Italian journalism about the 2007 riot, as I have examined previously.

NHK, Japan's national public broadcaster, made a television documentary titled イタリアブランド"を創りだせ ˜ファッションの都に生きる中国人~ (The creation of the "made in Italy" label: The Chinese who live in the fashion capital) (小黒雅宏) for its documentary series *WAVE*, which featured current social malaises and natural disasters around the world with a focus on China.[27] The documentary explores the Chinese redefinition of "Made in Italy" fashion through the narratives of two elite migrants and their middle-to-high-end brands: Wang Zengli's Eli Conf in Prato, which employed Italian designers, and the designer Xu Yuejuan's Delves-JK based in Campotto, near Bologna. In the segment focused on Prato in the only sequence to depict a police raid, with footage culled from Italian television, the voice-over notes migrants' illegal business activities without the moralizing undertones typical of Italian television news. Later, in footage from Prato's Chinatown obtained by NHK, the documentary questions the Italian officials' verdict about Chinese businesses' illegitimacy. As the voice-over sarcastically observes, a Chinese restaurant was closed down because it violated certain Italian rules, including the owners' inability to speak Italian.

This type of semantic subversion facilitated by montage also occurs in a scene set in a "Made in Italy" artisan workshop. At first, the camera admiringly captures the meticulous labour and craftsmanship of Italian tailors in several close-ups. It then cuts to an aging tailor who says that the Chinese were unable to replicate the high quality of genuine "Made in Italy" clothing. A moment later, Xu proudly shows her "Made in Italy" fashion certificate and demonstrates her skills in fashion design. If China's economic overtaking of Japan signalled the end of an era, the documentary intimates, then an earlier conception of the "Made in Italy" label might also give way. The cinematic juxtaposition of the middle-aged and energetic Xu and the aging and isolated Italian tailor reinforces this suggestion.

Praising Wang's and Xu's endeavours to integrate socially and economically in Italy, the documentary probes into the secrets of their success: their social and business skills. Wang employs Italian designers, socializes with Chinese compatriots in restaurants, dialogues with Prato's administrators about how to end economic crimes, parties with Italian friends, and takes advantage of business opportunities emerging in mainland China. In parallel, Xu prizes the fabrics' quality, appreciates her Chinese workers' skills, pays them wages equal to the Italian standards, experiments with numerous versions of a design before settling on the final one, holds her fashion show at a public venue in Italy, and earns a "Made in Italy" certificate from the Institute for the Protection of Italian Producers, the first award of its kind for a Chinese migrant in Italy. Like Xu Qiu Lin's media exposure, Wang's and Xu's appearance in the documentary demonstrated their positive attitude towards media coverage as a place to showcase their intercultural competencies in entrepreneurship. At the film's conclusion, as Wang and other Chinese migrants celebrate a contract with a mainland Chinese retailer, the voice-over claims in a crisp tone: "Chinese migrants living in the fashion capital overcame many obstacles and continue to create the 'Made in Italy' label. This is China Power!"

For Toshio Miyake, Japan's interest in Italy, and especially in Italian fashion since the 1980s, owed much to the country's need to express a modern cultural identity through contemplating Italy's status as the Other in the West. The background to this mechanism concerned Japan's challenge of Western modernity in the 1980s and 1990s which, in the critics David Morley and Kevin Robins's words, "confounded the assumption that modernity can only be articulated through the forms the West has constructed." Much of the Western disorientation and retaliation against Japan were re-enacted in the relationship between the West and China in the 2000s.[28] This phenomenon became even more meaningful as China overtook Japan as the world's second-largest economy in 2011, as Japan confronted its own economic slowdown, and as the global media spotlighted both topics.[29] Ultimately, the documentary interpreted Chinese migrants' success remaking the "Made in Italy" fashion as a model for the Japanese, while the old Italian tailor's apparent provincialism was a cautionary tale.

The idolization of the Chinese as Italy's model migrant entrepreneurs climaxed in *温州一家人/Legend of Entrepreneurship* (Kong Sheng and Li Xue).[30] Premiered in late 2012 in prime time on CCTV 1, the first channel of the state-owned China Central Television, the serial became one of the most-watched dramas of the year and won many national television awards. It features two main storylines involving Wenzhounese private entrepreneurship, with one in China and the other in continental Europe including Italy and France. Shot on location, the thirty-six-episode serial was inspired by real-life saga of the Wenzhounese Zhou family between 1981, roughly the beginning of Deng Xiaoping's Open Door policy, and 2002, before the mid-2000s explosion of media interest in Prato.[31] Therefore, the serial's narrative aims to provide a historical perspective on Chinese migrant entrepreneurship during the crucial years that led to the mediated controversies that I examine in this chapter.[32]

Praising their contributions to the local economy, the drama's narrative unambiguously defends Chinese migrants' rights to settle in Prato. As a young girl of thirteen, Zhou Ayu (Yin Tao) is sent by her family to Italy against her will, where she eventually becomes a garment entrepreneur. Mr Saishaer is a veteran Italian entrepreneur and Prato's largest fabric supplier, who shamelessly schemes to preserve his status by bringing down Ayu's various entrepreneurial attempts.[33] Initially, the narrative attributes all the negative qualities often associated with Chinese migrants to the Jewish-Italian entrepreneur, as he scrambles to fend off competition from Chinese start-ups using unethical ploys. Ayu loses her best friend to a car accident because of Mr Saishaer's business schemes. Just as she actively seeks revenge after the incident, he is obsessed with thwarting her. Ultimately, Mr Saishaer is saved from infamy as he apologizes to Ayu for his wrongdoing and accepts her invitation to become her business partner. Like pre-2009 media accounts examined in this chapter, the serial drama comments on the jealousy that a declining, aging Italy felt towards a rising, youthful China.

In *Legend of Entrepreneurship*, this generational gap and national difference is further gendered from a moralistic Chinese perspective: Ayu's honesty, industriousness, and generosity contrasts with Mr Saishaer's unfeelingness, greed, and cunning. In mobilizing his friends to hinder Ayu's entrepreneurial undertakings, Mr Saishaer took a moralizing stance on the supposed corrupting influence of the Chinese woman and "Made in China" production practices. The narrative mocks and criticizes Mr Saishaer's despicable behaviour before constructing the morally superior Ayu. Indeed, the drama hardly touches upon Chinese economic crimes, and the rare references to illegal Chinese migrants employed in sweatshops do not involve Ayu. Such an edifying story about a virtuous woman is in keeping with the Madonna-like Chinese female archetype, which also appears in novels by Chinese migrant women authors, like Yang Xiaping's *Come due farfalle in volo sulla Grande Muraglia* (Like two butterflies flying over the Great Wall) and Hu Lanbo's *Petali di orchidea* (Petals of orchid).[34]

Attributing time-honoured female virtues to Ayu, the serial offers her as a model citizen for overseas Chinese. She is a convincing spokeswoman on behalf of Prato's Chinese community. In their attempts to bar Chinese businesses from taking root in the city, Mr Saishaer and his friends present a motion at a public hearing. In court, Ayu defends her people by speaking about her own migration story and migrants' contributions to the city. For her, Italians who conspire against migrants are fuelled by envy and a sense of failure. The flight of Chinese from Prato would not compensate for the loss of opportunities caused by many Italian businesses' inertia and inability to innovate, she concludes. The applause at the end of her speech and the city council's decision to veto the motion by popular demand must have appeased the drama's Chinese viewers. At this point in the story, the viewer feels moved by Mr Saishaer's wrongdoing and deception and even more so by Ayu's resolve and clever corporate outmaneuvering.

Insofar as Ayu takes the first step to reconcile with Mr Saishaer, having overcome her own personal pain from their previous encounters, the drama makes her the model ethical entrepreneur for Prato's Italian industrialists. In the narrative, the connection between Ayu and the Italians in Prato is intriguingly established by deploying a positive Jewish-Wenzhounese mirroring. Just as Mr Saishaer is repeatedly typecast as a scheming Jew, Ayu is depicted as a representative of hardworking Wenzhounese merchants, nicknamed the "Jews of the East," as the drama calls them in the last on-screen caption.[35] To be sure, the supposed parallel between Chinese and Jewish cultures and peoples had ample popular, journalistic, and academic support in both China and the West since the 2000s.[36] Like some of those studies, the serial's ethnic mirroring articulates ethnocultural essentialism when it addresses the Chinese in Italy, and specifically exhibits positive stereotyping of both groups based on their presumed entrepreneurial spirits inherited from their homelands and ethnic origins. The journalist Federico Rampini used a similar ethnic matching to counter negative media coverage of

Chinatowns and Jewish ghettos (see chapter 3). With the two groups' ultimate economic and social plights paralleled in the narrative, the drama makes them confront a common destiny at its narrative end: an agreement to work together to address new local challenges in global capitalism within the textile and garment industries.

How should the Italians and the Chinese migrants work together in Prato? Ayu admires Italian excellence in fashion design and confines her activities to manufacturing and sales, a narrative detail that recalls Cenni's carrot policy. Before her arrival in Prato, Ayu works as an assistant in a fashion company in Paris. The chief designer praises her strong fashion sense and encourages her to design for him. After spending a night drawing designs, Ayu gives up and confesses her stronger desire to work in fashion sales. When she manages her first garment factory in Prato, she inadvertently uses a design very similar to one patented by a famous Italian designer. Mr Saishaer uses this mistake to take her to court. Having learned a lesson, she subsequently hires the same designer to work for her company. Moreover, Ayu's pact with Mr Saishaer at the end of the drama involves commissioning orders from his many textile factories, which had been on the verge of closing because of mainland Chinese competition and dwindling domestic and overseas orders.

Ayu's view of the Italians' imaginative capacity and of how it would contribute to her business resonates with Arjun Appadurai's observation about imagination in a post-national world both as a manifestation of individual agency and as a social practice. From this perspective, when "Made in Italy" was first conceptualized and systematically promoted in the 1980s, it was both an artistic expression and a survival strategy for Italian firms to expand export markets.[37] In more recent years, as the drama suggests, the label highlights the Italian artisanal expertise, especially in high-end fashion design and fabric production, and the employment of Chinese migrants in manufacturing.[38]

Except for the drama's approval of Ayu's ambitions in sales and distribution, this interpretation of "Made in Italy" aligned with Cenni's carrot policy to innovate "Made in Prato" garments by confining the Chinese to manufacturing. The drama's endorsement of business plans proposed by Prato's government was perhaps not coincidental. The Chinese government often promoted synergy between private Chinese migrant entrepreneurship and direct state investments in Western economies. *Xinhua Lianhe Shibao* quoted the CCTV and Phoenix TV commentator Song Xiaojun as saying: "China proposes the following strategy to us. Large-sized, state-owned companies will go abroad first to start up the production line. Small-sized, individual, and private enterprises will then follow and complement them. Only in this way can we create a relatively complete, protective layer abroad for our business interests."[39] In Chinese television dramas since the 1990s, this promotion expressed the state government's goal to maintain, in Ying Zhu's words, "social harmony, state benevolence, national stability, and family values," which would benefit "the political and economic self-reliance and self-regulation of individuals and communities" during migrations within China and to the West.[40] Indeed, the cooperation of Prato's Chinese with Cenni's government would have saved the Chinese consulate in Florence and the Chinese state a great deal of diplomatic negotiations with Italian authorities.

The Italian-Chinese commercial marriage would also pave the way for more of China's direct investment in Italy's fashion industry. The first time a Chinese company commissioned high-end fashion in Italy occurred in 2012. Upon launching the first Italian-Chinese luxury fashion brand, She Ji-Sorgere, Italian collaborators insisted on selling only the label "Made in Italy" and not the knowledge behind it. As *Panorama* reported, She Ji (nation in classical Chinese)-Sorgere (rebirth in Italian) was owned by China Garments of Beijing, but its entire production line remained in Italy. The Chinese company used Italian fabrics and employed Italian designers and artisans at the workshop Raffaele Caruso of Soragna in Parma, which the journalist Pieraccini once praised as one of the "great cultivators (and diffusers) of style and glamor" and a true producer of authentic "Made in Italy" fashion. As the German national daily *Die Welt* put it, She Ji-Sorgere represented "a reversal of global production streams," the opposite of more commonplace Italian fashion companies' outsourcing to Chinese factories.[41] She Ji-Sorgere rode high on a wave of business opportunities that emerged when selling "Made in Italy" products in China and to Chinese tourists in Italy, phenomena avidly covered by the Italian, Chinese, and international media.[42] Indeed, the brand's official promotional video dramatically presented China as a world power that owned and consumed Italian fashion.[43]

Nonetheless, She Ji-Sorgere sought a prestige that was rather orthodox in conception and practice: successful middle-class Chinese men and entrepreneurs influenced the destiny of the Chinese nation and therefore deserved "Made in Italy" products made by Italians in artisan workshops on Italian soil. This concept conformed to the contemporary tendency to link gendered Chinese cultural values to the country's economy ascendancy through men.[44] It also endorsed a restricted view of "Made in Italy" as one made by Italian artisans and revealed once again the economic and cultural tension among mainland Chinese, Italians, and Italy's Chinese migrants.

Chinese migrants who were unable to modify their business configurations, or to successfully integrate into Italian society, contemplated leaving the country. Those who sought new entrepreneurial opportunities elsewhere also packed up. Towards the end of 2011, according to the Chinese mainland newspaper *Huanqiu Shibao/The Global Times*, the Chinese left Prato because of its declining entrepreneurial opportunities. A police report indicated that more than 1,000 foreign residents left the city in 2011. At the beginning of 2012, as *Ouzhou Qiaobao* reported, the number of Chinese workers in Prato dwindled as a result of excessive Italian police raids and bias against local Chinese businesses.[45]

The significant departure of Chinese migrants from Prato in 2012 was certainly not an exodus. As Frank Pieke notes, there is no certainty that returned migrants will remain in China and cut off all ties with Italy, and since Chinese migrations manifest a "constantly evolving process as new areas of origin emerge and as migrants find new ways of migrating, new countries to go to and new things to do in these countries," Italy might become attractive for them again.[46] However, 2012 was the end of an era, especially for Prato's semi-informal Chinese fast-fashion manufacturing. According to Antonella Ceccagno, since 2011 that industry has been in crisis, as the number of orders from Italian and other European markets dropped, the limited number of skilled workers demanded higher salaries and more benefits, and the trust established between the manufacturers and clients eroded.[47]

In February 2013, the left-leaning French newspaper *Libération* published a story in which the journalist, perhaps inspired by a recent series of cultural events organized by a non-profit association in Prato, muses on the possible social and economic effects on the city if a substantial number of Chinese migrants were to leave. *Il Tirreno* immediately responded to *Libération*'s suggestion that Prato's closure would mean missed opportunities with China and Chinese migrants: "This is a thesis that certainly pleases a daily newspaper with a clear leftist inspiration." However, *Il Tirreno* goes on to acknowledge the sway that international opinions have over Prato's future: "But it would be wrong to respond to the questions raised by the article with a shrug. The opinions of the international media are certainly not insignificant."[48]

Through the Prato case study, the localism-globalization debates that Chinese migration in Italy engendered became much better-known to the international media and readership. This caused a news media transition, already under way, to intensify: the switch from the Chinese mafia to the model migrant entrepreneurs, and from casting Chinese migrants as villains to putting them on a pedestal. The case study in Rome, to which I turn next, indicates this improvement of Italy's media environment for Chinese migrants.

Chapter 7

Rome: The 2012 Chinese March

In January 2012, two Chinese migrants, one of whom was a baby girl, were killed by Moroccan criminals during a violent robbery in Torpignattara, an eastern suburb of Rome. Both the Italian and the Chinese migrant media devoted considerable attention to the tragedy and its aftermath. Like the 2007 riot analysed in chapters 3 and 4, the 2012 murder was a one-time event. But it was one of many robberies and other harassments that Italians and foreigners inflicted on Chinese migrants. The Rome murder was the most prominent social incident in Italy when mainstream Italian media nearly unanimously portrayed the Chinese as victims of unprovoked violence.

Later that month, Rome witnessed Italy's first Chinese-organized, large-scale commemorative march to involve Italians and non-Chinese migrants. Chinese activists meticulously planned this social and media event, facilitating Italian photojournalists' coverage. They aimed to pressure the local government to provide better safety for Chinese and other migrants in the country's capital.[1] The Rome march was similar in methods and goals to how Italian industrialists and politicians orchestrated television coverage of police raids and popular protests in Prato in 2009 and 2010 in order to push for more state intervention in the textile and garment industries (see chapter 5).

While the events in Milan and in Prato that I have analysed featured opposing media viewpoints of the Chinese diaspora in Italy, such polarity was all but gone in the coverage of the 2012 murder and march. The tension between Chinese and Italian merchants in the Roman neighbourhood of Esquilino was completely absent in the 2012 coverage.[2] Instead, both the Chinese migrant and the Italian media showed compassion for the community, praised how the organizers obtained official approval for the march and demonstrated peacefully, and emphasized the good blend of globalization and migrants' local integration in working-class neighbourhoods in Rome including Esquilino and Torpignattara.

What brought about such consensus around the murder and march in both media camps? What was it about the personal safety of Italy's Chinese that decentred the Italian media's obsession with this community's criminality and business activities? Was the sympathetic reading of the 2012 march the result of a fortuitous combination of external social factors, or was it germane to a media milieu that became more hospitable to Chinese migrants thanks to journalists' increasing intercultural competencies? Or both? In this chapter, I unpack these questions, giving closure to my discussion of Italian and Chinese migrant journalists' intercultural capacities in framing the Chinese migration for the public through crime reporting and victimhood narratives.

Crime Reporting, Victimhood Narratives, and Cultural Traumas

The Italian media coverage of the 2012 murder and its subsequent police investigation was in keeping with the genre requirements of crime reporting in contemporary global media. These requirements were given flesh and blood in relevant coverage that emphasized the randomness of the violence, the location of the murder in a working-class Roman neighbourhood, the cruelty of the victims' physical annihilation, and the widely accepted perception that Italy's Moroccans were criminally inclined. All of these elements must have struck a deep chord with the Italians and the Chinese alike, causing the media in both languages to downplay the victims' ethnicity, social status, and cultural and physical markers, and to emphasize the tragic circumstances in which migrants, like other residents of Rome, fell prey to arbitrary violence. These media put urgent pressure on Rome's municipal government, which they said had not done enough to curb increasing crimes.

The march that commemorated the victims was born of these political and media circumstances that helped to portray the Chinese as ordinary citizens with understandable concerns for their personal safety. It was an act of public mourning that involved an extensive walk through many parts of Rome, and thereby was a significant subject of news photography in all the major Italian news outlets. Italian journalists and photographers covered the march and shot certain visual elements, such as banners that publicized the Chinese migrants' perspectives on the murder, from angles that Chinese migrant activists and organizers suggested. Italian photographers and newspaper editors interpreted the murder and march as the peak of the criminality in Rome that had escalated in the preceding months.[3] In so doing, narratives about the victimhood of Rome's Chinese population emerged.

In the Chinese migrant media, these victimhood narratives were even more powerful. They expressed their perception of the "enemies" who threatened hardworking and law-abiding Chinese migrants, and who included Italian and international journalists who partially falsified their news stories, biased Italian citizens who made inflammatory comments on television, the Italian state that persecuted the politically weak Chinese migrant community, Chinese migrants who eschewed hard work in favour of criminal activities, and migrants of Arab or African origin.

Why did the media narratives about the victimhood of Italy's Chinese achieve considerable success in the aftermath of a murder? These narratives resonated historically and culturally because national victimhood narratives have been pronounced in post-Second World War China and Italy. A national victimhood narrative conjures an imagined community of citizens who share a common history as victims at the hands of external and internal opposition groups that, for purportedly illegitimate reasons, have sought to overtake the current ruling elite. In this way, victimhood narratives help to fashion the nation-state's official story from the perspective of the ruling class.

Victimhood narratives are central to modern Chinese official political discourse, which is predicated on, to quote Neil Renwick and Qing Cao, the "idea of China as the victim of hostile external and internal predators," including "ancient invasion, nineteenth century Occidental 'semi-colonialism,' counter-revolutionary dangers and late twentieth century criticisms of commercial piracy, human rights abuses and its Taiwan policy." Apart from supporting communist rule in post-1949 China, this victimhood narrative recounted a deeply ingrained "historical trauma" that became a "collective cultural memory" for the Chinese and transcended its original historical contexts.[4] Media coverage of the personal safety of overseas Chinese around the 2007 riot discussed in chapter 4 can be viewed as a contemporary continuation of the nationalist discourse about the Chinese victimization. Similar reporting renewed after the 2012 murder.

Likewise, victimhood narratives had taken a foundational role in modern Italian politics and culture since the country's unification in 1861. With reference to the experiences of Italian prisoners of war, Ruth Ben-Ghiat comments that "rhetoric of victimhood had long been part of the landscape of Italian political discourse, but gained new meaning and popularity in the wake of World War II," as there were "feelings of victimization among non-Jewish Italians, who endured the effects of German occupation, Allied invasion, and a bloody civil war." In postwar Italian politics and culture dominated by the centrist party Democrazia Cristiana (Christian democrats), Italian soldiers' brutality was removed from the collective memory and war atrocities were increasingly attributed to the Nazi Germans and to the fascists of the Republic of Salò.[5] Popular feelings of national victimhood sat comfortably with Christian-inspired humanism and racial tolerance. Symptomatic of this condition was the narrative premise of several internationally successful Italian films, including *Nuovo cinema paradiso/Cinema Paradiso* (Giuseppe Tornatore, 1988), *Mediterraneo* (Gabriele Salvatores, 1991), *Il Postino/The Postman* (Michael Radford, 1994), and *La vita è bella/Life Is Beautiful* (Roberto Benigni, 1997). These historical films created an account of the Italians during the Second World War as Italiani brava gente (good-hearted people), thereby strengthening the victimhood narratives already visible in postwar neorealist cinema.[6]

From 1992 to 2012, several more high-profile events upheld diverse Italian victimhood narratives, often at a national level. The early 1990s Tangentopoli scandals revealed widespread corruption in Italy's political class and made voters feel victimized by irresponsible politicians, a sentiment Silvio Berlusconi appropriated for his political rise. As I examined in chapter 2, during the 1990s and 2000s the "Chinese mafia" and migrants' illegal business practices were a way for Italians to claim to be casualties of globalization and international organized crime. In the late 2000s, victim-centred Italian narratives forcefully emerged, often focusing on the anni di piombo, the so-called years of lead (from the late 1960s to the early 1980s) in which a significant number of terrorist acts occurred in Italy.[7]

Since the 2000s, the intense media coverage of refugees on Italian shores; police raids on Romany camps; and criminal acts committed by the Romanians, Albanians, and North Africans may have indirectly legitimated the victimhood narratives about Italy's Chinese.[8] As I demonstrated in chapters 2 to 6, despite strong dissenting voices, journalists of diverse political persuasions frequently considered the Chinese a model minority and viewed their impact on Italy's economic and cultural globalization as at least somewhat positive. Much of this positive stereotyping was accomplished through implicit interethnic comparisons. Although such comparisons rarely surfaced explicitly in the coverage that I study in this book, to me they seem a premise of the social imagination of Italy's migrants that the media nurtured. Certainly, in private conversations I have observed journalists and readers make such comparisons. My point here is that it was the Chinese community in Italy, not other migrant communities, whose victimhood narratives in 2012 seemed plausible and particularly powerful to the broader public.

As I have shown, there was a fertile terrain upon which to construct the specific victimhood narratives about the 2012 murder and march. Past victimhood narratives served specific political and cultural objectives. What did the 2012 versions intend to achieve that would make a positive portrayal of Chinese migrants desirable for the media in general and for the Italian media in particular, given their tendency to claim victimhood for the Italians allegedly threatened by the Chinese? I argue that Italian and Chinese migrant journalists shared the 2012 victimhood narratives to help mould the murder and march into a cultural trauma that extensively involved the country's migrants, with an aim to provide considerably more extensive hospitality to the Chinese in the country's mainstream media.

According to Jeffrey C. Alexander, "cultural trauma occurs when members of a collectivity feel they have been subjected to a horrendous event that leaves indelible marks upon their group consciousness, marking their memories forever and changing their future identity in fundamental and irrevocable ways."[9] An example of a cultural trauma in Italy's migration history is the 1989 murder of Jerry Masslo, which contributed to the passing of the 1990 Legge Martelli and which led to a wave of publications about Italian racism against migrants in the 1990s.[10] Drawing on Alexander, I contend that the 2012 murder constituted a traumatic event for Italy's Chinese migrants, because this senseless bloodshed allowed them to express their fears publicly and collectively for the first time through a carefully designed march for a receptive and sympathetic mainstream Italian audience. The murder pointed to a worsening entrepreneurial environment in Italy for Chinese migrants, and indeed some left Rome and other cities throughout 2012 (see chapter 6). But the murder also convinced many more Chinese to better integrate into local communities, crucially because ordinary Italians who were interviewed in the media seemed more disposed to empathize and sympathize with the Chinese than ever before.

The trauma's scope was not confined to Italy's Chinese community. By asking their readers to think collectively about the murder's causes, and about the trauma it engendered for them, the Italian media expanded the field of Italian-identified persons to include Chinese migrants. For Alexander, "Insofar as they identity the cause of trauma, and thereby assume such moral responsibility, members of collectivities define their solidary relationships in ways that, in principle, allow them to share the sufferings of others. Is the suffering of others also our own? In thinking that it might in fact be, societies expand the circle of the we."[11] The Italian media repeatedly argued that it was the ineptitude of Rome's municipal administration, which was responsible for public safety, that made Chinese and other city residents victims of street violence. Italians, foreigners of other ethnicities, and Chinese migrants unrelated to the victims participated in the march, showing the popularity of this media interpretation.

Ultimately, I propose that this Italian-Chinese migrant cultural trauma formed a base for a new view of Chinese migrants as Italian residents that began to gain legitimacy within a large spectrum of mainstream Italian media. For the first time, Italy's Chinese, whether elite or less affluent, were accepted as understandable people in most media coverage, and not as profit-seeking merchants or socially isolated workers. In the long run, the 2012 murder and march may prove a watershed moment, after which it has no longer been possible for the Italian media to discuss topics typically assigned to Chinese migrants without more extensively critiquing related Italian social and cultural malaises. That is, since 2012 it has been increasingly untenable for Italian journalists to employ Chinese stereotypes that have largely been rejected elsewhere in the world, to cover the Chinese with a persistently accusatory tone that seeks more to provoke social tension and to procure political gains than to solve the concrete issues at hand, or to conflate Chinese migrants and mainland Chinese for political and business reasons that often have little relevance to migrants' daily concerns. However, because the hospitable media coverage of the 2012 murder and march was born from specific circumstances around that time, it may also prove to be but a one-time blip in the evolving mediascape about Italy's Chinese.

Crime Reporting and Newsworthiness, Roman Style

Since the 1990s, the Italian media has tended to view migration through the lens of criminality, thereby highlighting, if not inventing, a dichotomy between victimized Italians and unruly migrants. The connection between migrants and criminality then legitimized the institutional discipline of migrants' real and imagined social deviance. The logic that linked criminality to security measures ensured that the newsworthiness of immigration to Italy in recent decades was often associated with the crimes it caused. Therefore, migrations to Italy often appeared in crime reporting. Even when compared to the news media in Greece and Spain – like Italy, both countries began to receive immigrants on a large scale in the 1990s – the Italians used the sociocriminal perspective more extensively.[12] Variations of this perspective have appeared in all three case studies previously examined in this book.

Not surprisingly, the coverage of the 2012 murder revitalized the sociocriminal approach to Italy's Chinese. The initial accounts of the murder in *La Repubblica* and *Corriere della Sera* characterize it as a premeditated robbery, likely involving Chinese criminals, that went awry. The murder occurred around 9 p.m. on 4 January 2012 in Torpignattara. Holding his six-month-old daughter Joy in his arms, Zhou Zheng walked home with his wife Lia from their café and money transfer agency. Two young men with pistols intercepted the Zhous and asked for the day's earnings. Probably provoked by the couple's refusal to surrender the money, the two men shot and killed Zhou and Joy and injured Lia. The murderers, who were not professional killers but possibly addicts from a nearby substance abuse clinic, fled with Lia's handbag. Later, investigators found 3,000 euros in Zhou's pockets. Thanks to Lia's cell phone, the police retrieved her handbag in an abandoned house located several kilometres from the crime scene. In the handbag, they found either 10,000 or 16,000 euros, depending on the account, which the killers had left behind and possibly intended to retrieve later.[13] The initial reports focus on Joy, articulating the tenet of personalization in contemporary crime reporting that interprets an event through a key character. Following the principle of conventionalism, the media also lingered over the cash that the Zhous had with them, reinforcing the widely circulated Italian stereotype that the Chinese always carried an excessive amount of it.[14]

Drawing on further police investigations, Italian journalists wondered about the murderers' nationality. As the murderers were initially reported as Italians, the Italian media was careful not to incite unnecessary Italian-Chinese clashes. Quoting posts on the Chinese microblog Weibo, *La Repubblica* claimed that "there is no rage against the Italians. It is clear to all that the victims' Chinese citizenship is only incidental." The paper also quoted the Chinese consul in Florence, which attributed the rise of harassment experienced by Prato's and Rome's Chinese to Italy's deepening economic crisis.[15] Later on, the media speculated about whether the assassins could be Chinese nationals, since Zhou's money transfer agency managed the circulation of an unusually large sum of money. As I discussed in chapter 5, the Italian media examined illicit Chinese money in Prato's money transfer agencies. *La Repubblica* pursued the subject of Chinese criminal activities by quoting several Chinese merchants in Piazza Vittorio, who complained about the very frequent muggings and protection rackets that other Chinese migrants and the Italians forced on them. *Il Messaggero* repeatedly claimed that the murder was in fact "revenge" carried out by Zhou's "enemies," as money transfer activities made his family vulnerable to robberies. Based on statements by Zhou's family, *Corriere della Sera* surmised that he might have known his killers, since he apparently was not afraid to resist guns.[16] These newspapers thus fell back on illegal Chinese economic activities and organized crime to explain the senseless murder.

The sociocriminal approach to the Chinese gained currency when on 9 January the police identified the killers as two Moroccans with previous criminal records for theft and mugging, and when on 16 January Mohammed Nasiri, one of them, was found dead in an isolated house in Rome. Nasiri's death, which the investigators were not able to rule as a suicide or a homicide, immediately led the press to hypothesize that Zhou was connected with Rome's alleged Chinese organized crime. According to *La Repubblica*, this rumour supposedly circulated among Italian residents in Torpignattara. *La Repubblica*, *Il Messaggero*, and *Corriere della Sera* all called the discovery of Zhou's possible criminal background a *giallo* (crime fiction), emphasizing this literary genre's connection with Italian crime reporting as had the 1992 to 1995 coverage of the Chinese mafia. According to Italian newspapers, the police recovered a coded message from a telephone conversation in which Nasiri's "execution" was ordered. Based on this evidence, the police speculated about whether local Italian and Chinese criminal organizations had assassinated Nasiri to prevent increased police searches in areas where they conducted various illicit activities such as drug trade.[17] This twist showed the importance of novelty in crime reporting: news outlets, in striving to come up with fresh things to say about a familiar story – one concerning a prevalent perspective that associated the Chinese with criminality – tended to encourage speculation based on meager evidence.[18]

Viewed holistically, however, Italian readers largely anticipated the supposed novelty, as they already knew about possible contacts between Italian and Chinese organized crime and about a crime surge in Rome in that period. Thus, the media's sociocriminal approach to the 2012 murder can be more appropriately viewed as a "daily moral workout," a notion that Jack Katz uses to explain how reporting on a particular crime can function only when the media speaks "dramatically to issues that are of direct relevance to readers' existential challenges, whether or not readers are preoccupied with the possible personal misfortune of becoming victims to crime."[19] For the highly ideology-driven Italian news media, another daily moral workout at that time was to pressure Rome's municipal government, led between 2008 and 2013 by

Gianni Alemanno of the centre-right party PdL (Il Popolo della Libertà/The people of freedom), to strengthen public security in order to address increasing crime in the capital city. More generally, this focus was meant to challenge the Alemanno administration's credibility and to denounce Italian society's perceived moral disintegration, typical media arguments in the late 2000s and early 2010s.

The real newsworthiness in the 2012 coverage focused not on the national identity of the murderers, nor on their motives, but on the 10 January Chinese-organized march, which was featured on the front pages of all the major local and national newspapers.[20] If in the past Italy's Chinese were known for their willful distance from the Italian media, their silence about discrimination to which they were subjected, and their single-minded focus on work and entrepreneurship, then the march provided a singular moment for the camera to capture them acting in concert for a public cause. An estimated ten thousand Chinese migrants, other foreigners, and Italians walked from Piazza Vittorio to Via Giovannoli, where they held a vigil by Zhou's apartment building. As *Il Messaggero* memorably describes, Lia, dressed in a white shirt belonging to her husband, fell to the ground near the crime site, holding his shoes and yelling desperately.[21] The march showcased a community on emotional public display, countering the stereotype of Chinese migrants as isolated workers enclosed in workplaces and obsessed with economic pursuits. Moreover, in covering the march, journalists highlighted how Italians sympathized with Chinese migrants on the grounds that anyone could fall victim to random violence in a place insufficiently patrolled by the police. The 2012 march was an utterly novel event for the Italian media in its depictions of the country's Chinese community.

Italian Victimhood Narratives for Chinese Migrants

Through covering the march, Italy's conventional (print newspapers), dominant (television), and new (internet) media were all inclined to circulate an exceptionally sympathetic understanding of Chinese migrants' social plight and aspirations. The Italian media portrayed the Chinese as victims at the mercy of criminals of diverse national and ethnic backgrounds, be they Italian, Chinese, or North African. This depiction was vastly different from the other three case studies I have examined in this book, in which much media coverage told stories about Italian victims at the hands of Chinese migrants.

How and why did Italian journalism create convincing victimhood narratives on behalf of the Chinese migrant community, which the

Italians were able to comprehend? In this section, I suggest that diverse communication technologies, including photojournalism, television news, and web television programs, helped turn abstract concepts of mourning and trauma into images that were visually concrete and emotionally accessible to Italian audiences. Journalists deployed these technologies to highlight several images and moments that they considered to have significant news value, including the murder's unremarkable location in a dense working-class neighbourhood, the robbers-turned-killers' arbitrary targets, and the recognizable public spaces in Rome through which the demonstrators marched and the vigil they held to mourn the victims.

Torpignattara, the setting for the murder, was said to exemplify the no-frills, working-class neighbourhoods found throughout urban Italy, where Chinese and other migrants lived peacefully with the locals. This spirit and the challenges the neighbourhood faced were captured on the front page of *La Repubblica* on 6 January:

> This is a traditional, working-class ["popolare"] neighbourhood with its own rhythms, rules, and habits. This is a lively and sensible town ["borgata"], where one breathes in freedom and democracy. Many migrants, great racial integration, few and isolated gestures of intolerance. However, this is also an immense marginalized area where the police and the carabinieri, with little equipment and funding available, rarely make themselves seen.

Photographs and clips published on the websites of *La Repubblica* and *Il Messaggero* accentuated the unremarkable crime scene, with plain-looking streets and interchangeable apartment buildings in the background.[22] The murder's unexceptional location indicated its geographical "nearness" or "proximity," a key news value in contemporary media that enhanced the murder's relevance to Romans, and so integrated it into coverage of escalating violence in Rome in that period.[23]

As the Italian media conveyed, Italian Romans saw the murder as a random episode of violence that they too might experience. By encouraging this perspective, it further endorsed Chinese victimhood and ordinary Italians' appreciation of it. Explicit representations of Italian and foreign residents expressing their disbelief at the murder's atrocity and arbitrariness characterized Rai news. Scored by an elegant Chinese melody, a *Corriere della Sera* web television program showed several Italian women leaving bouquets of flowers for the victims. In *La Repubblica* as in *Xinhua Lianhe Shibao*, photographs of flowers placed at the crime scene and at the Chinese couple's café focused on the handwritten cards left by Italians, in which mourners expressed their sympathy and sorrow for the loss of the lives of their Chinese "neighbours" and "friends."[24]

To be sure, for some, Chinese migrants were not arbitrary targets. As one Chinese woman put it in a *La Repubblica* video: "Since the Chinese have money, all the foreigners are after them." The foreigners to whom she referred must have been non-Chinese nationals, and therefore the Italians and non-Chinese migrants. To prove her point, she showed the camera documents that she would submit that day to report a mugging she had recently experienced.[25] However, as journalists understood, even if robberies and muggings had been daily affairs for those perceived to be weak and defenceless, Zhou and Joy were still random targets among many such potential victims in a nondescript Roman suburb. While media coverage of Zhou's money transfer agency's potential illegal activities led to popular conjectures about possible collaboration between Roman and Chinese criminal groups in which Zhou might have been involved, this hypothesis was neither proven by the police nor conclusively reported in the press.

For the most part, the Italian media emphasized universal human suffering because of senseless deaths, viewing migrants' vigil as an act of mourning. An iconic photograph, which Italian photojournalism created and which the Italian and the Chinese migrant media prominently used, spoke to this idea eloquently. The image's composition is dominated by two family photographs of Zhou and Joy, placed above flowers people had left at the entrance to their apartment building. The victims' smiling faces in these two photographs are lit by warm candlelight in the darkness, a contrast that effectively recalls their deaths for the viewer of the news photograph. This photograph of photographs thus points to the gap between the two moments of production in order to comment on the rift between death and life. In a special issue on the 2012 murder and march, *Xinhua Lianhe Shibao* reprinted this photograph on its front page.[26] Apart from the empathy and consolation this photograph elicited, it also became iconic because Joy functioned as the "ideal victim" insofar as she was defenceless and too young to be aware of the circumstances in which she was killed. The media's depiction of Joy validated other Chinese migrants' victimization for the viewers.[27]

Italian photojournalism also narrated a truly newsworthy aspect of the Chinese victimhood: the unusual sight of large crowds of Italy's Chinese in a public march that they had organized. The carefully orchestrated march provided a counterpoint to the unexceptional crime scene and to the murder's randomness. *La Repubblica* published a slideshow on its website to depict the march's movement through familiar spaces in Rome from a third-person perspective. The editorial sequencing of these photographs invites the viewer to discover the march's all-important motives, and through them to appreciate its significance for the Chinese and others in Rome. The first photograph sets the elegiac tone by showing marchers holding pictures of Joy and banners with a slogan written in both Chinese and Italian: "No a violenza, sì a sicurezza" (No to violence, yes to security). Zooming from medium to extreme close-ups, subsequent photographs capture demonstrators against the backdrop of Piazza Vittorio, with buildings in the august Umbertine style befitting the solemn march. The overwhelming scale of Chinese crowds in these photographs encourages the viewer to find out what causes they were protesting. More photographs focus on the faces of sad non-Chinese in the crowds, further motivating the viewer to seek out this march's purpose. The final photographs confirm that the march was about crime and victimhood as lit candles cover the ground at the entrance to an apartment building. The images prominently frame people's faces glowing in the candlelight against the surrounding darkness, as if to comment on their innocence vis-à-vis increasing crime in the capital city. The highly emotional state in which these photographs depict their subjects added force and nuance to their claims of victimhood.[28]

Apart from culturally and psychologically inflected visual perspectives, photography's role in creating and digesting the Chinese victimhood for an Italian audience can be further appreciated from a temporal perspective associated with image technologies. Peter Wollen suggests that conventional photographs can signify events, processes, or states of the things photographed. In editorial sequence, the news photographs collect the march's significant moments to indicate the states of a process. A dossier of several photographs could thus signify the march as a social event, or the process of protestors banding together to better public security in Rome in the future.[29]

Further, the stasis of these news photographs allowed the viewer to look at them repeatedly, which considerably facilitated their memorization. In contrast, the mobility of televisual images shown in newscasts gave the viewer only fleeting glimpses, unless they watched newscasts throughout the day until the images repeated. The combined stasis and mobility of web video, which let the viewer opt to repeat, pause, and fast forward, created a hermeneutic flexibility that mirrored an average reader's viewing experiences more closely. The seeming ambiguity in interpreting specific images conveyed in diverse mediums allowed the viewer to experience the murder's commemoration on multiple levels and to remember the march's iconic moments. These communications technologies considerably strengthened media construction of the 2012 murder and march as a cultural trauma in the history of foreign immigration to Italy.

Chinese Victimhood Narratives for the Italian Media

Apart from their news values, the Italian media created victimhood narratives thanks to Chinese migrant elites' activism in the march. Having honed their professional skills in their coverage of the 2007 riot and of Prato, in 2012 Chinese community activists and journalists wasted no time in launching the march to seek legitimacy for Chinese migrants in Italy from mainstream Italian media and society. Positive coverage of the 2012 march in the Italian media meant that elite community leaders and journalists were successful intermediaries between ordinary Chinese and the Italian political and media establishments. Lucia Hui King, one of the march's organizers, was emblematic of first- and second-generation elite Chinese Italians who gained social prestige by engaging Italian society. King periodically appeared in both the Italian and the Chinese migrant media outlets as a representative of Rome's Chinese community. She was also the secretary general of the Federazione delle Associazioni delle Comunità Cinesi di Roma (Federation of associations of the Chinese communities in Rome), the president of the Soong Ching Ling Foundation of Italy, and a consultant to the Fondazione Marisa Bellisario. Like Xu Qiu Lin of Giupel and Hu Lanbo of *Cina in Italia*, King wielded significant public power within Italy's Chinese community by virtue of her networks in the country's media and public relations.[30]

To be sure, these community activists and leaders were not elected by average migrants. In the 2000s, Italy's heterogeneous Chinese migrant community lacked a centralized structure. Further, most Chinese had limited interaction with migrants' associations because they preferred to turn to family members, relatives, and friends in times of need.[31] Nevertheless, the organizers' mobilizing power, mainly through street advertising and notices in community newspapers, was such that thousands of Chinese migrants participated in the march.

During the march, Chinese migrants displayed an acute awareness of visual means of persuasion to create victimhood narratives for Italian photographers, as they tried to shape the Italian media's depictions of them.[32] A *La Repubblica* web television video reveals the care that migrant activists and community leaders, including King, put into selecting angles for Italian photographers.[33] King instructed demonstrators to line up so that photographers could shoot them head on. The resulting images show the marchers' grave facial expressions in contrast to the victims' smiling faces in the large photographs they held. Chinese organizers preferred these frontal shots, as they wanted to paint a positive image of their community. In Chinese, being frontal to one's face means being positive (*zheng mian*), an example of a common wordplay that draws on the same or similar sounds and intonation of two words that normally have different and unconnected meanings.

This particular camera angle appears to have inspired several similarly composed Italian news photographs, which capture the front of Chinese crowds at varying distances. The viewer witnesses demonstrators holding pictures of the two victims as they walk along a tramway in Esquilino; an extreme long shot of demonstrators who fill the street to the horizon; the unsettling feeling aroused by the Chinese who bear a white banner that collects black-inked signatures in commemoration of the victims; and the close warmth of the light that illuminates migrants' faces as they solemnly place candles on the pavement.[34]

Thus, the head-on camera angle produces a series of "decisive moments," a term that Henri Cartier-Bresson uses to describe "the simultaneous recognition, in a fraction of a second, of the significance of an event as well as a precise organization of forms which give that event its proper expression." Italian photographers fortuitously captured the moment, whose significance they recognized because Chinese activists had suggested it. This angle was the product of a marriage between the moment's immediacy and the journalists' immersion.[35] Such decisive moments have specific prominent formal features. When this particular camera angle is used in close-up and panoramic shots, it privileges a theatrical viewing position that would have been impossible for most protestors to access during the march. These shots are also psychologically confrontational in a way that heightens the march's elegiac mood and encourages the viewer to respond with emotion. Considering these factors, I also suggest that the decisive moments that this camera angle nurtures were instrumental in turning the 2012 march into a media event and spectacle.[36]

This angle and the photographs it inspired are but one example of how Chinese migrants successfully inserted a self-legitimating discourse about their victimhood into the mainstream Italian media by organizing the march and mobilizing attention. Another case is the Italian media's references to the Chinese migrant press. Chinese migrants from a relatively broad range of professions, including journalism, were interviewed by the national television news and press.[37] *Xinhua Lianhe*

Shibao published a special issue dedicated to the murder and especially to Joy's death, which appeared in the aforementioned *La Repubblica* web television.[38] The visuals and the bilingual text on the issue's front page portray the Chinese migrants and the Italians as interdependent. The page's left column bears the Chinese word "dian" (an offering to the spirits of the deceased) set in white against a black background, using the two colours of Chinese funeral rituals. The right-side column features a Christian cross above the title, forming part of a Chinese expression that translates to the word "cross" (*shi zi jia* with the character "shi," which means the number ten and takes the shape of a cross). The combination of traditional Chinese and Christian Italian elements in this design articulates a mutual Italian-Chinese understanding through victimhood narratives that the Chinese deployed and the Italians perpetuated.

The 2012 march showcased the organizational and media clout Chinese migrants were able to wield as a minority group to contest previous portrayals of them in the Italian media. The largely forgotten history of Chinese migrants as victims of petty and violent crimes in Italy could then become inscribed into the country's national consciousness. Historically, the fight of Chinese and other Asian migrant and diasporic communities for greater visibility in their adopted countries and in the mainstream media was a significant issue.[39] Although Chinese migrants had already contended with the Italian media during the 2007 riot and in Prato, their positions were largely antagonistic and reactive and, when covered by Italian journalists, were almost always used for negative purposes. The changed circumstances following the 2012 murder, however, gave migrant journalists a unique opportunity to speak more organically and proactively in the Italian mediascape – not to counter Italian media opinions, but to shape them from the outset.

By analysing the Chinese agency in claiming victimhood and in commemorating the trauma engendered by the murder, I do not wish to downplay the pain suffered by the victims' family members and others. Their claims of victimhood were empirical and justifiable. Rather, I have revealed the rhetorical mechanisms, social and political circumstances, and technological means by which these victimhood narratives conveyed human suffering convincingly to migrants and Italians who were not immediately affected by the murder, but who were nonetheless mobilized to join the march. These victimhood narratives also provide a key to understanding the political goals and operational modalities of their creators who were the elite Chinese migrant journalists and entrepreneurs living in Italy.

Positive Stereotyping in the Chinese Migrant Media

The 2012 murder and march provided elite Chinese migrants with an unprecedented opportunity to actively inscribe their trauma and public mourning into Italian national consciousness. *Ouhua Lianhe Shibao* did not shy away from calling the march "the most opportune moment for Italy's Chinese to express their demands" to the Italian government.[40] As the 2012 murder became part of the collective memory of civil violence in Italy, and the march became a building block of multicultural Italian national identity, the Chinese community had a chance to play a key role in shaping multi-ethnic Italian history.

Chinese migrant activists seized the opportunity without hesitation. They professed cultural allegiance to Italy in their media and, by mobilizing a large number of demonstrators, publicly performed the civic duty of protesting the local government's negligence of public security that imperiled all residents in Rome. These efforts expressed elite migrants' desire to underscore and legitimate the lawful residence of the Chinese in Italy for migrants and for Italians. Chinese journalists and activists believed that victimhood narratives were the best way to convey their self-authorization.

Under these circumstances, the Chinese migrant media sought to elucidate migrants' human, economic, and moral contributions to Italy's multicultural society, thereby exaggerating positive stereotyping in their own coverage of the 2012 march. A similar situation had occurred in connection with Prato (see chapters 5 and 6), where the Chinese migrant and the international news media lauded the role that these migrants' local-global economic capital played in revitalizing the city's industrial district.

To be sure, it was fair for Italy's Chinese migrant press to focus on positive images of their community. As Ella Shohat and Robert Stam argue regarding minority groups' positive self-stereotyping, "Given a dominant cinema that trades in heroes and heroines, 'minority' communities rightly ask for their fair share of the representational pie as a simple matter of representational parity." The pitfalls of doing so, however, were manifest in Chinese migrant coverage of the march. According to Shohat and Stam, such shortcomings include essentialism, ahistoricism, moralism, suppressed internal diversity, and the promotion of a particular social positioning.[41] In the rest of this section, I explore these shortcomings in relation to two stereotypes: first, Chinese migrants were good-hearted and hardworking residents in Italy; and second, Chinese migrants formed a more mature community compared to other foreigners in Italy.

According to the first stereotype, Italy's middle-class Chinese were fundamentally "good people" and "lawful citizens" who, like average Italian citizens, did not deserve to become victims of violence. An open letter addressed to "all citizens in Italy" following the murder and march appeared in *Xinhua Lianhe Shibao* and *Cina in Italia* in both Italian and Chinese.[42] It infuses sentimentalism into a problem-solving narrative to great effect. The opening paragraph sets an elegiac tone: "We cannot imagine the gaze of the baby girl as she left this world. Perhaps her eyes were still sparkling with thankfulness for Santa Claus's best wishes; perhaps she was not even able to look at her wounded mother for the last time." The future of this migrant family, whose sole intention was to settle in the "belpaese" (beautiful country), was shattered by the murder. The article argues that the Italian government must prevent similar "family tragedies" from happening again. Moreover, "the tragic destruction of an innocent family allowed the Italians and the Chinese to be so close for the first time. The anger at the cruel killers and the determination to track them down made good people forget about their previous misunderstandings." As Arthur G. Neal observes, "a national trauma is shared collectively and frequently has a cohesive effect as individuals gather in small and intimate groups to reflect on the tragedy and its consequences."[43] This open letter viewed the march as a collective trauma through which the Chinese migrants and the Italians were not only able to release emotional stress in a civil way, but also to reflect collectively on this traumatic experience in order to prevent future clashes between the two groups.

Chinese migrants' plea to the Italian state for stronger measures to protect their personal safety was genuine and urgent. By 2012, Chinese migrant and Italian newspapers had extensively covered how migrants attracted significant criminal attention on the streets and in their stores. This included robberies, muggings, kidnappings, and murders committed mostly by Italians and foreigners of other ethnicities but also by Chinese nationals. Stories of Chinese victims in Italy and elsewhere came painfully to life in these accounts. This media milieu, together with the luridness of the accounts, explained the topic's grip on the Chinese, reinforcing the rhetorical force of migrants' victimhood narratives.[44]

Zhongguo Xinwenshe (China news), the Chinese state news agency that focuses on overseas Chinese, offered an overview of lesser-known but shocking violent episodes involving Chinese migrants in Milan and Reggio Emilia after the 2012 murder. One of France's most influential Chinese migrant news portals, www.franceqw.com/portal.php, published a list of robberies and muggings victimizing the Chinese in Europe, particularly in Italy and Spain in 2012. *Zhongguo Xinwenshe* surveyed Greece, Britain, Argentina, Brazil, Japan, and Canada for the rising number of Chinese victims of violence there. The news agency attributed the phenomenon to the economic recession, overseas Chinese's habit of conspicuously displaying their wealth, and psychological problems that arose from migrants' sudden insertion into new societies and cultures.[45] In such reports, journalists often drew on nationalist sentiments to accentuate ethnoculturalism as the underlying reason that Chinese migrants experienced physical violence. They often did not articulate specific sociopolitical contexts for this widespread violence, but instead noted that, despite their desire to live peacefully in host countries, Chinese migrants were assaulted for being Chinese (who succeeded in their enterprises, flaunted their wealth, and failed to learn the local languages).

The perpetrators of this violence were of diverse origins. Since the 2000s, the Chinese in Italy and France had shared a strong bias against North African migrants, who they perceived as frequent robbers and petty criminals who targeted Chinese migrants.[46] In covering the 2012 Rome murder, the Chinese media often tried to tone down this bias. When the Italian media revealed that the two killers were Moroccans, *Xinhua Lianhe Shibao* immediately opined that the murder was unrelated to systematic racism and to anti-Chinese sentiments from other "races" in Italy. Canale 5's coverage of the march featured the aforementioned Chinese activist Lucia Hui King stating that Moroccan migrants, who attended the march in the spirit of solidarity, were very welcome.[47]

The Italian media also decoupled the 2012 murder from any suggestion of interethnic conflict between the Chinese and North African migrants in Italy. To be sure, *La Repubblica* reported on how Italian and Romanian petty criminals targeted Rome's Chinese, who then resorted to private guards instead of relying on the Italian police for protection. A Bengalese owner of a laundromat near the scene of the 2012 murder claimed that muggings and robberies directed at foreigners, Italian senior citizens, and women occurred almost daily. However, such details did not surface in most media coverage of the march. Instead, although the Chinese made up the majority of the demonstrators, *Corriere della Sera* hastened to mention the presence of the "Indians, North Africans, migrants of other nationalities, and Italians," and went so far as to state that "perhaps never before has the victims' nationality been a minor detail for the media. Nobody dwelled on the almond-shaped eyes of the father and the baby girl he held to his chest, when one bullet ended their lives."[48]

The Italian media first widely circulated racist stereotype that North African migrants were criminally inclined in the 1990s. It had already amply examined this topic in relation to the murder, depleting its usefulness in explaining the march's newsworthiness. However, why did the Chinese migrant media refrain from employing this racist formula after the 2012 murder, one that the majority of Italy's Chinese would have internalized from watching Italian television and reading Chinese migrant newspapers? In their media coverage, Chinese migrant elites tried to convert inevitable interethnic antagonism into an invitation to Italians and migrants of all ethnicities to join the march. To my mind, this media strategy was intended to show the Italian authorities Chinese migrants' measure and maturity when handling conflicts with other social groups, as a way to stress that the Chinese migration was desirable for Italy. By 2012, many Italian institutional actors would have agreed that Chinese migrants' economic prowess was valuable to the country. Elite Chinese migrants now wished to convey that they also had the sophistication and diplomacy to avoid potential conflicts that would be trouble for the authorities.

In demonstrating this point, I turn to the second positive stereotype of Italy's Chinese that emerged from their own coverage of the 2012 march. Chinese migrants were said to have learned to negotiate their public anger with more restraint than they had during the 2007 Milan riot, thereby priming themselves for long-overdue acceptance into mainstream Italian media and society. This thinking refashioned the 2007 riot as a blunder to highlight how the community had been morally fortified by remembering the murder and other tragedies between 2007 and 2012. In a key piece of coverage, Bo Yuan of *Xinhua Lianhe Shibao* claimed that "overseas Chinese formed a migrant group in Italy that not only was broad-minded but also possessed a high degree of social responsibility."[49] What did such good qualities as "broadmindedness" and "social responsibility" entail?

In the aforementioned article, Bo Yuan does not elaborate on what "broadmindedness" means. Presumably, given the context of the article, this quality conveys that, unlike during the 2007 riot, the Chinese in 2012 did not act rashly to revolt against the Italians or the Moroccans during the police investigations into the killers' nationality. Other articles from *Xinhua Lianhe Shibao* corroborated this interpretation. Lia was quoted as claiming that the murderers vowed, in Roman dialect, to kill her and her family "like dogs." According to speculation, Zhou did not give up the money because he erroneously believed a shooting was not possible in a busy neighbourhood at that hour of the night. But as *Xinhua Lianhe Shibao* reminded its Chinese readers, the Italians, unlike the

Chinese, were not brought up to believe that it was always necessary to intervene in such a dangerous dispute. This difference between "Western and Eastern values," the newspaper hastens to add, should not be interpreted as an intrinsic Italian "indifference" to the Chinese in danger. As Italian newspapers did not mention this detail, it is difficult to gauge its veracity. But since Chinese migrant newspapers mentioned it, we know that migrants discussed this ethnocultural detail. Ultimately, *Xinhua Lianhe Shibao* asked Chinese to take a broad view of this incident in order to prevent the tragedy from escalating into interethnic aggression against the Moroccans.[50]

In preaching "social responsibility" towards mainstream Italian society, *Xinhua Lianhe Shibao* recommended that the Chinese protect themselves "by strengthening intergovernmental communication, winning maximum sympathy and support from Italian citizens, and utilizing the power of the entire Italian society to protect personal safety." In keeping with the newspaper's social conservatism, the journalist Bo Yuan respected the authorities' actions after the murder, and commended both the Chinese embassy's close attention and the Italian police's eager manhunt. Ji Zhihai, the first Chinese migrant to have become a member of the parliament (in Forlì), believed that the march was an excellent opportunity both to inform Italian society about Chinese migrants' rights to protect themselves and also to seek a change in how Italian authorities treated them. The Guangzhou-based weekly *Shidai Zhoubao/Time Weekly* quoted in *Ouhua Lianhe Shibao*, hoped that the Italian state would implement more programs to help migrants incorporate into Italian society. As *Xinhua Lianhe Shibao* suggested, thanks to the confident showcase of an organized and unified Chinese migrant community during the march, whose leaders deftly consulted Italian officials and Chinese diplomats in Rome, the possibility that criminals would perceive migrants' "weakness" and "fear of attracting bad things to themselves" would be diminished in the future.[51]

These ideas resembled the "unity" tenet in modern Chinese political discourse, which aims to reduce "internal friction to a minimum level" and to sustain "a public consensus at the top levels of state and Party and the absolute suppression of oppositional discourses inside and outside the CCP [Chinese communist party]."[52] As *Xinhua Lianhe Shibao* suggested, in order for the Italian public to accept the Chinese migrant community as a socially responsible one, and to accept elite migrants as legitimate intermediaries between the community and Italian authorities, a suppression of dissent from both within and outside this community was a necessary evil. This practice was already evident in the Chinese migrant media response to the Italian depictions of the Chinese mafia that I analysed in chapter 2.

Overall, the examples cited in this section convey a message of self-legitimation: a conscientious migrant community such as Italy's Chinese deserved to be lauded by, and accepted into, mainstream Italian society. Indeed, by praising the Chinese community's social responsibility, *Xinhua Lianhe Shibao* transformed the march into an expression of the collective desire of a unified migrant group that suppressed personal anger both for the sake of the community's public image and for the benefit of all residents of Rome. This interpretation implicitly commented on the distance between Italy's Chinese community and its Moroccan and other North African communities, whom the Italian and the Chinese migrant media often viewed in a racist vein.

Favourable Institutional Milieus for Trauma Claims

So far, I have explored various factors that made it more possible for the media to portray the 2012 Rome murder and march as an Italian Chinese migrant cultural trauma, including the requirements of contemporary Italian crime reporting, the Italian and the Chinese migrant media's conceptions and narratives of victimhood, the employment of diverse communications technologies in news coverage, and the positive stereotyping of the Chinese as a model minority. In this section, to further explore why this trauma claim came into being, I examine specific Chinese and Italian institutional conditions around the time of the murder and march that temporarily overruled unresolved – and perhaps irresolvable – conflicts that arose from recent Italian-Chinese social and cultural encounters.[53]

The march's slogan illustrates the organizers' calculated performance of victimhood within institutional restraints. In Chinese it translates to "Harmonious Development, Refusal to Violence," while in Italian it translates to "Yes to Security, No to Violence," revealing accommodation to China's and Italy's respective social and political preoccupations. This positioning meant that this discursive act proved to be effective, as media coverage of the march often noted how Italian police diligently searched for the killers at the Chinese embassy's urgent request.[54] Above all, the slogans helped to mobilize many Chinese migrants and Italians to participate in the march, a condition that laid the foundation for the Chinese and their allies to claim the murder and march as a collective trauma shared by mainstream Italian society.

For the slogan's Chinese version, the organizers were apt to choose the term "harmony" when addressing the Chinese state.[55] Derived from ancient Chinese political philosophy that recommended nonconflictual social negotiation between the ruling classes and their subjects, the concept of harmony is often used in contemporary Chinese political discourse to emphasize the peaceful coexistence of the Han ethnic majority with China's ethnic minorities. Throughout the 2000s, ethnic riots and tension in China's border regions, including Tibet and Xinjiang, drove the ruling political class to stress harmony. The term was also a catchword in Chinese diplomacy that accentuated the country's willingness to cooperate, rather than enter into conflict, with other nations. By nominally adhering to official Chinese political discourses, this linguistic enactment allowed both the Chinese Central Government and the Chinese embassy in Rome to pressure the Italian government and police during their manhunt.

In the years leading up to the 2012 murder and march, Rome was the primary Italian city to promote harmony. The closing ceremony of the 2010 to 2011 edition of "L'anno culturale della Cina in Italia" (The cultural year of China in Italy) took place on 14 January 2012 to coincide with the Chinese New Year festivities, and because of the recent murder and march, it also commemorated the two victims. Modelled on "The Year of China in France" (2003 to 2004) and sponsored by both the Italian and the Chinese governments, activities ran from October 2010 to September 2011 in several Italian cities but were concentrated in Rome.[56] On 7 October 2010, then prime ministers Wen Jiabao and Silvio Berlusconi delivered speeches at the event's opening ceremony. Berlusconi's speech, which the Chinese embassy in Rome published on its website, praised contemporary China's meteoric economic and political rise by underlining the "national humiliation" that allegedly motivated Chinese politicians to shed the past and embrace international politics.[57] Victimhood narratives thus resurfaced in official discourses to reinforce the legitimacy of the Italian and the Chinese ruling political classes.

For the slogan's Italian version, the organizers opted to highlight public security, which since the 2000s has been a topical issue in the Italian media, particularly in coverage of migrants' criminal activities. The "Pacchetto Sicurezza" (Security package), which the then minister of internal affairs Roberto Maroni introduced in 2008, indirectly heightened the impression of an Italy under the siege by irregular migration and migrant criminals.[58] In the 5 January 2012 edition of the talk show *Italia sul Due* (Italy on Rai Due), guests argued that the murdered Chinese migrants were casualties of several small-scale criminal groups' activities in Rome. This and other television news on Canale 5, Italia 1, and Rete 4 used clips of crime films to figuratively reiterate this point. Because of the significant increase in violence in the capital in the months preceding the 2012 murder, *La Repubblica* described Torpignattara and nearby Pigneto as a "theatre for a long series of ambushes and shootings." According to media coverage, Walter Veltroni of Partito Democratico, Rome's former mayor, expressed indignation at the violence that hampered community solidarity. The then minister of the interior Annamaria Cancellieri also reportedly remarked on the crime scene's ordinariness and its impact on the local community.[59]

According to the Italian media, Alemanno won the mayoral elections because he promised to focus on Rome's public security.[60] Therefore, when the news media accentuated the increasing violence in the capital in connection with the murder of the Chinese migrants, it was a clear critique of Alemanno's governance. In response, Alemanno told the media that Rome was "militarized" in the search for the fugitive killers and urged state agencies to adopt "emergency" measures and to increase the size of the police force to combat crime. The sequencing of several Rai news reports about the 2012 murder also endorsed Alemanno's method: the reconstruction of the crime scene is followed by interviews with residents of Torpignattara, calls for more police investigations, and comments on the rising crime in Rome before the murder.[61]

As these events involving Alemanno suggest, the march's Italian slogan appealed to Italian locals because it articulated their protest against the government's inability to curb criminality, which in their opinion led to the Chinese migrants' murder and the risk that similar violence could befall them any day. The organizers anticipated the issue's connection with concerns about public and personal safety for Italians and others in Rome. From this perspective, they helped to accrue solidarity and empathy from non-Chinese marchers for Rome's Chinese and contributed to the formation of the Italian-Chinese migrant cultural trauma.

An Italian-Chinese Migrant Cultural Trauma

A traumatic event like the 2012 murder and march had the potential to lead to conflicts between Chinese and Moroccan migrants or between the Chinese and the Italians. But this did not occur because new narratives of social cohesion, a kind of repair work, appeared in both the Italian and the Chinese migrant media to bind Rome's residents.[62] These narratives painted Chinese migrants not as exploitative workers and entrepreneurs, but as innocent victims subjected to random physical violence. Migrants' trauma claims and Italian acceptance and reinforcement of those claims amply demonstrated their modernist belief in overcoming national, racial, and cultural barriers in the name of progress.[63] The collective trauma's "liberating effect" disrupted the existing social order that separated Italian citizens from Chinese migrants, and opened up new spaces in Italy's media milieu that ultimately welcomed the Chinese in a more comprehensive way than previously attempted.[64] The 2012 murder and march as a cultural trauma, to follow Alexander, "broaden[ed] the realm of social understanding and sympathy" and "provide[d] powerful avenues for new forms of social incorporation," which in my context concerned Chinese migrants' inclusion as regular residents in the Italian media.[65]

I propose that since the 2012 murder and march, the Italian media based in Rome would be hard pressed to speak of Chinese migrants disparagingly without risking its own credibility and legitimacy with the Italian public. I also suggest that given Rome's political and symbolic importance, the Italian media as a whole would be more measured in approaching issues related to Chinese migration. By interpreting the 2012 murder and march as a cultural trauma, most mainstream Italian media depicted Chinese migrants as comprehensible individuals and fellow residents within the space of Italy's mediascape. This change in hospitality depended on specific institutional, political, and cultural conditions at the time of the 2012 murder and march, which were either absent or unfocused during the 2007 Milan riot and in Prato. As the Rome march shows, it was indeed possible for a large spectrum of the Italian media to normalize Chinese migrants as unmarked and non-controversial subjects, free from the Italian-Chinese migrant cultural repertoire's constraining influence, and particularly from the ethnocultural approach.

However, these observations require immediate qualification. Caution is required when applying these insights to the Italian media as a whole (particularly not to extreme right-wing media outlets), or to most Italian journalism covering Chinese communities in cities other than Rome. For one thing, most press repressed the potential money laundering in the Zhous' money transfer agency for the sake of the victimhood narratives.[66] Illegal Chinese economic and business practices existed, and coverage of this issue depended on the specific circumstances in which it was raised and on the ideological and political leanings of media outlets raising it. This issue could haunt any unqualified, positive depictions of Italy's Chinese. In the end, the coverage of the 2012 murder and march may represent a qualitative leap in neither Italian journalistic knowledge of the Chinese migration nor journalistic practices in covering Italy's migrants.[67] Rather, it may merely indicate that the murder and march were quite interesting to the familiar crime reporting genre.

For another, while Italian media debates about the Chinese communities in Milan, Prato, and Rome employed and contributed to the Italian-Chinese migrant cultural repertoire, they differed greatly in their specifics. The specific content of these media topics and discourses, as well as their social and institutional circumstances, were what ultimately affected the reader the most. It would be difficult to imagine that embittered Italian journalists and entrepreneurs in Prato, who continued to interpret the Chinese fast-fashion sector as a "parallel district" to the native textile industry, experienced a sudden change of heart.

As Neal wryly observes, some collective "traumas have intense emotional effects at the time of the crisis, but tend to have less lasting effects on the social system … The degree to which a nation dwells upon a trauma depends on the degree of closure that is achieved." If the case is resolved soon after the incident, then people can put it behind them and move on; a successful national cultural trauma would need repeat and frequent mentions in public discourses that explain its relevance to and impact on our current age.[68] Did the Italian news media promptly close the case surrounding victimhood narratives and the personal security of Rome's Chinese? Did it frequently refer to the Rome march in subsequent depictions of the Chinese in Italy? To be sure, it readily identified the cause of the murder and empathized with the Chinese and others, and it did not recall the march often in subsequent accounts of Italy's Chinese community. This is a partial indication that the work on providing media hospitality to Italy's Chinese would continue.

A few significant examples in 2013 point to the persisting unevenness of media representations of Italy's Chinese, despite a general improvement. When a warehouse of Chinese migrant sweatshops in Prato's Macrolotto district burned down on 1 December in an accident that claimed the lives of several migrants, criticism of Prato's local government dominated the media coverage, much as it had around the 2012 Rome murder and march. In a prominent article published in *La Repubblica* on 10 July, the diffusion of Chinese-owned cafés in Milan served as a springboard for examining a variety of other supposedly illegal Chinese businesses in Italy, with mentions of the Chinese mafia and its relationship with Chinese migrant entrepreneurship lurking in the background. On 20 June, *L'Espresso* ran a cover story about Italians working both for mainland Chinese and for Italy's Chinese migrants, with most of the examples taken from Milan and elsewhere in Lombardy. It was the first time that a Chinese migrant, Francesco Wu, graced the cover of an influential mainstream Italian weekly, replicating Xu Qiu Lin's media celebrity from Prato a couple of years prior.[69]

Conclusion

In this book, I set out to revise the widespread view that, being a primarily social and economic phenomenon, recent Chinese migration in Italy has had no significant cultural history. I demonstrated that the Italian and the Chinese migrant news media produced a sizeable body of knowledge about Italy's Chinese and circulated it in the country's cultural sphere between 1992 and 2012. I fleshed out this point through a restorative analysis of media texts which were widely available in significant numbers in the public domain, but which previous scholarship did not examine in a comprehensive and systematic way. In evaluating this vast media and cultural production, I focused on four significant case studies concerning contemporary Chinese migration in Italy – namely, crime reporting about the "Chinese mafia" from 1992 to 2006, the 2007 riot in Milan's "Chinatown," Prato's Chinese migrant entrepreneurship from 2005 to 2012, and the 2012 Chinese-organized march in Rome to commemorate two murdered victims' legacy. In delving into the cultural, historical, and sociological specificities of these case studies, I read key texts using medium-specific criticism concerning television, news articles, photojournalism, and internet forums. My reading revealed that Chinese migration in Italy has lived varied, vital, and complicated cultural lives in the news media.

For much of the twenty-year period, media debates about this migration led to opposing viewpoints and irreconcilable positions on many issues. But fragmentary and yet persistent moments of compromise and adaptation in the media did lead to a significant improvement in Italians and Chinese migrants' mutual understanding, respect, and accommodation. From the supposed Chinese mafia in Italy as a metaphor in criminalizing migrants to the normalization of Prato's Chinese as a business strategy and a political exigency, and from opposing views of the 2007 Milan riot between Italian and Chinese migrant journalists to the 2012 Italian-Chinese trauma claim of a peaceful march in Rome, at each turn Italian-Chinese migrant encounters provided a window onto economic globalization and migrant integration in Italy.

As all my case studies showed, the economic stakes of Italy's negotiations with Chinese migrant entrepreneurs and workers from 1992 to 2012 were high. For Italian journalists, these negotiations provided a particularly thought-provoking and controversial example with which to highlight ongoing deep conflicts between the migrants and the Italians, be they ordinary citizens, merchants, politicians, activists, or academics. Indeed, by accentuating the two groups' ethnocultural differences and affinities, the media made pointed, and most often biased or even one-sided, judgments about conflicts that pertained to cross-cultural communication and to the local-global dynamics in today's business world.

That said, many cultural practitioners also employed the Chinese migration as a way to prove that Italy was coping with unexpected mass immigration relatively well on a short notice, a phenomenon that was neither explicitly demanded by Italian employers, nor sponsored by the Italian state, as occurred in Germany and elsewhere in the postwar period.[1] Italian journalists noted how archaic and discriminatory views of the Chinese and China were vigorously and immediately rejected, how Italian merchants flexibly responded to what appeared to be dual pressure from mainland China and from Italy's Chinese migrant community, and how migrants benefited from collaborating with Italians in many business contexts. They also educated the Italians on how to view and interact with Chinese migrants in order to better engage with China in the age of globalization.[2] Indeed, as Maurizio Ambrosini rightly observes, Italy has been living a "tension between aversion on principle and de facto evolution towards a multi-ethnic future that is full of contradictions."[3]

Indeed, if the mediated Italian-Chinese migrant encounters between 1992 and 2012 hold any significance for other Italian-migrant and European-Chinese migrant encounters, it is that the Italian-Chinese model illustrates particularly dramatically and convincingly how advocates for globalization and those for localism – the Italians and the Chinese migrants – clash with, as well as adapt to, one another. Such a conclusion is possible in this book because I took as my unit of analysis the existing dialogical transactions between Italian- and Chinese-language – and to some degree, American, German, and Japanese – media coverage. Only by analysing the contact zone, in which this media dialogue occurred and was negotiated, can we begin to appreciate the meanings and larger implications of these mediated episodes of abrasive confrontation and mutual accommodation.

Using this dialogical analysis, I clarified that Chinese migrants refused to be scapegoats for others' business failings, cultural biases, or political exigencies from the very beginning of their contestation of depictions of them in the Italian media. Elite migrants defended their rights to entrepreneurship and to social and cultural lives in Italy. Although Chinese entrepreneurs and journalists condemned the breach of Italian labour and business-related laws by some members of their community, they largely viewed such violations as by-products of the Italian business environment, which is significantly driven by its underground economy. That economy was what initially attracted the Chinese to Italy, because their migration agenda was to become entrepreneurs and to ascend economically and socially as quickly as possible. Therefore, in their media outlets Chinese migrant opinion-makers focused not on examining past errors and current illegal business practices, but on making pleas to fellow migrants to conduct completely legitimate business activities and on legitimating the ongoing expansion of their entrepreneurship.

In their press, elite Chinese migrants also encouraged their conationals to pursue careers as politicians and to participate in local elections in Italy. Doing so would help avert the harsh top-down disciplinary treatment that the Italian municipal authorities and police applied to the community. The 2007 riot and the Prato case study demonstrate this perceived necessity. If Milan's governing officials had consulted and informed the Chinese community better about street rules, then the riot might have been avoided. If the Chinese had been more influential in Prato's local government and industrialists' association, which often worked in concert for affairs relating to this industrial district, then the industrial and economic restructuring led by migrant workers and entrepreneurs might have encountered fewer fierce accusations of illegal conduct. Another benefit of having a voice in the deliberations of municipal political and civic programs concerned migrants' personal safety, as the 2012 murder and march led many to believe. If more Chinese migrants had served on city councils, many claimed, the community would have had more political capital to request reinforced police patrols, which would lower the frequency of the Chinese falling victim to petty crimes. In advocating for more effective political representation and participation, Chinese migrants highlighted the need for Italy to provide a pathway to obtain its national citizenship.

As Chinese migrants realized early on in their settlement in Italy, the most effective way to voice their discontent and to make their demands known to Italian authorities and the public was to engage them via the news media. In the aftermath of the 2007 riot and during the ongoing debate in Prato, Chinese migrants agreed to interviews in the Italian and the international media. Following the 2012 murder, the Chinese staged a march in which their perspectives led Italian photojournalists to interpret the event as a display of victimhood. In major national newspapers, Italian journalists translated and cited news penned by Chinese migrants. These media texts functioned as retrievable records whose malleable discourses could be contested and reshaped.

To my mind, the prolific Italian and Chinese migrant media coverage of this migration underscored a popular journalistic conviction from 1992 to 2012: media arguments and counterarguments, as well as accusations and recommendations, could sway the actions of social, business, and political stakeholders in the empirical world to the benefit of Italian-Chinese migrant relationships. For many Italian and Chinese migrant journalists, their impulse was both to leave past blunders behind and to move forward. Their common understanding was that win-win situations could be achieved and multiplied, and their goal was to incorporate the economically powerful and yet politically insignificant Chinese migrant community into Italian media and society. Thus, within the context of recent Chinese migration in Italy, the news media became the laboratory in which cultural actors including journalists, politicians, and entrepreneurs addressed issues concerning migrant integration and economic globalization that arose from a variety of institutions, particularly municipal governments, the police, local and national economies, and Italian and Chinese migrant cultures.

I contended that it was best to interpret the specific events and mechanisms in this laboratory by examining the Italian-Chinese migrant cultural repertoire's invention and reinforcement. Reformulating Ann Swidler's concept, I argued that this cultural repertoire provided topical issues, textual mechanisms, and frames to guide news production about Italy's Chinese. The concept of the cultural repertoire allowed me to shed light on journalists' agency as they covered municipal policies and regulations; market rules in the Italian economy; police, judicial, and political authorities; and Italian and Chinese cultural heritage. This conceptual tool also gave me flexibility and depth when analysing the motivations and modalities of cultural practitioners who addressed the Chinese migration. In particular, I highlighted the force of ethnocultural essentialism in Italian-Chinese encounters, which I define as the deployment of supposed ethnic and cultural differences between the two groups in articulating a variety of issues from essentialist standpoints that eventually serve larger government-involved projects of migrant integration and economic globalization. Thus, praise for Chinese migrants' global business competencies and transnational values in Italian society existed alongside denunciation of migrants' deep-rooted propensity for illegal economic and business practices.

Avenues for Future Research

Much research of consequence on Chinese migration to Italy remains to be done. The first area of future research can address the variety of Chinese migrant cultures in the country in terms of geography and history. Cultural representations and encounters in areas densely populated by Chinese migrants, such as the Veneto, Emilia-Romagna, Campania, and Piedmont, as well as those recently explored by them, such as Sicily, await detailed analyses. Related research might focus on migrants of Chinese ethnicity residing in Italy who are not from mainland China. Another point of entry into the study of Chinese migrant cultures concerns Italian cultural texts about the Chinese from the 1920s to the 1990s. Moreover, the number of Chinese students in Italian universities has recently grown. Do some students contemplate obtaining Italian residency? How do they view and interact with other Chinese migrants and the Chinese Italians? More media and cultural studies of bilingual Chinese Italians, including those who eventually go to live and work in China, will also provide insight into diverse Italian-Chinese migrant identities.[4]

Future research can combine, in more organic ways than previously attempted, theories and methodologies borrowed from both the humanities and social sciences and apply them towards analyses of this migration. Humanistic studies of cinematic and literary depictions of Italy's Chinese will continue to highlight Italian-language cultural production about them. But more interpretive anthropological research can illuminate the professional and creative practices of these filmmakers and novelists. Empirical research about the reception of these cultural texts by Italian and Chinese migrant audiences can shed further light on patterns of cultural consumption. Such a method may lead us to examine the meanings of cultural texts about China and the Chinese, such as Hong Kong martial arts movies and their transnational imitations, that have arguably been more influential than contemporary Italian films and novels in shaping the Italians' views of Chinese migrants. Similarly, research concerning migrants' use of social media, Chinese-language television, and other media formats available in Italy would cause scholars to rethink the cultural map on which migrants build their transnational lives.[5]

New scholarship can also focus on comparative cultural studies of Chinese migrations in other European countries. Such research will yield a useful guide for policy makers on the European Union level with a more sophisticated cultural perspective. This is especially so as Italian-Chinese cultural encounters reveal certain peculiarities when compared to those in France and Britain, which have a longer history of addressing Chinese migrations, as well as when compared to those in Spain, Portugal, and Greece, which like Italy only became significant immigrant-receiving countries after the 1970s. In addition, France, the other European country that has received significant numbers of Chinese migrants since the 1980s, nurtured a vibrant Chinese-managed garment sector, particularly in Paris. How did the French media address Chinese migrants? Such comparative studies will allow scholars to map out Chinese migrants' transnational cultural networks within European countries. Regarding these networks, a particular concern is migrants' use of civil services provided by various municipal governments and non-governmental organizations, as well as their interaction with various migrant, Chinese-European, and religious organizations.[6]

Yet another strand of future research can explore cultural conversations about Italy's non-Chinese migrant groups from both Italian and migrant perspectives. These studies would complement the observations made in my book and provide a more comprehensive picture of migrant activism in Italy. Several migrant groups publish newspapers, magazines, and websites in their own languages, or in major European languages, in Italy.[7] How do these outlets interact with Italian society and media? How do they justify their legitimacy and self-employment? Do they claim their cultural heritage and economic capital as conspicuously as Chinese migrants do, and why? How do they view social events important to their communities? How do they view and participate in globalization?

My aim in this book has been to show that, like related sociological and anthropological studies, media and cultural analyses of recent Chinese migration in Italy have much to contribute to a fuller appreciation of, and participation in, ongoing debates about migration and globalization, Italian style. Using diverse research methods in Italian studies, Chinese studies, cultural sociology, cultural studies, and media studies, I hope to open interdisciplinary and intercultural dialogues about Italian-Chinese migrant cultural encounters.

Coda

This book has been primarily concerned with the activities and journalism of first-generation elite Chinese migrants in Italy and with Italian views of them. What about the so-called second- and third-generation Chinese migrants, or Chinese Italians, who the media often views as the bridge generation for a better Italian Chinese migrant future? Two noteworthy trends in the late 2000s and early 2010s concerned the transnational dimension of these young people leaving Italy to pursue a career elsewhere. I close this book by examining two examples.

Having been educated in the Italian tradition, some of these young people now actively seek to reclaim their Chinese identity. They travel to China to perfect their Mandarin, deepen their knowledge of Chinese culture, and establish personal and business networks. A 2013 Rai Tre documentary, titled *Radici: L'altra faccia dell'immigrazione* (Roots: The other face of immigration), features one such young person. Malia Zheng contends with her migratory past and present in Campi Bisenzio and makes trips to China. In her parents' ancestral home, she tells viewers: "I feel a bit like being reborn." When asked whether she feels more Italian or Chinese, she replies that she felt more Italian in China and more Chinese in Italy. Her reply shows the cultural relativism and bicultural belonging that also marks the intercultural attitudes of Chinese migrants in other European countries, and for that matter of migrants everywhere.[1]

Chinese Italians like Zheng perform what Homi Bhabha describes as the "contest of narrative authority between the pedagogical and the performative." In validating and living out their intercultural identities in often-conflictual situations, these Chinese Italians resort to a double process: they assert their Chinese ethnic origins in the past (i.e., "nationalist pedagogy") and reiterate Italian values and symbols in the present (i.e., "the strategy of the performative"). This mechanism may represent a conscious tactic to evade racism's double binds – namely, following Ella Shohat and Robert Stam, the denial of difference and the denial of sameness. In the first denial, the Italians see the Chinese as too different, and therefore as inferior in Italian cultural competencies. In the second denial, if Chinese migrants act and think too much like Italians, then they cease to be Chinese. Some, like Zheng, also seek to regain a Beijing-centred Chinese identity in the present. It is at this intersection where, still following Bhabha, the question of cultural difference may be productively displaced from the differences between China and Italy to those within Italy (e.g., north and south) and within China (e.g., Wenzhou and Beijing).[2]

Ultimately, Zheng seems to use Chinese modernity to reimagine her life in Italy, an attempt to avert the Italian state's discipline and prejudice. Zheng's name is "Malia" because her parents were not able to properly roll the Italian "r" in "Maria" when they registered her name. As Zheng preserves "Malia," is there any wonder that, to borrow an observation by Stuart Hall, the supposed error "[set] the word in motion to new meanings yet without obscuring the trace of its other meanings in its past"? But can these migrants obtain public recognition of their multiple cultural identities in Italy, or must their identities always be questioned, such as when Zheng herself and people around her do in *Radici*?[3] Perhaps the only logical outcome of these processes is for Zheng to move to China to start a different career than that of a journalist in Italy; according to her LinkedIn profile, in 2014 she moved to Beijing to work as a project manager at a mobile social gaming start-up.

Some young Chinese Italians and Chinese migrants expanded their parents' migration trajectory by going to North America for school, like A., whom I interviewed in Los Angeles in 2014.[4] A.'s case points to a history since at least the early 2000s of Europe's Chinese sending their children to English-speaking countries for higher education.[5] This phenomenon exemplifies what Aihwa Ong terms flexible citizenship: "the strategies and effects of mobile managers, technocrats, and professionals seeking to both circumvent *and* benefit from different nation-state regimes by selecting different sites for investments, work, and family relocation."[6]

A. has always lived an Italian-Chinese-American life, a conscious move designed by their family. A.'s parents were among the first Chinese to arrive in Italy since the early 1980s, and lived there until the late 2000s. Following their success in the import-export trade, they returned to China but maintained tight social and business ties with Italy and moved back and forth between the two. Having attended Italian public elementary and middle schools, A. went to the Marymount

International School Rome where English and Italian are the languages of instruction, and later had a part-time stint in a Chinese-language school in Rome.[7] Unlike many young Chinese Italians, A. was not involved in their parents' family business. Instead, at the University of Southern California at the time of our interview, A. was majoring in business administration. They were eyeing a future in the United States and did not plan to pursue a career in Italy or elsewhere in Europe. In Los Angeles A. was attracted to the pulsating entrepreneurial spirit and welcoming social environment, but in Italy they felt like a member of an ethnic minority despite their citizenship. A. expressed a desire, however, to work in Italy as a teacher of English or American business ethics. They were also worried that not speaking Mandarin well enough might hinder potential integration in China. Although initially reluctant to work in China, A. had interned in a trade company in Shanghai.

Despite the generational gap between A. and their family, A. believed they shared an entrepreneurial spirit. A. was acutely aware of the linguistic, cultural, and social gaps between first-generation Chinese migrants and second-generation Chinese Italians, which they illustrated with an anecdote. Once A. joked to their father that, as a Chinese Italian, A. would get off from work on both Chinese and Italian holidays. Their father reasoned that since they lived in Italy, Chinese holidays were workdays, and because they were Chinese, Italian holidays did not apply to them. However, in our interview A. repeatedly pointed to the entrepreneurial spirit that bound the two generations together, a spirit associated with the culture of migration characteristic of the Wenzhou area from which A.'s parents had migrated. A. told a rags-to-riches story of their parents' migration from China to Italy, praising their father's rise from a peasant in Wencheng and their mother's skills in financial management. When I subsequently met A.'s parents in an elegant restaurant in Shanghai to sample seafood delicacies from Wenzhou, A.'s mother told their migration story in a vein similar to A.'s account, and both resembled Ayu's storyline in *Legend of Entrepreneurship* (see chapter 6), with which they were familiar.

A.'s family exhibited a positive construction of what James Clifford calls diaspora consciousness, as they were proud of their efforts to achieve economic prosperity and to enjoy higher education through strategic planning and overcoming hardships.[8] They had every reason to feel proud and global. At the dinner table in Shanghai, a relative of A.'s even joked about how she passed through border control at a European airport on her way to Italy for the first time thanks to her beauty, which allegedly dazzled and distracted the customs officer from questioning further the motives of her visit. Their hearty laughter and great achievements were the things that they most remembered and retold about their migration odyssey, continual migration, and increasing transnationalism.

Notes

Introduction

1 According to Li, *The Chinese Community in Europe*, 19–20, while at the beginning of the 1990s Italy was among the European countries with the lowest numbers of Chinese migrants, at the end it was among the highest. Based on the statistics released by the Council of Europe (Pieke, *Recent Trends in Chinese Migration to Europe*, 56), among all major European countries from 1996 to 1998, Italy recorded the highest net increase of Chinese migrants. In order to track the number of migrants from specific villages in Wenzhou county to various European countries, I use Wenzhou Institute of Overseas Chinese and Foreign Nationals of Chinese Origin, *Wenzhou huaqiao shi*, 179, 188–9, 192, 195, 206, 214, 220, 228, and 231. These locally collected Chinese data during the 1990s clearly indicate that Italy and France were the top destination countries for migrants.

2 The quoted figures are from Caritas, "XXIII Rapporto Migrazione 2013," 10–11; ISTAT, "Cittadini non comunitari regolarmente soggiornanti. Anni 2013–2014," 5; and Li and Li, "The Chinese Overseas Population," 23.

3 Xiang, "Emigration from China"; and Reyneri, "Migration and the Underground Economy in New Receiving South European Countries," 132–4.

4 Ceccagno, *City Making and Global Labor Regimes*, 93–4.

5 Bertuccioli and Masini, *Italia e Cina*.

6 Entman, "Framing," 52–3.

7 For an overview of sociological literature on Chinese migration to Italy, see Introvigne, "Tra speranze e paure," 31–53. The edited book, in which Introvigne's article appears, has a bibliography that lists individual studies of Chinese communities in various Italian cities and regions. For the rich scholarship on the Prato case study since the early 1990s, see Berti and Valzania, "La mobilità sociale degli migrati," 44–56. For overviews of the

Chinese diasporas elsewhere, see Tan, *Routledge Handbook of the Chinese Diaspora*; Li, "Zhongguo huaqiao huaren yanjiu de lishi yu xianzhuang gaishu"; and Wang, *The Chinese*. My differentiation among "migration," "diaspora," and "transnationalism" draws from Vertovec, *Transnationalism*, 136–7; and from Castles, de Haas, and Miller, *The Age of Migration*, 25–54.

8 For an overview of the study of the meaning-making in cultural sociology, see Lamont, "Meaning-Making in Cultural Sociology."

9 See subsequent chapters for the various theorists and critics that I draw on in relation to these scholarly fields.

10 Cohen and Jónsson, "Introduction," xiii–xxxii. For an introduction to research on migration in various social sciences, see Brettell and Hollifield, "Migration Theory," 1–36.

11 For example, Parati, *Migration Italy*; Parati and Tamburri, *The Cultures of Italian Migration*; and Schrader and Winkler, *The Cinemas of Italian Migration*.

12 Pieke, "Introduction," 15–17.

1 Chinese Migration to Italy, Globalization, and the News Media

1 For a concise English introduction to the history of Chinese migrants in Italy and their entrepreneurship, see Cologna, "Chinese Migrant Entrepreneurs in Italy," 262–84. For a brief history of Chinese migrants in Italy from the 1920s to the 1990s, see Breveglieri and Farina, "Crepe nella muraglia," 59–103. For a more detailed history of early Chinese migrants from Zhejiang Province to Europe, which uses Chinese sources, see Thunø, "Moving Stones from China to Europe," 159–80. For a detailed analysis of Chinese migrant entrepreneurship in Milan between the 1920s and the 1990s, see Cologna, "Un'economia etnica di successo," 105–55. For lists of early migrants (1920s to 1940s) from Wenzhou in European countries, see Wenzhou Institute of Overseas Chinese and Foreign Nationals of Chinese Origin, *Wenzhou huaqiao shi*, 64–73. These lists show that Italy, along with France, was a major destination for such villages as Rui'an and Wencheng. The number of Italy's Chinese in the 1940s is deduced from those interned in various fascist concentration camps. See Kwok, *I cinesi in Italia durante il fascismo*. For the general history of immigrants in Italy, see Colombo and Sciortino, "Italian Immigration"; and Einaudi, *Le politiche dell'immigrazione in Italia dall'Unità a oggi*.

2 Figures for Italy are from Colombo et al., *Wenzhou-Firenze*, 33; ISTAT, "Migrazioni internazionali e interne della popolazione residente," 10; and Caritas, "XXIII Rapporto Migrazione 2013," 10–11. For Britain, see Li and Li, "The Chinese Overseas Population," 23. According to this source, the Chinese population in France reached 233,000 in 2009, and

the Netherlands had more Chinese than Italy during the 1990s. Estimates for France are taken from Gao and Poisson, "Exploitation of Chinese Migrants' Vulnerabilities in France," 57; and from Picquart, "Les migrants de la diaspora chinoise." There are no official statistics available for the ethnic origins of migrants in France. For the difficulty of counting Chinese nationals in France, see Live, "The Chinese Community in France," 102. Note that statistics were collected using different methodologies in Britain, France, and Italy. The number of Chinese migrants in Russia in 2000 was estimated to be between 200,000 and 500,000. See Nyíri, *Chinese in Eastern Europe and Russia*, 69.

3 Caritas, "XXIII Rapporto Migrazione 2013," 10–11.

4 For English accounts of Italian immigration laws and policies, see Allievi, "Immigration and Cultural Pluralism in Italy," 92–5; and Zincone, "The Making of Policies." For an extended treatment of the subject in Italian, see Einaudi, *Le politiche dell'immigrazione in Italia dall'Unità a oggi*. On Chinese migrants and Italy's regularization schemes, see Ceccagno, *City Making and Global Labor Regimes*, 65–6.

5 Cologna, "Chinese Migrant Entrepreneurs in Italy."

6 For national statistics, see "Migrazione," 6. On Egyptian self-employment in Milan, see Bernasconi, "Presenza migratoria e processo di regolarizzazione in provincia di Milano." This source indicates that in the early 2000s, there were more Chinese businesses registered than Egyptian ones. On the Romanians in Rome, see Strozza, "Immigrati stranieri e inserimento nel mercato del lavoro nella provincia di Roma," 298.

7 Liu, "Changing Chinese Migration Law," 316–19.

8 For Zhejiang's culture of migration, see Li, *Seeing Transnationally*, 9–23; and Wenzhou Institute of Overseas Chinese and Foreign Nationals of Chinese Origin, *Wenzhou huaqiao shi*, 110–11.

9 For migrants of Chinese ethnicity who went to France and Britain from countries other than mainland China, see Ma Mung, "Chinese Migration and the (Ethnic) Labour Market in France." For the complex origins of Chinese migrants in major European countries, see Pieke, *Recent Trends in Chinese Migration to Europe*, 27–8; and relevant chapters in Benton and Pieke, *The Chinese in Europe*. For a concise introduction to major trends of Chinese migration in Europe in the 1990s and 2000s, see Pieke et al., *Transnational Chinese*, 70–6.

10 Strozza, "Immigrati stranieri e inserimento nel mercato del lavoro nella provincia di Roma," 299; and Caritas, *Dossier statistico immigrazione*, 316. Statistics concerning migrant enterprises are from Laj and Ribeiro Corossacz, *Imprenditori immigrati*, 92.

11 On the relationship between regularization schemes and migrant self-employment, see Reyneri, "Migration and the Underground Economy in

New Receiving South European Countries," 134–6. For the numbers of permits issued in these amnesties by country, see Caritas, *Dossier statistico immigrazione*, 133. For Chinese entrepreneurship in Italy in relation to Italy's regularization schemes, see Genova, "Non solo ristoranti: Lavoro e impresa tra vocazione e necessità," 151–4 and 196–8; and Marsden, "Il ruolo della famiglia nello sviluppo dell'imprenditoria cinese a Prato," 71–103.

12 Zincone, "The Making of Policies."

13 For the Chinese diaspora as trade and labour diasporas, see Cohen, *Global Diasporas*, 83–91. For Chinese migrant communities in Spain and Portugal, which were numerically inferior to but shared many similarities with those in Italy during the 1990s and 2000s, see Beltrán Antolín, "The Chinese in Spain," 211–37; and Teixeira, "Entrepreneurs of the Chinese Community in Portugal," 238–60. For a comparative case study of Wenzhounese migrant communities in Beijing and Florence, see Tomba, "Exporting the 'Wenzhou Model' to Beijing and Florence," 280–94.

14 Reyneri, "Migration and the Underground Economy in New Receiving South European Countries," 125–7; and Ceccagno, "New Chinese Migrants in Italy."

15 Guy Dinmore, "Migrants Abandoning Recession Hit Italy," *Financial Times*, 6 January 2013; Paolo Brogi, "Crisi e affari, i cinesi lasciano l'Italia: Serrande chiuse nella China Town di Roma," *Corriere della Sera*, 10 January 2013; and "Anche i cinesi scappano dall'Italia," La7, 29 January 2013, http://www.la7.it/laria-che-tira/video/anche-i-cinesi-scappano-dallitalia-29-01-2013-94608.

16 Cohen, *Global Diasporas*, 15–19; Safran, "Diasporas in Modern Societies," 83–4; Tan, "Introduction," 2–3; and Baumann, "Diaspora," 328–32.

17 On Chinese migrants' mobility, see Ceccagno, *City Making and the Global Labor Regimes*, 155–63.

18 Ceccagno, *Cinesi d'Italia*, 33–5; Pedone, *A Journey to the West*, 15–18; and Caritas, "XXIV Rapporto Immigrazione Caritas Migrantes 2014," 27.

19 I draw this observation from Portes and DeWind, "Conceptual and Methodological Developments in the Study of International Migration," 833.

20 This book will not discuss these issues. Instead, see Zhang, "Chinese Migrants, Morality, and Film Ethics in Italian Cinema"; and Zhang, "Contemporary Italian Novels on Chinese Immigration to Italy."

21 Burke, *What Is Cultural History?*, 121–3 and 134–5.

22 In order to compare the three Italian cities with the largest Chinese populations using statistics from a single report, I used the one released on 22 September 2011 by ISTAT. As far as I know, this is the only ISTAT document that has information on the Chinese in all three cities between 1992 and 2012. See ISTAT, "La popolazione straniera residente in Italia," 10.

23 Statistics from 2006 show that the first four residential areas in Milan with a large number of Chinese residents were Niguarda-Bicocca-Comasina, Fiera-Bovisa-Gallaratese, Stazione Centrale-Loreto-Via Padova-Viale Monza, and Duomo (including Milan's "Chinatown"). See Cologna, "Il caso Sarpi e la diversificazione dell'imprenditoria cinese," 5–6.

24 For detailed accounts of the Chinese community in Milan, see Cologna, "Chinese Migrant Entrepreneurs in Italy"; and Ceccagno, Rastrelli, and Salvati, "Exploitation of Chinese Migrants in Italy."

25 ISTAT, "La popolazione straniera residente in Italia," 4; Ceccagno, Rastrelli, and Salvati, "Exploitation of Chinese Migrants in Italy," 120 and 130; Ufficio di Statistica, "Tab. 1.9"; Ufficio di Statistica, "Tab. 1.1"; and Bo Yuan, "Yihuaren xi qian an shang dai sifa jieding 'hui se jingji' yin huoduan?," *Xinhua Lianhe Shibao*, 30 June 2010.

26 Ceccagno, "New Chinese Migrants in Italy," 198; and Ceccagno, "L'epopea veloce," 191.

27 ISTAT, "La popolazione straniera residente in Italia," 4. Other migrant communities in Rome greater than 10,000 in the 2010 official records included the Romanians (72,500), Filipinos (29,000), Poles (13,100), Peruvians (11,600), and Ukrainians (10,800). Lucchini, "Luoghi di residenza e di lavoro della comunità cinese a Roma," 27–44; Ceccagno, "L'epopea veloce," 191; Pedone, "La parabola dell'import-export cinese a Roma," 232–40; and Pedone, *A Journey to the West*, 21–39.

28 Downing and Husband, *Representing "Race,"* 145–59 and 194–7.

29 For a useful analysis of news articles addressing migrants and racism that parallels my methodology, see Dijk, *Elite Discourse and Racism*, 241–82.

30 For guidelines for investigating extreme right- and left-wing media, see Downing and Husband, *Representing "Race,"* 60–85; and Però, *Inclusionary Rhetoric/Exclusionary Practices*, 1–14.

31 I use the Chinese, Italian, and English titles that these newspapers employed themselves.

32 Chow, *Writing Diaspora*, 1–15. For an example of "orientalist melancholia," see Federico Rampini, "Le Pechino d'Italia," *La Repubblica*, 13 April 2007.

33 Shohat and Stam, *Unthinking Eurocentrism*, 7 and 346.

34 Clifford, *Routes*, 32–6; Greenblatt, "A Mobility Studies Manifesto," 250–3; and Bhabha, *The Location of Culture*, 1–27.

35 For critiques of theories of hybridization, of "in-betweenness," and Clifford, see respectively Tomlinson, *Globalization and Culture*, 141–8; Bauman, *Globalization*, 99–102; and Lukes, *Moral Relativism*, 112–22.

36 Geertz, *The Interpretation of Cultures*, 14.

37 I draw this and the next paragraphs from Andornino, "Strategic Ambitions in Times of Transition," 151–8; and Prodi, "Economic Relations between Italy and China."

38 Reyneri, "Migration and the Underground Economy in New Receiving South European Countries"; Bernasconi, "Presenza migratoria e processo di regolarizzazione in provincia di Milano," 177; Strozza, "Immigrati stranieri e inserimento nel mercato del lavoro nella provincia di Roma," 299; Zucchetti, "I caratteri salienti della regolarizzazione in Italia," 39–40; and Portes and Yiu, "Entrepreneurship, Transnationalism, and Development," 83–9.

39 On how mainland Chinese and Prato's Chinese competed on low-end fast fashion, see Ceccagno, *City Making and Global Labor Regimes*, 132–3.

40 Fulvio Migliaccio, "Stranieri Made in Italy," *Un mondo a colori*, Rai Due, 20–1 February 2008.

41 Nonini and Ong, "Chinese Transnationalism as an Alternative Modernity," 19–20.

42 Ceccagno, *City Making and Global Labor Regimes*, 101–2; and Reyneri, "Migration and the Underground Economy in New Receiving South European Countries," 127.

43 For a typology of news on migrants and their typical connotations, see Binotto, "Immagini dell'immigrazione," 40–1; and Uccellini, "Romanian Migration to Italy," 106–8.

44 Similar processes of interethnic comparison informed the activism of Chinese migrants in early twentieth-century Lima and Chicago. See McKeown, *Chinese Migrant Networks and Cultural Change*, 168–77, 220–1, and 279–82.

45 Zincone, "The Making of Policies," 351; Einaudi, *Le politiche dell'immigrazione in Italia dall'Unità a oggi*, 215–28; and Zincone, "Conclusion," 390–1.

46 Parati, *Migration Italy*, 39.

47 For an example of this line of argument, see Piero Colaprico, "I ragazzi di Paolo Sarpi: 'Noi ci sentiamo milanesi,'" *La Repubblica: Milano*, 14 April 2007.

48 This topic has deep historical and cultural roots. For recent analyses of multiple Italian mobilities, see Bouchard and Ferme, *Italy and the Mediterranean*, 43–69; Lombardi-Diop and Romeo, "The Italian Postcolonial"; Fogu and Re, "Italy in the Mediterranean Today"; Dainotto, *Europe (in Theory)*, 1–10; Moe, *The View from Vesuvius*; Schneider, "Introduction"; and Gabaccia, *Italy's Many Diasporas*. On race relations and the Italian nation in liberal and fascist Italy, see Wong, *Race and the Nation in Liberal Italy, 1861–1911*, especially 99–106; Gillette, *Racial Theories in Fascist Italy*; and Welch, *Vital Subjects*. On Chinese race and migrations, see Dikötter, "The Discourse of Race in Twentieth-Century China"; and Dikötter, *The Discourse of Race in Modern China*. For a comparison of Chinese nationalism promoted by Sun Yat-sen and the Italian nationalism

in Liberal Italy, see Gregor and Chang, "Nazionalfascismo and the Revolutionary Nationalism of Sun Yat-sen." For a comparison of Chinese and Italian immigrants in the United States from the perspective of race, see Gabaccia, "The 'Yellow Peril' and the 'Chinese of Europe.'"

49 Dal Lago, *Non-persone*, 9 and 15–17.

50 Portes, Guarnizo, and Landolt, "The Study of Transnationalism," 217–37; and Portes, "Introduction," 181–93. For brief biographies of successful migrants in Italy, see Wenzhou Institute of Overseas Chinese and Foreign Nationals of Chinese Origin, *Wenzhou huaqiao shi*, 124 and 130–1. Lists from this source (215 and 222) show a very limited number of migrants living in Italy in the mid-1990s who had a college degree.

51 Liu, "New Migrants and the Revival of Overseas Chinese Nationalism," 315.

52 Ong, *Flexible Citizenship*, 88–93.

53 Cologna, "Chinese Migrant Entrepreneurs in Italy," 275–6; Ma Mung, "Chinese Migration and the (Ethnic) Labour Market in France," 47–8; Beltrán Antolín, "Chinese Entrepreneurship in Spain," 288; and Ambrosini, "Migration in Italy."

54 Hall, "Culture, Community, Nation," 354.

55 Swidler, "Culture in Action," 273 and 276–8; and Swidler, *Talk of Love*, 24–40 and 71–88. On transnational competences, which draw on the theories of Swidler and of Pierre Bourdieu on "habitus," a notion related to "cultural repertoire," see Vertovec, *Transnationalism*, 66–74.

56 Swidler, *Talk of Love*, 1 and 24.

57 Giddens, *Runaway World*, 6–19; Tomlinson, *Globalization and Culture*, 9 (italics original).

58 Appadurai, *Modernity at Large*, 15–16. For a consideration of Appadurai's culturalism in connection with literature, see Jay, *Global Matters*, 58–61.

59 Bhabha, *The Location of Culture*, 1–27; and Gilroy, *The Black Atlantic*, 1–40 and 72–110. For an overview of critical works concerning ethnocultural essentialism in Euro-American contexts, see Vertovec, "The Cultural Politics of Nation and Migration." For comments related to Italy and the Italian media, see Grillo, "Immigration and the Politics of Recognizing Difference in Italy," 18–21; and Zinn, "*Pacem in Terris*."

60 Castles, de Haas, and Miller, *The Age of Migration*, 289–90; Einaudi, *Le politiche dell'immigrazione in Italia dall'Unità a oggi*, 186–7, 284–5, and 360–3; and Zincone, "Citizenship Policy Making in Mediterranean EU States," 2–5.

61 To use another categorization of migrant incorporation, note that the primordialist school views migrants as belonging to distinct ethnic groups, while the instrumentalist school seeks to incorporate migrants into the cultures of their destination countries. Christiansen, *Chinatown, Europe*, 21–4.

62 On the two incorporation models, see Castles, de Haas, and Miller, *The Age of Migration*, 66–8 and 264–70; and Bertossi, "Mistaken Models of Integration?" On ethnoculturalism in multicultural initiatives in Britain in the 1990s, see Vertovec, "Multiculturalism, Culturalism and Public Incorporation," 49–69; and in other European countries, see Martiniello, *Le società multietniche*, 79–90. On the two models' significance for Italy, see Einaudi, *Le politiche dell'immigrazione in Italia dall'Unità a oggi*, 281–5; and Fazzi, "Italiani brava gente?," 192–8. For the definition of "migration management," see https://www.iom.int/key-migration-terms.

63 For a similar argument in the context of the black diaspora in Britain in the 1950s and 1960s, see Hall, "Old and New Identities, Old and New Ethnicities," 51–4.

64 Such positive culturalist claims about Chinese civilization, especially as rooted in nationalism and racialization, are also part of the contemporary scholarly discourse on China. See Nonini and Ong, "Chinese Transnationalism as an Alternative Modernity," 5–9.

65 Giddens, *Runaway World*, 48–9.

66 My thinking here draws on Clifford, "Indigenous Diasporas," 51–2, 54–5, and 60.

67 Ong, "Chinese Modernities," 172.

2 The "Chinese Mafia" in Italy, 1992–2006

1 Enrico Mannucci, "Una patria cinese sull'Arno," *L'Europeo*, 23 November 1990, 24–6. For a bibliography of news coverage of the Chinese-Italian clash in San Donnino, see Galli, "Le comunità cinesi in Italia," 103n9. For a detailed account of this clash and subsequent institutional solutions, see Marsden, *Cinesi e fiorentini a confronto*, 161–82. For additional lists of related media accounts about Chinese migrants in Tuscany in the late 1980s and early 1990s, see Lucchesini, *Cinesi a Firenze*, 111–12; and Campani and Maddii, "Un monde à part, les Chinois en Toscane," 70–1. For an English-language overview of Italian media depictions of immigrants from the 1970s to the early 2000s, which also refers to important previous critical works in Italian, see Sciortino and Colombo, "The Flows and the Flood."

2 Breveglieri and Farina, "Crepe nella muraglia," 100–1. For a bibliography of similar reporting in Italy, see Galli, "Le comunità cinesi in Italia," 102–3n4, 102–3n7, and 102–3n10. For a panoramic view of coverage of Chinese migrants in *Corriere della Sera* from the 1920s to the 1990s, see Breveglieri and Farina, "Crepe nella muraglia," 96–101. For news coverage of the Chinese mafia in Spain during in the same period, see Beltrán Antolín, "The Chinese in Spain," 232–5.

3 The critic Renzo Rastrelli called for prudence when using the term "the Chinese mafia." See Rastrelli, "Immigrazione cinese e criminalità: Fonti e interpretazioni a confronto," 229–30. For the United Nations Office on Drugs and Crime's definition of transnational organized crime, see "Organized Crime," https://www.unodc.org/unodc/ar/organized-crime/index.html.
4 Ceccagno, Rastrelli, and Salvati, "Exploitation of Chinese Immigrants in Italy," 120–9; Cologna and Farina, "Dove si infrangono le onde dell'oceano ci sono cinesi d'oltremare," 48–9; and Bernasconi, "Presenza migratoria e processo di regolarizzazione in provincia di Milano," 153.
5 Many primary materials that I use in this chapter were brought to my attention by Daniele Cologna and by Pogliano and Zanini, "L'immaginario e le immagini degli immigrati," 103–87. For newspaper articles, I chose *La Repubblica* and *Corriere della Sera* because their websites feature well-organized, searchable archives from the 1990s.
6 Lakoff and Johnson, *Metaphors We Live By*, 139–46.
7 Appadurai, "Putting Hierarchy in Its Place," 36.
8 Li, *The Chinese Community in Europe*, 77–9.
9 *Spazio 5 (Il settimanale del TG5)*, Canale 5, episode no. 23, 17 March 1993.
10 Castles, de Haas, and Miller, *The Age of Migration*, 203.
11 King and Mai, *Out of Albania*, 101–26 (quotations from 102 and 123).
12 Dino Martirano, "Allarme 'sole rosso,' racket cinese," *Corriere della Sera*, 16 May 1992; and Gianfranco Ambrosini, "Milano gialla," *Sette*, 14 March 1992.
13 Guglielmo Sasinini, "La piovra dagli occhi a mandorla," *Famiglia Cristiana*, 12 July 1995; "Piovra cinese," *TG2 Dossier*, Rai Due, 28 May 1995; and "Mafia cinese," *Verissimo*, Canale 5, 18 June 1995 (episode 192).
14 Sciortino and Colombo, "The Flows and the Flood," 107–9.
15 I draw on an insight into different types of metaphors and how they organize human understanding from Lakoff and Johnson, *Metaphors We Live By*, 147–55.
16 The crash of the *Golden Venture* freighter near New York in 1993 further cemented the public view of the vast network of human trafficking organized by Chinese criminal groups. See Liang and Ye, "From Fujian to New York."
17 Buonanno, *Italian TV Drama and Beyond*, 56–9, 62, and 66–7.
18 Rastrelli, "Immigrazione cinese e criminalità," 243–5.
19 Biao, "'Zhejiang Village' in Beijing," 236–7.
20 Laura Maragnani and Katia Ferri, "Cosa nostla," *Panorama*, 31 May 1992.
21 On the importance of cinema in propagating the image of Fu Manchu and the Yellow Peril, see Mayer, *Serial Fu Manchu*, 59–89.

22 Tchen and Yeats, "Introduction," 1–15 and 350. Another prominent twentieth-century incarnation of the octopus metaphor is associated with the German illustrator Eric Schilling's print of an advancing Japanese empire in China in the satirical magazine *Simplicissimus*.
23 Belluati, *L'in/sicurezza dei quartieri*, 130–2.
24 Lavinia Di Gianvito, "Mafia dagli occhi a mandorla," *Corriere della Sera*, 1 February 1995. One of the criminals under investigation, Zhang Yiping, was a well-known figure in the Chinese community. See Christiansen, *Chinatown, Europe*, 61–3.
25 Papuzzi and Magone, *Professione giornalista*, 61–2.
26 Lavinia Di Gianvito, "I pentiti dagli occhi a mandorla," *Corriere della Sera*, 28 April 1997.
27 See "Presunzione d'innocenza" in "Carta dei doveri del giornalista." On the differences between the deontological and ethical obligations of journalists, see Papuzzi and Magone, *Professione giornalista*, 285. No mention of how to cover foreigners in Italy was present in the 1993 version of the "Carta." For the current version of the "Carta," where there are rules about how to cover foreigners, see Ordine dei Giornalisti, "Testo unico dei doveri del giornalista," http://www.odg.it/testo-unico-dei-doveri-del-giornalista/24288.
28 Zhang and Chin, *Characteristics of Chinese Human Smugglers*, 10–12.
29 Angelo Pergolini, "Grossi guai a Chinatown," *Panorama*, 4 December 2003; and Alessandro Rossi, "Reportage: Viaggio nelle Chinatown d'Italia," *Panorama*, 13 November 2003.
30 Cologna, "Un'economia etnica di successo," 149–51; and Xiang, "'Zhejiang Village' in Beijing," 236–7.
31 Anna Gennari, "La vita agra di Chinatown," *Grazia*, 9 April 1995, 44–6.
32 Photographs are viewable on the Lombardia Beni Culturali website. For example, Armando Rotoletti, "Capodanno cinese. Immigrazione cinese," 1989, http://www.lombardiabeniculturali.it/fotografie/schede/IMM-LOM60-0003834/?view=autori&offset=14&hid=4016&sort=sort_int. Photographs by Maurizio Berlincioni from 1994–5 in the Florence-Prato area have less of an ethnic connotation as they are focused on the spaces inhabited by Chinese migrants. See Colombo et al., *Wenzhou-Firenze*.
33 Ceccagno, Rastrelli, and Salvati, "Exploitation of Chinese Immigrants in Italy," 99–105; and Ceccagno and Rastrelli, *Ombre cinesi*, 39–66.
34 Pergolini, "Grossi guai a Chinatown."
35 Ong, *Flexible Citizenship*, 117 and 195. For further critiques of guanxi, see Nonini and Ong, "Chinese Transnationalism as an Alternative Modernity," 21–3; and Chan, *Migration, Ethnic Relations and Chinese Business*, 144–7.
36 Andornino, "Strategic Ambitions in Times of Transition," 151.

37 For examples concerning China, see Huntington, "The Clash of Civilizations?," 34 and 47. The Italian translation of Huntington's 1996 book of the same theme dates from 2000. For a critique of Huntington's essay, see Said, *Reflections on Exile and Other Essays*, 569–90; and Ong, *Flexible Citizenship*, 185–213.

38 Antonella Barina, "I cinesi della porta accanto," *Il Venerdì*, 14 July 1995. Such views must have also resulted from Chinese migrants' collaboration with the Italian journalist on this article. Evidence of this collaboration can be seen in the nuanced interpretations of a wealth of information about the Chinese community in Italy. The smiling faces of Chinese migrants shown in the article's photographs further underscore their willingness to collaborate with the Italian journalist.

39 Kim, *Ethnicity and Foreigners in Ancient Greece and China*, 100, 118, and 121–2.

40 I draw concepts of "diaspora" and "transnationalism" from Vertovec, *Transnationalism*, 136–7; and from Castles, de Haas, and Miller, *The Age of Migration*, 25–54.

41 *Maurizio Costanzo Show*, Canale 5, episode no. 61, 28 November 1995.

42 The mainstream Italian media's transition from a culture-based approach to a context-based one in interpreting Chinese immigration to Italy mirrors similar debates on ethnic businesses in academia. See Chan, *Migration, Ethnic Relations and Chinese Business*, 115–17.

43 Ceccagno, "New Chinese Migrants in Italy," 192–3.

44 Rossi, "Reportage"; and Pergolini, "Grossi guai a Chinatown."

45 Mariano Maugeri, "La Cina è vicinissima: Anzi, è già qui," *Ventiquattro*, 7 April 2001.

46 For examples, see Mirante, "Chinatown e 'mafia gialla,'" 81–5; and D'Agostino, "Il giallo dell'Esquilino," 215–20.

47 *Cina in Italia* is collected by the Biblioteca Nazionale (National library) in Rome, while all issues of *It's China* were available in the magazine's editorial office in Campi Bisenzio, near Prato, at the time of my research in 2013. For a similar understanding of the Chinese mafia by a Chinese migrant in 1997, see Zhu, "Dinamiche all'interno della comunità cinese a Roma," 41–3.

48 Pratt, *Imperial Eyes*, 9.

49 Xiang Jun, "Shetoumen de buguilu," *Cina in Italia*, January 2001.

50 Li, "An Overview of the Migration Mechanism between China and Europe," 19–32.

51 "Pulatuo jingchaju juzhang Giacomo Dentici xiansheng de zhuanfang/ Intervista con il Questore di Prato," *Wan Li*, June 2003; and "Juliu zheng beihou de bu zhengdang jiaoyi/Il business dei permessi di soggiorno," *Wan Li*, July 2004.

52 Shi Yi, "Huashang maoyi. shengcun? haishi siwang?," *Cina in Italia*, January 2001.

53 The pointed and antagonistic critique in *Ouhua Shibao* of certain Italian institutional practices alarmed Lega Nord's mouthpiece, *La Padania*. See Alessandro Morelli, "Ma siamo ancora padroni a casa nostra?," *La Padania*, 8 September 2005.

54 Xiang, "Emigration from China," 36–7.

55 Chen Jian, "Shou shou ba, shetoumen," *Cina in Italia*, January 2001; and Hu Lanbo, "'Wo jinsheng zui da de huihen jiu shi toudu lai Yidali'/'Il mio grande rimorso è stato quello di essere venuto in Italia come clandestino,'" *Cina in Italia*, January 2001. For a similar description of these journeys found in an Italian newspaper, see Alessandra Longo, "Da Pechino a Belgrado: Il cammino dei disperati," *La Repubblica*, 11 August 2000. On Hungary, the Czech Republic, and Yugoslavia as transit countries for human smuggling from China to Western Europe in the 1990s and 2000s, see Nyíri, *Chinese in Eastern Europe and Russia*, 63–8.

56 Ceccagno, *Cinesi d'Italia*, 67–72.

57 For a brief analysis, see Ceccagno, Rastrelli, and Salvati, "Exploitation of Chinese Immigrants in Italy," 132.

58 Hu Lanbo, "Perché i cinesi non muoiono?," *Cina in Italia*, January/February 2007; and "*Gomorra*: I cinesi morti trasportati nei container," Associna, 30 December 2006, http://www.associna.com/modules.php?file=article&name=News&sid=449.

59 Said, "Orientalism Reconsidered," 211; and Vukovich, *China and Orientalism*, 128–35.

60 According to the "Carta dei doveri del giornalista," under "Le fonti," journalists should name their sources unless there is a legitimate need to protect them. All subsequent page numbers refer to the English-language translation of *Gomorrah*.

61 Pergolini, "Grossi guai a Chinatown"; and Rossi, "Reportage."

62 Pergolini, "Grossi guai a Chinatown."

63 Introvigne, "Le società segrete cinesi nella ricerca storica e sociologica," 290.

64 For example, Maria Antonietta Calabrò, "La mafia cinese alleata alla camorra," *Corriere della Sera*, 29 October 2000; and Giovanni Marino, "La Chinatown del Vesuvio: Lavoro nero, affari e misteri," *La Repubblica*, 19 March 2003.

65 Sasinini, "La piovra dagli occhi a mandorla"; Attilio Giordano, "Si fa presto a dire mafie," *Il Venerdì*, 5 February 1999; Calabrò, "La mafia cinese alleata alla camorra"; Giuseppe Crimaldi, "L'allarme, c'è un piano per acquisire il controllo della Duchesca," *Il Mattino*, 9 December 2000; and Live, "The Chinese Community in France," 118–22.

66 Dal Lago, *Eroi di carta*, 48–9 and 123–5.

67 For this observation in another context, see Bauman, *Globalization*, 125–6. In the mid-2000s, Chinese migrants in Naples expressed discontent with petty crimes and police abuse. See Malavolti, "Integrazione cinese a Napoli," 150–2.

68 Said, *Orientalism*, 71–2.

69 Appadurai, "Putting Hierarchy in Its Place," 45–6 (italics original).

3 Milan: The 2007 "Chinatown" Riot in Italian Debates

1 ISTAT, "La popolazione straniera residente in Italia al 1 gennaio 2008," 11.

2 Hall, "Encoding/Decoding," 651 (italics original).

3 D'Orsi, "The 'Pacchetto Sicurezza' and the Process of Ethnogenesis," 5.

4 Campani, "Migrants and Media," 47–9.

5 Gianni Santucci, "Criminalità Cinese: Sesso, clandestini e merci contraffatte: Così la 'Triade' gestisce traffici e denaro," *Corriere della Sera*, 14 April 2007; Giangiacomo Schiavi, "La città separata," *Corriere della Sera*, 13 April 2007; and Carlo Lovati, "Dalle borse e gli involtini primavera agli affari ombra," *Corriere della Sera: Milano*, 13 April 2007.

6 Migliaccio, "Guerriglia a Chinatown." On *Un mondo a colori* in relation to migration, see Lombardo, "L'offerta multiculturale nei media a larga diffusione," 76–7; and Ardizzoni, *North/South, East/West*, 103–6.

7 Marco Belpoliti, "L'altra Gomorra," *La Stampa*, 13 April 2007; Alessandro Montanari, "Riciclaggio dei documenti dietro l'immortalità dagli occhi a mandorla?," *La Padania*, 14 April 2007; and Roberto Di Caro, "Porto franco Chinatown," *L'Espresso*, 23 April 2007.

8 Shohat and Stam, *Unthinking Eurocentrism*, 25.

9 Fiorenza Sarzanini, "Alleanza con la mafia albanese per il traffico dei clandestini: La nuova geografia del crimine," *Corriere della Sera*, 16 April 2007; and Enrico Bonerandi, "Così i giovani gangster danno l'assalto a Chinatown," *La Repubblica: Milano*, 28 April 2007.

10 Gianandrea Zagato, "Il quartiere dei mille affari dove nessuno muore mai," *Il Giornale*, 13 April 2007.

11 Maurizio Stefanini, "Mafioso un cinese su venti, 78 milioni affiliati alle Triadi," *Libero*, 14 April 2007; and Alessandro Montanari, "Le nostre banlieue pronte ad esplodere," *La Padania*, 14 April 2007.

12 Federico Rampini, "Ghetti razziali: Le leggende di Chinatown," *La Repubblica*, 15 April 2007.

13 Ong, *Flexible Citizenship*, 129–30. Such an import from the American context must have been made possible, among other things, by Rampini's work experience in the United States.

14 Cologna, "Il quartiere cinese di Milano," 134; Ricucci, "La diaspora cinese," 63–4; and Mudu and Li, "Recent Chinese Migration in the United States and Italy," 287–90.
15 Andrea Galli, "Le Vie Ghetto: Da via Padova al Corvetto: ecco le nuove enclave: Aumentano le strade 'occupate' dagli immigrati," *Corriere della Sera: Milano*, 14 April 2007; and Antonio Carnevale, "Cinesi, slavi, nordafricani, milanesi: un melting flop?," *Panorama* (online), 13 April 2007, http://italia.panorama.it/Cinesi-slavi-nordafricani-milanesi-un-melting-flop.
16 Claudio Schirinzi, "Scontri a Chinatown: Moratti: No a zone franche: L'enclave e le regole," *Corriere della Sera: Milano*, 13 April 2007; and Piero Colaprico, "Chinatown alla scoperta del mercato," *La Repubblica*, 13 April 2007.
17 Giacomo Susca, "Chinatown, controrivolta dei milanesi," *Il Giornale*, 14 April 2007. See also Francesca Cassani, "Era una delle vie più belle della città," *La Padania*, 13 April 2007.
18 Gerardo Fiorillo, "Scoprire di odiare il vicino, dopo," *Il Giorno*, 13 April 2007; and Canale 4, 12 April 2007.
19 Schiavi, "La città separata."
20 Giacomo Stucchi, "Preoccupante esempio per altre 'zone franche,'" *La Padania*, 13 April 2007; Roberto Cota, "Una 'risposta' a chi ha sottovalutato e tollerato il fenomeno dilagante della contraffazione," *La Padania*, 13 April 2007; Zagato, "Il quartiere dei mille affari dove nessuno muore mai"; Matteo Salvini, "Vogliono dettare legge," *La Padania*, 13 April 2007; Renato Besana, "Intervista con Paolo Madron, vice-president, *Panorama*," Rai, 20 April 2007; Salvatore Scarpino, "La sovranità non si vende," *Il Giornale*, 13 April 2007; Gianandrea Zagato, "La 'holding' dei 50 mandarini pronta a comprarsi mezza città," *Il Giornale*, 14 April 2007; and Renato Farina, "Quel drago è periocoloso: La sinistra non ci giochi," *Libero*, 15 April 2007.
21 Mayer, *Serial Fu Manchu*, 21–2.
22 Huysseune, "Masculinity and Secessionism in Italy," 599–603.
23 Biorcio, "The *Lega Nord* and the Italian Media System," 72–3; and Faloppa, *Razzisti a parole*, 40.
24 Canale 5, 12 and 13 April 2007; Italia 1, "Studio aperto 1," 12 and 13 April 2007; Alberto Taliani, "Milano, rivolta a Chinatown: 300 immigrati contro la polizia," *Il Giornale*, 12 April 2007; Ippolito Negri, "La febbre gialla: Non c'è voglia di integrazione," *Il Giorno: Milano metropoli*, 13 April 2007; and Gianni Stucchi, "Rivolta a Chinatown: Esplode la banlieue milanese," *La Padania*, 13 April 2007.
25 Faso, "La lingua del razzismo," 33–4.
26 Fulvio Migliaccio, "Guerriglia a Chinatown," *Un mondo a colori*, Rai Due, 17 April 2007; Rai TG3, primo piano, 12 April 2007, "Copertina: Brutto

Affare a Chinatown"; and Simona Ravizza, "Il vigile ferito," *Corriere della Sera: Milano*, 13 April 2007.

27 Anonymous, "Milano, rivolta a Chinatown," *La Repubblica*, 12 April 2007; "Guerriglia a Chinatown," *La Repubblica*, 13 April 2007, https://video.repubblica.it/copertina/guerriglia-a-chinatown/9077/10904; "Scontri in Via Sarpi" and "Scontri a Chinatown: La sequenza," *Corriere della Sera*, 12 April 2007, http://milano.corriere.it/gallery/Milano/vuoto.shtml?2007/04_Aprile/sarpi/1&1; Enrico Bonerandi, "Milano, cinesi in rivolta, Guerra con vigili e polizia," *La Repubblica*, 13 April 2007; "Bandiera rossa a Chinatown," La7, 2 May 2007, http://www.la7.it/linfedele/video/bandiera-rossa-a-chinatown-02-05-2007-94782; and Francesco Sisci, "Chinatown il giorno dopo: L'ira di Pechino: 'È stata una trappola,'" *La Stampa*, 14 April 2007.

28 Checchino Antonini, "Milano, comunità cinese in rivolta: Scontri con vigili urbani e polizia," *Liberazione*, 13 April 2007.

29 Cristaldi and Lucchini, "I cinesi a Roma," 216–17.

30 Schiavi, "La città separata"; Gianandrea Zagato, "Milano, nella Chinatown ogni due minuti si commette un'illegalità," *Il Giornale*, 14 April 2007; for Associazione ViviSarpi's slogan, see the photograph in *Il Giorno*, 13 April 2007; for photographs of racist slurs left by Forza Nuova, see Michele Focarete, "Scritte razziste a Chinatown: Mistero sul film degli scontri," *Corriere della Sera*, 15 April 2007; Stucchi, "Rivolta a Chinatown"; and Beppe Grillo, "Le bandiere rosse di via Paolo Sarpi," 12 April 2007, http://www.beppegrillo.it/2007/04/le_bandiere_ros.html#trackbacks.

31 Schirinzi, "Scontri a Chinatown"; Fabio Grosso, "Cinesi, rom e musulmani pronti a 'esplodere' da un momento all'altro," *La Padania*, 14 April 2007; Rai TG3, primo piano, 12 April 2007; Rai TG2, Giorno, 13 April 2007; and Rai TG1, 20.00, 17 April 2007.

32 Maneri, "Media Discourse on Migration," 91.

33 "Rivolta a Chinatown," *Il Giornale*, 12 April 2007, http://www.ilgiornale.it/fotogallery/rivolta_chinatown/id=121-foto=1-slideshow=0.

34 Focarete, "Scritte razziste a Chinatown."

35 On institutional racism, see Miles and Brown, *Racism*, 109–12.

36 Essed, *Understanding Everyday Racism*, 73, 110, 79–81, and 288.

37 Anon., "Milano, rivolta a Chinatown."

38 Paolo Berizzi, "Jian, una giornata in via Sarpi: 'La mia vita? Negozio e calcetto,'" *La Repubblica: Milano*, 15 April 2007.

39 Paolo Salom, "Pechino, il primo ministro: 'Voglio conoscere i fatti,'" *Corriere della Sera*, 13 April 2007.

40 Cariglio, "Stranieri impaginati," 61. See also Andall, "New Migrants, Old Conflicts"; and Cole, *The New Racism in Europe*, 5–10 and 100–29.

41 Giannino della Frattina, "L'ultimo abbaglio della sinistra schierata con i cinesi in rivolta," *Il Giornale*, 14 April 2007; and Luca Fazio, "Milano, rivolta made in China," *Il Manifesto*, 13 April 2007.
42 Federico Rampini, "Le Pechino d'Italia," *La Repubblica*, 13 April 2007; *Uno mattina*, Rai Uno, 13 April 2007; and "I due volti di Chinatown" in Rai TG3, 13 April 2007. On this positive stereotype, see Hatziprokopiou and Montagna, "Contested Chinatown," 724.
43 For an analysis of the employment of ethnic essentialism in connection with Prato, see Ceccagno, *City Making and the Global Labor Regimes*, 204–6.
44 Hall, "The Whites of Their Eyes," 83 (italics original); and Essed, *Understanding Everyday Racism*, 288.
45 For a detailed analysis of Chinese migrant women's Italian representations, see Zhang, "The Chinaman and the *cinesina*," 85–92.
46 Giacomo Susca, "Il racconto di un testimone: 'Ho visto la donna spintonare le vigilesse,'" *Il Giornale*, 13 April 2007; Marco Ruggiero, "Chinatown si ribella: Guerriglia a Milano: E tutto per una multa," *Il Giorno*, 13 April 2007; and Montanari, "Le nostre banlieue pronte ad esplodere."
47 Padovani, "The Extreme Right and Its Media in Italy," 764–5.
48 Michele Focarete, "La grinta di Ruowei e delle altre," *Corriere della Sera*, 13 April 2007; Giuseppe Caruso, "Scontri a Milano, Pechino chiede 'equilibrio,'" *L'Unità*, 14 April 2007; and "Rivolta a Chinatown," *Il Giornale*.
49 Paola Fucilieri, "Milano, guerriglia a Chinatown: I vigili assaliti da 400 migrati," *Il Giornale*, 13 April 2007; Italia 1, "Studio aperto 1," 12 April 2007; Giuseppina Piano, "Moratti: nessun passo indietro: Le regole devono valere per tutti," *La Repubblica: Milano*, 13 April 2007; Bonerandi, "Milano, cinesi in rivolta"; *Uno mattina*, 13 April 2007; and Giuseppina Piano, "L'altolà del sindaco Moratti: 'Non esistono zone franche,'" *La Repubblica*, 13 April 2007.
50 Cariglio, "Stranieri impaginati," 69; and Maneri, "I media nel razzismo consensuale," 48.
51 Andrea Accorsi, "Una comunità divisa e fondata sull'illegalità," *La Padania*, 13 April 2007.
52 Oscar Giannino, "La rivolta dei cinesi: Figli del comunismo più spietato cercano un liberismo senza regole," *Libero*, 14 April 2007; Cassani, "Era una delle vie più belle della città"; and Giovanni Seu and Alessandra Stoppa, "Il vero piano di Chinatown," *Libero*, 15 April 2007.
53 Lucia Bellaspiga, "Prima troppe licenze: Ora troppe multe," *Avvenire*, 13 April 2007; Luigina Venturelli, "Dalle lanterne rosse al groviglio dei carrelli," *L'Unità*, 13 April 2007; Daniele Cologna, "Via Sarpi: non è colpa della diversità culturale," *Liberazione*, 14 April 2007; Antonella Ceccagno, "Sindrome cinese," *L'Unità*, 13 April 2007; and Antonella Ceccagno, "Migranti di successo," *L'Unità*, 18 April 2007. See also Roberto Borgonovi, "Italia schizofrenica," *Cina aperta* 2, no. 4 (2007): 1–2.

54 Zincone, "The Making of Policies," 352, 359, and 366–7. See also Bigot and Fella, "The Prodi Government's Proposed Citizenship Reform, and the Debate on Migration and Its Impact in Italy," 306; and Ceccagno and Rastrelli, *Ombre cinesi?*, 34 and 157.

55 *Studio aperto 1*, Italia 1, 12 November 2005.

56 Giannelli, cartoon, *Corriere della Sera*, 14 April 2007.

57 Krancic, "La Cina è vicina," *Il Giornale*, 13 April 2007; and Krancic, "Rifonderemo il P.C.I.: Partito Cinese Italiano!," *Il Giornale*, 14 April 2007. For similar mockery in *Libero*, see Alessandra Stoppa, "Il Partito di Chinatown," *Libero*, 14 April 2007.

58 Lorenzo Salvia, "L'ambasciatore Dong Jinyi: 'Non tentino di cacciarci altrimenti rivedremo i nostri investimenti in Italia," *Corriere della Sera*, 15 April 2007.

59 Mario Giordano, "Una lezione da chi non può darne," *Il Giornale*, 16 April 2007; and Fiorello Provera, "In Cina la protesta di Milano sarebbe stata sedata con violenza," *La Padania*, 14 April 2007.

60 Zincone, "The Making of Policies," 351; and Shohat and Stam, *Unthinking Eurocentrism*, 208.

61 "Guerriglia a Chinatown"; "Copertina: Brutto Affare a Chinatown"; and "I due volti di Chinatown."

62 Mazzoleni and Sfardini, *Politica Pop*, 46 and 135.

63 Vittorio Romano and Andrea Sceresini, "Niente carrelli (cinesi) in via Paolo Sarpi," *CorriereTV: Milano*, 1 March 2007, http://video.corriere.it/media/c268cb08-c743-11db-86a4-0003ba99c53b; Vittorio Romano and Andrea Sceresini, "Qui le regole valgono solo per gli stranieri," *Corriere della Sera: Milano*, 13 April 2007; "Studio aperto 1," Italia 1, 13 April 2007; Luca Fazio, "Milano, rivolta made in China," *Il Manifesto*, 13 April 2007; and Fabio Poletti, "Quelli ci multano e intascano i soldi," *La Stampa*, 13 April 2007.

64 This analysis draws from Coleman and McCahill, *Surveillance and Crime*, 10–11.

65 Davide Carlucci, "Botte con i vigili, il mistero del video," *La Repubblica: Milano*, 15 April 2007; and Gianni Santucci, "Blackout di due ore nel film degli scontri," *Corriere della Sera*, 15 April 2007.

66 Foucault, *Discipline and Punish*, 206.

67 For a sociological study of this phenomenon in Turin, see Genova and Ricucci, "Abitare Torino," 93–148.

68 Vladimiro Polchi, "'Un mondo chiuso, ma serve dialogo,' Il ministro Amato: Vivono se stessi come città nelle città," *La Repubblica*, 13 April 2007; "Copertina: Brutto Affare a Chinatown"; Colaprico, "I ragazzi di Paolo Sarpi"; Colaprico, "Nella Chinatown milanese tra magia e olimpiadi"; and Laura Eduati, "Noi giovani cinesi aperti alla società," *Liberazione*, 14 April 2007.

69 For a rare report on youth gangs formed by Chinese migrants following the 2007 riot, see Alessandra Stoppa, "Giovani cinesi contro i padri: 'Siete chiusi e mafiosi,'" *Libero*, 18 April 2007. See also Piero Colaprico, "Le gang di Chinatown," *La Repubblica*, 27 February 2009.

70 Dario di Vico, "Il confronto nella comunità cinese in Italia: I figli ai padri: 'Questa è la nostra casa,'" *Corriere della Sera*, 2 November 2013; and Sun Wenlong, "Lettera ai genitori cinesi – un pezzo di storia dei Cinesi in Italia," Associna, 28 October 2013, http://www.associna.com/it/2013/10/28/lettera-ai-genitori-cinesi-un-pezzo-di-storia-dei-cinesi-in-italia.

71 On the importance of local governments in policy-making and its implementation concerning immigration to Italy, see Castelli Gattinara, *The Politics of Migration in Italy*, 64–5.

72 Checchino Antonini, "Per favore, non chiamateci Chinatown," *Liberazione*, 14 April 2007; Laura Eduati, "Noi giovani cinesi aperti alla società," *Liberazione*, 14 April 2007; and Matteo Durante, "Campi rom, la Stecca dei pusher, Chinatown: Milano sull'orlo di una crisi di nervi," *Panorama* (online), 13 April 2007, http://italia.panorama.it/video/Campi-rom-la-Stecca-dei-pusher-Chinatown-Milano-sull-orlo-di-una-crisi-di-nervi. In the Prato case study, some Italian journalists claimed that the textile and garment industry run by Chinese migrants was lagging behind the service sector managed by Chinese migrants in other major Italian cities. See Maria Novella Rossi, "Ombre cinesi," *Dossier*, Rai TG2, 23 January 2010.

73 Allievi, "Immigration and Cultural Pluralism in Italy," 98. See also Bertossi, "Mistaken Models of Integration?"; and Martiniello, *Le società multietniche*, 56–60.

74 Einaudi, *Le politiche dell'immigrazione in Italia dall'Unità a oggi*, 349–54.

75 Vertovec and Wessendorf, "Assessing the Backlash," 4.

76 Mazzoleni and Sfardini, *Politica Pop*, 149–50 and 81.

77 "Sortino: China Town. Un micromondo di sfruttamento. La mafia cinese a Roma," *Le Iene*, 2007, http://www.video.mediaset.it/video/iene/puntata/43783/sortino-china-town.html; and "Sortino: Chinatown: La realtà dei cinesi che vivono nelle Chinatown italiane," *Le Iene*, 2007, http://www.video.mediaset.it/video/iene/puntata/17446/sortino-chinatown.html and http://www.video.mediaset.it/video/iene/puntata/17451/sortino-chinatown.html. *Le Iene* featured a Chinese migrant character, Yang Shi, in 2012 and 2013.

78 Zincone, "The Making of Policies," 367–8; and Zincone, "Citizenship Policy Making in Mediterranean EU States," 12–15 and 28.

79 Renata Pisu, "Lo dice Confucio: La famiglia prima della legge," *La Repubblica*, 15 April 2007; and Rai TG1, 20.00, 15 April 2007. See also Ceccagno and Rastrelli, *Ombre cinesi?*, 32.

80 Giovanni Morandi, "Se permettete siamo in Italia," *Il Giorno*, 13 April 2007; Enrico Fovanna, "Salvini: 'Peggio dei Rom,'" *Il Giorno*, 13 April 2007; Vittorio Feltri, "Rimandate a Pechino chi non sta alle leggi," *Libero*, 15 April 2007; and Gilberto Oneto, "Attenti a questa comunità che non vuole essere milanese," *Libero*, 14 April 2007.

81 Both multicultural and nativist discourses can be considered forms of racism: respectively differentialist and discriminatory racisms in Robert Miles's distinction. See Miles and Brown, *Racism*, 65–6.

82 Editorial, "Migrazioni: Il caso Chinatown visto dal Cospe," *Vita*, 19 April 2007; and Mazzetta, "I bauscia in guerra con la Cina," *Altrenotizie*, 15 April 2007, http://altrenotizie.org/societa/1003-i-bauscia-in-guerra-con-la-cina.html.

4 Milan: The 2007 "Chinatown" Riot in Migrant Debates

1 King and Wood, "Media and Migration," 1–2.

2 Genova and Ricucci, "Abitare Torino," 138–41.

3 Sun, "Introduction," 1, 3, and 5. For a study of how Chinese migrants in Rome preserve their language, see Angeli, "La conservazione della lingua madre nei cinesi adulti di Roma," 101–15.

4 For an introduction to migrant media in Italy, see Maneri, "La stampa," 24–42. For a survey of Chinese migrant media active in Italy around 2005, see Santangelo, "L'immigrazione cinese in Italia," 12–17. I will not discuss Chinese-language radio and television stations in Italy because of the scarcity of pertinent information. But readers will be interested to know that television news in Chinese was broadcast on RTB Network. There was also Chinese-language radio in Prato in 1993 and in Bologna in 2005. See Paolo Fallai, "In Toscana c'è una radio che parla solo cinese," *Corriere della Sera*, 31 July 1993; and Elisabetta Pagani, "La prima Radio bolognese che parla cinese," *L'Unità*, 21 October 2005. The first Chinese-language television station in Italy was called Huayi zhongwen dianshitai, founded by Liao Zonglin. See Santangelo, "L'immigrazione cinese in Italia," 37; and "Liao Zonglin: Jinjun yiguo wenhua lingyu de Wenzhouren," http://www.chinaqw.com/node2/node116/node119/node153/userobject6ai43038.html.

5 For brief accounts of Chinese migrant reactions to Italian depictions of them, see Maneri, "I media multiculturali, riconsiderati," 94–5; Tarantino and Tosoni, "The Battle of Milan," 214–15; and Latham, "Media and Discourses of Chinese Integration in Prato, Italy." I have previously published preliminary results of the research I present in this chapter. See my "The Protest in Milan's Chinatown and the Chinese Immigrants in Italy in the Media (2007–2009)."

6 Information about the financial backing of these newspapers was provided by *Ouzhou Qiaobao*'s then editor-in-chief, Wu Jie, in our interview in the newspaper's headquarters at Via Morazzone 7 in Milan on 18 December 2012. The same information was published on the *Ouzhou Qiaobao* website, http://www.qiaobao.eu/bencandy.php?fid=26&aid=14066. On the birth of *Ouhua Lianhe Shibao* and its founder Liao Zonglin, see "Liao Zonglin." *Xinhua Lianhe Shibao* resulted from the merger of *Xinhua Shibao* and *Oulian Shibao* in 2010. From my research, the first publication dates of these two newspapers are uncertain. In my book, when referring to articles in both newspapers before 2010, I only use *Xinhua Lianhe Shibao* for convenience. For the Italian and English titles of the Chinese-language newspapers that I cite in this chapter, I follow the ones used by the newspapers themselves.

7 Sun, "Introduction," 7–8.

8 See Santangelo, "L'immigrazione cinese in Italia," 12–16. Statistics about other newspapers and magazines are unavailable.

9 For an analysis of Associna's history and the composition of its members, see Marsden, "Second-Generation Chinese and New Processes of Social Integration in Italy," 113–16.

10 Laguerre, "Virtual Diasporas."

11 Sun, "China's Rise and (Trans)national Connections," 440–1; and Nyíri, "Expatriating Is Patriotic?" 645 and 648–9.

12 For a comparison between *Xinhua Lianhe Shibao* and *Ouhua Lianhe Shibao* based on their business and ideological interests, see Berrocal, Cortellesi, and Marconi, "Vendere la vendita," 69–70.

13 Because of space restrictions and the lack of data, I will not discuss the impact of Chinese mainland satellite television and mobile phone technologies on Chinese migrants in Italy. For relevant discussions, see Latham, "Media and Discourses of Chinese Integration in Prato, Italy"; and Johanson and Fladrich, "Ties that Bond."

14 Pieke et al., *Transnational Chinese*, 189–91 (the quotation is from 191).

15 Bourdieu notes a similar situation in a different context. See Bourdieu, *Distinction*, 228.

16 See Portes and Yiu, "Entrepreneurship, Transnationalism, and Development," 75 on survival strategy and individual mobility; Kandel and Massey, "The Culture of Mexican Migration," 981–3 on the culture of migration; and Giambelli, "L'emigrazione cinese in Italia" on Chinese restaurants in Italy.

17 On such a model of Chinese-ethnic moral economy in Singapore, see Ong, "Chinese Modernities," 183–7. For Italy, see Cologna, *Bambini e famiglie cinesi a Milano*, 71–5; and Ceccagno, "Compressing Personal Time."

18 Hall, "Encoding/Decoding," 125–7.

19 Georgiou, "Mapping Diasporic Media across the EU," 35.

20 Fewsmith, *China Today, China Tomorrow*, 159; and Santangelo, "L'immigrazione cinese in Italia," 9. For empirical research on the Italians' and the Chinese migrants' perceptions of one another in Via Sarpi, conducted in the early 2000s, see Cologna, "Il quartiere Canonica Sarpi," 41–54.

21 For this strategy in Chinese-European contexts, see Pieke et al., *Transnational Chinese*, 182–3. On the role of overseas Chinese in the Republic of China and in the People's Republic of China, see Christiansen, *Chinatown, Europe*, 7–12. See also Ong, *Flexible Citizenship*, 18. Typically, migrant media in Italy exhibit little awareness of their political role. See Meli and Enwereuzor, "Conclusioni," 115–16.

22 Xu Jianguo, "Yige zhongguoren yan zhong de Zhongguocheng fengbo shimo/I disordini della Chinatown milanese agli occhi di un cinese," *Cina in Italia*, April 2007. My translation was made from the Chinese version of the text.

23 My claim here builds on insights from Laguerre, *Global Ethnopolis*, 4–8, 13–15; and Chan, *Migration, Ethnic Relations, and Chinese Business*, 33.

24 Shi Jie and Cai Qiong, "Milan huaren yu Yidali jingcha fasheng zhongda chongtu shijian zuixin baodao," *Ouhua Lianhe Shibao*, 18 April 2007; and Qiu and Li, "Hundreds of Overseas Chinese Protested the Police Authorities for Assault," *Guangzhou Daily*, 14 April 2007.

25 I do not mention the names of the editor and the newspaper to protect their identities. The interview was conducted in 2012.

26 Renwick and Cao, "China's Political Discourse Towards the 21st Century," 121.

27 Yu, "Milan baofa huashang da guimo kangyi langchao."

28 Renwick and Cao, "China's Political Discourse Towards the 21st Century," 120.

29 Fu Hongge, "'Musuolini' de gunzi," *Sohu*, 13 April 2007, http://news.sohu.com/20070413/n249419861.shtml; Paolo Salom, "La vignetta in un sito di Pechino: Poliziotti italiani come Mussolini," *Corriere della Sera*, 16 April 2007; and "Bandiera rossa a Chinatown."

30 Chen, *Occidentalism*, 3–5.

31 Cao Xin and Chen Chen, "'2007, Zhongguoren haiwai anquan baogao,' zou chu guo men, zhe ge shijie gengjia bu anquan," *Nanfang Zhoumuo*, 9 January 2008. As an official document, this report does not address Chinese migrant enterprises in its main text, but instead focuses on overseas branches of state-owned companies.

32 "Guanzhu haiwai huaren anquan," *Sohu*, 2007, http://news.sohu.com/s2007/huarenanquan/index.shtml; Li Wei, "The Question of the Security of Overseas Chinese Is Becoming Prominent Daily," *International Herald Leader*, 21 May 2007; and "Cong quanqiu zhanliu gaodu kan 'Milan shijian.'"

33 Fang Manqing, "BBC Chinese Channel Journalist Wick Interviews Vice-President Fang Manqing of Italy's *Ouhua Italy*," *BBC*, 12 April 2007, http://news.bbc.co.uk/chinese/simp/hi/newsid_6550000/newsid_6550700/6550713.stm.

34 Xi Bei, "Milan bufen huaren ren zifa jingzuo shiwei heping biaoda rongru yiyuan," *Ouhua Lianhe Shibao*, 23 April 2007.

35 Han Yu, "Milan baofa huashang da guimo kangyi langchao," *Ouzhou Qiaobao*, 13 April 2007; and "Women yao shenme?," *Ouzhou Qiaobao*, 26 April 2007.

36 lichunhaug, Associna forum post, 12 April 2007, http://www.associna.com/it/forum/index.php?topic=2701.30; and Tai Shan et al., "Milan huaren yu jingcha fasheng canlie chongtu," *Ouzhou Huaren Bao*, 14 April 2007.

37 linlin, Associna forum post, 12 April 2007, http://www.associna.com/it/forum/index.php?topic=2701.30; cri82 and dalang, Associna forum posts, 13 April 2007, http://www.associna.com/it/forum/index.php?topic=2701.45; and "Studio aperto 1," Italia 1, 13 April 2007.

38 Shi and Cai, "Milan huaren yu Yidali jingcha fasheng zhongda chongtu shijian zuixin baodao." Already in 2000, *Ouhua Lianhe Shibao* was vocal about being misrepresented by *Corriere della Sera*. See "La comunità cinese," *Corriere della Sera*, 2 December 2000.

39 Shi and Cai, "Milan huaren yu Yidali jingcha fasheng zhongda chongtu shijian zuixin baodao."

40 "Studio aperto 1," Italia 1, 13 April 2007; *Il Giornale*, 14 April 2007; *La Padania*, 16 April 2007; and "I loro quotidiani: Giusto protestare, la polizia italiana è violenta," *Libero*, 14 April 2007.

41 federep, Associna forum post, 13 April 2007, http://www.associna.com/it/forum/index.php?topic=2701.75.

42 Hu Lanbo, "Zhongguoren he Yidaliren neng gongtong shenghuo ma?/Cinesi e italiani possono convivere?," *Cina in Italia*, April 2007. I translated from the Chinese version of this article, which is slightly different from the Italian version.

43 Ibid.

44 Ceccagno, *Cinesi d'Italia*, 15–28.

45 Hall, "Cultural Identity and Diaspora," 223–5; and Chen, *Occidentalism*, 3–5.

46 Anderson, *Imagined Communities*; and Ong, *Flexible Citizenship*, 57–65.

47 Latham, "Media and Discourses of Chinese Integration in Prato, Italy," 148.

48 I draw this observation from Christiansen, *Chinatown, Europe*, 32–3.

49 Pieke et al., *Transnational Chinese*, 190–2; and Christiansen, *Chinatown, Europe*, 137–8.

50 Dirlik, "Chinese History and the Question of Orientalism," 113.

51 Qiu and Li, "Hundreds of Overseas Chinese Protested the Police Authorities for Assault"; Han Han, "Qing zai deng ji fenzhong, hao ma?," *Ouzhou Huaren Bao*, 26 April 2007; Cao and Chen, "2007, Zhongguoren haiwai anquan baogao"; and Li Shuang, "What Revelations Did the 'Milan Incident' in Italy Give Us?," *People's Daily* (overseas edition), 22 May 2007.

52 For example, "La rivolta di Chinatown" in episode 134, *Secondo voi*, which was broadcast on all three Mediaset channels on 18 April 2007 and featured Paolo del Debbio.

53 Qiu and Li, "Hundreds of Overseas Chinese Protested the Police Authorities for Assault."

54 Louie, *Theorising Chinese Masculinity*, 10–21 and 53–7; and Louie, *Chinese Masculinities in a Globalizing World*, 89–105. Women entrepreneurs are rarely mentioned in this context.

55 "Milan huashang shifou mianlin geng da de jiyu?," *Ouhua Lianhe Shibao*, 28 May 2007; and "Cong quanqiu zhanliu gaodu kan 'Milan shijian,'" *Ouhua Lianhe Shibao*, 18 April 2007.

56 Xi Bei, "Quan fangwei guanzhu Milan huaren yu jingfang chongtu shijian," *Ouhua Lianhe Shibao*, 18 April 2007; "Tuanjie jiu neng duguo nanguan," *Ouzhou Qiaobao*, 9 April 2007; and Tai Shan et al., "Milan huaren yu jingcha fasheng canlie chongtu."

57 Stefano Di Martino, 2012, http://www.stefanodimartino.it/ambasciatore/biografia-stefano-di-martino.html; Giuseppe Guastella, "'Fondi ad associazione fantasma': A giudizio Manca e Di Martino," *Corriere della Sera*, 26 October 2010; and "Truffa su fondi a onlus, condannati Di Martino e un ex assessore del Pdl," *La Repubblica*, 16 February 2012.

58 Cheng Liu, 31 March 2007, http://www.meltingpot.org/Ancona-La-faccia-felice-della-Cina-I-problemi-non-mancano.html#.WDUUmplyR0s; and Malia Zheng, 1 April 2014, http://iltirreno.gelocal.it/prato/cronaca/2014/04/01/news/un-consigliere-comunale-cinese-per-campi-1.8963465. For other candidates of Chinese origins in Tuscany in 2014, see http://www.redattoresociale.it/Notiziario/Articolo/460149/Elezioni-boom-di-candidati-cinesi-tra-Firenze-e-Prato.

59 Andall, "The G2 Network and Other Second-Generation Voices," 184–9.

60 "Milano: Rivolta a Milano," Associna forum thread, http://www.associna.com/it/forum/index.php?topic=2701.0. The last reply is dated 16 April 2007.

61 feilong, Associna forum post, 16 April 2007, http://www.associna.com/it/forum/index.php?topic=2701.435; and lichunhaug, Associna forum post, 12, 13, and 14 April 2007, http://www.associna.com/it/forum/index.php?topic=2701.30, http://www.associna.com/it/forum/index

.php?topic=2701.90, and http://www.associna.com/it/forum/index.php?topic=2701.240.

62 For the concepts of multiculturalism in relation to citizenship which I draw upon here, see Kymlicka, "The Rise and Fall of Multiculturalism?"

63 On the definition of "contact zones," see Pratt, *Imperial Eyes*, 7–8. Chinese Italians' hybrid cultural identities and career interests recall those of overseas Chinese during the sixteenth century, when the latter helped Portuguese, Spanish, Dutch, and English fleets navigate routes to China and Japan and establish commercial relations with them. See Clifford, *Routes*, 188–219; and Carioti, "Haiwai huaren," 79–86.

64 Yu, "Milan baofa huashang da guimo kangyi langchao."

65 Zincone, "Citizenship Policy Making in Mediterranean EU States," 26.

66 "I nostri video," vivisarpi.it, http://www.vivisarpi.it/wb/pages/i-nostri-video/tra-degrado-e-illegalita.php; and Dan, "Huaren re le shei?," *Ouhua Qiaobao*, 28 May 2007.

67 Davide Carlucci, "Rivolta in Sarpi, 38 condanne nove mesi a Di Martino del Pdl," *La Repubblica*, 24 June 2010; and "'Milan shijian' haiwai huaren wei quan shi shang yi ci xue de jiaoxun," *Xinhua Lianhe Shibao*, 2 July 2010.

68 Fazio, "Milano, rivolta made in China"; and Cassani, "Era una delle vie più belle della città."

69 Glick Schiller and Çaglar, "Towards a Comparative Theory of Locality in Migration Studies," 186–8.

70 Paola Calvetti, "'L'isola che non c'è': Come fallische il progetto di una nuova Paolo Sarpi," *Corriere della Sera*, 16 November 2011; and "Milano: Chinatown quattro anni dopo," La7, 5 October 2011, http://www.la7.it/coffee-break/video/milano-chinatown-quattro-anni-dopo-05-10-2011-122067.

5 Prato: Local Debates on "Made in Italy" by the Chinese, 2005–2012

1 For concise summaries of the Chinese insertion in Prato's local economy, see Dei Ottati and Cologna, "The Chinese in Prato and the Current Outlook on the Chinese-Italian Experience," 39–40; Dei Ottati, "An Industrial District Facing the Challenges of Globalization"; and Dei Ottati, "A Transnational Fast Fashion Industrial District." For the most authoritative account of the Prato case study, see Ceccagno, *City Making and Global Labor Regimes*, 39–146. The information I present in the introduction to this chapter draw on analyses presented in this literature. For the history of Prato's textile industry before the 1990s, see Hamilton and Fels, "The Social Sources of Migration and Enterprise," 273–7.

2 On the "Made in Italy" ready-to-wear sector and on the distinction between the ready-to-wear and fast fashion sectors, see Segre Reinach, "China and Italy" and "Italian Fashion."
3 Ceccagno, "The Hidden Crisis," 45–6.
4 Figures are respectively from Ceccagno, "The Hidden Crisis," 50; "Le aziende cinesi? Una risorsa per la nostra economia," *La Nazione*, 5 March 2013; Ceccagno, "The Hidden Crisis," 46–9; and Ufficio di Statistica, "Tab. 1.9."
5 Dei Ottati, "An Industrial District Facing the Challenges of Globalization," 1828; and Ceccagno, *City Making and Global Labor Regimes*, 104–7 and 135–8.
6 Ceccagno, *City Making and Global Labor Regimes*, 132.
7 Dei Ottati, "An Industrial District Facing the Challenges of Globalization," 1826–7. For recent statistics concerning the entire economic output of Prato's textile and garment industries, and those of the ready-to-wear industry in particular, see Ceccagno, "The Hidden Crisis," 46.
8 For Zara's production model, one of the most imitated in the fast-fashion sector, see McCarthy, 541–6. For Italian fast fashion, see Ceccagno, *City Making and Global Labor Regimes*, 56–8, 130–3, and 157–8.
9 Bianca Stancanelli, "Il cinese dell'azienda accanto," *Panorama*, 12 December 2004.
10 Tomlinson, *Globalization and Culture*, 24. See also Hall, "Old and New Identities, Old and New Ethnicities."
11 Butler, *Excitable Speech*, 2 and 12.
12 "Sindaco, sorpasso del centrodestra: Cenni è il nuovo primo cittadino," *La Nazione*, 22 June 2009. In 2014, Prato elected a centre-left government with Matteo Biffoni as mayor.
13 "'Prato non deve chiudere': 8000 i manifestanti in città," *La Nazione*, 28 February 2009; Prato TV, "Manifestazione Tessile," 28 February 2009; Rai TG1, 13.30, 28 February 2009; Rai TG3, 19.00, 28 February 2009; and "Prato, una bandiera lunga un chilometro contro la crisi. Foto e Video," 28 February 2009, http://firenze.repubblica.it/multimedia/home/4971902/1/1. Edoardo Nesi's Strega award-winning book, *Storia della mia gente* (Story of my people) (Milano: Bompiani, 2010), also describes this event.
14 Hadjimichalis, "The End of Third Italy as We Know It?," 82.
15 *Annozero*, "Il rosso e il nero," Rai Due, 19 March 2009.
16 Ambrosini, "Immigration in Italy," 184–5; and Blim, *Made in Italy*, 3 and 162–71.
17 Mazzoleni and Sfardini, *Politica Pop*, 48–50 and 140–1.
18 For an analysis of a similarly jarring pairing on the same talk show concerning Islam, see Cere, "Globalization vs. Localization," 236–7.

19 "Telecamere del 04/01/2010," *Telecamere*, Rai Tre, 4 January 2010; and *Le Storie: Diario italiano/Stories: Italian Diary*, Rai Tre, 5 December 2011.
20 Ferri and Gronchi, "La comunità cinese a Prato: Analisi di alcuni spazi etnicamente connotati," 306–8.
21 Ceccagno, "The Hidden Crisis," 61.
22 Papuzzi and Magone, *Professione giornalista*, 117 and 298–300.
23 Butler, *Excitable Speech*, 27–8 and 40.
24 "Carta di Roma" and "Professionisti."
25 For examples of the use of "blitz," see Cotesta, "Mass media, conflitti etnici e identità degli italiani," 459.
26 Prefettura di Prato, Comune di Prato, Provincia di Prato, and Regione Toscana, "Patto per Prato sicura," 2.
27 Elena Duranti, "Blitz da record contro l'industria di Chinatown," *La Nazione*, 30 April 2009; and Prato TV, Telegiornale, 29 April 2009.
28 "Maxi operazione della GdF. Sei aziende sequestrate," *La Nazione*, 29 April 2009; "Nuova maxi operazione della GdF in quattro province 110 denunce," *La Nazione*, 30 April 2009; Rai TG 1, 17.00, 29 April 2009; Rai TGR, Toscana Edizione Serale, 29 April 2009; and Prato TV, "Blitz cinesi," 29 April 2009. For an account of the Chinese insertion into the local economy in Campi Bisenzio, see Carchedi and Tripodi, "La comunità cinese a Campi Bisenzio," 329–30.
29 Leonardo Biagiotti, "Abiti pratesi-cinesi per i grandi marchi," *La Nazione*, 23 January 2010.
30 Biagiotti, "Abiti pratesi-cinesi per i grandi marchi"; Ilenia Reali, "Il sindaco anti-cinesi va a produrre in Cina," *L'Espresso*, 23 September 2009; Editoriale, "Kongju rang quanju dedao le chenggong. Keneng yao changjiu zhizheng le/La paura vince le elezioni e forse governerà a lungo," *It's China*, July 2009; Giacomo Cocchi, "L'intervista: Parla Silvia Pieraccini, autrice di uno studio sul 'distretto parallelo': Da manodopera a imprenditori illegali," *Toscana Oggi*, 27 January 2010; and Guy Dinmore, "Tuscan Town Turns against Chinese Migrants," *Financial Times*, 9 February 2010. For an analysis on a possible Italian-Chinese migrant integrated fashion industry in Prato, see Ceccagno, *City Making and the Global Labor Regimes*, 232–4.
31 Stefano Cecchi, "Pratesi e cinesi alleati nel tessile," *La Nazione*, 3 February 2010; Cristina Orsini, "Blitz a Chinatown, spot pericoloso," *Il Tirreno*, 24 January 2010; Prato TV, "Gente di Prato," 22 December 2011, http://www.tvprato.it/2011/12/gente-di-prato-16/; "Rang women jianli yi zhong fangzhi hezi/Facciamo la joint venture italo-cinese nel tessile," *It's China*, October 2008; and "Fanzhi he shizhuang: Pulatuo jiang shi yi ge da gongchang/Tessile e moda: Prato sarà un grande laboratorio," *It's China*, November 2008.

32 Dario di Vico, "Il patto di Prato con i "nemici' cinesi," *Corriere della Sera*, 25 January 2010; and Cecchi, "Assedio a Chinatown. Basta illegalità."

33 Hall, "The Local and the Global," 33; and Robertson, *Globalization*, 26. See also Robertson, *Globalization*, 177–9.

34 Damiano Fedeli, "Prato e il blitz contro i cinesi," *Toscana Oggi*, 27 January 2010.

35 Dai Xiaozhang, "Yidali huashang zonghui mishu-zhang Dai Xiaozhang: Tan Yidali huashang jingji," *Xinhua Lianhe Shibao*, 12 March 2011.

36 Maria Lardara, "Guerra ai cinesi con le scritte," *L'Espresso*, 3 July 2009. These slurs also referred to the unhygienic conditions in Prato's Via Pistoiese, where garbage visibly piled up in 2009. The incident gave the impression that the area was a ghetto. See Raffaetà and Baldassar, "Spaces Speak Louder than Words."

37 For the application of Taoist and Confucian notions to Chinese-language communication, see Hwang, "Masculinity Index and Communication Style," 85–101. On the notions of the yin and yang as applied to the female and the male in Chinese culture, see Louie, *Theorising Chinese Masculinity*, 9–10.

38 You Zi, "Huashang ying cong 'youjidui" zhuan wei 'zhengguijun,'" *Xinhua Lianhe Shibao*, 28 October 2010.

39 Bo Yuan, "Yi huaren qiye yinggai bian 'lianjia' xingxiang," *Xinhua Lianhe Shibao*, 7 July 2011; and Bo Yuan, "Liyi bu shi haiwai huaren jingji wei yi zhuiqiu," *Xinhua Lianhe Shibao*, 8 April 2011.

40 Federica Bianchi, "Ma cosa fanno i cinesi in Italia?," *L'Espresso*, 3 January 2011. For examples of Rai newscast, see Rai TG2 Notte, 20 January 2010; and Rai TGR Toscana, Edizione Notturna, 19 January 2010.

41 "Aldo Milone: Gongbu ta de qingli feifa xianxiang de zhanliu/Aldo Milone: 'Vi spiego la mia guerra per la legalità," *It's China*, July 2009.

42 "Minacce al sindaco di Prato firmate Br-Pcc," *La Repubblica*, 6 January 2010; Paolo Nencioni, "Mega-blitz nella Chinatown, quartiere blindato a Prato," *Il Tirreno*, 19 January 2010; Stefano Cecchi, "Assedio a Chinatown: Basta illegalità," *La Nazione*, 20 January 2010; Cesare Peruzzi, "Blitz anti-sommerso a Prato," *Il Sole 24 Ore*, 20 January 2010; Luigi Caroppo, "I blitz prevengono il conflitto sociale," *La Nazione*, 21 January 2010; Fabio Evangelisti, "L'Italia sta scivolando nell'intolleranza razziale," *Il Tirreno*, 22 January 2010; and "Maxi-Blitz nella Chinatown pratese e Wong non ci sta: 'Solo repressione,'" *Corriere Fiorentino*, 19 January 2010.

43 Nencioni, "Mega-blitz nella Chinatown, quartiere blindato a Prato"; and Cecchi, "Pratesi e cinesi alleati nel tessile."

44 Bo Yuan, "Puladuo jiancha shi daliang huaren liuluo jie tou, huaren xu yi fa wei quan," *Xinhua Lianhe Shibao*, 25 January 2010; and Cui Yinhui, "Mian-dui-mian, bu yao bei-dui-bei/Faccia a faccia, non schiena contro

schiena," *Cina in Italia*, March 2010. For Chinese migrants' testimonies on Italian officials' bias towards them, see Chen, "Made in Italy (by the Chinese)," 121–2.

45 Cesare Peruzzi, "Una moratoria per Prato," *Il Sole 24 Ore*, 19 January 2010; Giovanni Ciattini, "Nuovo colpo all'illegalità cinese," *Il Tirreno*, 20 January 2010; Giovanni Ciattini, "Come un rastrellamento Ss," *Il Tirreno*, 20 January 2010; Caroppo, "I blitz prevengono il conflitto sociale"; and Luigi Caroppo, "Bufera sul console Gu Honglin," *Il Tirreno*, 21 January 2010.

46 "'Chinatown non dorme mai': In arrivo controlli di notte," *La Nazione*, 7 May 2010.

47 Marco Bazzichi, "Maxi blitz contro la mafia cinese: 24 arresti tra Firenze e Prato," *Corriere Fiorentino*, 29 June 2010.

48 In keeping with the national trend, the Chinese mafia was the foremost topic in news widely read in Prato and Florence between 1988 and 1994. See Marsden, "Le comunità cinesi viste dalla stampa," 213–17. The French international television channel *France 24* also covered Prato's Chinese mafia in late 2008. See Geraldine Quidu-Desqueyroux and Livio Capra, "In the Hell of an Italian Chinatown," *France 24*, 5 December 2008, http://www.france24.com/en/20081205-hell-italian-chinatown-italy-immigration.

49 Giovanni Spano, "'E a Chinatown è Guerra per bande': Il procuratore antimafia, Pietro Grasso," *La Nazione*, 29 June 2010; Prato TV, Telegiornale, 28 June 2010; and "La protesta della Lega: 'Via l'ambasciatore Ding Wei,'" *La Nazione*, 28 June 2010.

50 Zhu Lin, "Ru ci dadong-gange dou shi wei le qian," *Ouzhou Qiaobao*, 2–6 July 2010. *Nanfang Zhoumou*, however, published a feature story explaining this phenomenon. See Qin Xuan and Liu Bin, "Haiwai huaren heibang diaocha," *Nanfang Zhoumou*, 5 August 2010.

51 Bo Yuan, "Yidali 'xi qian an' yu wan huaren shou sun, zhongfang gaodu guanzhu," *Xinhua Lianhe Shibao*, 2 July 2010; and Chen Jun, "Yidali zhengfu shishi zhengdui huaren fanzui tuanhuo dahei ying Zhengyi/Giro di vite del governo italiano contro i gruppi criminali cinesi, scoppiano le polemiche," *China Newsweek*, July 2010; and *Cina in Italia*, September 2010.

52 Bo Yuan, "Yi huaren xi qian an shang dai sifa jieding, 'hui se jingji' ying huo duan?," *Xinhua Lianhe Shibao*, 21 July 2011; and You Zi, "Huaren 'wei gui' hui kuan jiujin shi shei de cuo?," *Xinhua Lianhe Shibao*, 12 October 2010.

53 Bo Yuan, "Yi huaren xi qian an shang dai sifa jieding, 'hui se jingji' ying huo duan?"; Bo Yuan, "Yi huaren jingji quan diaocha: Kao xinyu yunzuo, fumian xingxiang zao er chao," *Xinhua Lianhe Shibao*, 29 September 2010; Chen, "Yidali zhengfu shishi zhengdui huaren fanzui tuanhuo dahei ying Zhengyi"; You Zi, "Huashang heyi chengwei le Yidali shuaitui jingji de

'tizui-gaoyang'?," *Xinhua Lianhe Shibao*, 8 October 2010; and Bo Yuan, "Lushi jiedu 'xi qian an': Zhenzheng yingjia shi Yidali meiti," *Xinhua Lianhe Shibao*, 6 July 2010.

54 You Zi, "Zuoren yao didiao," *Xinhua Lianhe Shibao*, 3 July 2010.

55 You Zi, "Zhongguoren: Bie xingzai-lehuo," *Xinhua Lianhe Shibao*, 19 July 2010; and You Zi, "Pizhibuzun, maojiangyanfu," *Xinhua Lianhe Shibao*, 10 October 2010. For a case study of "class consciousness" among Chinese migrant workers in relation to Chinese migrant entrepreneurs in the Veneto area, see Wu and Liu, "Bringing Class Back In," 8 and 13.

56 "Tisheng zhonghua wenhua ruan shili shi Zhongguo yu haiwai huaren gongtong zhize," *Xinhua Lianhe Shibao*, 10 September 2010; and Mario Lancisi, "Il sogno: Un sindaco cinese a Prato," *L'Espresso*, 21 September 2009.

57 Bo Yuan, "Yi Pulatuo tangrenjie caomu-jiebin, da jiancha ling huashang qianjing kan you," *Xinhua Lianhe Shibao*, 1 July 2010.

58 Cui, "Mian-dui-mian, bu yao bei-dui-bei"; Bo Yuan, "Ba buli jumian biancheng wanshan zisheng de dongli – Yi ge zhongguoren dui Pulatuo jiancha de fansi/Tramutare una situazione sfavorevole in una forza per migliorare: Considerazioni di un cinese sui controlli di Prato," *Cina in Italia*, March 2010; Bo Yuan, "Puladuo jia da dui huaren qiye jiancha lidu, suashang qiantu kanyou," *Xinhua Lianhe Shibao*, 21 January 2010; Bo Yuan, "Puladuo huaren mianlin xin de jueze yu kaoyan," *Xinhua Lianhe Shibao*, 22 January 2010; and Bo Yuan, "Huaren ying zhuan buli jumian wei wanshan zisheng dongli," *Xinhua Lianhe Shibao*, 26 January 2010.

6 Prato: Global Debates on "Made in Italy" by the Chinese, 2005–2012

1 The international media tended to focus on a limited number of topics concerning Italy. See Pannocchia, "Il giornalismo italiano visto dall'estero," 276–8.

2 Peter Gumbel, "Twilight in Italy," *Time*, 5 December 2005. For related articles, see Susan Jakes, "Italy vs. China: Sitting Pretty," *Time*, 19 March 2006; and "Italian Textiles and China: Material Fitness," *Economist*, 23 February 2006.

3 To view an image of this cover, visit http://content.time.com/time/covers/europe/0,16641,20051205,00.html.

4 See the endnotes of the next sections for examples of this coverage.

5 WTO, "Agreement on Textiles and Clothing," www.wto.org; and Directorate General for Trade of the European Commission, 2 October 2006, "Evolution of EU Textile Imports from China in 2005 and the First 7 Months of 2006."

6 Ross, "Made in Italy," 210; Di Tommaso and Rubini, "'Made in Italy' and 'Made in China,'" 1 and 7; and Ceccagno, *City Making and Global Labor Regime*, 51.
7 Stancanelli, "Il cinese dell'azienda accanto"; and William Underhill, "The Chinese Are Coming," *Newsweek*, 15 October 2006.
8 Antonio Galdo, "Ma quale Prato, questa è Chinatown," *Panorama*, 9 December 1999; Rossi, "Reportage: Viaggio nelle Chinatown d'Italia," 43; and "Intervista con il Questore di Prato." See also Rastrelli, "L'immigrazione a Prato fra società, istituzioni ed economia," 70–9. In the early 2000s, the governments of Prato and Wenzhou instituted a series of friendly official agreements in the areas of fabrics, tourism, agriculture, education, health, and sister cities. See Lombardi, *Sulla Via della Tela*, 118–39.
9 Barbie Nadeau, "Made by Foreign Hands," *Newsweek*, 23 June 2007; and John Hooper, "Made in Little Wenzhou, Italy: The Latest Label from Tuscany," *Guardian*, 17 November 2010.
10 Sabrina Giannini, "Schiavi del lusso," *Report*, Rai Tre, 2 December 2007; and Sabrina Giannini, "Disoccupati del lusso," *Report*, Rai Tre, 18 May 2008. For an update on these two episodes, see Sabrina Giannini, "Schiavi del lusso – Aggiornamento del 2/12/2007," *Report*, Rai Tre, 1 November 2009. On the style of *Report*'s investigative journalism, see Bianda, "Verso un ritorno del giornalismo d'approfondimento," 248–9 and 252–3.
11 Ross, "Made in Italy," 212.
12 Thomas Schmid, "Die Chinesen kommen," *Die Zeit*, 5 February 2008. The title may also be a reference to a 1987 German film, *Die Chinesen kommen*, by Manfred Stelzer. The translation from German to English is mine. On Prato's real estate, see Ceccagno, *City Making and Global Labor Regimes*, 93–4.
13 Fiona Ehlers, "The New Wave of Globalization: Made in Italy at Chinese Prices," *Der Spiegel*, 7 September 2006.
14 Ben-Ghiat, "The Secret Histories of Roberto Benigni's *Life Is Beautiful*."
15 "Tempi moderni," Rete 4, 17 March 2007; and Mario Portanova, "Siamo cinesi e molto borghesi," *L'Espresso*, 7 October 2008. Similar observations are made in Zhong Wenyi, "Zhan zai 'Yidali zhizao' beihou de huaren/ Immigrati cinesi dietro il Made in Italy," *Cina in Italia*, July 2008.
16 "Prato sui media mondiali: Un'opportunità di crescita," *La Nazione*, 7 July 2010.
17 Rachel Donadio, "Chinese Remake the 'Made in Italy' Fashion Label," *New York Times*, 12 September 2010; Guy Dinmore, "Negative Effects," *Financial Times*, 9 June 2011; Henry Ridgwell, "Ancient Italian Town Turns against Chinese Migrants," *Voice of America*, 22 October 2010; and Nina Burleigh, "Italian Jobs, Chinese Illegals," *Bloomberg Businessweek*, 3 November 2011.

See also Philipp Bilsky, "Chinesische Textilproduktion in Italien," *Deutsche Welle*, 3 April 2011. On the *New York Times*'s role in agenda-setting, see McCombs, *Setting the Agenda*, 128–9.

18 "Il *New York Times*: Allarme Prato," *La Repubblica*, 14 September 2010; Prato TV, Telegiornale, 13 September 2013; Bo Yuan, "'Xi qian an' deng shijian zhongchuang Yidali huashe, huaren mianlin xin kaoyan," *Xinhua Lianhe Shibao*, 21 September 2010; Bo Yuan, "Zhenshi de Pulatuo haren zhuangkuang/La reale situazione dei cinesi a Prato," *Cina in Italia*, October 2010; Ilenia Reali, "Mani cinesi cuciono abiti di Prada," *Il Tirreno*, 5 September 2007; Nina Burleigh, "L'Italia salvata dai cinesi," *Internazionale*, 25 November–1 December 2011; and Associna, 25 November 2011, http://www.associna.com/it/2011/11/25/l%E2%80%99italia-salvata-dai-cinesi/.

19 Burleigh, "Italian Jobs, Chinese Illegals."

20 Raffaella Galvani, "Così la Cina ci rovina," *Panorama*, 3 June 2005; and Monica Camozzi, "Aiuto, il tessile si sfila," *Panorama*, 6 May 2005.

21 Song Jian and Wang Junjia, "Pulatuo: Haiwai 'xin tangrenjie' shengzhang yangben," *Xinhuanet*, 22 August 2011, http://news.xinhuanet.com/overseas/2011-08/22/c_121892101.htm; and Su, *Hu Yundi jiazu qiao pu*.

22 Hooper, "Made in Little Wenzhou, Italy"; Duncan Kennedy, "Italy's Fashion 'Challenged' by Chinese Factories," *BBC News*, 26 October 2010; and Philippe Ridet, "Made in Italy à la chinoise," *Le Monde*, 4 November 2010. Xu Qiu Lin is erroneously spelt as "Hu Qui Lin" in the *Guardian*, as "Xu Quilin" in *Le Monde*, and as "Xu Lin" in *BBC News*. For a list of major international news outlets covering Prato, see Baldassar, Johanson, McAuliffe, and Bressan, "Chinese Migration to the *New* Europe," 12 and 23–5.

23 Bourdieu, *The Field of Cultural Production*, 68.

24 Cariglio, "Stranieri impaginati," 74; and Ahmed, "Home and Away," 338.

25 *Guipel*, http://www.giupel.it/.

26 These two media texts are mentioned in Chen Yiming, "Wenti jiu zai yu: Zhongguo ren 'guoyu qinlao': Wenzhou ren zai Yidali," *Nanfang Zhoumou*, 21 December 2012.

27 NKH, http://www.nhk.or.jp/documentary/1207.html. Apart from the documentary on Prato, Italy was also featured in a story about African refugees on the island of Lampedusa in 2011. See NKH, "地中海・難民島~ジャスミン革命は何をもたらしたのか~," http://www.nhk.or.jp/documentary/1105.html.

28 Miyake, "Italy Made in Japan," 202–6; and Morley and Robins, *Spaces of Identity*, 160 and 165–6.

29 For example, Andrew Monahan, "China Overtakes Japan as World's No. 2 Economy," *Wall Street Journal*, 14 February 2011.

30 I use the official English title of the television serial. The literal translation of the Chinese title is "a family from Wenzhou."

31 For television news that claims a certain Wenzhounese entrepreneur as the model for the father character in *Legend of Entrepreneurship*, see http://www.wcbtv.com.cn/wcgd/lmsp/lmzt/2013-03-01/8967.html. On the parallels between Wenzhounese migration to elsewhere in China and to Europe, see Thunø, "Moving Stones from China to Europe," 159–80; and Biao, "Zhejiang Village in Beijing," 215–50.

32 Starring the famous Taiwanese actor Li Lichun and featuring the family melodrama, a genre most associated with Taiwanese serial dramas, the drama was clearly geared towards Chinese-speaking communities worldwide, the concept of the "big Chinese family" analysed in chapter 4. See Zhu, *Television in Post-Reform China*, 105–8.

33 Since the Italian entrepreneur's name never appears in its original language, here I transliterate his Chinese name into pinyin, as Mr Saishaer. The list of Italian actors was not available at the time of my research for this chapter. Zhou Ayu's storyline mainly takes places during the serial's final nine episodes. Chinese mainland television drama has previously addressed overseas Chinese's lives in other countries, the most famous being 1993's *Beijing ren zai Niu Yue* (A Beijing native in New York).

34 Zhang, "Contemporary Italian Novels on Chinese Immigration to Italy," 18–20 and 25–8. It is notable that in one of the earliest Western depictions of China, a passage in Pliny the Elder's *National History*, the author condemns imported Chinese silk for enticing Roman patrician women to breach social decorum and to squander financial sources that would put Roman society at financial risk. Pliny the Elder, *National History*, cited in Leslie and Gardiner, *The Roman Empire in Chinese Sources*, 123.

35 The comparison between Italian Jews and the Wenzhounese is particularly pronounced in the serials' episodes 32 and 33.

36 For example, Amy Chua's best-selling parenting book, *Battle Hymn of the Tiger Mother* (New York: Penguin Books, 2011); *Sohu*'s article on Chinese-Jewish business competition, Anonymous, "Zhongguo zhenzheng de duishou shi Youtairen, du wan ruleiguanding!," http://www.sohu.com/a/111649142_466904; and M. Avrum Ehrlich, ed., *The Jewish-Chinese Nexus: A Meeting of Civilizations* (London: Routledge, 2008).

37 Appadurai, *Modernity at Large*, 31; and Ross, "Made in Italy."

38 The concern for Italian expertise articulates some of the industrialists' fear of Chinese infringements on Italian intellectual property rights, a concern exacerbated by a proposed Chinese Italian textile research centre in Prato in 2012. See Silvia Pieraccini, "Ricerca e artigianalità sostengono il tessile made in Italy," *Il Sole 24 Ore*, 5 July 2012.

39 Bo Yuan, "Yang shi tan 'Luoma jie sha an': Huaren ying jiji can zheng yibao zisheng quanyi," *Xinhua Lianhe Shibao*, 12 January 2012.

40 Zhu, *Television in Post-Reform China*, 131–2.

41 Raffaella Galvani, "Made in Italy in Cina: Ora Mao veste Caruso," *Panorama*, 1 March 2012; Silvia Pieraccini, "Caruso, stile su misura per il cliente italiano più sofisticato," *Il Sole 24 Ore*, 4 January 2013; and Florian Eder, "Cultural Revolution: A Chinese Functionary Creates His Own Luxury Label," *Die Welt*, 4 June 2012.

42 Enrico Maria Albamonte, "Il Made in Italy corteggia il Dragone," *L'Espresso*, 19 January 2011; Lu Chang, "'Made in Italy' Has Prestige in China," *China Daily*, 5 October 2010; "Tra Italia e Cina alleanza nel fashion," *AGI China 24*, 26 October 2011; Vanessa Friedman, "Can China Save Made in Italy?," *Financial Times*, 9 April 2012; and Paolo Cagnan, "Turisti cinesi, che li ha visti?," *L'Espresso*, 23 August 2012.

43 China Garments, Inc., http://www.chinagarments.net.cn. See also Dominique Muret, "She Ji Sorgere, a Chinese Label Made in Italy," www.fashionmag.com, 10 April 2012.

44 Louie, *Chinese Masculinities in a Globalizing World*, 6.

45 Xu Tianran, "'Chinese Backyard' of Italy about to Go Bust," *Huanqiu Shibao*, 23 November 2011; Ceccagno, "The Hidden Crisis," 49; and "Fangzhiye weiji: Qianming huaren likai Pulatuo," *Ouzhou Qiaobào*, 6–10 January 2012. Published in Chinese- and English-language editions, *Huanqiu Shibao* is an influential newspaper that specializes in international affairs. Affiliated with *People's Daily*, it often adopts a pragmatic approach to current affairs with a tendency to appeal to Chinese nationalism. See for example Sun Fang and Tian Pingsha, "San wan huaren ku shou Yidali 'Wenzhou cheng,'" *Huanqiu Shibao*, 12 August 2011.

46 Pieke, *Recent Trends in Chinese Migration to Europe*, 34.

47 Ceccagno, "The Hidden Crisis," 54–7.

48 Eric Jozsef, "Si les Chinois s'en vont, Prato va fermer," *Libération*, 18 February 2013; and Carlo Bartoli, "Se i cinesi se ne vanno, Prato chiude," *Il Tirreno*, 23 February 2013. "Io sono qui perché" is the title of a 2012 series of encounters between Chinese migrants and Italians who were engaged in a sociological simulation of daily Italian-Chinese interaction.

7 Rome: The 2012 Chinese March

1 The Rome march made demands similar to those of a 2010 Chinese demonstration in Paris following a violent encounter between Chinese migrants and Parisians of Arab and African origins. Elise Vincent, "La communauté chinoise defile contre 'l'insécurité,'" *Le Monde*, 21 June 2010; and Situ Beichen, "Faguo huaren fan baoli da youxing jie mi," *Nanfang Zhoumou*, 24 June 2010.

2 Lucchini, "Luoghi di residenza e di lavoro della comunità cinese a Roma," 42–3; and Berrocal, Cortellesi, and Marconi, "Vendere la vendita," 68.
3 In Italy, editors, not photo editors or art directors, select news photographs. See Cariglio, "Stranieri impaginati," 77–8.
4 Renwick and Cao, "China's Political Discourse towards the 21st Century," 112–14.
5 Ben-Ghiat, "The Secret Histories of Roberto Benigni's *Life Is Beautiful*," 256 and 260. See also my discussion in chapter 6.
6 Galt, *The New European Cinema*, 42.
7 Glynn, "The 'Turn to the Victim' in Italian Culture," 373–90.
8 See Uccellini, "Romanian Migration to Italy," 113–18 for the Romanians and the Romany; King and Mai, *Out of Albania* for the Albanians; and Sibhatu, *Il cittadino che non c'è* for the Africans.
9 Alexander, "Toward a Theory of Cultural Trauma," 1.
10 For example, Balbo et al., *I razzismi possibili*.
11 Alexander, "Toward a Theory of Cultural Trauma," 1.
12 McGuire, "Crimes of Diction"; Morcellini, *Sintesi del rapporto di ricerca*, 2; Batziou, *Picturing Migration*, 84–6; and Sredanovic, "Fotografia," 38–41.
13 Federica Angeli and Emilio Orlando, "Roma, rapina e terrore a Tor Pignattara, uccisi padre e bimba di sei mesi," *La Repubblica*, 4 January 2012; Valeria Forgnone and Emilio Orlando, "Roma, uccisi padre e figlia durante una rapina con un solo colpo sparato al volto della bimba," *La Repubblica*, 5 January 2012; Fiorenza Sarzanini, "Di chi sono i soldi che Zhou aveva con sé," *Corriere della Sera*, 7 January 2012. In some accounts, Joy was nine months old. In the Italian media, the man's name was often erroneously transliterated as "Zhou Zeng."
14 Chibnall, "Press Ideology," 206–7 and 209–10; Jewkes, *Media and Crime*, 56.
15 "La rabbia della Cina sui social network. Gli appelli alle autorità: 'Trovate i killer,'" *La Repubblica*, 7 January 2012; Valeria Forgnone and Manuel Massimo, "Zhou e Joy, 10mila al corteo delle luci. Il Campidoglio: 'Non vi lasceremo soli,'" *La Repubblica*, 10 January 2012.
16 Federica Angeli and Martina di Berardino, "Sulla borsa le impronte dei killer, dentro c'erano diecimila euro," *La Repubblica*, 7 January 2012; Laura Mari, "La comunità è un bersaglio facile: Racket e assalti anche in pieno giorno," *La Repubblica*, 8 January 2012; Nino Cirillo and Valentina Errante, "E' caccia ai killer di Joy e del papà: Spunta l'ipotesi di una vendetta," *Il Messaggero*, 7 January 2012; "Roma dà l'ultimo saluto a Zhou e Joy: La madre Lia cede al dolore," *Il Messaggero*, 9 February 2012; and Sarzanini, "Di chi sono i soldi che Zhou aveva con sé." On 7 January, Lia claimed that the murderers could come from eastern Europe and, according to one account, since she "does not speak our language perfectly, it could be that she was not able to understand whether they were Italians, or

simply well-integrated foreigners, or second-generation migrants." See Forgnone and Orlando, "Roma, uccisi padre e figlia durante una rapina"; and "Il delitto di Torpignattara: 'I killer italiani o dell'Est,'" *La Repubblica*, 7 January 2012.

17 Sarzanini, "Di chi sono i soldi che Zhou aveva con sé"; "Nel quartiere della rapina: 'E' stata la mafia cinese,'" *La Repubblica*, 16 January 2012; Martina di Berardino, "E' arrivata prima la mafia cinese: La madre di Joy: nessun sollievo," *La Repubblica*, 17 January 2012; Maria Elena Vincenzi, "Il ministero del suicidio del killer dei cinesi: La procura è pronta a indagare per omicidio," *La Repubblica*, 17 January 2012; "Torpignattara, giallo sulla morte del killer: Trovato impiccato a Boccea," *Il Messaggero*, 17 January 2012; "Padre e figlia cinesi uccisi per rapina: Trovato impiccato uno di ricercati," *Corriere della Sera*, 16 January 2012; and Federica Angeli and Maria Elena Vincenzi, "La telefonata al boss cinese: 'Ci vediamo a Boccea,'" *La Repubblica*, 20 January 2012.

18 Chibnall, "Press Ideology," 211.

19 Katz, "What Makes Crime 'News'?," 235 and 232.

20 After the reporting on the march trailed off, news came out in October 2012 that the other convicted killer, Moustafà Betit, was found in Morocco. Because of certain bilateral agreements between Italy and Morocco, Betit could not be extradited to Italy and thus remained at large. On the anniversary of the murder in January 2013, *La Repubblica* ran a piece about Zhou's wife's unrelenting calling for justice. Federica Angeli and Angela Maria Erba, "Uccise per rapina padre e figlia di 9 mesi: Libero in Maghreb il killer di Torpignattara," *La Repubblica*, 25 October 2012; and Luca Monaco, "Da quel giorno non ho più pace, l'assassino di Joy ancora libero," *La Repubblica*, 5 January 2013.

21 To throw the public mourning into a dramatic relief was Rome's large Chinese New Year celebration in Via Corso and in the Piazza del Popolo on 14 January, which coincided with the closure of the Year of China in Italy. "Roma dà l'ultimo saluto a Zhou e Joy"; "Capodanno cinese, la festa al Corso e in piazza del Popolo," *La Repubblica*, 11 January 2012; Alessandra Paolini, "Capodanno cinese, sfilata in centro in corteo anche i familiari di Zhou e Joy," *La Repubblica*, 14 January 2012; and Carlotta De Leo, "Sarà dedicata a Zeng e alla piccola Joy la grande festa del Capodanno cinese," *Corriere della Sera*, 7 January 2012.

22 Daniele Mastrogiacomo, "La città delle pistole," *La Repubblica*, 6 January 2012; "Notte di sangue al Pigneto, uccisi padre e figlia di sei mesi," *La Repubblica*, 5 January 2012, http://roma.repubblica.it/cronaca/2012/01/04/foto/notte_di_sangue_al_pigneto_uccisi_padre_e_figlia_di_due_anni-27608948/1 and http://roma.repubblica.it/cronaca/2012/01/05/foto/

la_notte_di_terrore_al_pigneto_padre_e_figlia_uccisi_per_rapina-27610427/1; Zeppetella and Toiati, "L'omicidio in via Giovannoli," *Il Messaggero*, 5 January 2012, http://foto.ilmessaggero.it/italia/lomicidio_in_via_giovannoli/0-6440.shtml?idArticolo=175674#0; and "Roma, nel quartiere della tragedia," *La Repubblica*, 5 January 2012, http://video.repubblica.it/edizione/roma/roma-nel-quartiere-della-tragedia/85090?video.

23 Jewkes, *Crime and Media*, 51–3.

24 Rai TG3, 19:00, 5 January 2012; Rai TG2, 18:15, 5 January 2012; Rai TG1, 20:00, 5 January 2012; Rai TG3, 19:00, 6 January 2012; Rai TG3, Pomeriggio, 6 January 2012; Mario Proto, "Fiori e lacrime," *Corriere della Ser*, 6 January 2012, http://roma.corriere.it/roma/notizie/cronaca/12_gennaio_6/tor-pignattara-manifestazione-1902762786549.shtml; "Torpignattara, fiori e commozione per la piccola Joy e suo padre," *La Repubblica*, 5 January 2012, http://roma.repubblica.it/cronaca/2012/01/05/foto/fiori_omicidio_tor_pignattara-27643376/1/; and "Shiguan chixu shi ya, yi zhengfu jiji huiying," *Xinhua Lianhe Shibao*, "Haowai," special issue, 10–20 January 2012.

25 "Torpignattara, le voci del quartiere," *La Repubblica*, 5 January 2012, http://video.repubblica.it/edizione/roma/torpignattara-le-voci-del-quartiere/85084/83473.

26 "Torpignattara, la fiaccolata per ricordare la piccola Joy," *Il Messaggero*, 7 January 2012, http://foto.ilmessaggero.it/italia/torpignattara_la_fiaccolata_per_ricordare_la_piccola_joy/0-6449.shtml?idArticolo=175965#6 (photograph 7); and "Shiguan Chixushiya, Yizhengfu Jijihuiyin."

27 Christie, "The Ideal Victim," 18–21.

28 "Da piazza Vittorio a Torpignattara, fiaccolata per Zhou e Joy uccisi dai banditi," *La Repubblica*, 10 January 2012, http://roma.repubblica.it/cronaca/2012/01/10/foto/piazza_vittorio_la_fiaccolata_per_zhou_e_joy_uccisi_dai_banditi-27871537/1.

29 Wollen, "Fire and Ice," 118.

30 King, Xu, and Hu were the examples of Italy's successful Chinese migrants mentioned in a 2009 conference organized by the Fondazione Italia Cina (Italy-China foundation in Milan). See "Storie di successo cinesi in Italia," http://www.codiciricerche.it/download/analisi/loc016%202009_03_16%20Cinesiinitalia%20Milano.pdf. While King and Hu have a migration trajectory vastly different from that of most of Italy's Chinese, Xu's story as a self-made entrepreneur is one to which many aspire.

31 For a discussion of Italy's Chinese associations and their work, see Genova and Ricucci, "Abitare Torino," 113–18 and 130–1.

32 In comparison, for example, Italy's Romany photographed by the Europeans did not enjoy such activism. Forgacs, *Italy's Margins*, 266–72.

33 Pasquale Notargiacomo, "Roma, candele e solidarietà alla comunità cinese," *La Repubblica*, 10 January 2012, https://video.repubblica.it/edizione/roma/roma-candele-e-solidarieta-alla-comunita-cinese/85413/83802; and television news on Italia 1 on 10 January 2012.

34 "Torpignattara, la fiaccolata per ricordare la piccola Joy," *Il Messaggero*, 10 January 2012, https://foto.ilmessaggero.it/italia/la_fiaccolata_per_zhou_e_joy/0-6498.shtml?idArticolo=177370 (see photographs 2, 3, 5, and 6) and https://foto.ilmessaggero.it/italia/torpignattara_la_fiaccolata_per_ricordare_la_piccola_joy/0-6449.shtml?idArticolo=175965 (see photograph 4); "Lutto, fiaccolata e corteo per Joy e Zhou," *Corriere della Sera*, 10 January 2012, https://roma.corriere.it/gallery/roma/01-2012/fiaccolata/1/lutto-fiaccolata-corteo-joy-zhou-_53577fe0-3b9a-11e1-9a5f-c5745a18f471.shtml (see photographs 4, 6, 10, 11); "Da piazza Vittorio a Torpignattara," *La Repubblica*, 10 January 2012, https://roma.repubblica.it/cronaca/2012/01/10/foto/piazza_vittorio_la_fiaccolata_per_zhou_e_joy_uccisi_dai_banditi-27871537/1. The angle in the first photograph mentioned here is reminiscent of several photographs published during the protest following the assassination of Jerry Essan Masslo. See Pogliano and Zanini, "L'immaginario e le immagini degli migrati," 114.

35 Cartier-Bresson, *The Decisive Moment*; and Ferrell and de Voorde, "The Decisive Moment," 46–7.

36 Greer, "News Media, Victims and Crime," 29.

37 For example, Rai TG2, 20:30, 6 January 2012; and "Italia Sul Due," Rai Due, 10 January 2012.

38 "Shiguan chixu shi ya, Yi zhengfu jiji huiying"; and "Roma, candele e solidarietà alla comunità cinese." See also "Torpignattara, la fiaccolata per ricordare la piccola Joy," *Il Messaggero*, 7 January 2012, http://foto.ilmessaggero.it/italia/torpignattara_la_fiaccolata_per_ricordare_la_piccola_joy/0-6449.shtml?idArticolo=175965#6.

39 Kwong and Miscevic, *Chinese America*, x–xi.

40 Yan Xu, "'Luoma can an' zhi hou, huaren gai fanxi shenme?," *Ouhua Lianhe Shibao*, 19 January 2012.

41 Shohat and Stam, *Unthinking Eurocentrism*, 198–208.

42 "Yidali huaren fabiao gao quanti gongmin shu: gongtong xieshou hanwei pingan," *Xinhua Lianhe Shibao*, 12 January 2012; and "Yidali huaren gao quanti gongmin shu/Lettera aperta a tutti cittadini italiani," *Cina in Italia*, January 2012. I translated from the Chinese-language version.

43 Neal, *National Trauma and Collective Memory*, 4.

44 Although I do not cite specific news articles here, the veracity of this observation can be easily grasped when one looks at coverage in the four major Chinese migrant newspapers. For examples of this issue in the Italian media, see the references in note 48.

45 Shi Ci, "Yidali zhendui huaren fanzui xu zeng: Qiao jie huyu zhengfu gaishan zhi'an," *China News*, 28 February 2012, http://www.chinanews.com/hr/2012/02-28/3703369.shtml; "Jingti! Nian wei Ouzhou huaren dao qiang duo fa!," http://www.franceqw.com/portal.php, 5 December 2012, http://www.franceqw.com/article-25324-1.html; and Shi Ci, "Jingji di mi zhendui huren fanzui xu zeng. Haiwai huaren anquan xingshi kanyou," *China News*, 29 February 2012, http://www.chinanews.com/hr/2012/02-29/3707160.shtml. These reports updated the information in similar reports in *Nanfang Zhoumou* (see chapter 4).

46 Ye Weiming, "Tuanjie shiyan qiantu nan pu, Faguo huaren da youxing zhi hou," *Nanfang Zhoumou*, 5 August 2010.

47 Zhang Xia, "Zhongguo zhu Yi shiguan guanzhu huaren zao qiang ji an xi tufa xingshi anjian," *Xinhua Lianhe Shibao*, 7 January 2012; and TG5, Canale 5, 10 January 2012.

48 Lorenzo D'Albergo and Maria Elena Vincenzi, "La paura dei cinesi: Ora ci minacciano," *La Repubblica*, 6 January 2012; Aldo Gianfrate, "Biglietti e fiori per la piccola Joy: Torpignattara, il giorno dell'ira," *La Repubblica*, 6 January 2012; Forgnone and Orlando, "Il delitto di Torpignattara"; "'No alla violenza, sì alla sicurezza': Migliaia in corteo per Joy e Zhou," *Corriere della Sera*, 10 January 2012. See also Sredanovic, "The 2012 Killing of Chinese Citizens in Rome and the Ambivalence of Italian Journalism," 70–2.

49 Bo Yuan, "Cong 'Milan shijian' dao 'Luoma heping qiusu,' Yi hua she jian jin chengshu," *Xinhua Lianhe Shibao*, 12 January 2012.

50 Bo Yuan, "Luoma qiang jie qiang sha huarenan shehui fanying qianglie: Minzhong zifa diao nian," *Xinhua Lianhe Shibao*, 6 January 2012; and Bo Yuan, "Luoma xue an hou de sikao: Haiwai huaren anquan baozhang gai yikao shenme?," *Xinhua Lianhe Shibao*, 7 January 2012.

51 The quote is from Bo Yuan, "Luoma xue an hou de sikao." Cai Yanfei and Chen Wei, "Qiao shang tan Yidali huaren youxing: Tuanjie cai you liliang quanyi yao zhengqu," *Xinhua Lianhe Shibao*, 16 January 2012; Zhang Ziyu and Ma Huan, "Wenzhou ren zai Luoma: Jie tou mie meng xue an baolu kunjin," *Shidai Zhoubao*, 12 January 2012; *Ouhua Lianhe Shibao*, http://www.ouhuaitaly.com/?action-viewnews-itemid-71107; Yan Xu, "Luoma can an' zhi hou, huaren gai fanxing shenme?"; and You Zi, "Huaren: 'Gai chu shou shi jiu chu shou,'" *Xinhua Lianhe Shibao*, 11 January 2012.

52 Renwick and Cao, "China's Political Discourse towards the 21st Century," 121.

53 On why a cultural trauma comes into being, see Alexander, "Toward a Theory of Cultural Trauma," 24–7.

54 Rai TG3, Linea Notte, 10 January 2012; Giuseppe Ferrante, "Roma, cinesi in corteo: 'Basta violenze,'" *La Repubblica*, 10 January 2012, http://video.repubblica.it/edizione/roma/

roma-cinesi-in-corteo-basta-violenze/85397/83786; "Shiguan chixu shi ya, Yi zhengfu jiji huiying"; and Federica Angeli and Francesco Viviano, "'Così morì il killer dei cinesi': Il pm nel casale dei misteri," *La Repubblica*, 9 February 2012.

55 The slogan used during a 2010 march organized by Paris's Chinese, which was "Against Violence, I Need Security," conceptually similar to the French-language version "Stop Violence, Security for All," made no linguistic effort at enlisting the assistance of the Chinese government. See "Chinese Migrants March through Paris to Protest Insecurity," *France 24*, 22 June 2010, http://observers.france24.com/content/20100622-paris-belleville-chinese-march-against-insecurity; and "Chinese Protest in the Streets of Paris," *China Daily*, 21 June 2010.

56 "Conferenza stampa di presentazione per l'Anno Culturale della Cina in Italia," http://it.china-embassy.org, 6 October 2010, http://it.china-embassy.org/ita/acdc01/t758720.htm.

57 "Calendario dei principali eventi dell'Anno Culturale della Cina," http://it.china-embassy.org, 4 October 2010, http://it.china-embassy.org/ita/acdc01/t758613.htm. For the Year of China in France, see http://english.cri.cn/events/culture/china-france/. Silvio Berlusconi, "Intervento del Presidente del Consiglio Silvio Berlusconi," 7 October 2012, http://it.china-embassy.org/ita/acdc01/t760303.htm.

58 Ministero dell'Interno, "Pacchetto Sicurezza. Misure per rendere più sicura la vita dei cittadini. Patti per la sicureazza," 2008, http://www1.interno.gov.it/mininterno/export/sites/default/it/sezioni/sala_stampa/speciali/Pacchetto_sicurezza/index_2.html.

59 "Italia sul Due," Rai Due, 6 January 2012; Angeli and Orlando, "Roma, rapina e terrore a Tor Pignattara"; and Federica Angeli and Laura Vivian, "Roma blindata e posti di blocco, è caccia ai killer del Pigneto," *La Repubblica*, 5 January 2012.

60 "Capodanno cinese, migliaia di romani in piazza per ricordare Joy e Zheng," *Il Messaggero*, 14 January 2012.

61 "Torpignattara, Alemanno: 'Fermate le belve.' Il ministro: 'Lo stato è presente e lo dimostrerà,'" *La Repubblica*, 5 January 2012; Rai TG1, 13:30, 5 January 2012; and Rai TG2, 20:30, 5 January 2012.

62 I draw this idea from Neal, *National Trauma and Collective Memory*, 21.

63 Renwick and Cao, "China's Political Discourse towards the 21st Century," 114.

64 I build this observation on Neal, *National Trauma and Collective Memory*, 17; and on Silverstone, *Media and Morality*.

65 Alexander, "Toward a Theory of Cultural Trauma," 24.

66 For an exception, see Angeli and Berardino, "Sulla borsa le impronte dei killer."

67 Cospe, "Italy," 296–7.

68 Neal, *National Trauma and Collective Memory*, 6–7. On the value of contingencies in Mobility Studies, see Greenblatt, "Cultural Mobility," 16. For an example of negative and misinformed English-language journalism about Prato in 2013, see Barbie Latza Nadeau, "The Dark Side of Italy's Garment Business: Human Trafficking," *Daily Beast*, 20 August 2013, https://www.thedailybeast.com/italys-garment-factory-slaves.

69 Ilenia Reali, Paolo Nencioni, and Danilo Fastelli, "Prato, incendio in fabbrica al Macrolotto: 7 morti," *Il Tirreno*, 1 December 2013; Laura Montanari and Michele Bocci, "Prato, rogo in fabbrica. Procura: qui far west," *La Repubblica*, 2 December 2013; Riccardo Staglianò, "I cinesi di Prato: i nostri morti non erano schiavi," *Il Venerdì*, 10 January 2014; Malia Zheng, "Non chiamateci schiavi, stiamo cercando il riscatto sociale (e voi non ci aiutate)," *Panorama*, 18 December 2013; Carlo Verdelli, "Il bar cinese: Oriente espresso," *La Repubblica*, 10 July 2013; and Fabrizio Gatti, "Se il padrone è cinese," *L'Espresso*, 20 June 2013.

Conclusion

1 Ambrosini, "The Role of Immigrants in the Italian Labour Market."

2 For an overview of Italy's largely failed attempts at better engaging with China in recent decades, see Coralluzzo, "Italy's Foreign Policy toward China," 6–24; and Marinelli, "Introduction," 491–501.

3 Ambrosini, "Immigration to Italy," 192.

4 For new research directions in global Chinese diasporas, see Li, "Zhongguo huaqiao huaren yanjiu de lishi yu xianzhuang gaishu," 1035. For the values of a geographical approach to migrant writings, see Papotti, "L'approccio della geografia alla letteratura dell'immigrazione." A prominent public figure of Taiwanese origin active on Italian television is Silvia Hsieh. Mario Tchou's life between Italy and the United States in the first half of the twentieth century is an example of what one can learn from the early history of Chinese in Italy. On the development of the coverage of Chinese migrants in *Corriere della Sera* from the 1920s through 1990s, see Breveglieri and Farina, "Crepe nella muraglia," 96–101; and Cologna, "L'immigrazione cinese nell'Italia fascista." For empirical studies of Chinese's religious practices in Italy, see Cecchini, *Lanterne amiche*, 94–6; Parnanzone, "La spiritualità e i luoghi di culto della comunità cinese di Roma," 87–100; Zoccatelli, "Religione e religiosità fra i cinesi a Torino," 203–54; and Vicziany, Fladrich, and Di Castro, "Religion and the Lives of the Overseas Chinese."

5 For Italian films and novels about Chinese migrants, see my "Contemporary Italian Novels on Chinese Immigration to Italy" and "Chinese Migrants, Morality, and Film Ethics in Italian Cinema." For a preliminary study of

Chinese migrants' use of technology in Italy, see Denison and Johanson, "Community Connections," 161–73. For an example of interpretive empirical research on the Chinese media's influence on Australia's Chinese, see Sinclair et al., "Chinese Cosmpolitanism and Media Use," 35–90.

6 Early twentieth-century associations in Italy are examined in Thunø, "Chinese Emigration to Europe," 285–6. For summaries of Chinese migrant associations in Europe and in Italy in the 1990s, see Li, *The Chinese Community in Europe*, 57–75; Li, *Seeing Transnationally*, 111–31; Lombardi, *Sulla Via della Tela*, 20–4; and Wenzhou Institute of Overseas Chinese and Foreign Nationals of Chinese Origin, *Wenzhou huaqiao shi*, 158–61 and 171. For preliminary sociological studies of Italy's contemporary migrant associations, see Cecchini, *Lanterne amiche*, 44–6 and 88–91. On geographically specific associations, see Cecchini, *Lanterne amiche*, 99–123 for Reggio Emilia; Malavolti, "Integrazione cinese a Napoli," 117–25 for Naples; Ricucci, "La diaspora cinese," 78–84 for Turin; Ceccagno and Omodeo, "Il Centro di ricerca e servizi per la comunità cinese di Prato," 81–110 for Prato; and Ghisalberti, "Alla conquista del mercato," 129–34 for Bergamo. On Italy's pro-migrant activities in the 1990s, see Cole, *The New Racism in Europe*, 105–15; and Pojmann, *Immigrant Women and Feminism in Italy*, 101–2. Pojmann's analysis of Chinese migrant associations in relation to the community's supposed closure towards Italy is misleading and deterministic. This analysis does not explain, for instance, why an association for Chinese women has existed in Italy since 2000. *HS98*, http://www.hs98.com/bencandy.php?fid=144&id=13137.

7 Roma Multietnica, http://www.romamultietnica.it/ provides much information on these media outlets.

Coda

1 For an analysis of the sense of home among second-generation Chinese migrants in Germany, which combines literature and ethnography, see Leung, *Chinese Migration in Germany*, 53–67.

2 Bhabha, *The Location of Culture*, 212, 208–9, and 214–17; and Shohat and Stam, *Unthinking Eurocentrism*, 24–5.

3 Hall, "Old and New Identities, Old and New Ethnicities," 49; and Vertovec, *Transnationalism*, 83. On Chinese migrants' negotiations with nation-states, the family network, *guanxi*, and imaginaries in non-Italian contexts, see Nonini and Ong, "Chinese Transnationalism as an Alternative Modernity," 24–7.

4 In order to protect the identity of my interviewee and the immediate and extended family, I name my subject A.

5 Pieke et al., *Transnational Chinese*, 163.

6 Ong, *Flexible Citizenship*, 112 (italics original).

7 A. also mentioned the American Overseas School of Rome and the St George's British International School as two other English-language schools that have been popular with Italy's Chinese. Several of A.'s friends studied in various North American universities.

8 Clifford, *Routes*, 256–7.

Bibliography

Ahmed, Sara. "Home and Away: Narratives of Migration and Estrangement." *International Journal of Cultural Studies* 2, no. 3 (1999): 329–47.

Alexander, Jeffrey C. "Toward a Theory of Cultural Trauma." In *Cultural Trauma and Collective Identity*, edited by Jeffrey C. Alexander et al., 1–30. Berkeley: University of California Press, 2004.

Allievi, Stefano. "Immigration and Cultural Pluralism in Italy: Multiculturalism as a Missing Model." *Italian Culture* 28, no. 2 (2010): 85–103.

Ambrosini, Maurizio. "The Role of Immigrants in the Italian Labour Market." *International Migration* 39, no. 3 (2001): 61–84.

– "Immigration in Italy: Between Economic Acceptance and Political Rejection." *International Migration & Integration* 14 (2013): 175–94.

Andall, Jacqueline. "New Migrants, Old Conflicts: The Recent Immigration into Italy." *Italianist* 10 (1990): 151–74.

– "The G2 Network and Other Second-Generation Voices: Claiming Rights and Transforming Identities." In *National Belongings: Hybridity in Italian Colonial and Postcolonial Cultures*, edited by Jacqueline Andall and Derek Duncan, 171–93. Oxford; Bern: Peter Lang, 2010.

Anderson, Benedict. *Imagined Communities: Reflections on the Origins and Spread of Nationalism*. 2nd ed. London: Verso, 1991.

Andornino, Giovanni. "Strategic Ambitions in Times of Transition: Key Patterns in Contemporary Italy-China Relations." In Marinelli and Andornino, *Italy's Encounters with Modern China*, 147–70.

Angeli, Silvia. "La conservazione della lingua madre nei cinesi adulti di Roma." In Pedone, *Il vicino cinese*, 101–15.

Appadurai, Arjun. "Putting Hierarchy in Its Place." *Cultural Anthropology* 3, no. 1 (1988): 36–49.

– *Modernity at Large: Cultural Dimensions of Globalization*. Minneapolis: University of Minnesota Press. 1996.

Ardizzoni, Michela. *North/South, East/West: Mapping Italianness on Television*. Lanham, MD: Lexington Books, 2007.

Balbo, Laura, Luigi Manconi, Marina Forti, and Bruno Nascimbene. *I razzismi possibili*. Milano: Feltrinelli, 1990.

Baldassar, Loretta, Graeme Johanson, Narelle McAuliffe, and Massimo Bressan. "Chinese Migration to the New Europe: The Case of Prato." In Baldassar et al., *Chinese Migration to Europe*, 1–25.

–, eds. *Chinese Migration to Europe: Prato, Italy, and Beyond*. Basingstoke, Hampshire: Palgrave Macmillan, 2015.

Barthes, Roland. *Image, Music, Text*. Translated by Stephen Heath. New York: Hill and Wang, 1977.

Basili, Marzia. "Sull'integrazione della popolazione immigrate." In *L'immigrazione straniera: Indicatori e misure di integrazione*, edited by Antonio Golini, 9–52. Bologna: Il Mulino, 2006.

Batziou, Athansia. *Picturing Immigration: Photojournalistic Representation of Immigrants in Greek and Spanish Press*. Bristol: Intellect, 2011.

Bauman, Zygmunt. *Globalization: The Human Consequences*. New York: Columbia University Press, 1998.

Baumann, Martin. "Diaspora: Genealogies of Semantics and Transcultural Comparison." *Numen* 47, no. 3 (2000): 313–37.

Belluati, Marinella. *L'in/sicurezza dei quartieri: Media, territorio e percezioni d'insicurezza*. Milano: Franco Angeli, 2004.

Beltrán Antolín, Joaquín. "The Chinese in Spain." In Benton and Pieke, *The Chinese in Europe*, 211–37.

– "Chinese Entrepreneurship in Spain: The Seeds of Chinatown." In Spaan, Hillmann, and van Naerssen, *Asian Migrants*, 285–308.

Ben-Ghiat, Ruth. "The Secret Histories of Roberto Benigni's *Life Is Beautiful*." *Yale Journal of Criticism* 14, no. 1 (2001): 253–66.

Benton, Gregor, and Frank N. Pieke, eds. *The Chinese in Europe*. London: Macmillan, 1998.

Bernasconi, Mauro. "Presenza migratoria e processo di regolarizzazione in provincia di Milano." In Zucchetti, *La regolarizzazzione degli stranieri*, 107–83.

Berrocal, Emilio Giacomo, Giulia Cortellesi, and Silvio Marconi. "Vendere la vendita: Rappresentazioni e stereotipi sulla presenza cinese all'Esquilino." In Pedone, *Il vicino cinese*, 59–72.

Berti, Fabio, and Andrea Valzania. "La mobilità sociale degli immigrati: Un'introduzione al tema attraverso l'analisi dei costumi e del commercio." In *Vendere e comprare: Processi di mobilità sociale dei cinesi a Prato*, edited by Fabio Berti, Valentina Pedone, and Andrea Valzania, 15–58. Pisa: Pacini Editore, 2013.

Bertossi, Christophe. "Mistaken Models of Integration? A Critical Perspective on the Crisis of Multiculturalism in Europe." In *European Multiculturalism Revisited*, edited by Alessandro Silj, 235–51. London: Zen Books, 2010.

Bertuccioli, Giuliano, and Federico Masini. *Italia e Cina*. Roma: L'Asino d'Oro, 2014.

Berzano, Luigi, Carlo Genova, Massimo Introvigne, Roberta Ricucci, and PierLuigi Zoccatelli, eds. *Cinesi a Torino: La crescita di un arcipelago*. Roma: Il Mulino, 2010.

Bhabha, Homi. *The Location of Culture*. London: Routledge, 1994.

Bianda, Enrico. "Verso un ritorno del giornalismo d'approfondimento." In Sorrentino, *Il giornalismo in Italia*, 245–59.

Bigot, Giulia, and Stefano Fella. "The Prodi Government's Proposed Citizenship Reform, and the Debate on Immigration and Its Impact in Italy." *Modern Italy* 13, no. 3 (2008): 305–15.

Binotto, Marco. "Immagini dell'immigrazione." In Binotto and Martino, *Fuoriluogo*, 31–43.

Binotto, Marco, and Valentina Martino. "Se la notizia è clandestine: Il Monitor su informazione e immigrazione." In Binotto and Martino, *Fuoriluogo*, 13–28.

–, eds. *Fuoriluogo: L'immigrazione e i media italiani*. Cosenza: Pellegrini; Roma: Rai-ERI, 2004.

Biorcio, Roberto. "The *Lega Nord* and the Italian Media System." In *The Media and Neo-populism: A Contemporary Comparative Analysis*, edited by Gianpietro Mazzoleni, Julianne Stewart, and Bruce Horsfield, 71–94. Westport, CT: Praeger, 2003.

Blim, Michael L. *Made in Italy: Small-Scale Industrialization and Its Consequences*. New York: Praeger, 1990.

Bouchard, Norma, and Valerio Ferme. *Italy and the Mediterranean: Words, Sounds, and Images of the Post-Cold War Era*. New York: Palgrave Macmillan, 2013.

Bourdieu, Pierre. *Distinction: A Social Critique of the Judgement of Taste*. Translated by Richard Nice. Cambridge, MA: Harvard University Press, 1984.

– *The Field of Cultural Production*. Edited by Randal Johnson. New York: Columbia University Press, 1993.

Brettell, Caroline B., and James F. Hollifield. "Migration Theory: Talking across Disciplines." In *Migration Theory: Talking across Disciplines*, edited by Caroline B. Brettell and James F. Hollifield, 1–36. 3rd ed. New York: Routledge, 2015.

Breveglieri, Lorenzo, and Patrizia Farina. "Crepe nella muraglia." In Farina et al., *Cina a Milano*, 61–103.

Buonanno, Milly. *Italian TV Drama and Beyond: Stories from the Soil, Stories from the Sea*. Translated by Jennifer Radice. Bristol: Intellect, 2012.

Burke, Peter. *What Is Cultural History?* 2nd ed. Cambridge, UK: Polity Press, 2008.

Butler, Judith. *Excitable Speech: A Politics of the Performative*. New York: Routledge, 1997.

Campani, Giovanna. "Migrants and Media: The Italian Case." In Russell and Wood, *Media and Migration*, 38–52.

Campani, Giovanna, and Lucia Maddii. "Un monde à part, les Chinois en Toscane." *Revue Européenne des Migrazions Internationales* 8, no. 3 (1992): 51–72.

Carchedi, Francesco, and M.L. Tripodi. "La comunità cinese a Campi Bisenzio: Le interviste ai testimony privilegiati." In *Politiche sociali e bisogni degli immigrati*, edited by Laboratorio per le politiche sociali, 319–38. Roma: TER, 1991.

Carini, Stefania. "La fiction italiana tra immaginario e reputazione." In Grasso and Agostini, *Storie e culture della televisione italiana*, 290–301.

Carioti, Patrizia. "Haiwai huaren: La diaspora cinese, dall'antichità ai primi Qing." In Paolo and Varriano, *Dal Zhejiang alla Campania*, 62–107.

Caritas. *Dossier statistico immigrazione*. Roma: Sinnos, 2013.

– "XXIII Rapporto Immigrazione 2013." 2014.

– "XXIV Rapporto Immigrazione 2014." 2015.

Cartier-Bresson, Henri. *The Decisive Moment*. New York: Simon & Schuster, 1952.

Castelli Gattinara, Pietro. *The Politics of Migration in Italy: Perspectives on Local Debates and Party Competition*. London: Routledge, 2016.

Castles, Stephen, Hein de Haas, and Mark J. Miller. *The Age of Migration: International Population Movements in the Modern World*. 5th ed. New York: The Guilford Press, 2014.

Ceccagno, Antonella. *Cinesi d'Italia: Storie in bilico tra due culture*. Milano: Manifestolibri, 1998.

– "New Chinese Migrants in Italy." *International Migration* 41, no. 3 (2003): 187–213.

–, ed. *Migranti a Prato: Il distretto tessile multietnico*. Milano: Franco Angeli, 2003.

– *Giovani migranti cinesi (la seconda generazione a Prato)*. Milano: Franco Angeli, 2004.

– "L'epopea veloce: Adeguamenti, crisi e successi dei nuovi migranti cinesi." In Trentin, *La Cina che arriva*, 172–206.

– "Compressing Personal Time: Ethnicity and Gender within a Chinese Niche in Italy." *Journal of Ethnic and Migration Studies* 33, no. 4 (2007): 635–54.

– "The Hidden Crisis: The Prato Industrial District and the Once Thriving Chinese Garment Industry." *Revue européenne des migrations internationales* 28, no. 4 (2012): 43–65.

– *City Making and Global Labor Regimes: Chinese Immigrants and Italy's Fast Fashion Industry*. Cham, Switzerland: Palgrave Macmillan, 2017.

–, ed. *Il caso delle comunità cinesi: Comunicazione interculturale ed istituzioni*. Roma: Armando, 1997.

Ceccagno, Antonella, and Maria Omodeo. "Il Centro di ricerca e servizi per la comunità cinese di Prato: Attività di consulenza ed assistenza." In Ceccagno, *Il caso delle comunità cinesi*, 81–110.

Ceccagno, Antonella, and Renzo Rastrelli. *Ombre cinesi? Dinamiche migratorie della diaspora cinese in Italia*. Roma: Carocci Editore, 2008.

Ceccagno, Antonella, Renzo Rastrelli, and Alessandra Salvati. "Exploitation of Chinese Immigrants in Italy." In Gao, *Concealed Chains*, 89–138.

Cecchini, Rossella. *Lanterne amiche: Immigrazione cinese e mediazione interculturale a Reggio Emilia*. Reggio Emilia: Edizioni Diabasis, 2009.

Cere, Rinella. "Globalization vs. Localization: Anti-immigrant and Hate Discourses in Italy." In *Beyond Monopoly: Globalization and Contemporary Italian Media*, edited by Michela Ardizzoni and Chiara Ferrari, 225–44. Lanham: Lexington Books, 2010.

Chan, Kwok B. *Migration, Ethnic Relations, and Chinese Business*. London: Routledge, 2005.

Chen, Calvin. "Made in Italy (by the Chinese): Migration and the Rebirth of Textiles and Apparel." *Journal of Modern Italian Studies* 20, no. 1 (2015): 111–26.

Chen, Xiaomei. *Occidentalism: A Theory of Counter-Discourse in Post-Mao China*. 2nd ed. Lanham, MD: Rowman & Littlefield, 2002.

Chibnall, Steve. "Press Ideology: The Politics of Professionalism." In Greer, *Crime and Media*, 203–14.

Chow, Rey. *Writing Diaspora: Tactics of Intervention in Contemporary Cultural Studies*. Bloomington: Indiana University Press, 1993.

Christie, Nils. "The Ideal Victim." In *From Crime Policy to Victim Policy*, edited by Ezzat A. Fattah, 17–30. New York: St Martin's Press, 1986.

Christiansen, Flemming. *Chinatown, Europe: An Exploration of Overseas Chinese Identity in the 1990s*. London: Routledge, 2003.

Clifford, James. *Routes: Travel and Translation in the Late Twentieth Century*. Cambridge, MA: Harvard University Press, 1997.

– "Indigenous Diasporas." In *Les diasporas dans le monde contemporain*, edited by William Berthomière and Christine Chivallon, 49–64. Paris: Karthala and Maison des Sciences de l'Homme, Bordeaux, Pessac, 2006.

Cohen, Robin. *Global Diasporas: An Introduction*. 2nd ed. London: Routledge, 2008.

Cohen, Robin, and Gunvor Jónsson, "Introduction: Connecting Culture and Migration." In *Migration and Culture*, edited by Robin Cohen and Gunvor Jónsson, xiii–xxxii. Cheltenham, UK: Edward Elgar Publishing, 2011.

Colaprico, Piero. "Nella Chinatown Milanese tra magia e olimpiadi." *Limes* 4 (2008): 271–6.

Cole, Jeffrey. *The New Racism in Europe: A Sicilian Ethnography*. Cambridge: Cambridge University Press, 1997.

Coleman, Roy, and Mike McCahill. *Surveillance and Crime*. Newbury Park, CA: Sage Publications, 2010.

Cologna, Daniele. "Un'economia etnica di successo." In Farina et al., *Cina a Milano*, 105–55.

– *Bambini e famiglie cinesi a Milano: Materiali per la formazione degli insegnanti del materno infantile e della scuola dell'obbligo*. Milano: Franco Angeli, 2002.

– "Il quartiere Canonica Sarpi: 'Mirano a impossessarsi del quartiere.'" In *La Cina sotto casa: Convivenza e conflitti tra cinesi e italiani in due quartieri di Milano*, edited by Daniele Cologna, 41–54. Milano: Franco Angeli, 2002.

– "Chinese Immigrant Entrepreneurs in Italy: Strengths and Weaknesses of an Ethnic Enclave Economy." In Spaan, Hillmann, and van Naerssen, *Asian Migrants*, 262–84.

– "Il quartiere cinese di Milano." *Mondo cinese* 134 (2008): http://www.tuttocina.it/mondo_cinese/134/134_colo.htm.

– "L'immigrazione cinese nell'Italia fascista." PhD dissertation, Sapienza University of Rome, 2018.

Cologna, Daniele, and Patrizia Farina. "Dove si infrangono le onde dell'oceano ci sono cinesi d'oltremare." In Farina et al., *Cina a Milano*, 15–57.

Colombo, Asher, and Giuseppe Sciortino. "Italian Immigration: The Origins, Nature and Evolution of Italy's Migratory Systems." *Journal of Modern Italian Studies* 9, no. 1 (2004): 49–70.

Colombo, Massimo, Corrado Marcetti, Maria Omodeo, and Nicola Solimano. *Wenzhou-Firenze: Identità, imprese e modalità di insediamento dei cinesi in Toscana*. Firenze: Angelo Pontecorbolli, 1995.

Contino, Maria Assunta. "Made in China: Il caso Napoli." In Paolo and Varriano, *Dal Zhejiang alla Campania*, 164–79.

Coralluzzo, Valter. "Italy's Foreign Policy toward China: Missed Opportunities and New Chances." *Journal of Modern Italian Studies* 13, no. 1 (2008): 6–24.

Cospe. "Italy: Freedom of the Press and Racial Discrimination: A Review of the Legislation and an Analysis of the Role of Codes of Conduct." In *Turning into Diversity: The Representation of Immigrants and Ethnic Minorities in Italian Mass Media*, edited by Censis, 289–314. Rome: Censis, 2002.

Cotesta, Vittorio. "Mass media, conflitti etnici e identità degli italiani." *Studi Emigrazione* 36, no. 135 (1999): 443–71.

Cristaldi, Flavia, and Giulio Lucchini. "I cinesi a Roma: Una comunità di ristoratori e commercianti." *Studi emigrazione* 44, no. 165 (2007): 197–218.

D'Agostino, Federico. "Il giallo dell'Esquilino." *Limes* 2 (2005): 215–20.

Dainotto, Roberto. *Europe (in Theory)*. Durham, NC: Duke University Press, 2007.

Dal Lago, Alessandro. *Non-persone: L'esclusione dei migranti in una società globale*. Milano: Feltrinelli, 1999.

– *Eroi di carta: Il caso Gomorra e altre epopee*. Roma: Manifestolibri, 2010.

D'Aloia, Adriano. "Piccolo grande schermo: Quando la televisione fa il cinema." In Grasso and Agostini, *Storie e culture della televisione italiana*, 269–89.

Dei Ottati, Gabi. "An Industrial District Facing the Challenges of Globalization: Prato Today." *European Planning Studies* 17, no. 12 (December 2009): 1817–35.

– "A Transnational Fast Fashion Industrial District: An Analysis of the Chinese Businesses in Prato." *Cambridge Journal of Economics* 38 (2014): 1247–74.

Dei Ottati, Gabi and Daniele Cologna. "The Chinese in Prato and the Current Outlook on the Chinese-Italian Experience." In Baldassar et al., *Chinese Migration to Europe*, 29–48.

Denison, Tom, and Graeme Johanson. "Community Connections: The Chinese Community in Prato, Italy and Their Use of Technology." In Johanson, Smyth, and French, *Living outside the Walls*, 161–73.

Di Tommaso, Marco R., and Lauretta Rubini. "'Made in Italy' and 'Made in China': Empirical Analysis and Industrial Policy Implications." *c.MET* working paper 2 (2009): 1–20.

Dijk, Teun A. van. *Elite Discourse and Racism*. Newbury Park, CA: Sage Publications, 1993.

Dikötter, Frank. "The Discourse of Race in Twentieth-Century China." In *Race and Racism in Modern East Asia: Western and Eastern Constructions*, edited by Rotem Kowner and Walter Demel, 351–68. Leiden: Brill, 2013.

– *The Discourse of Race in Modern China*. New York, NY: Oxford University Press, 2015.

Dionisio, Patrizia, and Francesco Sisci. *Piovra gialla: La mafia cinese alla conquista del mondo*. Corteolona: Liber Internazionale, 1994.

Directorate General for Trade of the European Commission. "Evolution of EU Textile Imports from China in 2005 and the First 7 Months of 2006, Brussels, 2 October 2006." http://trade.ec.europa.eu/doclib/docs/2006/october/tradoc_128999.pdf.

Dirlik, Arif. "Chinese History and the Question of Orientalism." In "Chinese Historiography in Comparative Perspective," theme issue, *History and Theory* 35, no. 4 (December 1996): 96–118.

D'Orsi, Lorenzo. "The 'Pacchetto Sicurezza' and the Process of Ethnogenesis." Network Migration in Europe, 2010. http://www.migrationeducation.org/fileadmin/uploads/d__orsi__ethnogenesis.pdf.

Downing, John, and Charles Husband. *Representing "Race": Racisms, Ethnicities, and Media*. Thousand Oaks: Sage Publications, 2005.

Downing, Lisa, and Libby Saxton. *Film and Ethics: Foreclosed Encounters*. London: Routledge, 2010.

Einaudi, Luca. *Le politiche dell'immigrazione in Italia dall'Unità a oggi*. Bari: Laterza, 2007.

Entman, Robert M. "Framing: Toward Clarification of a Fractured Paradigm." *Journal of Communication* 43, no. 4 (1993): 51–8.

Essed, Philomena. *Understanding Everyday Racism: An Interdisciplinary Theory*. Newbury Park, CA: Sage Publications, 1991.

European Federation of Chinese Organisations. *The Chinese Community in Europe*. Amsterdam: EFCO, 1999.

Faloppa, Federico. *Razzisti a parole (per tacer dei fatti)*. Roma: Laterza, 2011.

Farina, Patrizia, Daniele Cologna, Arturo Lanzani, and Lorenzo Breveglieri, eds. *Cina a Milano: Famiglie, ambienti e lavori della popolazione cinese a Milano*. Milano: Abitare Segesta, 1997.

Faso, Giuseppe. "La lingua del razzismo: Alcune parole chiave." In *Rapporto sul razzismo in Italia*, edited by Grazia Naletto, 29–36. Roma: Manifestolibri, 2009.

Fazzi, Gabriella. "Italiani brava gente?" In Pitrone, Martire, and Fazzi, *Come ci vedono e come ci raccontano*, 178–98.

Ferrell, Jeff, and Cécile Van de Voorde. "The Decisive Moment: Documentary Photography and Cultural Criminology." In Hayward and Presdee, *Framing Crime*, 36–52.

Ferri, Cristiano, and Marta Gronchi. "La comunità cinese a Prato: Analisi di alcuni spazi etnicamente connotati." In Ceccagno, *Migranti a Prato*, 301–17.

Fewsmith, Joseph. *China Today, China Tomorrow: Domestic Politics, Economy, and Society*. Lanham: Rowman & Littlefield Publishers, 2010.

Fogu, Claudio, and Lucia Re. "Italy in the Mediterranean Today: A New Critical Topography." *California Italian Studies* 1, no. 1 (2010): https://escholarship.org/uc/item/6dk918sn.

Forgacs, David. *Italy's Margins: Social Exclusion and Nation Formation since 1861*. New York: Cambridge University Press, 2014.

Foucault, Michel. *Discipline and Punish: The Birth of the Prison*. Translated by Alan Sheridan. New York: Vintage Books, 1995.

Gabaccia, Donna. "The 'Yellow Peril' and the 'Chinese of Europe': Global Perspectives on Race and Labor, 1815–1930." In *Migration, Migration History, History: Old Paradigms and New Perspectives*, edited by Jan Lucassen and Leo Lucassen. New York: Peter Lang, 1997.

– *Italy's Many Diasporas*. Seattle: University of Washing Press, 2000.

Galli, Susanna. "Le comunità cinesi in Italia: Caratteristiche organizzative e culturali." In *L'immigrazione silenziosa: Le comunità cinesi in Italia*, edited by

Giovanna Campani, Francesco Carchedi, and Alberto Tassinari, 75–104. Torino: Edizioni della Fondazione Giovanni Agnelli, 1997.

Galt, Rosalind. *The New European Cinema: Redrawing the Map*. New York: Columbia University Press, 2006.

Gao, Yun. "Conclusion." In Gao, *Concealed Chains*, 169–75.

–, ed. *Concealed Chains: Labour Exploitation and Chinese Migrants in Europe*. Geneva: International Labour Office, 2010.

Ge, Jianxiong. "Daolun." In *Zhongguo yimin shi*, edited by Ge Jianxiong, 3–165. Fuzhou: Fujian ren min chu ban she, 1997.

Geertz, Clifford. *The Interpretation of Cultures: Selected Essays*. New York: Basic Books, 1973.

Genova, Carlo. "Non solo ristorante: Lavoro e impresa tra vocazione e necessità." In Berzano et al., *Cinesi a Torino*, 149–202.

Genova, Carlo, and Roberta Ricucci. "Abitare Torino: Percorsi, integrazione, vita quotidiana." In Berzano et al., *Cinesi a Torino*, 93–148.

Georgiou, Myria. "Mapping Diasporic Media across the EU: Addressing Cultural Exclusion." 2003. http://www.lse.ac.uk/media@lse/research/EMTEL/reports/georgiou_2003_emtel.pdf.

Ghisalberti, Alessandra. "Alla conquista del mercato: Un processo di territorializzazione economica." In *Atlante dell'immigrazione a Bergamo: La diaspora cinese*, edited by Emanuela Casti and Giuliano Bernini, 129–34. Bergamo: Università degli studi; Ancona: Il lavoro editoriale, 2008.

Giambelli, Rodolfo A. "L'emigrazione cinese in Italia: il caso di Milano." *Mondo Cinese* 48 (1984). http://www.tuttocina.it/mondo_cinese/048/048_giam.htm#.VTAE75TF_ns.

Giddens, Anthony. *Runaway World: How Globalisation Is Reshaping Our Lives*. 2nd ed. London: Profile, 2002.

Gillette, Aaron. *Racial Theories in Fascist Italy*. London: Routledge, 2002.

Gilroy, Paul. *The Black Atlantic: Modernity and Double Consciousness*. London: Verso, 1993.

Glynn, Ruth. "The 'Turn to the Victim' in Italian Culture: Victim-Centered Narratives of the *anni di piombo*." *Modern Italy* 18, no. 4 (2013): 373–90.

Grasso, Aldo. "Il dissodatore appassionato." In Grasso and Agostini, *Storie e culture della televisione italiana*, 5–25.

Grasso, Aldo, and Angelo Agostini, eds. *Storie e culture della televisione italiana*. Milano: Mondadori, 2013.

Greenblatt, Stephen. "A Mobility Studies Manifesto." In Greenblatt, *Cultural Mobility*, 250–3.

– "Cultural Mobility: An Introduction." In Greenblatt, *Cultural Mobility*, 1–23.

–, ed. *Cultural Mobility: A Manifesto*. Cambridge, UK: Cambridge University Press, 2010.

Greer, Chris, ed. *Crime and Media: A Reader*. London: Routledge, 2010.

– "News Media, Victims and Crime." In *Victims, Crime, and Society*, edited by Pamela Davies, Peter Francis, and Chris Greer, 20–49. London: Sage, 2007.

Gregor, A. James, and Maria Hsia Chang. "Nazionalfascismo and the Revolutionary Nationalism of Sun Yat-sen." *The Journal of Asian Studies* 39, no. 1 (1979): 21–37.

Grillo, Ralph. "Immigration and the Politics of Recognizing Difference in Italy." In Grillo and Pratt, *The Politics of Recognizing Difference*, 1–24.

Grillo, Ralph, and Jeff Pratt, eds. *The Politics of Recognizing Difference: Multiculturalism Italian-Style*. Aldershot: Ashgate, 2002.

Hadjimichalis, Costis. "The End of Third Italy As We Know It?" *Antipode* 38, no. 1 (2006): 82–106.

Hall, Stuart. "Encoding/Decoding." In *Culture, Media, Language: Working Papers in Cultural Studies, 1972–1979*, edited by Stuart Hall, 117–27. London: Routledge, 1980.

– "Cultural Identity and Diaspora." In *Identity: Community, Culture, Difference*, edited by Jonathan Rutherford, 222–37. London: Lawrence & Wishart, 1990.

– "Culture, Community, Nation." *Cultural Studies* 7, no. 3 (1993): 349–63.

– "The Local and the Global: Globalization and Ethnicity." In King, *Culture, Globalization, and the World-System*, 19–39.

– "Old and New Identities, Old and New Ethnicities." In King, *Culture, Globalization, and the World-System*, 41–68.

– "The Whites of Their Eyes: Racist Ideologies and the Media." In *Gender, Race, and Class in Media: A Critical Reader*, edited by Gail Dines and Jean McMahon Humez, 81–4. Thousand Oaks: Sage Publications, 2011.

Hamilton, Gary G., and Donald Fels. "The Social Sources of Migration and Enterprise: Italian Peasants and Chinese Migrants in Prato." *East Asia* 31 (2014): 269–87.

Harrington, Peter. *Peking 1900: The Boxer Rebellion*. Westport, CT: Praeger, 2005.

Hatziprokopiou, Panos, and Nicola Montagna. "Contested Chinatown: Chinese Migrants' Incorporation and the Urban Space in London and Milan." *Ethnicities* 12, no. 6 (2012): 706–29.

Hayward, Keith J., and Mike Presdee, eds. *Framing Crime: Cultural Criminology and the Image*. New York: Routledge, 2010.

Hu, Lanbo. "Perché i cinesi non muoiono?" *Cina in Italia*, no. 1/2 (January/February 2007): 52–4.

Huntington, Samuel P. "The Clash of Civilizations?" *Foreign Affairs* 72, no. 3 (Summer 1993): 22–49.

Huysseune, Michel. "Masculinity and Secessionism in Italy: An Assessment." *Nations and Nationalism* 6, no. 4 (2000): 591–610.

Hwang, John C. "Masculinity Index and Communication Style: An East Asian Perspective." In *Chinese Communication Theory and Research:*

Reflections, New Frontiers, and New Directions, edited by Wenshan Jia, Xing Lu, and D. Ray Heisey, 85–101. Westport, CO: Ablex Publishing, 2002.

Introvigne, Massimo. "La società segrete cinesi nella ricerca storica e sociologica." In Berzano et al., *Cinesi a Torino*, 279–91.

– "Tra speranze e paure: L'immigrazione cinese nella letteratura sociologica." In Berzano et al., *Cinesi a Torino*, 31–53.

ISTAT. "Cittadini non comunitari regolarmente soggiornanti: Anni 2013–2014." 5 August 2014.

– "Migrazioni internazionali e interne della popolazione residente." 27 January 2014, 1–13.

– "La popolazione straniera residente in Italia." 22 September 2011, 1–11.

– "La popolazione straniera residente in Italia al 1 gennaio 2008." 9 October 2008, 1–17.

Jay, Paul. *Global Matters: The Transnational Turn in Literary Studies*. Ithaca: Cornell University Press, 2010.

Jewkes, Yvonne. *Media and Crime*. London: Sage, 2004.

Johanson, Graeme, and Anja Michaela Fladrich. "Ties that Bond: Mobile Phones and the Chinese in Prato." In Baldassar et al., *Chinese Migration to Europe*, 177–97.

Johanson, Graeme, Russell Smyth, and Rebecca French, eds. *Living outside the Walls: The Chinese in Prato*. Newcastle: Cambridge Scholars Publishing, 2009.

Kandel, William, and Douglas S. Massey. "The Culture of Mexican Migration: A Theoretical and Empirical Analysis." *Social Forces* 80, no. 3 (2002): 981–1004.

Katz, Jack. "What Makes Crime 'News'?" In Greer, *Crime and Media*, 228–38.

Kim, Hyun Jin. *Ethnicity and Foreigners in Ancient Greece and China*. London: Duckworth, 2009.

King, Anthony D., ed. *Culture, Globalization, and the World-System*. Minneapolis: University of Minnesota Press, 1997.

King, Russell, and Nicola Mai. *Out of Albania: From Crisis Migration to Social Inclusion in Italy*. New York: Berghahn Books, 2008.

King, Russell, and Nancy Wood. "Media and Migration: An Overview." In Russell and Wood, *Media and Migration*, 1–22.

–, eds. *Media and Migration: Constructions of Mobility and Difference*. London: Routledge, 2001.

Kwok, Philip W.L. *I cinesi in Italia durante il fascism: Il campo di concentramento*. Napoli: Marotta, 1984.

Kwong, Peter, and Dušanka Miščevič. *Chinese America: The Untold Story of America's Oldest New Community*. New York: New Press, 2005.

Kymlicka, Will. "The Rise and Fall of Multiculturalism? New Debates on Inclusion and Accommodation in Diverse Societies." In Vertovec and Wessendorf, *The Multiculturalism Backlash*, 32–49.

Laguerre, Michel S. "Virtual Diasporas: A New Frontier of National Security." The Nautilus Institute. http://oldsite.nautilus.org/gps/virtual-diasporas/paper/Laguerre.html.

– *Global Ethnopolis: Chinatown, Japantown, and Manilatown in American Society.* Houndmills: Macmillan; New York: St Martin's Press, 2000.

Laj, S., and Valeria Ribeirio Corossacz. *Imprenditori immigrati: Il dibattito scientifico e le evidenze dell'indagine.* Roma: ISFOL, 2006.

Lakoff, George, and Mark Johnson. *Metaphors We Live By.* Chicago: University of Chicago Press, 2003.

Lamont, Michèle. "Meaning-Making in Cultural Sociology: Broadening Our Agenda." *Contemporary Sociology* 29, 4 (2000): 602–7.

Latham, Kevin. "Media and Discourses of Chinese Integration in Prato, Italy: Some Preliminary Thoughts." In Baldassar et al., *Chinese Migration to Europe,* 139–57.

Leslie, D.D., and K.H.J. Gardiner. *The Roman Empire in Chinese Sources.* Roma: Bardi, 1996.

Leung, Maggi Wai-Han. *Chinese Migration in Germany: Making Home in Transnational Space.* Frankfurt: IKO Verlag, 2004.

Li, Anshan. "Zhongguo huaqiao huaren yanjiu de lishi yu xianzhuang gaishu." In *Huaqiao huaren baike quanshu, Zonglunjuan,* edited by Zhou Nanjing, 997–1036. Beijing: Zhongguo Huaqiao Chubanshe, 1990.

Li, Minghuan. *The Chinese Community in Europe.* Amsterdam: European Federation of Chinese Organisations, 1999.

– "An Overview of the Migration Mechanism between China and Europe." In Gao, *Concealed Chains,* 19–32.

– *Seeing Transnationally: How Chinese Migrants Make Their Dreams Come True.* Leuven: Leuven University Press; Hangzhou: Zhejiang University Press, 2013.

Li, Peter S., and Eva Xiaoling Li. "The Chinese Overseas Population." In Tan, *Routledge Handbook of the Chinese Diaspora,* 15–28.

Liang, Zai, and Wenzhen Ye. "From Fujian to New York: Understanding the New Chinese Immigration." In *Global Human Smuggling: Comparative Perspectives,* edited by David Kyle and Rey Koslowski, 187–215. Baltimore: Johns Hopkins University Press, 2001.

Liu, Guofu. "Changing Chinese Migration Law: From Restriction to Relaxation." *Migration & Integration* 10 (2009): 311–33.

Liu, Hong. "New Migrants and the Revival of Overseas Chinese Nationalism." *Journal of Contemporary China* 14, no. 43 (2005): 291–316.

Live, Yu-Sion. "The Chinese Community in France: Immigration, Economic Activity, Cultural Organization, and Representations." In Benton and Pieke, *The Chinese in Europe,* 96–124.

Lombardi, Rosa. *Sulla Via della Tela: Immigrazione cinese e integrazione, una nuova prospettiva: L'esperienza della Provincia di Prato.* Firenze: Nova Arti Grafiche, 2004.

Lombardi-Diop, Cristina, and Caterina Romeo. "The Italian Postcolonial: A Manifesto." *Italian Studies* 69, no. 3 (2014): 425–33.

Lombardo, Valentina. "L'offerta multiculturale nei media a larga diffusione." In Maneri and Meli, *Un diverso parlare*, 73–86.

López, Kathleen. *Chinese Cubans: A Transnational History*. Chapel Hill: University of North Carolina Press, 2013.

Louie, Kam. *Theorising Chinese Masculinity: Society and Gender in China.* Cambridge: Cambridge University Press, 2002.

– *Chinese Masculinities in a Globalizing World*. New York: Routledge, 2015.

Lucchesini, Alessandro. *Cinesi a Firenze: Storia e biodemografia di una colonia di immigrati.* Firenze: Pontecorboli, 1993.

Lucchini, Giulio. "Luoghi di residenza e di lavoro della comunità cinese a Roma." In Pedone, *Il vicino cinese*, 27–44.

Malavolti, Eva. "Integrazione cinese a Napoli." In Paolo and Varriano, *Dal Zhejiang alla Campania*, 108–63.

Ma Mung, Emanuel. "Territorializzazzione commerciale delle identità: I cinesi a Parigi." *La Critica Sociologica* 117–18 (1996): 64–79.

– "Chinese Immigration and the (Ethnic) Labour Market in France." In Spaan, Hillmann, and van Naerssen, *Asian Migrants*, 42–55.

Maneri, Marcello. "I media multiculturali, riconsiderati." In Maneri and Meli, *Un diverso parlare*, 87–113.

– "La stampa." In Maneri and Meli, *Un diverso parlare*, 24–42.

– "I media nel razzismo consensuale." In *Rapporto sul razzismo in Italia*, edited by Grazia Naletto, 47–51. Roma: Manifestolibri, 2009.

– "Media Discourse on Immigration: Control Practices and the Language We Live." In Palidda, *Racial Criminalization*, 77–93.

Maneri, Marcello, and Anna Meli, eds. *Un diverso parlare: Il fenomeno dei media multiculturali in Italia.* Roma: Carocci, 2007.

Marinelli, Maurizio. "Introduction: The Encounter between Italy and China: Two Countries, Multiple Stories." *Journal of Modern Italian Studies* 15, no. 4 (2010): 491–501.

– "The Genesis of the Italian Concession in Tianjin." *Journal of Modern Italian Studies* 15, no. 4 (2010): 536–56.

Marinelli, Maurizio, and Giovanni Andornino, eds. *Italy's Encounters with Modern China: Imperial Dreams, Strategic Ambitions.* New York: Palgrave Macmillan, 2014.

Marsden, Anna. *Cinesi e fiorentini a confronto.* Firenze: Firenze Libri, 1994.

– "Le comunità cinesi viste dalla stampa: Informazioni e stereotipi." In Ceccagno, *Il caso delle comunità cinesi*, 207–22.

– "Il ruolo della famiglia nello sviluppo dell'imprenditoria cinese a Prato." In *L'imprenditoria cinese nel distretto industriale di Prato*, edited by Massimo Colombi, 71–103. Firenze: Leo S. Olschki, 2002.

– "Chinese Descendants in Italy: Emergence, Role, and Uncertain Identity." *Ethnic and Racial Studies* 37, no. 7 (2014): 1239–52.

– "Second-Generation Chinese and New Processes of Social Integration in Italy." In Baldassar et al., *Chinese Migration to Europe*, 101–18.

Martiniello, Marco. *Le società multietniche*. Translated by Roberta Ferrara. Bologna: Il Mulino, 2000.

Mayer, Ruth. *Serial Fu Manchu: The Chinese Supervillain and the Spread of Yellow Peril Ideology*. Philadelphia: Temple University Press, 2014.

Mazzoleni, Gianpietro, and Anna Sfardini. *Politica Pop: Da "Porta a Porta" a "L'Isola dei famosi."* Bologna: Il Mulino, 2009.

McCarthy, Teresa M. "Zara: The Business Model for Fast Fashion." In *The Fashion Reader*, edited by Linda Welters and Abby Lillethun, 541–7. Oxford: Berg, 2011.

McCombs, Maxwell. *Setting the Agenda: The Mass Media and Public Opinion*. Cambridge, UK: Polity, 2014.

McGuire, Valerie. "Crimes of Diction: Language and National Belonging in the Fiction of Amara Lakhous." *Journal of Romance Studies* 15, no. 2 (2015): 1–21.

McKeown, Adam. *Chinese Migrant Networks and Cultural Change: Peru, Chicago, Hawaii, 1900–1936*. Chicago: University of Chicago Press, 2001.

Meli, Anna, and Ugo Enwereuzor. "Conclusioni." In Maneri and Meli, *Un diverso parlare*, 114–20.

Memmi, Albert. *Racism*. Minneapolis: University of Minnesota Press, 2000.

Miles, Robert, and Malcolm Brown. *Racism*. London: Routledge, 2003.

Ministero dell'Interno, "Pacchetto Sicurezza: Misure per rendere più sicura la vita dei cittadini: Patti per la sicureazza." 2008, http://www1.interno.gov.it/mininterno/export/sites/default/it/sezioni/sala_stampa/speciali/Pacchetto_sicurezza/index_2.html.

Miranda, Adelina. "Les Chinois dans la région de Naples: Altérités et identitiés dans une économie locale en mutation." In *La fin des norias? Réseaux migrants dans les économies marchandes de la Méditerranée*, edited by M. Péraldi, 431–51. Paris: Maisonneuve et Larose, 2002.

– "La commerce chinois: Conflits et adaptations au sein de la structure socio-économique napolitaine." In *Nouvelles migrations chinoises et travail en Europe*, edited by Laurence Roulleau-Berger, 160–77. Toulouse: Presses Universitaires du Mirail, 2007.

Mirante, Elsa. "'Chinatown e 'mafia gialla': La comunità dell'Esquilino nella cronaca romana." In Pedone, *Il vicino cinese*, 73–86.

Miyake, Toshio. "Italy Made in Japan: Occidentalism, Self-Orientalism, and Italianism in Contemporary Japan." In *New Perspectives in Italian Cultural*

Studies, vol. 1, *Definitions, Theory, and Accented Practices*, edited by Graziella Parati, 195–213. Madison: Fairleigh Dickinson University Press, 2012.

Moe, Nelson. *The View from Vesuvius: Italian Culture and the Southern Question*. Berkeley: University of California Press, 2002.

Morcellini, Mario et al. *Sintesi del rapporto di ricerca: Ricerca nazionale su immigrazione e asilo nei media italiani*. Roma: Sapienza Università di Roma, 2009. https://cattivenotizie.wordpress.com/2009/12/20/in-poche-parole/.

Morley, David, and Kevin Robins. *Spaces of Identity: Global Media, Electronic Landscapes and Cultural Boundaries*. London: Routledge, 1995.

Mudu, Pierpaolo, and Wei Li. "Recent Chinese Immigration in the United States and Italy: Settlement Patterns and Local Resistance." In *Crossing Over: Comparing Recent Migration in the United States and Europe*, edited by Holger Henke, 277–302. Lanham: Lexington Books, 2005.

Neal, Arthur G. *National Trauma and Collective Memory: Extraordinary Events in the American Experience*. Armonk, NY: M.E. Sharpe, 2005.

Nonini, Donald M., and Aihwa Ong. "Chinese Transnationalism as an Alternative Modernity." In Ong and Nonini, *Ungrounded Empires*, 3–33.

Nyíri, Pál. "Expatriating Is Patriotic? The Discourse on 'New Migrants' in the People's Republic of China and Identity Construction among Recent Migrants from the PRC." *Journal of Ethnic and Migration Studies* 27, no. 4 (October 2001): 635–53.

– *Chinese in Eastern Europe and Russia: A Middleman Minority in a Transnational Era*. London: Routledge, 2007.

Omodeo, Maria. "Toscana terra 'cinese.'" *Mondo Cinese* 131 (2007), http://www.tuttocina.it/mondo_cinese/131/131_omod.htm#.VTAFD5TF_ns.

Ong, Aihwa. "Chinese Modernities: Narratives of Nation and of Capitalism." In Ong and Nonini, *Ungrounded Empires*, 171–202.

– *Flexible Citizenship: The Cultural Logics of Transnationality*. Durham, NC: Duke University Press, 1999.

Ong, Aihwa, and Donald Nonini, eds. *Ungrounded Empires: The Cultural Politics of Modern Chinese Transnationalism*. New York: Routledge, 1997.

Ordine dei Giornalisti. "Carta dei doveri del giornalista: Documento CNOG-FNSI dell'8 luglio 1993." http://www.odg.it/content/carta-dei-doveri-del-giornalista.

– "Carta di Roma. Protocollo deontologico concernente richiedente asilo, rifugiati, vittime della tratta e migranti: Protocollo d'intesa 13 giugno 2008." http://www.odg.it/content/carta-di-roma.

– "Testo unico dei doveri del giornalista." http://www.odg.it/content/testo-unico-dei-doveri-del-giornalista.

Padovani, Cinzia. "The Extreme Right and Its Media in Italy." *International Journal of Communication* 2 (2008): 753–70.

Palidda, Salvatore. "The Italian Crime Deal." In Palidda, *Racial Criminalization*, 213–33.

–, ed. *Racial Criminalization of Migrants in the 21st Century*. Burlington, VT: Ashgate, 2011.

Pannocchia, Andrea. "Il giornalismo italiano visto dall'estero." In Sorrentino, *Il giornalismo in Italia*, 273–9.

Papotti, David. "L'approccio della geografia alla letteratura dell'immigrazione: Riflessioni su alcune potenziali direzioni di ricerca." In *Leggere il testo e il mondo: Vent'anni di scritture della migrazione in Italia*, edited by Fulvio Pezzarossa and Ilaria Rossini, 65–84. Bologna: CLUEB, 2011.

Papuzzi, Alberto, and Annalisa Magone. *Professione giornalista: Le tecniche, i media, le regole*. Roma: Donzelli Editore, 2010.

Parati, Graziella. *Migration Italy: The Art of Talking Back in a Destination Culture*. Toronto: University of Toronto, 2005.

Parati, Graziella, and Anthony Julian Tamburri, eds. *The Cultures of Italian Migration: Diverse Trajectories and Discrete Perspectives*. Madison: Fairleigh Dickinson University Press, 2011.

Parnanzone, Ilenia. "La spiritualità e i luoghi di culto della comunità cinese di Roma." In Pedone, *Il vicino cinese*, 87–100.

Pedone, Valentina. "La parabola dell'import-export cinese a Roma: Ascesa, apogeo e decadenza della capitale europea del commercio cinese." In *Osservatorio Romano sulle migrazioni*, VI Rapporto, edited by Caritas, 232–40. Roma: Anterem, 2010.

– "'As a Rice Plant in a Wheat Field': Identity Negotiation among Children of Chinese Immigrants." *Journal of Modern Italian Studies* 16, no. 4 (2011): 492–503.

–, ed. *Il vicino cinese: La comunità cinese a Roma*. Roma: Nuove Edizioni Romane, 2008.

– "L'Italia nella letteratura sinoitaliana." In Pitrone, Martire, and Fazzi, *Come ci vedono e come ci raccontano*, 42–64.

– *A Journey to the West: Observations on the Chinese Migration to Italy*. Firenze: Firenze University Press, 2013.

Però, Davide. *Inclusionary Rhetoric/Exclusionary Practices: Left-Wing Politics and Migrants in Italy*. New York: Berghan Books, 2007.

Pezzotti, Barbara. *The Importance of Place in Contemporary Italian Crime Fiction: A Bloody Journey*. Madison: Fairleigh Dickinson University Press, 2012.

Picquart, Pierre. "Les migrants de la diaspora chinoise." *Chinois de France*, http://www.chinoisdefrance.com/migrants-chinois-chine.html.

Pieke, Frank. "Introduction: Chinese Migrations Compared." In Pieke and Mallee, *Internal and International Migration*, 1–26.

– *Recent Trends in Chinese Migration to Europe: Fujianese Migration in Perspective*. International Organization for Migration (IOM), Research Series 6. Geneva: IOM, 2002.

Pieke, Frank, and Hein Mallee, eds. *Internal and International Migration: Chinese Perspectives*. Richmond: Curzon Press, 1999.

Pieke, Frank, N., Pál Nyíri, Mette Thuno, and Antonella Ceccagno. *Transnational Chinese: Fujianese Migrants in Europe*. Stanford: Stanford University Press, 2004.

Pitrone, Maria Concetta, Fabrizio Martire, and Gabriella Fazzi, eds. *Come ci vedono e come ci raccontano: Rappresentazioni sociali degli immigrati cinesi a Roma*. Milano: Franco Angeli, 2012.

Pogliano, Andrea, and Riccardo Zanini. "L'immaginario e le immagini degli immigrati: Un percorso qualitativo." In *Facce da straniero: 30 anni di fotografia e giornalismo sull'immigrazione in Italia*, edited by Luigi Gariglio, Andrea Pogliano, and Riccardo Zanini, 103–87. Milano: Mondadori, 2010.

Pojmann, Wendy Ann. *Immigrant Women and Feminism in Italy*. Burlington, VT: Ashgate, 2006.

Portes, Alejandro. "Introduction: The Debates and Significance of Immigrant Transnationalism." *Global Networks* 1 (2001): 181–93.

Portes, Alejandro, and Josh DeWind. "Conceptual and Methodological Developments in the Study of International Migration." *International Migration Review* 38, no. 3 (2006): 828–51.

Portes, Alejandro, Luis E. Guarnizo, and Patricia Landolt. "The Study of Transnationalism: Pitfalls and Promise of an Emergent Research Field." *Ethnic and Racial Studies* 22, no. 2 (1999): 217–37.

Portes, Alejandro, and Jessica Yiu. "Entrepreneurship, Transnationalism, and Development." *Migration Studies* 1, no. 1 (2013): 75–95.

Posner, Gerald. *Warlords of Crime: Chinese Secret Societies: The New Mafia*. New York: McGraw-Hill, 1988.

– *Il sole bianco: La mafia cinese sulla pista della droga*. Milano: SugarCo, 1990.

Pratt, Mary Louise. *Imperial Eyes: Travel Writing and Transculturation*. 2nd ed. London: Routledge, 2008.

Prefettura di Prato, Comune di Prato, Provincia di Prato, and Regione Toscana. "Patto per Prato sicura, 2008–2009." http://www.regione.toscana.it/documents/10180/23718/Patto%20Prato%20Sicura%202008/d879227e-1f76-410f-bb7b-cb8d10257832.

Prodi, Giorgio. "Economic Relations between Italy and China." In Marinelli and Andornino, *Italy's Encounters with Modern China*, 171–99.

"Professionisti." Ordine dei giornalisti. http://www.odg.it/files/PROFESSIONISTI_GENNAIO_2015_0.pdf.

Raffaetà, Roberta, and Loretta Baldassar. "Spaces Speak Louder than Words: Contesting Social Inclusion through Conflicting Rhetoric about Prato's Chinatown." In Baldassar et al., *Chinese Migration to Europe*, 119–37.

Rastrelli, Renzo. "L'immigrazione a Prato fra società, istituzioni ed economia." In Ceccagno, *Migranti a Prato*, 69–104.

– "Immigrazione cinese e criminalità. Fonti e interpretazioni a confronto." In Trentin, *La Cina che arriva*, 207–55.

Regione Toscana – IRES Toscana. *Immigrati a Firenze: Inserimento lavorativo, la collettività cinese*. Provincia di Firenze, 1992.

Renwick, Neil, and Qing Cao. "China's Political Discourse towards the 21st Century: Victimhood, Identity, and Political Power." *East Asia* 17, no. 4 (1999): 111–43.

Reyneri, Emilio. "Immigration and the Underground Economy in New Receiving South European Countries: Manifold Negative Effects, Manifold Deep-Rooted Causes." *International Review of Sociology* 13, no. 1 (2003): 117–43.

Ricucci, Roberta. "La diaspora cinese: Dinamiche internazionali ed esiti locali." In Berzano et al., *Cinesi a Torino*, 55–91.

Robertson, Roland. *Globalization: Social Theory and Global Culture*. London: Sage, 1992.

Ross, Andrew. "Made in Italy: The Trouble with Craft Capitalism." *Antipode* 36, no. 2 (2004): 209–16.

Safran, William. "Diasporas in Modern Societies: Myths of Homeland and Return." *Diaspora* 1, no. 1 (1991): 83–99.

Said, Edward. "Orientalism Reconsidered." In *Literature, Politics, and Theory: Papers from the Essex Conference, 1976–84*, edited by Francis Barker et al. London: Methuen, 1986.

– *Reflections on Exile and Other Essays*. Cambridge, MA: Harvard University Press, 2000.

Santangelo, Paolo. "L'immigrazione cinese in Italia: Come le comunità cinesi in Italia presentano se stesse: Valori e immagini dalla stampa cinese." In Paolo and Varriano, *Dal Zhejiang alla Campania*, 7–61.

Santangelo, Paolo, and Valeria Varriano, eds. *Dal Zhejiang alla Campania: Alcuni aspetti dell'immigrazione cinese*. Roma: Edizioni Nuova Cultura, 2006.

Saviano, Roberto. *Gomorra: Viaggio nell'impero economico e nel sogno di dominio della camorra*. Milano: Mondadori, 2006.

– *Gomorrah*. Translated by Virginia Jewiss. New York: Farrar, Straus and Giroux, 2007.

Schneider, Jane. "Introduction: The Dynamics of Neo-Orientalism in Italy (1848–1995)." In *Italy's "Southern Question": Orientalism in One Country*, edited by Jane Schneider, 1–23. Oxford: Berg, 1998.

Sciortino, Giuseppe, and Asher Colombo. "The Flows and the Flood: The Public Discourse on Immigration in Italy, 1969–2001." *Journal of Modern Italian Studies* 9, no. 1 (2004): 94–113.

Segre Reinach, Simona. "China and Italy: Fast Fashion versus Prêt à Porter: Towards a New Culture of Fashion." *Fashion Theory* 9, no. 1 (2005): 43–56.

– "Italian Fashion: The Metamorphosis of a Cultural Industry." In *Made in Italy: Rethinking a Century of Italian Design*, 239–54. London: Bloomsbury Academic, 2014.

Shohat, Ella, and Robert Stam. *Unthinking Eurocentrism: Multiculturalism and the Media*. London: Routledge, 1994.

Sibhatu, Ribka. *Il cittadino che non c'è: L'immigrazione nei media italiani*. Roma: EDUP, 2004.

Silverstone, Roger. *Media and Morality: On the Rise of the Mediàpolis*. Cambridge: Polity Press, 2007.

Sinclair, John, Audrey Yue, Gay Hawkins, Kee Pookong, and Josephine Fox. "Chinese Cosmpolitanism and Media Use." In *Floating Lives: The Media and Asian Diasporas*, edited by Stuart Cunningham and John Sinclair, 35–90. Lanham, MD: Rowman & Littlefield Publishers, 2001.

Smith, Shirley Ann. *Imperial Designs: Italians in China, 1900–1947*. Madison, NJ: Fairleigh Dickinson University Press; Lanham, MD: Rowman & Littlefield, 2012.

Sorrentino, Carlo, ed. *Il giornalismo in Italia: Aspetti, processi produttivi, tendenze*. Roma: Carocci, 2003.

Spann, Ernst, Felicitas Hillmann, and Ton van Naerssen, eds. *Asian Migrants and European Labour Market: Patterns and Processes of Immigrant Labour Market Insertion in Europe*. London: Routledge, 2005.

Sredanovic, Djordje. "Fotografia: Media e immigrazione nel 2012." In *Notizie fuori dal ghetto: Primo rapporto annuale*, edited by Associazione Carta di Roma, 17–50. Roma: Edizioni Ponte Sisto, 2013. http://www.cartadiroma.org/wp-content/uploads/2014/01/libro-rapporto-carta-di-roma-versione-genn-2014.pdf.

– "The 2012 Killing of Chinese Citizens in Rome and the Ambivalence of Italian Journalism." *Patterns of Prejudice* 50, no. 1 (2016): 61–81.

Strozza, Salvatore. "Immigrati stranieri e inserimento nel mercato del lavoro nella provincia di Roma: La situazione prima e dopo la 'grande regolarizzazione.'" In Zucchetti, *La regolarizzazzione degli stranieri*, 261–346.

Su, Hong, ed. *Hu Yundi jiazu qiao pu*. Wenzhou: Wenzhou Institute of Overseas Chinese and Foreign Nationals of Chinese Origin, 1997.

Sun, Wanning. "Introduction: Transnationalism and a Global Diasporic Chinese Mediasphere." In *Media and the Chinese Diaspora: Community, Communications, and Commerce*, edited by Wanning Sun, 1–25. London: Routledge, 2006.

– "China's Rise and (Trans)national Connections: The Global Diasporic Chinese Mediasphere." In Tan, *Routledge Handbook of the Chinese Diaspora*, 433–45.

Swidler, Ann. "Culture in Action: Symbols and Strategies." *American Sociological Review* 51, no. 2 (1986): 273–86.

– *Talk of Love: How Culture Matters*. Chicago: University of Chicago Press, 2001.

Tan, Chee-Beng. "Introduction." In Tan, *Routledge Handbook of the Chinese Diaspora*, 1–12.

–, ed. *Routledge Handbook of the Chinese Diaspora*. London: Routledge, 2013.

Tarantino, Matteo, and Simone Tosoni. "The Battle of Milan: Social Representations of the April 2007 Riots by Two Chinese Communities." In Johanson, Smyth, and French, *Living outside the Walls*, 202–19.

Tchen, John Kuo Wei, and Dylan Yeats. "Introduction: Yellow Peril Incarnate." In *Yellow Peril! An Archive of Anti-Asian Fear*, edited by John Kuo Wei Tchen and Dylan Yeats, 1–32. London; Brooklyn: Verso, 2014.

Teixeira, Ana. "Entrepreneurs of the Chinese Community in Portugal." In Benton and Pieke, *The Chinese in Europe*, 238–60.

Thunø, Mette. "Chinese Emigration to Europe. Combining European and Chinese Sources." *Revue Européenne des Migrations Internationales* 12, no. 2 (1996): 275–96.

– "Moving Stones from China to Europe: The Dynamics of Emigration from Zhejiang to Europe." In Pieke and Mallee, *Internal and International Migration*, 159–80.

Tomba, Luigi. "Exporting the 'Wenzhou Model' to Beijing and Florence: Suggestions for a Comparative Perspective on Labour and Economic Organization in Two Migrant Communities." In Pieke and Mallee, *Internal and International Migration*, 280–94.

Tomlinson, John. *Globalization and Culture*. Chicago: University of Chicago Press, 1999.

Trentin, Giorgio, ed. *La Cina che arriva: Il sistema del dragone*. Napoli: Avagliano, 2005.

Uccellini, Cara. "Romanian Migration to Italy: Insiders and Outsiders." In *Globalisation, Migration, and the Future of Europe: Insiders and Outsiders*, edited by Leila Simona Talani, 101–23. New York: Routledge, 2012.

Ufficio di Statistica. "Tab. 1.1 – Comune di Prato – Popolazione italiana e straniera residente a fine anno dal 1995 al 2010." 2010. http://allegatistatistica.comune.prato.it/dl/20090924103235853/tab1_1.pdf.

– "Tab. 1.9 – Comune di Prato – Cittadini stranieri per cittadinanza dal 1995 al 2010." 2010. http://allegatistatistica.comune.prato.it/dl/20090924105506396/tab1_3.pdf.

The United Nations Office on Drugs and Crime. "Organized Crime." https://www.unodc.org/unodc/en/organized-crime/index.html.

Varriano, Valeria. "Gli italiani nell'immaginario cinese: scene di un serial televisivo." In *La Cina e il mondo: Atti del XII Convegno dell'Associazione Italiana di Studi Cinesi*, edited by Paolo De Troia, 495–516. Roma: Nuova Cultura, 2010.

Vertovec, Steven. "Multiculturalism, Culturalism, and Public Incorporation." *Ethnic and Racial Studies* 19, no. 1 (1996): 49–69.

– *Transnationalism.* London: Routledge, 2009.

– "The Cultural Politics of Nation and Migration." *Annual Review of Anthropology* 40 (2011): 241–56.

Vertovec, Steven, and Susanne Wessendorf. "Assessing the Backlash against Multiculturalism in Europe." In Vertovec and Wessendorf, *The Multiculturalism Backlash,* 1–31.

–, eds. *The Multiculturalism Backlash: European Discourses, Policies, and Practices.* New York: Routledge, 2010.

Vicziany, Marika, Anja Michaela Fladrich, and A. Andrea Di Castro. "Religion and the Lives of the Overseas Chinese: What Explains the 'Great Silence' of Prato." In Baldassar et al., *Chinese Migration to Europe,* 215–31.

Vukovich, Daniel F. *China and Orientalism: Western Knowledge Production and the P.R.C.* London: Routledge, 2012.

Wang, Gungwu. *The Chinese Overseas: From Earthbound China to the Quest for Autonomy.* Cambridge, MA: Harvard University Press, 2000.

Wenzhou Institute of Overseas Chinese and Foreign Nationals of Chinese Origin, ed. *Wenzhou huaqiao shi/History of Overseas Chinese from Wenzhou.* Beijing: Jinri zhongguo chubanshe/China Today Press, 1999.

Wollen, Peter. "Fire and Ice." *Photographies* (1984): 118–20.

Wong, Aliza S. *Race and the Nation in Liberal Italy, 1861–1911: Meridionalism, Empire, and Diaspora.* New York: Palgrave Macmillan, 2006.

Wu, Bin, and Hong Liu. "Bringing Class Back In: Class Consciousness and Solidarity among Chinese Migrant Workers in Italy and the UK." *Ethnic and Racial Studies* 37, no. 8 (2014): 1391–408.

World Trade Organization. "Agreement on Textiles and Clothing." 2005. http://www.wto.org/english/docs_e/legal_e/16-tex_e.htm.

Xiang, Biao. "'Zhejiang Village in Beijing': Creating a Visible Non-state Space through Migration and Marketized Networks." In Pieke and Mallee, *Internal and International Migration,* 215–50.

– "Emigration from China: A Sending Country Perspective." *International Migration* 41, no. 3 (2003): 21–48.

Yar, Majid. "Screening Crime: Cultural Criminology Goes to the Movies." In Hayward and Presdee, *Framing Crime,* 68–82.

Yow, Cheun Hoe. "Chinese Diasporas and Their Literature in Chinese." In Tan, *Routledge Handbook of the Chinese Diaspora,* 459–74.

Zhang, Gaoheng. "The Three Riddles in Puccini's *Turandot*: Masculinity, Empire, and Orientalism." In *Der musikalisch modellierte Mann: Interkulturelle und interdisziplinäre Männlichkeitsstudien zur Oper und Literatur des 19. und frühen 20. Jahrhunderts,* edited by Ester Saletta and Barbara Hindinger, 397–416. Vienna: Praesens, 2012.

– "The Protest in Milan's Chinatown and the Chinese Immigrants in Italy in the Media (2007–2009)." *Journal of Italian Cinema and Media Studies* 1, no. 1 (2013): 21–37.

– "Contemporary Italian Novels on Chinese Immigration to Italy." *California Italian Studies* 4, no. 2 (2013): 1–38. https://escholarship.org/uc/item/0jr1m8k3.

– "Chinese Migrants, Morality, and Film Ethics in Italian Cinema." *Journal of Modern Italian Studies* 22, no. 3 (2017): 385–405.

– "The Chinaman and the *cinesina*: Gendering Chinese Migrants in Italian Novels." *Journal of Romance Studies* 19, no. 1 (2019): 69–97.

Zhang, Sheldon, and Ko-lin Chin. *Characteristics of Chinese Human Smugglers.* Washington: US Department of Justice, Office of Justice Programs, 2004. https://www.ncjrs.gov/pdffiles1/nij/204989.pdf.

Zhu, Dinglong. "Dinamiche all'interno della comunità cinese a Roma." In Ceccagno, *Il caso delle comunità cinesi*, 37–44.

Zhu, Ying. *Television in Post-Reform China: Serial Dramas, Confucian Leadership, and the Global Television Market*. London: Routledge, 2008.

Zincone, Giovanna. "The Making of Policies: Immigration and Immigrants in Italy." *Journal of Ethnic and Migration Studies* 32 (2006): 347–75.

– "Citizenship Policy Making in Mediterranean EU States: Italy." Florence: European University Institute, 2010. http://eudo-citizenship.eu/docs/EUDOcom-Italy.pdf.

– "Conclusion: Comparing the Making of Migration Policies." In *Migration Policymaking in Europe: The Dynamics of Actors and Contexts in Past and Present*, edited by Giovanna Zincone, Rinus Penninx, and Maren Borkert, 377–441. Amsterdam: Amsterdam University Press, 2011.

Zinn, Dorothy Louise. "*Pacem in Terris*: Problems in Reading a '*Multi-ethnic*' Television Variety Show." In Grillo and Pratt, *The Politics of Recognizing Difference*, 197–217.

Zoccatelli, PierLuigi. "Religione e religiosità fra i cinesi a Torino: 'Religione cinese,' identità secolare e presenze di origine cristiana." In Berzano et al., *Cinesi a Torino*, 203–54.

Zucchetti, Eugenio. "I caratteri salienti della regolarizzazione in Italia." In Zucchetti, *La regolarizzazzione degli stranieri*, 15–58.

–, ed. *La regolarizzazzione degli stranieri: Nuovi attori nel mercato del lavoro italiano*. Milano: Fondazione ISMU, 2004.

Index

Cultural Spaces

Cultural Spaces explores the rapidly changing temporal, spatial, and theoretical boundaries of contemporary cultural studies. Culture has long been understood as the force that defines and delimits societies in fixed spaces. The recent intensification of globalizing processes, however, has meant that it is no longer possible – if it ever was – to imagine the world as a collection of autonomous, monadic spaces, whether these are imagined as localities, nations, regions within nations, or cultures demarcated by region or nation. One of the major challenges of studying contemporary culture is to understand the new relationships of culture to space that are produced today. The aim of this series is to publish bold new analyses and theories of the spaces of culture, as well as investigations of the historical construction of those cultural spaces that have influenced the shape of the contemporary world.

General Editor: Jasmin Habib, University of Waterloo

Books in the Series:

Peter Ives, *Gramsci's Politics of Language: Engaging the Bakhtin Circle and the Frankfurt School*

Sarah Brophy, *Witnessing AIDS: Writing, Testimony, and the Work of Mourning*

Shane Gunster, *Capitalizing on Culture: Critical Theory for Cultural Studies*

Jasmin Habib, *Israel, Diaspora, and the Routes of National Belonging*

Serra Tinic, *On Location: Canada's Television Industry in a Global Market*

Evelyn Ruppert, *The Moral Economy of Cities: Shaping Good Citizens*

Mark Coté, Richard J.F. Day, and Greg de Peuter, eds., *Utopian Pedagogy: Radical Experiments against Neoliberal Globalization*

David Jefferess, *Postcolonial Resistance: Culture, Liberation, and Transformation*

Mary Gallagher, ed., *World Writing: Poetics, Ethics, Globalization*

Maureen Moynagh, *Political Tourism and Its Texts*

Lily Cho, *Eating Chinese: Culture on the Menu in Small Town Canada*

Rhona Richman Kenneally and Johanne Sloan, eds., *Expo 67: Not Just a Souvenir*

Erin Hurley, *National Performance: Representing Quebec from Expo 67 to Céline Dion*

Gillian Roberts, *Prizing Literature: The Celebration and Circulation of National Culture*

Lianne McTavish, *Defining the Modern Museum: A Case Study of the Challenges of Exchange*

Misao Dean, *Inheriting a Canoe Paddle: The Canoe in Discourses of English-Canadian Nationalism*

Michael McKinnie, *City Stages: Theatre and the Urban Space in a Global City*

Sarah Brophy and Janice Hladki, eds., *Embodied Politics in Visual Autobiography*

Robin Pickering-Iazzi, *The Mafia in Italian Lives and Literature: Life Sentences and Their Geographies*

Kyle Conway, Little Mosque on the Prairie *and the Paradoxes of Cultural Translation*

Ajay Heble, ed., *Classroom Action: Human Rights, Critical Activism, and Community-Based Education*

Claudette Lauzon, *The Unmaking of Home in Contemporary Art*

Jason Demers, *The American Politics of French Theory: Derrida, Deleuze, Guattari, and Foucault in Translation*

Gaoheng Zhang, *Migration and the Media: Debating Chinese Migration to Italy, 1992–2012*

www.ingramcontent.com/pod-product-compliance
Lightning Source LLC
LaVergne TN
LVHW090153080826
844660LV00013B/783/J

* 9 7 8 1 4 4 2 6 3 0 4 3 7 *